AMERICAN DOMESTICITY

AMERICAN
DOMESTICITY

From How-to Manual to Hollywood Melodrama

Kathleen Anne McHugh

New York   Oxford
Oxford University Press
1999

Oxford University Press

Oxford   New York

Athens   Auckland   Bangkok   Bogotá   Buenos Aires   Calcutta
Cape Town   Chennai   Dar es Salaam   Delhi   Florence   Hong Kong   Istanbul
Karachi   Kuala Lumpur   Madrid   Melbourne   Mexico City   Mumbai
Nairobi   Paris   São Paulo   Singapore   Taipei   Tokyo   Toronto   Warsaw

and associated companies in

Berlin   Ibadan

Library of Congress Cataloging-in-Publication Data
McHugh, Kathleen Anne.
American domesticity: From how-to manual to Hollywood melodrama /
Kathleen Anne McHugh.
p.   cm.
Includes bibliographical references and index.
ISBN 0-19-512261-5
1. Women in motion pictures.   2. Housework in motion pictures.
3. Feminism in motion pictures.   I. Title.
PN1995.9.W6M38   1999
791.43'652042—dc21   98-25603

Parts of chapter 5 have appeared as "Housekeeping in Hollywood:
The Case of *Craig's Wife*," *Screen* 35, no. 2. Used by permission.

Parts of chapter 9 have appeared in "Subjectivity and Space
in the Films of Patricia Gruben," *Jump Cut*, no. 35, and as a
section of "One cleans, the other doesn't," *Cultural Studies* 11,
no. 1. Used by permission.

1 3 5 7 9 8 6 4 2
Printed in the United States of America
on acid-free paper

*In loving memory of
my grandmother*

Dorothy McHugh

1902–1998

Acknowledgments

Many people have assisted me in the completion of this book, and I include those who, while not having any direct involvement, offered support, encouragement, or inspiration along the way. My sister, Donna Neville, literally moved me into academia, and my uncle Laurence McHugh helped me pay the rent with an unexpected and generous gift. My interest in the paradoxical relationship between domesticity and social justice has been inspired by my parents, Margret and Kenneth McHugh. Karen Waters, Norma Bowles, and Eleanor Oths have sustained me with their warmth and friendship. In very different ways, Konda Mason and Roger Melton have kept me sane. Robert B. Ray, Barrie Ruth Straus, John Leavey, Gregory Ulmer, Alistair Duckworth, and Brandon Kershner were early and important mentors. The wit and wisdom of Gail Shepherd, Cathy Griggers, Helen Kirklin, Stacey Breheny, Nancy Davidson, and Bonnie Jo DeCourcey shaped my nascent feminist consciousness.

Manuscripts evolve. Advising me through the project's earliest manifestation, my dissertation, Susan Gubar insisted I address the race question; Claudia Gorbman noted the absence of considerations of maternity; Barbara Klinger's incisive mind and extensive grasp of contemporary theory helped shape my approach; and James Naremore guided me, with clarity, brilliance, and kindness, through every aspect, conceptual and pragmatic, of the process. I continue to benefit from his insights and those of Barbara Klinger as they have both seen the project through to its end.

Generous readings and feedback by Nancy Abelmann, Cathy Davidson, Janet Lyons, Jon McKenzie, David James, Carol Neely, John Izod, Glenna Matthews, Sarah Stage, and Sharon Salinger shaped the direction of later revisions and saved me from making an array of theoretical and historical errors. Erika Suderburg and Carole-Anne Tyler discussed the project with me extensively and offered emotional and intellectual encouragement. Jennifer Brody, Piya Chatterjee, and Tiffany Ana López's close and astute readings of the manuscript improved it immensely, readying it for the editorial consideration that Emory Elliott helped bring about.

Various readers offered me important advice that guided my final revisions. Chuck Kleinhans encouraged me to clarify the scope and intent of my project. Lisa Cartwright, Ramona Curry, and Christine Holmlund's readings were stunning for their generosity, insight, and detail. Lisa Cartwright's feedback was especially helpful in relation to the earlier sections of the book and important transitions, and Christine Holmlund's comments guided my revisions of the final section. Although all of Ramona Curry's suggestions were valuable, I am particularly grateful for her observations about chapter 5. In implementing her advice, I was able to turn what had been one of the weakest chapters into one of the strongest.

In the course of writing this book, I have had generous support from a number of sources. At the University of California, Riverside, Academic Senate and Faculty Development Grants have provided funding for research and teaching release. A Resident Fellowship at the Center for Ideas and Society at UC Riverside allowed me to refine a number of ideas connected to this project. I also appreciate the congenial and supportive character of the administration at UC Riverside. I am grateful to Associate Dean Carl Cranor, Dean Carlos Vélez-Ibáñez, and the chair of my department, Thomas Scanlon, for their support, advice, and encouragement. I have also had the benefit of wonderful research assistants and would like to thank Robert D'Alonzo, Lisa Forsyth, Michael Maloney, and especially Erla Marteinsdottir.

An author could not wish for a better experience than I have had with Oxford University Press. I want to thank Susie Chang for facilitating the manuscript's acquisition, and Will Moore and Amanda Heller for superb copyediting. Special thanks to Will Moore also for the book's design and for his warmth and humor throughout the production process.

Finally, to Lisa Duggan and Chon Noriega I owe the deepest thanks. While others have shaped my manuscript, Lisa Duggan has shaped my thought with her prodigious intellect, wit, insight, and compassion. Her influence marks the best of this manuscript, as does that of Chon Noriega, who has patiently read and reread every one of these pages, substantially improving them at every pass. As generous as he is brilliant, Chon has transformed both the work itself and my relationship to it, the first a gift for now, the second for a lifetime.

Riverside, California   K. A. M.
July 1998

Contents

AMERICAN DOMESTICITY

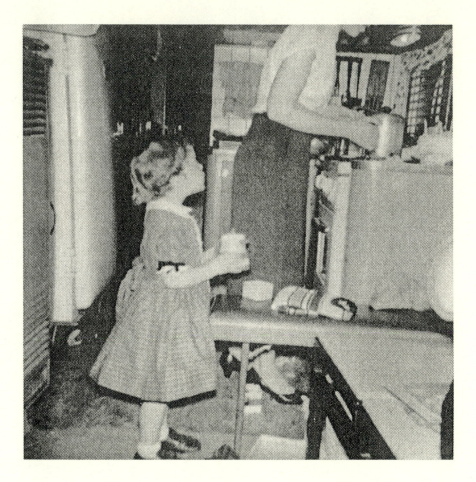

Swept Away

The Truth about Dirt

Housekeeping as Autobiography: Two Kinds of Invisibility

Here, a photograph found by chance in an old family scrapbook, detailing a moment perhaps completely forgotten by both participants. A mother and daughter. Coffee. Date? The 1950s, the era of domesticity, of the baby boom, denoted by the clothing, the round bulky lines of the refrigerator, the serrated edges of the black-and-white photo. A memento from the private sphere, from the space of the family, the photo depicts a mute pedagogy, knowledge passed on by a miming of the mother, by a wordless exchange. The child's chin cranes upward, looking on to adapt her pose to that of her mother. The mother is working, preparing coffee for absent others. Her work; a child's play.

I came upon this photo when I was well into the project—a study of film melodrama and representations of housework—that would become this text. Someone, charmed at the sight of me imitating my mother, had recorded the moment. The framing focuses on me, cutting my mother's head out of the image. Her housework, in and of itself, would not warrant a photograph; my imitation of her motivates the snapshot, centers it, transforms inherently boring labor into something "cute."

I have no memory of this scene. Indeed, it delighted me to find that a personal connection to my subject, lost to my memory and conscious mind, had been documented and preserved. I found in the photo everything I wanted to discuss at that time: housekeeping as a form of labor whose affective and erotic components (maternity, sexuality) obscure its identity as labor; its involvement in the family romance (my mother is making coffee for my father); its function as a pedagogy of the feminine, shaping the relationships between some mothers and daughters; its affiliation with the private, personal, and familial; its sentimental and trivial status in visual representations. As a consequence of this discovery, I reconceived my manuscript as a series of sweeps, a series of readings, back and forth across this photo.

In the image my family, my personal history, surfaced in my academic subject area. The coincidence of personal and professional identities, though pleasing and, in some sense, inevitable, was also unnerving. There were risks in taking up or excluding either the professional or the personal: on the one hand, that of abstraction, the cold-bloodedness of facts without flesh, the dubious mastery of a speaker with no position or obvious investment; on the other, the risk of sentiment, a maudlin rendering of a subject too close to understand or to see with a sufficient degree of dispassion. My fears (the embarrassment of autobiography, of the sentimental) were countered by the desire to tell the story of this photo affirmatively as well as critically, to describe my mother's tradition, to fashion my accomplishments in relation to hers.

But the narrative of this photo is not only my mother's narrative; it is mine as well. I look at the image again and a fundamental ambivalence surfaces: this is me; it is not me. I have no empathy for this little body, no memory of her. Certainly no memory of any proclivity for housework. Quite the contrary; as I write this project, I take the position of my father—a professional with an advanced degree—to write about my mother, to acknowledge and analyze the great differences that separate her life from mine. The photo documents a particularly fortuitous moment. My father is writing his dissertation, perhaps even as I imitate my mother with the coffee. Discovering the photo years later, I find it proleptic, its image a differently and belatedly realized primal scene. I found the photo as I was writing my dissertation, taking the position of the father, yet writing about my mother's profession, her activities, and her pedagogical relation to me.

As I continued reading and sweeping, what emerged as the photo's most valuable information was what I could *not* see in it. In the first writing, the first sweep across the photo, I found what had not been or could not be said about housekeepers by thinkers, such as Marx and Freud, whose critical perspectives shaped my own feminist thought. Academic writing on movies in the 1970s and 1980s was influenced by Marx, who theorizes labor and work, and even more strongly by Freud, who analyzes the psychodynamics of bourgeois family life; but neither of these theoretical approaches can account for housework, and this I began to see as their structuring absence. As labor performed without remuneration in the private sphere, housekeeping is a practice lying within, but exceeding, the libidinal and political economies described by classical theory.[1] Its practices literalize the paradoxical condition—both inside and other—often invoked to describe women's position in patriarchy.

Yet the feminist methodology that enabled me to see the link between housework's invisibility as labor and problematic notions of femininity simultaneously facilitated another blind spot: my emphasis on gender obscured other differences evident in the image. The photo depicts a tiny, constricted space; my mother perhaps does not have enough room to be a very good housekeeper. Her clothing seems somewhat out of place in this very small, very messy kitchen. The class codes of her attire (tailored straight wool skirt, linen blouse, pumps) are at odds with her cramped surroundings. My father is in graduate school. We live in a travel trailer. When he finishes, he (and my family) will ascend to my mother's middle-class status, and I will live out my childhood in segregated suburbs. Read in this way, the photo emphatically reminds me that housekeeping, as it is predominantly represented, has a history that includes me and that excludes many others. The obviousness of the photo's social implications eluded me on first, second, and third sweeps. This scene that apprehends my topic and aspects of gender formation, that renders me in relation to my mother and my father, that marks a certain destiny, also frames me within the social conventions and psychic structures of a white bourgeois domesticity. This is me; however I might wish it, it cannot not be me.

The photo, then, documents two kinds of invisibility, both related to labor and constructions of femininity. First, the scene depicted in it indicates how the affectively oriented roles of mother and wife sentimentalize domestic labor and make it very difficult to see or understand as labor qua labor. The second invisibility concerns my identity as a woman and as a feminist film scholar *trained* to read images. My experience with reading this photo and *not* seeing its very clearly articulated class narrative (a narrative I was born into and lived) indicates that both gender identity (femininity) and the analysis of gender relations (feminism) function to obscure class difference. In this book I propose that these two aberrations of seeing are historically and discursively codependent. Thus, if this framing has been difficult to see, its function within social relations has been even more so. Since a feminist perspective compromised my ability to discern other facets of my identity clearly represented in the photo, I resolved to theorize, to historicize, what I could *not* see: housework as labor; femininity *and* feminism as a category and a method, respectively, that obscure other social differences.[2]

My interest in this topic originally derived from an absence I noted in classical film melodramas. Though set in the home and featuring female protagonists as wives and mothers, these films routinely transformed representations of domestic labor into acts with pathetic, symbolic, or romantic import, rendering their function as labor invisible and irrelevant. Yet, rather than simply document and diagnose the invisibility of housework in classical film melodramas, I decided to track down the historical underpinnings of these related invisibilities, a task that necessarily took me back to the nineteenth century in order to uncover a critical genealogy that takes women's labor into account.[3]

In the United States, nineteenth-century formulations of domestic labor made possible constructions of a seemingly classless domestic femininity, a gender entity that helped forge a coherent democratic nationalism. Significantly, this tradition of women's writing increasingly emphasized the importance of the housewife's pleasing *appearance* in discussions of women's domestic labor. If she labors, they assert, she must appear *not* to labor. Thus these writings wed the importance of women's appearance to mystifications of household labor. They therefore provide a cogent historical context for the invisibility of women's housework in the domestic film melodramas that were the original focus of my project. The value of my foray into "nineteenth-century film studies" is that it puts the theoretical "lack" that has dominated feminist film studies—women's iconic representation of castration—in the context of another materially and sociohistorically specific lack, that of representations of certain women's domestic labor. My approach takes the photo and the films out of the sentimental, bio-spiritual timelessness of the personal and historicizes both that timelessness and the lack of laboring activity these images represent.

Certain questions have guided my study. How is domestic labor and its invisibility related to an intensely moralized and sentimentalized construction of maternity that completely colonizes modern American understandings of femininity? How is this moralistic colonization related to femininity and feminism's role in the exclusion of other social differences? Why is it so hard to go from the personal scene depicted in the photo to its historical moment? The fifties in America were a decade that saw simultaneously the bleaching and the dumbing down of the feminine while at the same time the stultifying environment of domesticity, in which my mother lived, gave rise to what would be feminism and the reorientation in American culture of white bourgeois women, of which I am an example. Part of the process of writing this book has been to understand how *American* a certain construction of both femininity and domesticity is and how certain historical particularities shaped feminist thought in this country. The questions raised, while directly posed vis-à-vis film studies, resonate more generally with American, cultural, and women's studies.

Housekeeping as Text

Housework. Domesticity. Though related, the two words considered independently conjure up extremely different sets of associations and values. Housework is trivial, dull, stultifying labor, work only a woman in love or impoverished would willingly do, repetitive, strenuous, endless, infantilizing. Domesticity, by contrast, refers to home, family, maternity, warmth, hearth, to the creation of a private place where we can be who we really are, to a set of experiences, possessions, and sentiments that are highly symbolically valued in our culture. Though inextricably related—domesticity *includes* housework—the two words represent values and experiences that are profoundly opposed. In this book I assert that domestic discourses have been a primary determinant of feminine identity over the last two centuries in America. Furthermore, the affiliation of (white bourgeois) femininity with a certain location (the home) and ethos (moralized sentimentality) has had a profound ideological effectivity in organizing our nation primarily around gender distinctions.

American Domesticity is first and foremost a book about female gender construction and the mechanics of class mystification in America. I locate this mystification within the critical conundrum of domestic labor: it is both labor and love, it constitutes an imbrication of the concerns of Marx and Freud, and it involves criteria related to both class and gender construction. The book begins from the insight that in Hollywood melodramas focused on female protagonists, housework is consistently rendered *invisible* as labor and transformed into emotional, sentimental acts saturated with pathos. I then make use of an interdisciplinary and diachronic analysis focused on representations of housework as labor to trace the historical and ideological roots of the affiliation between sentimentalized femininity and housework.

Thus the book gives a historical, discursive, and material context for an underrepresented and untheorized issue in film studies: domestic labor.

This analysis affords several crucial insights that are foreclosed by conventional disciplinary boundaries. The book locates within nineteenth-century domestic housekeeping manuals and their social, economic, and political contexts the rise of a morally inflected appearance standard for white bourgeois women that specifically involves the erasure of their identity as laborers. This insight radically recontextualizes and alters what have been two theoretical cornerstones of female gender representation in the cinema: the woman as object of the gaze and, more recently, woman as spectator. My analysis opens up these universalized and hence ahistorical conceptions to their specific national, racial, and class-based functions. In addition to providing an explication for what David James argues in *The Hidden Foundation* is the unspeakability of class difference within cinema studies, this insight also makes a significant contribution to American studies and women's studies via its placement of the cult of domesticity.[4] Conventionally understood as related to "women's history" or the history of the *private* sphere, the cult of domesticity has not generally been considered by historians in relation to the concerns of the *public* sphere in the nineteenth century — for example, abolition, universal (white male) suffrage, and regional conflicts between North and South. I suggest that the overarching function of the cult had everything to do with the push for universal white male suffrage. Through the idealization of privileged womanhood, the cult essentially reestablished in the private sphere the inequities that no longer structured civic and political privilege in the public sphere. This period also saw the new nation trying to reconcile the pronounced contradictions between capitalism and democracy, contradictions also tellingly ameliorated by the distinctions between "public" and "private." As I discuss in part I, domestic femininity discursively operates to preserve and mystify class inequities in the delicate bodies of middle-class white women; it effectively sentimentalizes the relationship between a landowner and his property; and it sets up the terms for the construction of racial difference in America.[5] White middle-class women's delicate appearance and the spiritualization of their domestic labor were crucial to all these functions.

In sum, in *American Domesticity* I reject a universalized gender binary that overrides and substitutes for all other social differences by identifying the moment and context of its inception in the United States, a moment wherein gender was wedded to a public-private distinction in the ideology of separate spheres. I reveal through a careful analysis of the changing representations of women's domestic labor how the construction of American (white bourgeois) femininity is inextricably linked to class mystification and its very racialized and racist manifestations.

My overarching thesis is that post–industrial revolution domestic discourses construct and naturalize a hierarchical matrix of vital cultural binaries — male/female, public/private, work/leisure, nature/culture, gender/class, production/consumption, and so on — whose obvious problems and contradictions are articulated (and therefore mystified) as properties of femininity. I would assert, with Thomas Streeter, that "discussions of dichotomies such as production/consumption, work/home, public/private, and masculine/feminine are not intended as descriptions of empirical social structures . . . but as descriptions of ways that people in our society, particularly elites in decision-making capacities, *imagine* social relations."[6] The suppression of women's domestic labor within a moralized, sentimentalized construction of femininity is vital to the preservation and efficacy of these binaries. Sampling different generic and historical representations of domesticity and housework, I indicate the social, economic, and political forces served by the intricate ideological matrices and paradoxes that femininity secures.

Combining a chronological and a generic approach, I examine representations of domesticity and housekeeping in three specific discursive locations. Embodying historical, popular, and feminist perspectives, respectively, these locations consist of, first, the didactic literature on housework written by white middle-class American women in the nineteenth and early twentieth centuries; second, the images of housekeeping promulgated by classical Hollywood melodramas in the twentieth century; and third, feminist films' constructions and revisions of housework, both aesthetic and political, which emerged in the late twentieth century. I consider both American and European feminist filmmakers in the final section to stress both the ideological priorities of their American reception and the international character of feminism which predicates itself on a universalized notion of gender.

Because my interests are ideological, diachronic, and discursive, I limit my considerations in the first two parts of the book to texts involved in hegemonic, dominant constructions of domestic femininity. Although many historians and cultural critics have asserted that such discourses were internally fractured and open to a variety of appropriations and receptions (assertions I would not contest), my interest in the paradoxical character of domestic femininity has an altogether different aim and orientation. I am attempting to provide a map that shows how feminine gender construction, via domestic discourses, both displays and masks the property relations that underpin class and racial difference in the nineteenth century. Although middle-class white women deployed domestic discourses to gain position and power, my analysis suggests that they were at the same time inscribing classist and racist inequality into the very core of their identities and discourses because of their structural relation to changes in civic privilege. In the twentieth century, the culture industry and feminism both inherited the femininity of the nineteenth, each employing it to different purposes. The former weds its classist and racist ethos to iconographies of consumer desire, subtly moralizing and essentializing women's relation to the market. The latter assumes gender as the primordial social difference, to the exclusion of other differences.

In part I, titled "Housekeeping by the Book," I consider the historical role of domestic discourses in the production of the American nation. Spanning the nineteenth and early twentieth centuries, these chapters chronicle the incremental transformation of housekeeping into the publicly acknowledged, quasi-scientific discipline known as home economics. This discipline was established by housewives writing about their work and simultaneously formulating a place for women in an American democracy that did not see them as citizens. Among nineteenth-century American writers on domesticity, Lydia Child and Catharine Beecher are obvious choices, Child for being one of the first writers on housework, and Beecher for being the most influential.

I analyze their texts in the context of the dramatic political and social changes characterizing America's first century, indicating how the discursive construction of the domestic woman and of the feminine private sphere organized and managed articulations of class and racial difference. For example, in the chapter on Catharine Beecher's work, I consider her perspective in relation to the fact that the rise of the cult of domesticity and the push for universal white male suffrage occurred during the same time period in U.S. history. Using Beecher's vision of domesticity to illustrate my points, I argue that the sentimentalized relationship to property developed by the cult of domesticity reestablished in the private sphere the class hierarchy formerly maintained in the public sphere by property requirements for suffrage. In the historical construction of domestic femininity in America, the particulars of feminine gender identity are derived not only from transformed and transforming property relations and shifting class identities, but also from religious changes that imbue both femininity and the domestic sphere with inordinate moral weight. Nineteenth-century Victorianism identified women (white middle-class women) as precisely more moral, spiritual, and compassionate, as well as more delicate, than others: white middle-class men, the lower classes, "colored" races. This delicacy located class privilege within the standards of appropriate femininity and, by inference, within the bodies of middle-class white women. These standards would be difficult if not impossible to achieve for a woman who was not white or middle-class. Finally, nineteenth-century American writers on domesticity conceived of and developed an "invisible style" of self-representation for the bourgeois housewife and her home which set the terms for their representation in twentieth-century cinema.

At the beginning of the twentieth century, the influence of the nascent culture industry, particularly the cinema and advertising, on appropriate domesticity superseded that of "scribbling women." In part II, "Housekeeping in Hollywood," I look at domesticity's role in the production of desire, specifically commodity desire, by examining specific domestic melodramas that foreground housework, maternity, or both. Domestic melodramas sustained moralized constructions of the domestic woman while also insinuating into this morality desires and values related to spectacle, commodities, and appearance. The work of D. W. Griffith, an important figure in early cinema, weds nineteenth-century Victorian moralism and melodrama to the spectacular, fetishistic, desiring apparatus of film. What results is a perverse construction of domestic femininity ultimately positioned at the intersection of two irresolvable imperatives—those of acquisitive desire and moral restraint. Beginning with Griffith's domestic melodramas, I analyze key films—*The Making of an American Citizen* (1912), *The Mothering Heart* (1913), *Broken Blossoms* (1919), *Way Down East* (1920), *Too Wise Wives* (1921), *Craig's Wife* (1936), *Stella Dallas* (1937), *Mildred Pierce* (1945), and *Imitation of Life* (1934, 1959)—for the ways in which they progressively convert housework from a form of physical labor to one of purely expressive emotional labor. My discussions point to how the sentimentalization of white middle-class women and their domesticity fostered and maintained illusory, moralistic, and highly seductive conventions of consumption that set the terms for (mis)understanding the relation of gender to other social classes and identities.[7]

In part III, "Housekeeping against the Grain," I examine domesticity's role in the production of a political aesthetic, specifically that of feminism. In looking at self-conscious, politically motivated representations of housework and domesticity in feminist films and visual texts, I consider how these texts attempt to deconstruct the conventions of a moralized, domestic femininity. Feminist revisions of domesticity, which emerged with particular force in the 1970s, contest popular culture images and narratives by investigating alternative symbolic, aesthetic, and political implications of women's work. In some of these films, the problem of a "feminine aesthetic" is depicted as deriving from women's historically privatized situation and practices. Other texts expose the inherent race and class biases present in images of white middle-class housewives. Finally, these representations of domesticity make manifest the ways in which "women's work" has been shaped and evaluated by an aesthetics and politics of invisibility. Using very different approaches, contemporary feminist film-makers such as Patricia Gruben, Zeinabu Davis, Chantal Akerman, and Marleen Gorris render this work and its effects emphatically visible. Although only Davis is American (Gruben was born in the United States but emigrated to Canada), all of these filmmakers speak back to Hollywood's hegemonic constructions of domestic femininity while also critiquing the very psychoanalytic discourse that secures these constructions within the canon of American feminist film theory.[8]

The re-readings of classical Hollywood melodrama and avant-garde feminist films proffered in parts II and III supplement feminist readings of these texts that ulti-mately secure their meanings in relation to gender. My readings implement the insights of Stuart Hall and Paul Gilroy, respectively, that "race is the modality in which class is lived," and "gender is the modality in which race is lived," by demon-strating how gender functions to erase racial and class differences and inequities when it is considered as a difference in and of itself.[9] The particular readings of parts II and III absolutely depend on the framing in part I to show how the interpretive methods that dominate film studies have not understood or been able to articulate race, class, and gender as other than an idealized mantra of discrete and self-evident differences. My readings insist on these interpretive categories as interrelated modal-ities whose significance to our national imaginary finds its roots in the political and economic machinations of nineteenth-century America and its gendered division of public and private spheres, a division facilitated by the idealization and mystification of domestic labor.

Domestic discourses have served an array of conflicting social forces and posi-tions, all involved in some way with the articulation of feminine identity and women's proper place. Chronology allows me to give feminist artists and filmmakers the last word. Although the history of housework and domesticity by no means ends with that word, the preeminence that domestic discourses have maintained in the construction of feminine gender identity is slowly and incrementally being disman-tled and swept away.

Housekeeping as Method

What has the woman to do with truth?

FRIEDRICH NIETZSCHE

Where there is dirt, there is system.

MARY DOUGLAS

A recurrent tendency of domestic discourse produced by women, from Lydia Child to Chantal Akerman, is to use housekeeping as a strategy, a form, an aesthetic, and a method, and my text is no exception. Housework is supradisciplinary, as it includes many disparate tasks and crosses over delineations of leisure, labor, and love; while responsible for setting clear boundaries, it also exceeds them. I adopted an analogous multidisciplinary approach for this "film" book because I could not have historicized the American cinema's representations of domestic labor without looking beyond that particular medium. The crossing of disciplinary boundaries allowed me to place both labor and race at the center of the usual distinctions between private and public, domestic and socioeconomic, feminine and masculine. As I have argued, this perspective provided a context for representations of femininity that accounts for the invisibility of women's domestic labor in specific social and historical moments over the last two centuries. Furthermore, this context puts Hollywood, independent, and experimental films into a dynamic historical relationship to one another while also locating "film" in a cogent discursive relationship to nineteenth-century texts.

This book demonstrates that the importance of women's appearance in America has roots in the history of their domestic labor as well as of their sexuality, that is, in considerations of their sweeping as well as of their being swept away. Consequently, women's appearance has a textual as well as visual history, one that bears, finally, on constructions of nation, class, and race as well as gender. In both fiction and nonfiction, sentimentality and melodrama, the predominant modes that bring bourgeois domestic femininity into being, keep us from seeing beyond women's appearance. Thus pathos, sentiment, and sensation lie, whereas dirt is about the truth. Domestic femininity generates a system to remove the "dirty secrets" necessary for keeping up appearances—of a coherent national character, of masculine and feminine spheres, of a homogeneous and democratic social order—but these secrets are ultimately as much about labor, about who does the dirty work, as they are about sex. I use the materiality of housekeeping, its supradisciplinary labor, as a means to sweep away the sentimentality and sensation from discourses of domesticity and to lay out the mystifications they engender. Preeminent among these has been the fantasy of a leisured, lily-white gender, whose delicacy is unsullied by labor, whose identity is transcendent, untouched by history or messy social differences. Thus, if I found in the photo everything I wanted to discuss, as well as things I could not see at first, I am left answering another question in this book: "How to tell this story differently?"[10]

• PART I •

HOUSEKEEPING BY THE BOOK

One

Housekeeping by the Book

From Hints to Home Economics

Housekeeping ain't no joke.

LOUISA MAY ALCOTT

If housekeeping is not a joke, the question then becomes how to take it seriously. Nineteenth-century American culture generated an array of texts concerned with domesticity and women's role in it. Sermons, religious literature, novels, diaries, auto-biographies, magazine articles, and textbooks by, for, and about women and the home all contributed to the construction and dissemination of what is now tellingly referred to as both "the cult of True Womanhood" and "the cult of domesticity."[1] Yet, as the designation "cult" and Nathaniel Hawthorne's outraged injunctions against "mobs of damned scribbling women" suggest, this work and its topic were dismissed at that time and have been ever since in traditional approaches to history and literature.[2] Feminist scholars, however, have taken domesticity, housekeeping, and women's writings about them very seriously, but their significance has often been understood in a limited way: as related exclusively to the private sphere—the home and femininity. The joke that informs this section of the book and that lays the foundation for all the material that follows is that housekeeping has never been taken seriously, though it in fact organizes and puts in place all the major questions and political problems facing the American nation in the nineteenth century.

In the body of work that has come to delimit the field of domestic economy in America, books by women predominate. Early advice books tended to pass on their wisdom about housekeeping in the form of hints and personal anecdotes. Yet these texts rapidly evolved, assumed different formal appearances, and, in conjunction with other sociohistorical forces, transformed the localized, informal practices of housekeeping into the general science of home economics. These books, their rhetorical strategies, and the discursive contexts of which they were a part are the subject of this section.

What interests me about these texts and their historical moment is neither the social experience of housekeeping nor its institutionalization in home economics per se, but rather the extremely productive encounter between "women's" writing and their social experience. Specifically, I will show how literate, well-educated white middle-class women, in different historical moments, conceived themselves, literally invented themselves, in relation to work that they began to write of as "theirs." Alternatively, "their" writing constructed domestic space and their function, their identity within it, in very particular ways. Finally, a politically and economically crucial gender identity took shape, in part through these representations, and shaped American politics and economics in relation to the discourses of housekeeping and domestic femininity that proliferated in this period. I will argue that this very socially effective construction of femininity arose out of several interrelated phenomena involving women's work and function in the United States. Housework, though always *necessary* labor, became increasingly *useless* in a market economy as industrialization moved productive activities outside the home. The writings on domesticity in nineteenth-century America wed this labor to a moralized construction of femininity that worked to solidify and justify different class positions, while at the same time class distinctions were increasingly obscured by the now overarching distinction between the genders.

These coincident developments raise two significant questions. First, how did conceptions of American domesticity operate to distinguish it from European models, an issue evident in the work of both Lydia Child and Catharine Beecher? Second, how did these conceptions organize and unify regional, political, and ideological contradictions within the new nation? The intersecting needs of establishing a nation both sufficiently distinct from other nations (but particularly England) yet also sufficiently coherent to encompass its own fragmented and diverse social body found common ground in the idea of home, an idea wherein individual identity and origins are wedded to nation. In the texts I discuss, American identity is a persistent focus, one that generalizes and subsumes individual concerns within a nationalistic discourse. It does so by establishing individual origins—the home, the family, maternity, and so forth—as humanist universals that give rise to a similarly universalized citizen, divorced from historical and social contingencies. American domesticity consequently acquires a paradoxical character. Although it is conservative in function (it both implements and participates in constructing the ideological foundations for nation formation), its identity is initially articulated in opposition both to a market economy and nascent capitalism *and* to the privileges of an aristocratic social order (the so-called servant problem that has structured American domesticity since its discursive inception). The home is frequently represented as a haven, in that it is presumed to foster and maintain values distinctly at odds with and threatened by capitalism. As I will show, it is precisely in these "humane" manifestations that the concept is most profoundly conservative, racist, and classist in its social effectivity. I therefore consider in this book the influence of domestic discourses on ideas about national identity, property, citizenship, slavery, and technology in the newly formed American nation.

Lydia Child's Frugal Housekeeping:
Hints and a Patchwork Economy

Lydia Maria Child, one of the earliest American writers on housekeeping, achieved considerable, if controversial, public stature in the nineteenth century. William Lloyd Garrison called her "the first woman in the republic," and her biographer Carolyn Karcher notes that Child "pioneered almost every department of nineteenth-century American letters: the historical novel, the short story, children's literature, the domestic advice book, women's history, antislavery fiction, and journalism."[3] A baker's daughter, Child identified herself with that class of people who "work with their *hands*," yet her early literary successes propelled her to the higher echelons of Boston society.[4] Her publication of *The American Frugal Housewife* (1829) established her as a "national authority on homemaking," an authority and livelihood she later sacrificed for her committed abolitionist efforts.[5]

Though explicitly written for women of a particular class, Child's book nevertheless participated in the discursive alchemy that ultimately constructed a particularized version of "womanhood" as a category that transcended class, race, region, and other specific circumstances. Less obviously, Child's text also contributed to the formulation of a national character, consisting of American idiosyncracies and attitudes that she located within a nascent and resistant private sphere—that of frugal housekeeping.

In the mid-nineteenth century, however, as well as in historical accounts written today, Child's importance as a writer on domesticity is eclipsed by that of her successor Catharine Beecher. It is my argument that Child's work and its reception are vital to an understanding of what is at stake in the disciplining of American domesticity. Her book takes shape from an array of competing discourses not yet organized or placed as they will be in the "cult of domesticity." Thus her text demonstrates in microcosm the contradictory economic underpinnings and social ambivalences that domesticity ultimately contains and manages, contradictions that would be resolved in Beecher's much more systematic ideological construction. Using Foucault's criteria for disciplinary effectivity, whereby disciplines "reduce what in a multiplicity makes it much less manageable than a unity," we can say that Beecher's book participates in the articulation of a unity, while in Child's work multiplicity is still very much in evidence.[6] Still, Child's book does participate in a disciplinary trajectory in that it gives visibility to or puts into discursive circulation the idea of an explicitly American domesticity. Yet it is marked by the chaotic multiplicities of the new republic that manifested themselves in the discourses surrounding both the publication and reception of Child's book and in the content and rhetoric of the book itself. The most pointed of these issues involved class, regionalism, and the economic and social transformations that were completely changing the lives of women. These issues shaped Child's life and in turn were shaped and influenced by her work.

For obvious geographical, historical, and economic reasons, New England was the most influential region in the early years of the United States. Influence presumes representation of some sort, and not only were the most salient economic and political forces located in this area, but so too were the most lucrative publishing networks. Publishing firms in New York, Boston, and Philadelphia garnered the lion's share of the market in the first half of the nineteenth century.[7] Child's upbringing in New England and early literary successes in Boston mapped her own dramatic class rise onto what would become a significant factor in writings on domesticity: that the views of a regionally specific group and class—privileged New Englanders—would become the national model for a standardized notion of the proper home and the woman within it.

Child both was and was not a privileged New Englander. Largely self-educated, she came from a stern Calvinist family whose livelihood depended on substantial amounts of manual labor. Her father had developed his bakery into a successful business by the time Lydia Maria was born, but he nevertheless required his children's participation in "a thriving household enterprise and family farm" that taught them how to "make hay, weed the garden, set the hens, tend the shop, turn the 'dumb-betty,' and hang out the clothes."[8] Although Child's older brother's intellectual talents secured him a Harvard education from a father who did not particularly value education, her own considerable intelligence and precocity went unrewarded. Ultimately her brother's patronage, her own passionate pursuit of knowledge, and her publication, at the age of twenty-two, of her first novel, *Hobomok*, resulted in her introduction into the genteel upper class in Boston. Amply intellectually suited for these circles, Child nevertheless did not share their upbringing, their formal education, or their financial resources.

Writing was not an avocation for Child, nor was her belief in frugality conceived in abstraction. Child wrote and published "in order to support herself and her husband" because of the financial difficulties they encountered throughout their marriage.[9] Child experienced firsthand the economic instability of the period, an instability that affected large segments of the population in the depression that began in 1819.[10] The fact that her own troubles were precipitated by her marriage to a man laden with debt enhanced her insights regarding women's particular vulnerability in the dramatic transformations that characterized the early nineteenth century.[11] In her fiction, journalism, and domestic advice, Child theorized, narrativized, and generalized ambiguities concerning class, region, race, and feminine identity that drew on, but extended far beyond, her own situation.[12] Her formulations of some of these issues affected both the publication of *The American Frugal Housewife* and its construction of American domesticity.

Initially, Child had trouble getting her book accepted by publishers; they saw it as just another cookbook, like many that were available at the time. She persuaded them of its uniqueness and importance by pointing out both its attention to an ignored sector of the population and its appeal to the needs of Americans overall. All the books available on the market, either by British or by American writers, were addressed to the wealthy, to those who could afford servants. None of them, Child later asserted, were "suited to the wants of the middling class in our own country." Child's critique of the most popular of these books, Frances Parkes's *Domestic Duties* (1825), stressed its inappropriateness for Americans in general. Parkes's book, Child wrote, was addressed to the needs of "wealthy, aristocratic England. . . . [T]he economy, the benevolence, all the duties inculcated, presuppose great wealth, high station, and fashionable habits. We should indeed tremble for the twenty four *Disunited States* of this Republic, if we thought such books would become necessary here."[13]

When Child's book was finally published, it provided a "striking contrast" to all the other recipe and domestic advice books on the market because it did not presume to advise a housewife with servants.[14] Significantly, this difference was discursively framed as uniquely American in such a way that a specific class—the "middling" class—was seen to represent America overall far more accurately than the privileged or the wealthy. Child's housekeeping promised unity of the nation. Thus the title of her book, *The Frugal Housewife*, identifies frugality as a uniquely American virtue, a connection she made explicit in her title change to *The American Frugal Housewife* in 1835.[15] Published accounts of its significance also emphasized a notion of American housewifery distinct from that of England, a distinction articulated as deriving from the needs and the necessary autonomy of a particular class and its housewives.

Child's book did very well, selling more than six thousand copies in its first year and establishing her as a national expert on domesticity. By the time it went out of print in 1850, it had gone through thirty-five editions.[16] Written prior to the "second" industrial revolution, which most historians date at around 1850, her text formulates conceptions of economy, domesticity, and the housewife that predate the advent of consumer society. The economy overall was a mixed one, with domesticity still not completely differentiated from the growing market economy. Child distinguished the household economy from the marketplace in regionally and class-marked terms which prepared the way for, but were still very different from, those that the cult of domesticity would establish. Writing from, to, and for the "middling" classes, she dictated that the household economy should maintain a relation of abstention and autonomy from the market. She dedicated *The American Frugal Housewife* "to those who are not ashamed of economy," and cited on her title page Benjamin Franklin's dictum that "a fat kitchen maketh a lean will."

Child explicitly attempted to distinguish her domestic advice book from others available on the market at that time both in its format and content. Her competition combined information about the management of servants with considerations of etiquette and proper attitudes and tended to include recipes calling for very expensive ingredients.[17] Several aspects of Child's text were significant to her very different articulation of a uniquely American domesticity, specifically her emphasis on frugality, ingenuity, and self-reliance promoted in a text patched together from discursive forms available in the home such as recipes, hints, and lists. Beyond its promotion and reception, I am interested in these differences, both in *what* the text says and in *how* it dispenses its advice. What kind of advice does it include, what values does it imbue housekeeping with, and what image of the housewife emerges? What discursive format does it employ, and what are the epistemological and sociological implications of that format?

"Gathering up All the Fragments"

Though clearly offered as a strategy for housekeeping, *The American Frugal Housewife* situates itself and its advice within a nascent market economy. Not mincing any words, Child gets right to the truth of housekeeping in the opening lines of her introductory chapter:

> The true economy of housekeeping is simply the art of gathering up all the frag-
> ments, so that nothing be lost. I mean fragments of *time* as well as *materials*. Nothing
> should be thrown away so long as it is possible to make any use of it, however trifling
> that use might be: and whatever be the size of a family, every member should be
> employed either in earning or saving money.[18]

As her review of *Domestic Duties* indicates, Child saw the housewife's "gathering up
all the fragments" as necessary to family survival and as staving off the "*Disunited
States* of this Republic." In reviewing Child's advice to the housewife, I mean to show
how it uses the middle-class home and domesticity to strike a balance between competing modes of production in the early nineteenth century. In this light, the white
middle-class housewife becomes a central figure and role model in the period's
socioeconomic transformations, charged with "gathering up all the fragments" of the
home and, by extension, of the nation.

For Child, good housekeeping manages without resources per se, that is, without
the possession of materials already determined to be valuable. The housekeeper must
instead make an art out of gathering together all that would otherwise be lost. Her
material resources, the basis of her economy, consist of fragments, throwaways,
things that would be wasted without her intervention. Housekeeping carefully, art-
fully prevents waste by preserving what would be discarded and reusing it. Child
stresses that fragments of time as well as of materials make up her housekeeper's
paradoxical resources — lost or potentially wasted material, labor, and time that
require her agency to become valuable. Child's housewife creates use for the useless,
triumphing even in trifles, as imminent loss or waste is the determinant of her
resources and their only measure.

Only after she considers materials, time, and labor does Child mention housekeeping's relation to money — that all family members should be employed in earning or saving it. Money is the last of a housekeeper's resources and the one for which
she must scrupulously *avoid* creating a use. Good housekeeping saves money, earns
money, but never spends it freely; while a market economy exchanges, her domestic
economy keeps and saves — saving in the sense of rescuing from loss or non-use
rather than hoarding. For example, she advises that children be taught to "save everything — not for their *own* use, for that would make them selfish — but for *some* use"
(6).

Child's housekeeper is not a consumer, though her household economy coexists
with a nascent market economy. Even the notion that preindustrial colonial households were self-sufficient is grossly inaccurate; purchase and barter were housekeeping tasks from at least the early eighteenth century.[19] Nevertheless, the items purchased
and their significance to the household distinguish them from commodities as they
were conceived in the later consumer economy. Typically, housewives bought or
bartered for subsistence items or those that they needed for household production
and manufacturing. Jeanne Boydston writes of this period:

> Capitalized manufacturing was still in its early stages. The products it provided to fam-
> ilies were useful and often necessary. Wethersfield, Connecticut, women used their
> onions to purchase store credit toward cloth, food, and ribbon. Theodora Orcutt of
> Whateley, Massachusetts, kept a running account with shopkeeper Wells, trading her
> yarn for beef, pork, cheese, and occasionally, even cash. As the continuing volume of

women's household manufacture indicates, however, the goods of the marketplace were neither of a quantity nor of a nature to offset the bulk of the wife's work.[20]

In the situation that Boydston describes, production and consumption are not discrete and oppositional functions. Housewives produce in order to acquire goods they cannot make at home. The shopkeeper sells goods from them as well as to them. Often their purchases faciliate home manufacturing rather than replacing it.

By the time Child wrote her book, manufacturing in the Northeast had begun to compete very successfully with household production, especially of textiles.[21] While the upper-class housewife could easily fill the new role of consumer, for the middling class, for rural or frontier families, or for those just setting up housekeeping, consumption represented a hardship. Child's construction of this still mixed and transitional economy (which had both regional and class implications) attempts to render the market incidental to the home production that was still vital to many families' survival.

Thus, the frugal housewife acts, spends *within* her means, indeed well within them, for even if she has only "half a dollar a day," Child exhorts her to "be satisfied to spend forty cents" (4). The value of making do, of getting by, seems here to overshadow the very question of necessity itself. No objective standards of a minimum income circumscribe Child's notion of a viable household. What you have must always be more than enough: "Self-denial, in proportion to the narrowness of your income, will eventually be the happiest and most respectable course for you and yours" (5). Housekeeping, as Child describes it, has no definite place, resources, or absolute needs of its own. Represented as a subsistence economy within a growing market economy, an accommodation with always unpredictable circumstances, it nevertheless makes do; it works with whatever it has.

The primary impulse of Child's housekeeping seems geared to averting economic ruin and disaster; ceaseless and tireless activity and frugality of manner are her tactics for avoiding poverty. Her message articulates not only her own unstable situation but also that of the economy overall, bringing the home and housewife into that economy in very specific ways. Her emphasis on the importance and urgency of good housekeeping publicizes, puts into discursive circulation, an alternative model of the household that indicates the limits of upper-class urban accounts of proper domesticity. Her comments point to new forces in the changing economy that differentiate the tasks of the frugal housewife from those of a wealthier woman, those of "mediating between the demands of the cash market and the often-quite-different imperatives of family survival."[22]

Writing of the contribution of working-class and middle-class housewives to their households in the early years of the nineteenth century, Boydston observes that it was definitely in the interests of men of both classes to marry. Working-class wives' income and labor doubled the value of a husband's sub-subsistence wages and allowed families to survive. As economic conditions improved throughout the early decades of the century, the labors and income of middle-class women supplemented their husbands' ability to provide for the family's maintenance:

Overseeing patterns of both purchase and consumption, substituting her own labor in home manufacturing for the labor value contained in the price of commodities, allowing the household to avoid altogether or to decrease payment for cooking, laundry, child care, and cleaning, and often also adding outright to the family's cash income, the wife's labor created the surplus that could be translated into home ownership, an expanded business operation, savings or investment.[23]

Child's overall message in the early years of this transitional phase is to resist purchasing goods whenever possible and produce them at home. While this message seems to place the home *outside* the market economy, in many respects it facilitated the development of industry in the Northeast by allowing employers to pay married male workers below subsistence wages.[24] The housewife was left "gathering up all the fragments" of an emerging industrial and market economy.

"Time is Money"

In a telling aphorism, Child herself draws an equivalence between market and domestic currency:

> "Time is money." For this reason, cheap as stockings are, it is good economy to knit them. Cotton and woollen yarn are both cheap; hose that are knit wear twice as long as woven ones; and can be done at odd minutes of time, which would not be otherwise employed. Where there are children, or aged people, it is sufficient to recommend knitting, that it is an *employment*. (3)

Child's literate readership would not easily miss the citation of Benjamin Franklin's famous dictum "Remember, that *time* is money," written almost a century earlier, but still relevant as what Max Weber calls an expression of the spirit of capitalism "in almost classical purity."[25] Thus, in referring to Franklin's articulation of economy, Child's book explicitly draws a comparison between the values of market economy and what she outlines as the values of the frugal housekeeper. But for Child, the economy of housekeeping takes shape in reaction to the "the spirit of capitalism," making her application of this aphorism differ markedly from Franklin's. In his *Advice to a Young Tradesman*, money is fecund; put to wise use, it reproduces itself. Further, its accumulation, which can be assured only by use and investment, is the highest economic value. The aphorism expresses Franklin's belief that any work time not spent making money is time wasted, and is therefore worth quoting in full: "Remember, that *time* is money; Remember that *credit* is money; Remember that money is of the prolific, generating character."[26]

In contrast, Child's interpretation of Franklin's dictum formulates a very different relationship between time and money for the housewife. Rather than being a resource most fully exploited in making money, time can and should, whenever possible, *replace* money. "Cheap as stockings are," the frugal housekeeper makes them, substituting expenditures of time for those of money. The time spent finds its reward in stockings that "wear twice as long." Just as money makes more money in a market economy, so does time reap more time in the household. Here the benefits of "homemade" have not yet been completely sentimentalized; home production still competes with manufacture. The cumulative nature of knitting gathers together "odd minutes" to make a finished garment from a patchwork of stitches and time that would "otherwise" be lost. And in knitting stockings, members of the extended family who would be idle and nonproductive participate in housekeeping: they *spend* their time wisely.

The differing advice given the housewife and tradesman positions their economic practices in very different relations not just to money but to time and, consequently, to social space. Whereas the young tradesman is advised to cultivate monetary inter-actions, the housewife of the same class is cautioned to scrupulously avoid or sub-stitute for them. Franklin advises the young tradesman to exploit the workday fully, but the inference is that that day, though much longer than our modern workday, does come to an end—when he enters the home![27] In Child's description of house-keeping, the workday is never mentioned; time is not a measure that demarcates "work" from "leisure." For the housewife, the home is outside time as such.[28]

In some respects, housework seems to maintain the relationship with time charac-teristic of preindustrial, agrarian labor—the type of labor that predominated in colonial America.[29] In "Time, Work-Discipline, and Industrial Capitalism," E. P. Thompson defines preindustrial labor and outlines the ways in which the new work habits demanded by industrial capitalism necessitated a completely different under-standing of time. Preindustrial labor was governed by "task-orientation," that is, by the amount and intensity of work required by a given task. Harvest time required intense labor "from dawn to dusk," while at other times the agrarian workload would, of necessity, be lighter.[30] The demarcation between work and life is much less pro-nounced in task orientation, as "social intercourse and labour are intermingled—the working-day lengthens or contracts according to the task—and there is no great sense of conflict between labour and 'passing the time of day.'" But, to those disciplined in timed labor, task orientation "appears to be wasteful and lacking in urgency." Tellingly, Thompson (writing in the 1960s), remarks that, even today the work rhythms of the housewife and mother retain elements of preindustrial society.[31] But this analogy is deceptive, revealing the limits of socioeconomic analysis; it cannot apprehend house-work in historic terms because the analytical terms themselves are predicated on a gen-dered public-private split. That is, Thompson assumes a housewife and mother who does not also work outside the home in some form of industrial or wage labor; he thus unwittingly presumes that all housewives and mothers are middle class.

Reading through Child's text, with its insistence that every moment be filled with busy, if not useful, activity, one does not get the sense that the frugal housewife's day or night ever contracts or that her household could ever be found wasteful or lack-ing in urgency. Although her housekeeping is task oriented, it is also imbued through and through with the same Protestant work ethic that disciplined the practices of industrial capitalism. Child clearly shares the values that inform Benjamin Franklin's pristine rendition of the "spirit of capitalism." These virtues—honesty, frugality, industry, and an aversion to "any spontaneous enjoyment in life"—constitute the major tenets of the Protestant ethic, derived most directly from Calvinism.[32] For Franklin, for the capitalist, the virtues of industry and frugality pay off in substan-tial monetary accumulation. In Child's housekeeping, the busy use of all available time does not accumulate surplus time but rather purchases autonomy and self-reliance for the household, defined in this context as a lack of dependence on the market and money.

Family Value: "Kept out of Idleness"

In *The American Frugal Housewife* we see the moral and ethical structuring of the home and of work within the home as markedly devoid of the motivations that spur economic activity and shore up the values of Franklin's tradesman. Yet Child's references to Franklin and the values that permeate her text indicate a shared moral frame of reference, deriving from the religious forces that shaped New England, its values, and its ideas of work and community. But whereas domesticity in colonial times or in a frontier or rural setting was integrated within all productive and economic activity, we can see clearly in Child the fissure which would separate the discursively discrete public and private spheres. That fissure, as I have shown, constitutes home and market around radically different positions and attitudes toward money. And its location is in marriage, in the sanctioned relations between the tradesman and his frugal housewife.

Max Weber's interest in Franklin concerns the paradoxical character of the ethos that emerges from his writings. On the one hand, the values that Franklin celebrates are profoundly utilitarian: if one is honest, frugal, industrious, and diligent, one will reap material rewards; virtues are above all else useful to a man's worldly endeavors. On the other hand, Franklin advocates the accumulation of wealth beyond any consideration of material needs, even as he advances a staunchly ascetic lifestyle. The "absolutely irrational" consequence, in Weber's opinion, is that monetary acquisition is no longer subordinated to human needs or pleasure but exists as an end in itself, while the capitalist's morals are tainted with the very use value that has disappeared from his economic activity.[33]

But these motivations appear completely alien in noncapitalist economies such as that of the frugal housekeeper. Child advocates knitting even for those whose hands may be too young and undeveloped or too aged and stiff to do so competently. Such a view attributes value to actions that make use of time and human labor yet do not necessarily produce capital or a useful product as their end or purpose. In the misshapen length of knitted yarn hanging from Child's recommendation, we can see that the "true" economy of housekeeping prizes and generates symbolic values that extend beyond considerations of materially based utility or the accumulation of wealth. In distinguishing between what he calls "economic and symbolic capital," Pierre Bourdieu argues that "activity is as much a duty of communal life as an economic necessity."[34] That is to say that the impetus of necessity cooperates with a "charge" or force of bonding, of belonging, predicated or dependent not upon utility but upon economic activity or practices in and of themselves. For hands otherwise too old or too young to be included in the household economy, simply that they are employed is sufficient.

In setting all its members to tasks, even purely symbolic ones, Child's household economy constitutes its difference from the nascent capitalist market in a very specific way. Housekeeping retains values left over from a colonial economy in which symbolic and economic practices and capital were integrated within the home. Yet in the mixed transitional economy that Child describes, these values are no longer attached to productive activity. The alienation of value (money) from necessity essential to the spirit of capitalism and a market economy corresponds to the alienation of the household from productivity. Thus, in the home, the housewife's servicing of needs is no longer valued as materially productive and useful, while in the marketplace, the accumulation of value exceeds the satisfaction of needs as the goal of economic man. Utility, the basis of colonial and postrevolutionary subsistence economies, disappears as a standard from both the market and housekeeping economies as their functions are discursively differentiated. In this early construction of American housekeeping, Child formulates the value of housekeeping solely as its resistance to and autonomy from the value standard of the marketplace—money—in her insistence on frugality and economy. The paradox of housekeeping, which mirrors that of the marketplace, has to do with the cultivation of economic values—frugality, industry, and useful activity—in the interests of avoiding economic interactions. The value of domestic practices comes to be their *lack* of evident material value. Thus the domesticity that Child describes cultivates symbolic values in excess of standards of use or productivity—that is, it cultivates family values.

Housekeeping occurs where wit meets waste, where a canny sensibility can always discern not just the future blanket in the vestiges of the worn gown but the family that such an activity makes:

> In this point of view, patchwork is good economy. It is indeed a foolish waste of time to tear cloth into bits for the sake of arranging it anew in fantastic figures; but a large family may be kept out of idleness, and a few shillings saved, by this using scraps of gowns, curtains, & c. (3)

In this respect Child's housekeeper fits Lévi-Strauss's description of a bricoleur:

> The "bricoleur" is adept at performing a large number of diverse tasks; but, unlike the engineer, he does not subordinate each of them to the availability of raw materials and tools conceived for the purpose of the project. His universe of instruments is closed and the rules of his game are always to make do with "whatever is at hand," that is to say with a set of tools and materials which is always finite and is also heterogeneous because what it contains bears no relation to the current project, or indeed to any project, but is the contingent result of all the occasions there have been to renew or enrich the stock or to maintain it with the remains of previous constructions or destructions.[35]

The economic tool not available to the frugal housewife is money, and that constraint closes down or defines the universe of her instruments. The frugal household must rely on contingencies, on the nature of whatever happens to be at hand. In the measure of housekeeping's symbolic capital, waste and gain complement rather than oppose each other, the one the raw material of the other. Practices considered good economy derive from situations, from the clever orchestration "on the spot" of unpredictable variables. In making patchwork, the housekeeper gathers together a large family and her worn-out curtains and gowns, setting many hands to tear the fabric "to bits" and rearrange them in "fantastic figures." The original function of these objects, exhausted and worn, is obliterated, to be refigured, reinvented colorfully, fantastically, like the family itself.

Interestingly, though, Child's text lacks any definitive construction of a normative domestic space or situation; instead it presents housekeeping in and as a *spatial* patchwork, a collection or gathering together of tasks that vary from place to place and from situation to situation. Child offers no generalized, idealized notion of "the family" that transcends the idiosyncrasies of region. Instead, circumstance and class emerge from her text. Laid out with an almost incantatory rhythm, a series of hints demonstrates the contingent character of frugal housewifery in relation to place or location:

> Where grain is raised, it is a good plan to teach children to prepare and braid straw for their own bonnets and their brothers' hats.
> Where turkey and geese are kept, handsome feather fans may as well be made by the younger members of a family, as to be bought. (3)

Noting the collective use to which children and various remains—straw and feathers—can be put, Child also reveals other features of her housekeeping that are related to notions of place. Her repeated use of "where" underscores the fact that good housekeeping must adapt itself to its location and structure its tasks in relation to geography, to context, to social class, to whatever animals or crops happen to be in the yard. The housekeeper therefore makes do with her surroundings, with whatever circumstances confront her, with whatever chance (marriage, family) leaves to her: "In the city . . . it is better to exchange ashes and grease for soap; but in the country . . . it is good economy to make one's own soap" (24). Child's housekeeping consists of variable tasks that are usually not performed in any set or explicitly articulated space; rather they take their shape from their environment (urban or rural). She rarely refers to explicitly defined spaces; a specific home and rooms within it are rarely mentioned. Instead, "where one lives near a slaughterhouse, it is worthwhile to buy cheap, fading goods and set them in this way" (9).

But domesticity is proposed as a *gendered* knowledge, one that can transcend class, bridge the traumas of class distinction, and work to define and therefore standardize women's experience and identity across an array of social and economic circumstances. Still, Child does not offer a generalized notion of the feminine. The only references to marked identity in *The Frugal Housewife* consist of hints regarding the education of daughters. Touching on a theme that would persist through all the major American writers on domestic economy, Child calls for daughters to have "home education," to be apprenticed to their mothers "for two or three years" that they might learn their trade (92). One anecdote concerns a daughter of uncertain fortunes who does not know how to sew, and whose mother is more concerned that her daughter enjoy her youth in socializing rather than learn housekeeping. Her mother pays for someone to come in and do the sewing for her. Child remarks: "But why have you suffered your daughter to be ignorant of so useful an employment? If she is poor, the knowledge will be necessary to her; if she is rich, . . . she will merely be a better judge whether her work is well done by others" (94–95). This anecdote, and Child's text overall, implicitly formulate *gender* as contingent, making the position and character of femininity subject to an array of volatile and uncontrollable forces, most notably class and regional distinctions. Its discourse proposes that a set of values, particularly frugality, and certain practices deriving from those values, can help control and standardize the necessarily uncertain future of daughters. In addressing and attempting to ameliorate the problems of a certain class of housekeepers, Child's text inadvertently articulates the instability and fluidity of female gender construction in relation to class ("if she be poor . . . if she be rich"). Her solution is to conceptualize, under a rudimentary gender/knowledge construction (the frugal housewife), a set of values and practices that will serve daughters, and hence families, across any class.

The Grammar of Gender/Knowledge:
Lists, Hints, and Recipes

Lydia Child's frugal American housewife emerges from a matrix of distinct, if transitory and chaotic, social relations involving nation formation and transformation to a market economy. Her designation of this gender/knowledge explicitly invokes these contexts, bringing together national identity ("The American"), a certain kind of economy ("Frugal"), and domesticity ("Housewife"). As a knowledge formed within these specific socioeconomic relations within the United States, *The American Frugal Housewife* expresses a particular understanding of them, conceived from the perspective of domestic economy. As Child herself articulates it, domestic gender/knowledge constitutes the necessary complement to a market economy, an essential counterpart that can compensate for or ameliorate the market's destabilizing, undemocratic, or hierarchical effects. Thus Child's text, in its format and grammar, embodies the particulars of a certain material, economic, and discursive milieu— the home—in the midst of radical social change. But it also speaks beyond the immediacy of the domestic sphere, giving a sense of its relation to the market economy that it constituted and that now supersedes it.

Lydia Child brings together the material and discursive, economy and grammar, by inventing a text from the toil of her day. Her biographer characterizes the arrangement of her text as marked by the erratic patterns of a housekeeper's life: "*The Frugal Housewife* reads as if Child had flown between her kitchen and her desk, jotting down whatever ideas came to mind while she was performing her household tasks."[36] Certainly for Child, both her housekeeping hints and her writings were means of survival. Their union of grammar and economy is effected by a process of discursive imitation analogous to Child's model of pedagogy. Child's text mimes the rhythms, the ordering, the logic of the tasks she describes, and constructs itself from discourses already present in the home.

If we consider the kind of text that Child maintains by today's standards, it must be said that things appear to be in a bit of a mess. Hints, suggestions, recipes all haphazardly litter the pages, perfunctorily grouped in the most general of categories. Nothing has a precise place. Seemingly, in the cluttered piles of tasks and hints that constitute her text, only the principle of frugality gathers and holds tasks and text together. Yet *The American Frugal Housewife* is not completely bereft of organization. We can look closely at a typical excerpt drawn from "Odd scraps for the Economical" to discern the ordering of the text:

> See that the beef and pork are always *under* brine; and that the brine is sweet and clean. Count towels, sheets, spoons, & c. occasionally; that those who use them may not become careless. See that the vegetables are neither sprouting nor decaying: if they are so, remove them to a drier place, and spread them. (8)

As Child's section title leads us to expect, we find a collection of prescriptions for economy listed here. While any reader might characterize this passage as leaping "from topic to topic," to call it "unsystematic" excludes the list as a system capable of gathering and organizing material.

The combination of the list and the prescription found in this section—which consists of short, summary directives for particular actions arranged in a vertical series—recalls a familiar domestic text, the cookbook. Publishers mistook *The American Frugal Housewife* for a cookery book perhaps because Child takes from that genre the organization of the list and formats akin to the recipe to present information even in parts of her text that are not concerned with the preparation of food or medical remedies. These organizational formats, copied from discursive sources in the home and then used to represent its overall economy, shape the vision of housekeeping that emerges. They constitute its grammar.

But this grammar results in a paradox similar to the one Child addresses vis-à-vis the emerging market economy. Child's text intervenes in and transforms a pedagogy that she herself approves. Under "Education of Daughters," she recommends that girls be apprenticed to their mothers, and she seizes upon familial mimicry as an opportune model for domestic education. Her pedagogical model is oral, mimetic, and maternal. Her information is "common," that is, based on common sense; she has simply gathered it together so that these hints, this oral knowledge, will not be lost. But by putting this knowledge in writing, Child transforms it. The passage from task to text implies a kindred passage from immediate and historically mute (because unrecorded) modes of expression and transmission (mimicry, conversation, hearsay) to formal, "public," recorded transcription. Child, writing for a heretofore unaddressed and unarticulated middling-class housewife, faces a task with nothing but inappropriate textual models (etiquette books on the management of servants) to guide her. How does she effect an autonomous, self-reliant housekeeping in her writing?

First of all, the technology of writing gave rise to formats that did not exist in speech and, further, that changed the functional capacity of language and human cognition over time. Chief among these formats were the list and the recipe.[37] These forms, as Jack Goody argues, were "not simply the by-products of the interaction between writing and, say, the economy. . . . [T]hey represented a significant change not only in the nature of transactions but also in the 'modes of thought' that accompanied them."[38] As reference material, recipes can be "tried" and evaluated by their users. "Experiment, assessment, the isolation of common elements, all are encouraged by the written recipes, whose very existence changes the course and nature of teaching."[39] Printed recipes (or housekeeping hints) supplement and can alleviate altogether one's dependence on participatory learning and the limitations of one's social experience. Written recipes, hints, or instructions for housekeeping tasks are therefore empowering to their users in two ways: they provide a vehicle for autonomous learning divorced from a fixed interpersonal context, and they facilitate the reader's evaluation of and possible innovation on traditional modes of performing a task.[40]

These functions of the recipe suggest the cultural role played by books such as Child's, which were especially helpful to families migrating west, a situation that often separated mothers from daughters and removed women from an established social context. In inscribing and circulating instructions for activities learned and performed in a familial context, writers such as Child "depersonalize" this knowledge and position it for use, but also for evaluation, review, and change. Finally, ironically, in that the recipe fosters solitary learning, it facilitates the privatization of housework, the isolation of housewives from one another. The written recipe obviates the need for interpersonal demonstration or instruction.

In this way Child's written text produces a practical gender/knowledge that is impersonal, though not yet scientific, in the face of the emerging market economy. The list gathers its material and arranges it by category. This arrangement is non-hierarchical, predicated on an almost completely democratic dispersal of value. The categorical list provides a discursive rendering of housekeeping as nonspecialized, characterized by bewildering diversity, by the sense that no task is more or less important than any other, that they all simply need to be done. And while the principle of frugality does motivate Child's text, its value as an ideal is consistently dispersed and subsumed in hints that present concrete practical advice about specific situations and problems. That is to say, the hints that constitute Child's text have an independent practical value that exceeds their function as examples of the abstract concept of frugality. Child's reader will not find in this book a logically constructed conceptual apparatus that, once learned, will allow her to deduce the proper resolution to any given housekeeping problem. In its series of equally valuable individuated hints, the text recounts a housekeeper's wisdom as piecemeal, as arising in, and being inextricable from, specific occasions of practice.

Child's voice, authorship, and authority, deriving from the grammar of this gender/knowledge, is also congruent with the liminal positioning of the domestic in relation to the emerging market economy. Focused on the tasks themselves, her hints do not issue from the identity of their speaker. Rather, Child makes use of the hint in its prescriptive, didactic form. As the final section of her book illustrates, this form can be anecdotal but is not necessarily so. The hint presents knowledge in discrete increments. Usually advising a specific course of action or detailing its procedure, it requires little context or frame and easily fits into the serial arrangement of the list. Certain grammatical tendencies of the hint also bear on the voice, the paradoxical subjectivity of the writer-housekeeper produced by this text.

> Attend to all the mending in the house, once a week, if possible. Never put out sewing. If it be impossible to do it in your own family, hire someone into the house, and work with them. Make your own bread and cake. Some people think it just as cheap to buy of the baker and confectioner; but it is not half as cheap. (9)

Adopting the conventions of the recipe's instructional section, Child frequently writes her hints in the second-person imperative. Her text commands, and in so doing stresses the action to be performed and the person to whom these instructions are addressed. The speaker remains invisible, obscured by the grammar of the imperative, if concurrently inferred by its prescriptive tones.

Even in the more descriptive passages of her text, Child scrupulously avoids direct references to herself. Indeed, she explicitly disowns the authority of the imperative voice that should accrue to her as expert or author. She never introduces herself in her text, even as a frugal housewife; she merely states her intentions in writing her book, emphasizing the identity and needs of her readers. A selfless authority, she writes for "young housekeepers" and "the poor," those whose experience has not afforded them the range of "common knowledge" she has been able to gather together in her book. She thereby signifies herself as a collector, not the author or owner, of her information. It is not *her* knowledge or *her* property. A writer who gathers and saves and prevents hints from being lost, Child is like her subject, the frugal housewife.

The Author-ity of the American Frugal Housewife

But who, exactly, is this housewife? Not anywhere defined or identified in the text that bears her name, the American frugal housewife exists only as an accumulation, a culmination of lists of activities, hints, and advice. As Goody notes:

> The list has a clear cut beginning and a precise end, that is, a boundary, an edge, like a piece of cloth. It encourages the ordering of the items by number, by initial sound, by category etc. And the existence of boundaries, internal and external, brings a greater visibility to categories, at the same time making them more abstract.[41]

A category, a keeper, a saver, with an edge or boundary coming into view "like a piece of cloth," Child's housewife might also be listed as a "hinter," one who seizes and uses hints, in the word's archaic sense of an opportunity or occasion. Child's housekeeper, a bricoleur, is herself a product of bricolage: a writer's invention from bits of house-keeping and a housekeeper's invention in bits of writing, a subject pulled together from whatever fragments, tasks, and hints happened to be around. From a sewing basket comes Child's model for housekeeping and for writing: everything she knows—economy, text, and subject—is figured as a kind of patchwork. Child writes of the literal task, the ripping and recycling of disparate threads and fabric; yet this task figures the logic and the paradoxes of her housekeeper's art. It figures, too, the tactics of her text, which is fragmented and nonhierarchical, claiming no resources or system of its own.

And Child's housekeeper? A textual accumulation, "she" joins together the array of scrappy and colorful fragments that make her up. Reanimating a jumble of waste material, Child's housekeeper makes use of time, of scraps, of the idle. Seizing the moment, she motivates hands and objects to new tasks, ceaselessly converting what is destined to be left out to what she can keep. Identified only as an agent of frugal-ity, identifiable only by her effects, this housekeeper has no respect for the object in itself (in herself). Patchworker, remotivator, she lives by a logic of the "other-wise," of unforeseen and unforeseeable alternatives that depend on her wit and cleverness to be conceived and realized. Her wisdom relies on chance; her invention mothers necessity. She invents an asystematic model of a waste economy from a household task—patchwork. She constructs her text from discursive models found in the home—the recipe, the list, and the hint. These epistemological forms present knowledge aphoristically, incrementally, rather than as the product of a hierarchi-cally structured conceptual system. In this her text constructs an economy not yet explicitly rationalized or organized by the overarching categories of gender and "private space" that will increasing characterize and define domesticity.

In both the structure and the rhetoric of the text, in its formulation and promotion, *The American Frugal Housewife* gives modern readers a sense of the many discursive sources and influences that culminated in this rudimentary construction of American domesticity. Class interests in frugality become national interests in an "American" housekeeping, as opposed to British aristocratic norms. The idea of the autonomous American housewife begins to take shape from Child's formulation of more expedient and accessible housekeeping tactics. Instances of domestic practices span an array of environments—urban, rural, middle class, working class—and unite them in a common ethic of getting by, of adapting to disparate circumstances.

This ethic draws from Calvinism, from the frontier survivalist spirit (what James Fenimore Cooper and others were articulating during these very years as the essence of the American character, what distinguished it from Europe and its literature), and from a colonial, agrarian imperative to live off the land, all ideas seemingly hostile to market forces.[42] It gives rise to the rural/urban, country/city binaries that, like gendered domesticity, locate capitalism, the market, and its ills as somewhere else or something else than what is truly American.[43] Its diverse discursive sources all derive from a colonial social order not yet characterized by the economically discrete, much less gender-discrete, environments of market and domicile. Child's text constitutes one formulation of the terms whereby these discourses and their "market resistance" would be rationalized, privatized, and in some sense domesticated.

Significantly, gender was not yet one of those terms. That is, the profession of housewifery and its practices were not yet overtly tied to explicit discourses of essentialized femininity. The criticisms of Child's book by proper Boston matrons—that it was too crude for ladies' ears—and, alternatively, the criticism of aristocratic mannerisms as effeminate indicate how strongly femininity was inflected by class discourses and resistances. That is to say, the American frugal housewife constitutes a challenge to the aristocratic leisured femininity that Child explicitly contests based on the national character. Her American housewife is implicitly enjoined to make innovative use of natural resources, to work hard, to survive with whatever she has to work with, to prevail by any means at hand.

In so doing, Child's text disseminates a vision of the specifically *American* frugal housewife as independent, autonomous, innovative, and self-reliant. Just as the name, the framing, the exposition, and the promotion of her text inflated or infused class, region, and religiously marked values and concerns ("frugality") into elements of the national character, so had the similarly marked qualities of independence, industriousness, and self-reliance with which Child imbues the frugal housewife not yet been fully masculinized. This figure and the discourses she comprises signal the simultaneous construction and conflation of class- and gender-marked concerns. A discourse of economic constraints (class) fosters a construction of autonomous housewifery (gender) that synthesizes an array of concerns related to ethics and regional and national character. Child's text indicates the way in which discourses articulated as hostile or alien to market forces and values (frontier, agrarian) coalesce in the construction of a privatized, distinctly American domestic character. Yet the opposition to the market is much more apparent than real. Capitalism begins as agrarian capitalism, frontier expansion is primarily market driven, and the housewife's frugality provides for monetary surpluses that facilitate capitalist investment. What is striking is how a nascent domesticity organizes and ultimately embodies as *distinctly American* an ideology of market resistance in what will become the most rapaciously capitalist country in the world. Yet in Child these ideologies are not yet rigorously gendered.

In that Child's text is addressed to the American frugal housewife and concerns itself with educating daughters, the type of knowledge and the values it articulates do participate discursively in the "becoming feminine" of domesticity and the private sphere. Yet it would remain for her critics and her successors to institute the generalization "woman" and to explicate and sentimentalize both her identity and her "place." In Child we can see the foundations of that process in the problematic character of the housekeeper's particular trade: alienated from both market value and the material productivity of a subsistence economy, housekeeping has a worth that can be measured only negatively—by what isn't needed, by how much money isn't spent. A negative standard can gauge only intangible, symbolic value. *The Frugal Housewife* documents that the becoming feminine of domesticity coincides with the becoming *immaterial*, becoming symbolic economy, of housework. Both lay the discursive foundations for the moralization of housework, housewife, and home in the domesticity cult. But Child's housewife, though a woman, is not yet feminized in the ways in which we have come to understand the feminine. She is more American than feminine in her gender/knowledge.

Child's text participates in stereotypes of *American* ingenuity—of the ability to make do, to get by with whatever resources are at hand—which can trace some of their roots to the Protestant ethic applied to constrained circumstances, whether the frontier, rural life, or the articulation of a "home front" resistant to the encroachments of capital. As the emphasis on concrete science throughout Child's text indicates, a uniquely American bricolage arose as a resistant discursive residue to the market forces that utterly transformed agrarian colonial life. Against the imperative to accumulate, to have more, a nascent domesticity, accommodating economic inequity, countered, "What you have must always be more than enough." This reactive imperative was an imperative to bricolage. It also served capitalist market interests as well as those of a struggling "middling" class by facilitating economic accumulation and investment among the more privileged classes. Finally, this imperative and its various consequences point to a persistent and fundamental paradox of American domesticity; although it was constructed ideologically from the beginning as a resistant discourse to market capitalism, its resistance functioned conservatively, as an accommodation with or ameliorization of threatening market forces rather than a direct contestation of them.

From the Frugal to the Feminine

The American Frugal Housewife dominated the domestic advice market in the 1830s and probably "addressed . . . a majority of the nation's adult female population" at that time.[44] Yet the value of this text for helping us understand the construction of American domesticity derives not only from its popularity but also from the criticisms that attended its publication. In the particulars of its reception, we can see how conflicted and contested discourses of class and region articulated and resolved themselves in gendered terms. In other words, a distinctly Eurocentric urban upper-class discourse of femininity permeated the critical reviews of Child's text. The specifics of these critiques spell out in microcosm the ways in which the cult of domesticity would subsume and eradicate questions of class and regional specificity within the construction of American femininity and domesticity.

First and foremost, Boston critics called attention to Child's insistent focus on frugality and money. Sarah Josepha Hale remonstrated, "Now we do not think that either in earning or saving money consists the chief importance of life. . . . Our men are sufficiently money-making. Let us keep our women and children from the contagion as long as possible." She encouraged Child to focus not on an economy predicated on money but on one "which is seeking to enrich or assist others," a pointed allusion to maternal duties. Hale and others also upbraided Child for the book's directness, its vulgarity and lack of taste, and its disorganized format. The book was not suitable for "delicate" ears; it contained recipes "at which a palate of tolerable nicety would revolt."[45]

Although class is not a disguised discourse in these reviews, the notion of appropriate femininity emerges from them as a gender identity whose essence is to transcend considerations of class. A woman should not degrade herself or her husband (or father) by thinking or worrying about money. A "contagion" that threatens her and her children, money impedes her ability to mother, and represents a distortion of the truly feminine economy that should be her only concern. Hale's review identifies the currency that should "run" the household: sentimentality and maternal love. The criticisms of vulgarity and bad taste leveled at Child's text reframe its pragmatic reaction to economic difference as aberrations in the representation of a properly feminine sensibility and domesticity, or in other words, as a failure to render sexual difference accurately.

Domesticity arises as a subject and a discursive site wherein competing, conflicted discourses concerning gender and class subsume the constitutive elements of the latter (material measures of difference, such as money) within the terms of the former (symbolic capital, love, sentiment). Rather than opposing this discursive development, Child's class-based articulation of American domesticity actually voices its foundation—the inverted and apparently resistant relationship of the domicile to the currency of the marketplace. The cult of domesticity, whose discourse is invoked by Child's critics, overwrites her class-based aversion to the market ("frugality") with an embodied, characterological, gender-based aversion ("femininity").

Child's vision of housework expresses the contours of a vanishing economy whose significance lies in the fact that its discursive matrix had not produced a self-consciously gendered vision of labor. That is, even though there was a general sense that women performed certain kinds of labor and men performed other kinds, there was also a recognition that women worked, and worked hard, and that their labor was valuable and necessary as a material resource.[46] *The American Frugal Housewife* is an early construction of American housekeeping that can be read for the way it prepares for but does not yet fully assume the generalizations that the cult of domesticity would institute: the idea of "women" as a universal group, untrammeled by divisions of class, race, region, and so on, and a notion of domesticity conceived as an unchanging, transcendent, gendered institution. In Catharine Beecher's work, these transformations would be fully articulated.

Making Home, Making Nation

Catharine Beecher's Domestic Economy

> This is the true nature of the home—it is the place of peace; the shelter,
> not only from all injury, but from all terror, doubt and division. In so far
> as it is not this, it is not home.
>
> JOHN RUSKIN

> I do not hesitate to avow, that, although the women of the United States
> are confined within the narrow circle of domestic life, and their situation
> is one of extreme dependence, I have nowhere seen women occupying a
> loftier position; if I were asked . . . to what the singular prosperity and
> growing strength of that people ought mainly to be attributed, I should
> reply—*to the superiority of their women.*
>
> ALEXIS DE TOCQUEVILLE

Catharine Beecher is the most famous nineteenth-century writer on domesticity.
Were it necessary to summarize her significance to the construction of domesticity in America, that summary would be this: Catharine Beecher made a place for
(middle-class white) women by synthesizing political, philosophical, and religious
discourses with those concerning domestic labor, architecture, and design.[1] The format of her work, its vision, and its import help explain how nineteenth-century constructions of domestic femininity, deriving from specific class (middle and upper),
regional (the Northeast), and religious formations, were generalized across the entire
U.S. population and reproduced across generations. Contemporary scholars all consider her work on domestic economy much more important and influential than
Child's pioneering endeavors.[2] In attempting to understand Beecher's success in relation to her historical situation, I use a framework suggested by Michel Foucault, who
asserts that the relation of any discursive formation to power can be determined by
asking, "Who does it serve?"[3] I address this question to the discursive formation
known as the cult of domesticity using Catharine Beecher's work, specifically her
groundbreaking *Treatise on Domestic Economy* (1841), as an exemplar of the cult's
most strongly held beliefs and contradictions.

    The cult of domesticity was a ubiquitous, multifaceted, complicated, and con-

35

flicted discursive phenomenon. Indeed, it overlapped with feminist and abolitionist discourses, while it also participated in the formation of a dichotomized, gendered American political economy. This political economy incorporated universalized bourgeois values in such a way that class difference was constituted as invisible at the level of the individual subject. The cult of domesticity also formulated and promoted gender as *the* representationally dominant social difference at a time in U.S. history when the construction of racial difference had greatly intensified owing to increasing social conflict over slavery. One result of this discursive "coincidence," amply demonstrated in a book such as *Uncle Tom's Cabin*, is that the most popular representations of the abhorrent character of slavery frame it as a domestic problem, involving transgressive sentiments and moral sensibilities, rather than a problem of civil or human rights. In this chapter I trace the relations and obfuscations among articulations of gender, race, and class as they are effected within discourses of domesticity.

Catharine Beecher is credited with inventing a distinct type of text within the much larger diverse discursive formation on domesticity. Unlike the sentimental and religious productions of the cult of domesticity, Beecher's writings directly confront and attempt to systematize women's domestic labor. For reasons that will become evident, women's housework is central to class and gender transformations performed by domestic discourses. Thus Beecher's work demonstrates crucial ideological dynamics that are not at issue in sentimental domestic fiction and religious tracts; it construes domesticity as a discipline in the Foucauldian sense. Beecher's text therefore provides an exemplary instance of the discursive mechanisms that effectively organized and legitimized a set of practices previously characterized by contingency and multiplicity, for example, Child's concept of housekeeping. Beecher's work also calls for the institutionalization of domesticity within the disciplinary regime of the school. The rhetoric she employs to construct a place and an identity for American women lays bare the paradoxical power that domestic femininity attributed to middle-class white women; it also indicates how this domesticity affected, and in some sense subsumed, other profound national conflicts related to race and class.

Beecher's extraordinary influence on the construction of nineteenth-century domesticity is often noted in conjunction with the remarkable influence exerted by her entire family over national ideas and events throughout the century. Catharine was the firstborn of the famous Calvinist minister Lyman Beecher; her younger siblings included Harriet Beecher Stowe, Isabella Beecher Hooker, and Henry Ward Beecher, whose collective cultural impact, Kathryn Kish Sklar observes, certainly warrants comparison of the Beechers in the nineteenth century with the Adamses in the eighteenth and the Kennedys in the twentieth.[4]

In approaching Catharine Beecher's work, I consider its success in terms of the forces it served in all areas of nineteenth-century American political and social life. Historians, if they think about domesticity at all, tend to limit those forces and that success to the certifiable but ambiguous advances domesticity secured for middle-class white women.[5] Yet to do so is both to underestimate the power and the scope of domestic discourses and also to succumb to them by accepting the gendered dichotomous political economy that they construct. Catharine Beecher argued that the housewife's importance lay at the heart of American democracy. Taking her at her word, I consider her disciplining of domesticity from two very different perspectives, woven together. I first outline the debates about citizenship that constituted the "heart" of American democracy. This discussion then provides the frame for a consideration of Beecher's work that indicates how her construction of domesticity, within the larger cult, organizes or positions some of the major political questions in nineteenth-century America, such as suffrage, slavery, and the woman question. This reading points to the disciplinary strategies her text promotes that provide the framework within which these larger issues come to be understood.

Gendering Deference

The symptomatic legacy of the cult of domesticity haunts even the best-intentioned contemporary texts, requiring a second look at the underside of academic discourse itself. Consider, for example, a recent study of voting rights in the United States:

> And so, except for a short period in the early years of the nineteenth century in New Jersey, and in a few far western states at the end of the nineteenth century, *women were largely excluded from public life* until the Nineteenth Amendment granted them the vote in 1920.[6]

Here, women's participation in the abolitionist movement, in the temperance movement, in all areas of social reform are eradicated by this narrowly focused account of public life. Woman's effectivity is limited to the private sphere, a focus which suggests that it is there we must look for her history and identity. This historiographic premise, whether expressed by social or by political historians, is predicated on the imbrication of domesticity and womanhood, a premise perfected and hyperbolized in this country in the nineteenth century. The consequences of this union are so endemic to our social imaginary even today that it is hard to sustain thought outside of them.[7] The idea that public life and private life are truly distinct, not just discursively constructed as such, and the notion of a homogeneous gender identity called "woman" are powerful enabling fictions that continue to have profound efficacy in the organization of knowledge and power.[8] What I want to argue, however, is that whether they had the vote or not, white middle-class women had a significant role in public life and policy throughout the nineteenth century; but much of their influence and power, their very identity as moral guardians, was generated by domestic discourses.[9] I first consider briefly how this gendered power came about in the United States.

The semantic fortunes of the word *deference* quickly pinpoint the salient character of the relationship between citizenship and gender construction in colonial America and the early years of the republic. During the colonial period, *deference* referred to a social practice whereby small landowners "deferred" their votes to their social betters, whose larger stake in society (because they owned more land) supposedly entitled them to this privilege.[10] By the nineteenth century, *deference* indicated the proper respect one showed to a lady. This semantic shift—from a class-based privilege with civic import to a gendered attitude that at once conveyed yet obscured class privilege behind a lady's skirts—encapsulates the nature of the political and discursive transformations I outline here.[11]

The coincident rise of the "middling classes" and the domestic woman took place in a context wherein the United States was engaged in distinguishing itself, by both force and discourse, from Britain. The articulation and rise of an intensely sentimentalized domesticity made its presence strongly felt in the late eighteenth and early nineteenth centuries in a volatile and chaotic milieu concerned precisely with formulating these differences.[12] Necessarily constituted against the semiotics of an aristocratic social order, this colonial-cum-revolutionary milieu addressed itself to the fundamentals of its own national constitution. Rejecting the idea of a mixed government, postrevolutionary rhetoric debated the proper basis for citizenship and suffrage, and the best way to implement the values of democracy, while also avoiding its most significant risk—the overtaking of government by the ignorant, unprincipled, and incompetent masses.

Although the founding fathers reasoned that the governing of the state should be predicated on the will of its citizens, they limited the more dangerous extensions of democracy by imposing qualifications on the citizenry: "In their view, women, slaves, and propertyless men, along with children and the mentally ill, lacked the capacity for independent and rational judgement for the general good."[13] Property ownership served as the preeminent criterion of suffrage because it grounded (literally and figuratively) the rationale whereby other qualities of the propertyless were found deficient. John Adams theorized in a letter to a friend that "women and children, like men without property, were lacking in independent judgement."[14] The reasoning was twofold. First, those who did not own property and who therefore would pay little or no tax had no vested interest in government, unlike property owners, who had a material stake in society. Second, suffrage based on property ownership guaranteed a citizenry not economically, and therefore not politically, dependent on or beholden to anyone.[15]

A rather obvious paradox inhabits this logic: that those who have a vested interest are those who are independent, or, better, those who have a vested economic interest are precisely those who possess political disinterestedness ("the capacity for independent and rational judgement for the general good"). This paradox, naturalized and familiarized in a word wherein possession and individuality are wedded (*own*), shaped the initial legal identity of the U.S. citizen. The possession of property provided a material guarantee of a properly individuated man beholden to no one, one who was thus utterly "self-possessed" and therefore capable of independent, objective judgment.

According to this logic, women's entitlement to suffrage was compromised both by their relationship to property and by legal and religious dicta that rendered them subject to husbands and fathers: they were both propertyless and dependent.[16] In some rare instances, in both the colonies and the states, propertied widows (who therefore had outlived both their dependent and their propertyless status) were allowed to vote up until the early nineteenth century.[17] Neither in the colonies nor in the Constitution itself were there laws that excluded either Native American or free African American men from suffrage. This situation persisted until the first several decades of the nineteenth century.[18]

The overt links between the possession of property, citizenship, and individual integrity and merit that initially formed the basis of the social contract in America were challenged and seemingly completely overthrown by the push for universal white manhood suffrage, achieved throughout the country in the 1840s.[19] Significantly, as suffrage for white men was extended, laws were passed in both slave and free states explicitly disenfranchising free black men. In New Jersey, where a legal technicality had allowed some women to vote, all suffrage for women was eliminated, along with that for free blacks, in 1807.[20] All the free states that joined the Union between 1800 and 1860, except Maine, restricted suffrage to white males. The heinous 1857 *Dred Scott* decision that deprived all African Americans of citizenship foreclosed any suffrage privileges that free blacks still enjoyed.

What have slavery, suffrage, and citizenship to do with domesticity? In the period between 1787 and 1840, the rise of the cult of domesticity coincided almost exactly with the fight for universal white manhood suffrage. This fight entailed a profound transformation in what constituted the basis for American citizenship. The tangible criterion of property ownership that had formerly rationalized exclusions to "equality" disappeared, forcing these exclusions to be directly articulated and legislated. Race and, to a lesser extent, gender became explicit juridical distinctions that now constituted limits to civil rights.[21] From a legal situation in which class privilege (property ownership) included entitlement to suffrage rights, the extension of the franchise to propertyless white men resulted in another situation in which large segments of the population were overtly denied the right to vote because of who they were. In other words, the criterion for the franchise shifted from exclusions based on unequal distribution of property to exclusions that legally constituted *identity itself* as the legal premise for inequality. The imposition of legal constraints to suffrage based explicitly on formulations of racial difference also coincided with increasingly heated national debate on the "peculiar institution" of slavery. In this coincidence we also see gross inequalities founded in property ownership (slavery) being otherwise articulated as inequalities based on newly constituted identity distinctions (race).[22]

The paradoxical and class-based logic that produced propertied man as disinterested citizen, vested interests as independent and objective arbiters of public good, and owners as the only proper individuals (*own*-ers) was necessarily compromised by universal white manhood suffrage. The coincident cult of domesticity and the relationship it fabricates between identity and property were a vital component in this political transformation, establishing the terms whereby civic privilege would be privatized and therefore maintained no matter how apparently democratic the state.

Prior to universal white manhood suffrage, property had a public function: it secured citizenship privileges for its owner. State-sanctioned religious and political discourses rationalized this privilege in terms of the natural merit accruing to the man born to a higher station in life. The symbolic architecture that equated autonomous civic individuality with landownership constructed the "public" as a group selected by inherited merit—by their vested interests—from the unpropertied masses. The as yet unformulated private sphere was marked by legally defined states of *deprivation* (poverty, dependency, immaturity, or deficiency, and in the case of slaves, total lack of legal subjectivity) that rendered its members unfit for fully individuated civic status. Universal white manhood suffrage dismantled the integrated economic, religious, and social hierarchy that served as the basis for such civic status. It transformed the criterion that organized this hierarchy by depriving property of its public, civic function.

Concurrent with the political struggle for universal white manhood suffrage, the cult of domesticity transformed the character of domestic property relations, a transformation that rendered the private sphere in much more affirmative terms. As vital productive and economic functions were moved to workplaces distinct from the home, domestic discourses formulated and celebrated the value of private property or the domicile as precisely dematerialized and idealized. These discourses, derived from middle-class, upper-class, and religious milieux, subsumed market-reactive articulations of domesticity, such as Lydia Marie Child's, within highly moralized and sentimental visions of the American home.[23]

The most significant production of this confluence of class and religious forces was a moral and highly sentimental conception of motherhood and child rearing. Prior to this time, religious perspectives viewed infancy and its instinctual character as a problem to be resolved by rigorously breaking children's will at age two. The idea of a child's dependency and innocence, its receptivity to conversion and salvation, developed in tandem with the construction and celebration of the mother's nurturant role in her child's physical and spiritual growth. In the patriarchal structure of colonial families, fathers tended to their children's religious education, mothers to their physical needs. Mary Ryan argues that relations between the ages and sexes were substantially altered by religious transformations in the early decades of the nineteenth century: "The transition from patriarchal authority to maternal affection as the focal point of childhood socialization was the linchpin of this transformation."[24] The years of these transformations also saw dramatic alterations in the venues wherein these changes were formulated and articulated. While evangelical publications and missionary associations, authored or convened by clergy and upper- and middle-class women, predominated in the century's first three decades, these were superseded after the 1830s by mothers' magazines, maternal associations, and sentimental fiction primarily generated by women.[25]

What emerged from these phenomena and has since organized our perception of them were new, powerful, and socially effective conceptions of both domesticity and femininity.[26] These idealized and sentimentalized place and gender identities took shape from displaced religious discourses, and from the writings and activities of women whose class (middle or upper) and location (urban) had relieved them of more onerous domestic or productive duties. Women's magazines and associations, evangelical work, novels, and religious tracts all conceived the values of "femininity" and "domesticity" as uniquely moral and sentimental; naturalized through the bio-spiritual trope of maternity, both the domicile itself and all its functions (housekeeping, child rearing, and so on) became explicitly gendered. Middle- and upper-class urban women became feminine, that is, they became active religious and social agents who articulated and were articulated by domestic discourses and their constructions of women's "special relationship" to spirituality.[27] Yet that strong spirituality became paradoxically linked to physical and emotional delicacy, dependency, and the shelter of the domestic sphere.

The cult of domesticity transformed women's enforced legal subjection and material, economic dependency into an idealized spiritual, emotional, and physical state of dependency called "femininity" or "true womanhood." That through the perpetuation of this ideal power and influence accrued to middle-class white women in the nineteenth century, however ambiguous that power, is without question. But this paradoxical formulation also changed the idea of the home. The property that once secured economic sustenance and political privilege was transmuted into a place whose worth was measured by standards of morality and propriety. Nineteenth-century domestic femininity provided a conceptual framework wherein the individual (white male) citizen's relationship to his property and his home shifted from the pragmatics of production and the privilege of citizenship to a wholly sentimental, moral relation embodied in the identity of his wife and the mother of his children. The domestic sphere, rising from these myriad sources as etherealized, above all worldly concerns, now provided a gendered, moralized location constituted in opposition to a democratic public sphere, contaminated as it was by the economic machinations of the market. Distinctions among citizens formerly based on property and privilege and civic status now were reoriented to the private sphere, where the future (male) individual was developed and nurtured to maturity. The cult of domesticity ensured that the social, political, economic, and religious transformations of the early nineteenth century would be discursively configured, and therefore understood, in terms of masculinity and femininity. Property, which had once secured state-sanctioned class privilege, now became bifurcated into two distinct measures of value related to gender identity. Thus, while ownership attested to successful manhood, a mode of habitation infused with both moralized and ornamental values measured successful womanhood.

Discipling Domesticity

Unlike sentimental fiction or spiritual tracts produced in this period, Catharine Beecher's text focuses precisely on women's housework and the onerous labor it involved. It thus potentially challenged both the image of the delicate, dependent, feminine wife and mother and the ideological fabrication that all work is masculine, a fabrication on which the significance of the public sphere was predicated.[28] Thus her *Treatise* demonstrates particularly well the paradoxical machinations of domestic discourses that affirmed as they effaced women's labor, that consequently promoted femininity as a dematerialized sign of class difference, and that finally operated to construct race as a domestic issue. In answer to Foucault's query, it seems obvious that nineteenth-century domestic discourses served an array of social forces. My reading of Catharine Beecher's work examines how her construction of domestic economy organizes, endorses, complements, explicates, and implements the shifting terms of civic privilege and merit being outlined concurrently by public political and legal discourse.

Several features of Beecher's work and biography account for her unprecedented influence within and centrality to domestic discourses. Synthesizing material from an array of authoritative sources (religious and philosophical), Beecher legitimizes and rationalizes the sentimental values of the cult of domesticity.[29] She formulates domestic economy not only within the organs and rhetoric of mass media but also within the epistemological apparatus of the school. Beecher's staunch lifelong advocacy of education for girls, coupled with her active participation as a teacher in and founder of several female seminaries, accounts in part for her influence. Her most stunning successes in promoting female education came from linking that cause to the demands of domestic economy.[30]

Never a traditional housewife, Beecher did not marry but instead built a life for herself as an educator and author on subjects that ranged from theology to home economics. After publishing *Treatise*, she later co-authored a revision, *The American Woman's Home*, with her sister Harriet in 1869. As her initial title signals, Beecher was interested not in housekeeping but in domestic economy, and not in the aleatory wisdom of the hint but in the systemic rigor of the treatise. Unlike Child's *Frugal Housewife*, which merits only passing reference in feminist histories of American domesticity and housework, Beecher's work on domestic economy holds a significant place in the histories of architecture, design, and American feminism; many historians see her and her work as marking the founding moment of home economics.[31]

The facility with which Beecher articulates domesticity as a national institution vital to the interests of democracy derives in part from the format her text employs and the resulting construction of domesticity it produces. Her book differs from contemporaneous literary and religious productions pertaining to domesticity in that she conceives of her subject as a kind of knowledge requiring education and training.[32] Beecher's work formulates domestic economy through and with discursive tools related to the disciplinary regime of the school. Written as a textbook, *Treatise* organizes domesticity according to the regulatory structures of educational publications. Not only did this organization facilitate the perpetuation of Beecher's "domestic economy" in schools, but also it produced domesticity as knowledge in accord with quasi-disciplinary techniques.

This knowledge becomes integral to yet in certain ways at odds with the construction of the private sphere perpetuated by the cult of domesticity—that of a spiritualized, feminized, otherworldly place. One of the transformations effected by the cult was that it converted the private sphere from a place of deprivation (both *private* and *deprivation* share the etymological root *privus*, which means both "individual" and "deprived of") to one of sentimentalized privilege. Beecher's disciplining of domesticity insists on the utility of housewives' knowledge and their physical labor. Written at a time when science, education, and a commercial infrastructure were being constructed in a public sphere that greatly exceeded exclusively civic functions, Beecher's work articulates a complementary, not oppositional, construction of the private sphere. Bringing Foucault's work on disciplinary structures to bear on Beecher's work illuminates how domesticity functions paradoxically as both an ur-discipline and one that ultimately fails.[33] It fails because the housewife's iconic, representational function must ultimately eclipse and exceed her function as a laborer. Beecher's disciplinary model of domestic economy illustrates clearly the reasons for this eclipse. It also indicates how Foucault's investigations are limited to public institutions and therefore evade questions of subjectivity and gender construction.[34]

According to Foucault, disciplinary regimes (such as the school, the military, and the hospital) which came to fruition in eighteenth-century Europe subjected bodies to four sets of techniques: the distribution of individuals in space; the control of activity in terms of time, movement, and the manipulation of objects; the organization of geneses or progressive evolutions; and the coordination of diverse forces.[35] In that Catharine Beecher's text promotes a disciplinary regime of domesticity, written as a textbook and designed for women's education, it can be examined for how it implements these techniques of power. Of the four techniques outlined by Foucault, the two that are most relevant to Beecher's *Treatise* and that register the most far-reaching effects involve her construction and organization of domestic space and her positioning of the American housewife in relation to the evolution and development of future American citizens. Significantly, both of these concerns—the character and function of domestic space and the housewife's role in the development of future American citizens—necessitate the housewife's absence from both public life and citizenship. Thus the discipline of domesticity produces femininity as paradoxically subordinate and privileged. I consider first Beecher's construction of domestic space and then her vision of the housewife's place.

The Particularity of the Domestic Feminine Body

The highly organized format of the textbook compels Beecher the writer to "keep" her text in the same way that Beecher the domestic economist suggests a home should be maintained. "There is no one thing more necessary to a housekeeper, in performing her varied duties, than *a habit of system and order*," she writes.[36] Her book models this advice; the *Treatise* consists of forty chapters, copiously outlined in a table of contents, which divides every imaginable aspect of housekeeping into neatly organized and indexed sections. While early chapters present the conceptual, ethical, and organizational foundations of her book, later ones chart a passage through the house, noting the housewife's duties from parlor to kitchen, then out the back door from garden to barn, finally ending with a consideration of manure. Moving from principles to particulars, from lofty to low, Beecher's text institutes hierarchical priorities (from concepts to specific practices) in its articulation of domestic economy. Significantly, these articulations wed a cogent conceptual apparatus to another system, another order—a housewife's movement and performance of tasks throughout the space of her home.

Both the precise layout and partitioning of space and the mixing of conceptual and pragmatic concerns accomplished in Beecher's text are symptomatic of disciplinary transformations of space. Foucault argues that disciplines frequently enclose a space such that it is designated as different from all others (for example, the classroom or the factory floor). Frequently this space is partitioned ("each individual has his own place, each place its own individual") in such a way that individuals are precisely located for both supervision and intelligibility (for example, by disease in the hospital, by rank or grade in the military and in school). The organization of space is above all functional; architecture now creates *useful* space. The real partitioning and organization of physical space supports ideal distributions based on "characterizations, assessments and hierarchies." Finally, this use of space joins a "technique of power" (distribution, location of bodies, supervision) to a "procedure of knowledge"—the organization of analytical, intelligible space.[37]

This mixture of conceptual and pragmatic concerns brings together a mode of thinking about bodies that combines physical and metaphysical explanation (for example, medicine and philosophy) and empirically oriented procedures to regulate and control those bodies (military and educational disciplines). Thus disciplines construct a place where the analyzable body is joined to the manipulable body, or better, where the notion of bodies as entities to be understood is united with practices that fashion bodies to be useful.[38]

Treatise, by focusing insistently on a particular body—the housewife's—insinuates a political, philosophical explanation of her place and function within a set of practical directions that render that body more useful. Yet, unlike Foucault's soldiers, students, factory workers, and medical patients, whose bodies are multiple and anonymous, Beecher's housewife is a singular, highly spiritualized female worker in charge of a domain rendered visible and intelligible by her movement, function, and presence within it. The rendering of domesticity within disciplinary boundaries results in a body whose distribution in space is atomistic, yet whose singularity is generalized throughout the domestic sphere. Unlike in Foucault utility is not being wrested from many bodies located and coordinated in a partitioned homogenous space; instead, the housewife's body performs an array of tasks in a decidedly heterogenous space.

The discipline of domesticity that emerges from Beecher's conception deviates from the models Foucault identifies: those of the school, the prison, the hospital, and the factory. First and foremost, domestic space is not homogeneous. Not only does it accommodate many diverse activities, but also its function as Beecher constructs it is radically bifurcated. It is a place of leisure for men, a workplace for women. Thus the disciplinary function of partitioning space and distributing bodies discretely and according to schemas of use within that space produces two different bodies (masculine and feminine) with very different relations to domestic space and destined for two very different life trajectories. Whereas a man is educated for adult participation in the public *and* private spheres, Beecher argues that a woman needs to be sufficiently educated to know her place (the home) and to return there. Even more significantly, as I will argue, the utility of the properly disciplined domestic feminine body deviates from the model Foucault articulates: the domestic feminine body must appear to be a body that does not labor, that is not useful, however onerous that body's domestic labors actually are.

Disciplinary Paradoxes of the Private Sphere

The home that Beecher's text represents is bereft of productive functions; it assumes a husband who works elsewhere. Those chapters that are modeled on a home's floor plan designate that, for the housewife, unlike other members of the family, different rooms indicate the areas where different tasks are performed. This organization, in and of itself, delimits what Child's text does not: the space and context in which housekeeping occurs. Beecher's text defines that space in such a way that its pragmatic and metaphysical implications are fully integrated by and located in the entity and agency of the housewife. It accomplishes this integration by situating delimitations of useful space and practices within spiritual and political explanations of the housewife's and the home's significance (their *place* in American democracy).

Concern with placement, space, and its utility informs every level of Beecher's domestic economy, from her suggestions about specific housekeeping practices to her overarching philosophy of domestic economy. The spaces of chapters are analogous to the spaces of rooms, a metaphoric organization of discourse according to the dimensions of physical space. Chapter 32, for example, is titled "The Care of Chambers and Bedrooms." In this section Beecher emphasizes the importance of "well-ventilated sleeping rooms" and describes the means to ensure airflow in any bedroom, the relative qualities of different types of carpet, the proper height of bedsteads. She details the construction of wardrobes in rooms lacking closets and outlines the proper way to make a bed (358–63). These disparate tasks and concerns are organized by the space in which they occur. The frame of the room shapes the discussion of these chores; the coherence of its architecture provides boundaries and continuity within the chapter.

"On Habits of System and Order" organizes household tasks at a more abstract spatial level than that afforded by different rooms. This chapter begins with a lengthy list of a housewife's responsibilities, followed by an assertion that she "is the sovereign of an empire demanding as varied cares, and involving more difficult duties" than those of a "Queen's empire" (144). Reiterating the space-discourse relationship, the chapter generalizes the space of the home to that of an empire; invoking a hyperbolic regal metaphor, Beecher subjects this domain to a sovereign authoritative body. This particular disciplining of space differs dramatically from the partitioning of space and subjects Foucault describes. Here again the space-subject relation is singular; the partitioning of space and discourse produces the housewife's body not as an increment within a multitude but as the monarchical supervisor of a pointedly heterogeneous domain. A telling metaphor to characterize democratic housewifery and its domain, it emphatically introduces hierarchy as a necessary part of efficiency and organization. Hierarchy is in fact crucial to Beecher's understanding of women's place in American democracy, as my analysis will reveal.

Having identified domestic space as the woman's place, Beecher gives advice about how to manage properly and economically all the myriad tasks this space involves. She identifies various systems within which the housewife can place or order her duties. From Christianity she borrows a conventional religious hierarchy: the housewife should attend first to spiritual needs, then to the care of the "intellect and social affections," and finally to the "gratification of sense" (145–46). Although such a hierarchy drastically inverts what would appear to be housework's primary function, to serve bodily needs, Beecher ends with the observation that caring for the health of herself and her family is the highest spiritual task a housewife can perform. This perspective equates spiritual needs with the gratification of the senses, the metaphysical with the physical, and finds their meeting point in the functions and ultimately the body of the housewife and mother.

Beecher's text demonstrates several paradoxes fundamental to discourses of domesticity. Adopting a spiritual, philosophical hierachical binary—physical/

metaphysical—*Treatise* articulates the very special relation of these elements in the democratic nonproductive gendered home. In the personage of the wife and mother, they become the same. This mapping of the spiritual onto basic physical needs explains the contradictory representations of housekeeping and motherhood, familiar to us even today, as both the most transcendental and important of all endeavors and the most trivial, boring, and banal. It also explains the confusion of moral and economic issues that the cult of domesticity levies on the (middle-class white) housewife-mother's body. As we will see in the next section on popular culture, the twentieth century is rife with tales of housewives who "fall" because their sexuality or labor (or both) takes them outside the home. The cult of domesticity constructs women's sexuality *and* their labor as moral issues in ways men's sexuality and labor are not. Just as Beecher's text subsumes physical priorities under metaphysical injunctions, so the facts of the housewife's physical labor are obscured by her moral identity and position. Most important, the moral injunctions that beset women's bodies are all instituted through the disciplining of the home as women's place. Yet the middle-class white woman benefits from the moral sanction that defines her place.

The housewife accrues special authority through domestic discourses and their moral infusions of the home and its keeper. In her preface Beecher addresses this issue, one that Child tried to avoid altogether in her allusions to "common knowledge." Beecher locates her qualifications for proposing solutions to women's housekeeping problems in her own life experiences. As the eldest in her family, she was entrusted with the care of her younger siblings. She has always lived with "exemplary housekeepers" and has performed, often under their tutelage, most of the "domestic operations" she outlines in her book. On the few subjects she considers beyond the scope of women's experience, she has consulted "the highest authorities" for their expert information (viii–xi).

In identifying "exemplary housekeepers" as the source of her own authority, Beecher's call for better education for women avoids the implication that all housekeepers are ignorant, inept, and desperately in need of training. Rather, her argument manages to validate women's domestic tradition and experience explicitly as authoritative *and* to call for women's formalized education primarily by finding fault with the erratic and ineffectual way that domestic knowledge is transmitted.[39] As Beecher later argues, expert mothers and housekeepers do not have the time or resources necessary to train their daughters adequately (44). The extensive duties involved in keeping house warrant the same educational training as that provided for any other professional career. Her text makes housekeeping knowledge "proper" by assigning it an origin and a location, thereby inserting it into conventional discourses of legitimation. Also, in citing exemplary housekeepers as the source from which it derives, the text invents an authority for its claims. And the authority it invents is a housekeeper's.

Keeping House, Making Citizens

The construction of a housewife's authority and tradition fits another of Foucault's disciplinary techniques, that which "accumulates time in bodies." Disciplines distinguish bodies on a temporal as well as a spatial axis, Foucault argues, and this results in an "evolutive historicity" or progress mapped onto bodies in time (different grades in school or ranks in the military).[40] Beecher's call for women's education in the domestic profession in and of itself institutes this evolutive historicity, in that it advocates a regime of training for (female) bodies that inserts these bodies in seriated linear time involving practice and training that culminates in an end point, here a profession and a state of knowledge. But this body, ultimately, is being trained to produce a product—a product that constructs the "private" sphere in a significant temporal relation to the public sphere. *Treatise* articulates this relation within its overarching consideration of women's place.

Beecher characterizes women's place as peculiar. In the opening chapter of her book, "The Peculiar Responsibilities of American Women," she begins by noting the similarities between the principles of Christianity and those of democracy. In both the ideal of equality is fundamental. Yet this principle can be guaranteed only by a system of laws "which sustain certain relations and dependencies in social and civil life." These hierarchical relations are established "solely with reference to the general good of all," so both individual and public interests are served. The relation between "husband and wife, parent and child, teacher and pupil, employer and employed" all involve "duties of subordination." Beecher asserts that "society could never go forward, harmoniously, nor could any craft or profession be successfully pursued, unless these superior and subordinate relations be instituted and sustained" (2).

Beecher resolves the rather glaring paradox in this argument (that equality depends on hierarchy) by asserting that the equality democracy ensures provides that every individual can "choose for himself, who shall take the position of his superior" (3). This very localized rationalization completely ignores the situation of slaves and the working class (for whom financial compunction precludes or overrides choice), predicating its assertion entirely on the newfound freedoms of middle-class white women.[41] Women may choose the husband they wish to obey, or may choose to stay single. Within this frame she then explains why American women have a special interest in democracy:

> In this Country, it is established, both by opinion and by practice, that women have an equal interest in all social and civil concerns; and that no domestic, civil, or political institution is right, that sacrifices her interest to promote that of the other sex. But in order to secure her the more firmly in all these privileges, it is decided that, in the domestic relation, she take a subordinate station, and that, in civil and political concerns, her interests be intrusted to the other sex, without her taking any part in voting, or in making and administering laws. (4)

To support this argument, Beecher refers to Alexis de Tocqueville's thoughts on men and women in his *Democracy in America.* She extensively cites passages in which Tocqueville discriminates between the gender systems as they are practiced in Europe and in America. In Europe, many try to make the sexes "not only equal but alike. They would give to both the same functions, impose on both the same duties, and grant to both the same rights . . . thus . . . both are degraded." Americans, by contrast, separate the duties of the sexes according to their respective abilities and therefore ensure their equality. "American women never manage the outward concerns of the family, or conduct a business, or take a part in political life" (5). They also never contest the husband's conjugal authority. In exchange, American men repay them with much greater respect than that accorded European women by European men (6).

Beecher concurs with Tocqueville that the treatment of the sexes distinguishes American democracy from European sociopolitical systems. Yet both of these influential and widely published authors formulate this national distinction based on omissions that their discourses manifestly share: each completely excludes the situation of working-class and slave women from their respective considerations of American women. Both also use the category "women" and ideas about their "place" to promote a coherent conception of the American nation. In what each writer omits and what each presumes, we can see how domestic femininity is articulated and mobilized as a discursive homogenizing device which assists in shaping these two constructions of a cohesive national American identity.[42] If we pursue this line of analysis a bit further, we can see how the discipline of domestic economy organizes and positions understandings of class and racial differences in relation to property, status, and manhood in America.

Tocqueville concludes his argument with the statement:

> If I were asked . . . to what the singular prosperity and growing strength of that people ought mainly to be attributed, I should reply—*to the superiority of their women.* (9)

Embracing Tocqueville's argument that women's place is in the home, that they are not fit to govern, Beecher lays out an argument for the importance of women's education predicated on the implications of his ideas. Insofar as "the success of democratic institutions . . . depends on the intellectual and moral character of the mass of the people," and insofar as women bear the primary responsibility for "the formation of the moral and intellectual character of the young," the success or failure of democracy rests on women's ability to fulfill their domestic responsibilities (13).

In shrewd economic terms, Beecher observes that "the proper education of a man decides the welfare of an individual; but educate a woman, and the interests of a whole family are secured" (13). Denying women domestic education, Beecher suggests, is tantamount to obstructing the function of the democratic system. Everyone, especially women themselves, should recognize that women's work, far from being insignificant drudgery, lays the very foundation for democracy. But, Beecher asserts, women's education and social function mean nothing to them as self-interested individuals and citizens, which they are not. Housewives must be educated not for themselves but to help them prepare their sons for public life. Thus their knowledge, by definition, is not disinterested. In this way Beecher brokers a paradoxical civic identity for women that is based on negating that role itself. As a subjectivity *dispossessed* of both self-interest and disinterestedness, women (as Beecher and the cult of domesticity render them) form the perfect paradoxical complement to the citizen: a man both self and disinterested.

The Utility of a Housekeeper's Healthy Body

Beecher's assertion of women's civic selflessness allows her to make a cogent argument for women's education. So, too, do her arguments about household space and women's health facilitate a transformation of class issues into those exclusively concerned with a proper gender binary. Beecher's perceptions regarding the relationships between domestic space and housekeeping earned for her the accolade of "a precursor of modern architecture" from architectural historians.[43] Writing on the history of the idea of domestic comfort, Witold Rybczynski asserts that Beecher challenges architects' conventional perspective by discussing the home from the "point of view . . . of the user." Enriching the "European image of the home as a male preserve" for leisure and relaxation, Beecher presents a feminine version of this image—the home as "dynamic" and, most significantly, as a place where work occurs.[44]

In the chapter titled "On the Construction of Houses," Beecher begins by stating, "There is no matter of domestic economy, which more seriously involves the health and daily comfort of American women, than the proper construction of houses" (268). The size of a house, she maintains, must be suited to the income of those who live in it. Many Americans live in houses whose size greatly exceeds their economic means to care for it, and undue physical responsibilities therefore fall on the housewife. Similarly, she notes that in the design of homes, little thought is given to the "arrangement of rooms" and to the amount of walking and carrying such arrangements require a housekeeper to perform in the execution of her duties (269). Beecher points out that kitchens are often located in the basement and nurseries on the second floor, necessitating much wasted labor and energy in climbing stairs. She registers similar complaints about wells and cisterns located at a distance from the house (both unhealthy and wasteful), about dark kitchens, the placement of sitting rooms, and so on (270–73). In the physical spaces that Beecher describes, and in Rybczynksi's ideal of domestic comfort (conceived a century and half after Beecher), we can see middle- and upper-class standards being enveloped and enshrined in a economically undifferentiated gender binary. Beecher, advocating smaller homes (which can be managed without servants if need be) and stressing the importance of income to effective home management, *assumes* the ownership of a house with many rooms. Her assertion that the home is the woman's place tacitly presumes that that home is her *own*.

Beecher's housekeeper therefore is middle class; she does not worry about money. Instead the economic anxiety that haunted Child's text surfaces in *Treatise* as a concern about housewives' bodies and health. In her preface Beecher enumerates the reasons that motivated her to write her book. In her work as a teacher and in her travels she has noticed the appalling condition of women's health in America. She attributes women's suffering to their inadequate education and preparation for the substantial domestic duties they must assume as wives and mothers (vii–viii). American women suffer because, in a sense, they do not adequately know their place. Their ignorance, however, is not their fault, but is symptomatic of aspects of American culture. Later in the text Beecher explains that American women have particular difficulties because, though they are descended from excellent English housekeepers, they do not enjoy the cultural stability and fixed class rank offered by a "monarchical, aristocratic" society, a stability assured over generations. In America, "prosperity and democratic tendencies" allow social status and financial fortunes to rise and fall like a see-saw, with the twofold consequence that a housewife cannot expect to find sufficient domestic help or count on a stable standard of living. In all this social upheaval, she notes, many an American woman's health is ruined by age thirty-five (16–23).

Beecher, like Child before her, wrote her book to ameliorate the specific problems that American housewives confronted in a democracy. Yet the differences in their perspectives are striking. Beecher seems to regret the loss of stability and security afforded by an aristocratic order. Instead of offering admonitions regarding money and frugality, she formulates her cause as a concern for the health of housewives who are obviously at least middle class. Whereas Child's frugal housekeeping is meant to save or avoid expenditures of money, Beecher's domestic economy promises to preserve and protect women's bodies. The displacement is telling. Child's housewifery reasserts symbolic values (frugality, industry) divorced from their material context by the evolution of a market economy distinct from the home. For Beecher, the symbolic value of domestic economy is located in and measured by the housewife's health. The function of domestic economy is to eradicate the signs of labor that mark the bodies of women whose social status in an aristocratic order would usually protect them from such labor and its debilitating marks. The frugal housewife has a productive body whose practices have economic effects, albeit of a negative kind. Domestic economy produces a sovereign gendered body within a gendered private sphere whose success is determined by another negative measure: that that sovereign body displays no signs of the labor necessary to maintain and govern its sphere.

What is the utility of the domestic feminine body, of the body that keeps house in Beecher's domestic economy? Unlike the useful disciplined bodies of the student, the factory worker, and the soldier, who, in concert with kindred bodies, produce certain measurable effects (knowledge, manufactured goods, military force), the domestic feminine body works to appear as if "she" did not work. She must maintain aristocratic conventions of feminine appearance in a democracy where economic conditions can demand backbreaking domestic labor of her.[45] In the conceptual and manipulable bodies joined by Beecher's disciplining of domesticity, contradictory class imperatives are wedded and absorbed in the entity of the properly domestic, properly feminine woman. Beecher's assertion that a woman's body is to be understood as a body that does not work indiscriminately feminizes the privilege accorded to upper-class women and their bodies. Her pragmatic housekeeping advice, by contrast, attempts to make this a possibility, if not at the level of economic reality, then at least at the level of the sign. Her book indicates one path whereby status formerly gauged and secured by property ownership and acknowledged in the public sphere (by civic privilege) becomes privatized and feminized. What Beecher's *Treatise* suggests is that in a democracy, the middle-class woman must synthesize disparate tasks relegated in other socioeconomic orders to distinct social classes.[46]

In comparing Child and Beecher, we can see how domestic discourses progressively convert economic issues into gender issues through and with the agency of the housewife's body. Child's book attempted to articulate *economic* differences, both between domicile and market and among possible class-based responses to this new distinction. Her housewife could survive in physically taxing circumstances; she was hardy and independent. Boston book reviewers, urban and upper class, found this construction of womanhood "vulgar" and "indelicate." Child's housewife was not "feminine"; she paid attention to money, and her body was capable of hard work.

Beecher and the cult of domesticity reformulate economic differences as gender difference in such a way that the concept of femininity becomes incompatible with those of labor and work. This incompatibility derives from the class distinctions absorbed and diffused in "democratic" constructions of masculinity and femininity, constructions mapped onto the spaces and practices of public and private spheres.

Once suffrage became universalized across classes for white men, property ownership secured hierarchical status exclusively in the private sphere. Thus inequality, for white men, ceased to be a political, civic issue and persisted "only" in terms of private economic measures such as property ownership, wealth, and earning power.[47] Domestic discourses gendered work and labor in such a way that the private economic markers of class hierarchy became understood as measures of manhood. But successful manhood, finally, was manifested socially in the condition, the appearance, and the propriety of men's wives and the homes they kept. Thus the cult of domesticity ensured that class differences would be read and understood not in the register of wealth, property, or material differences but rather in terms of successful or failed gender performance. While the masculine body became the laboring economic body, measured in terms of monetary success, the feminine body was gauged by an altogether different standard.

An entity or agent whose value is identified by Beecher as precisely more apparent than real, the domestic woman came to function as a sign of immaterial, nonproductive value per se. Increasingly identified with a social location (the home) that had been progressively deprived of productive economic functions, feminine worth was constructed from the precipitation of dismantled or compromised value systems (religious and political) that could no longer operate in the public sphere with democratic governmental sanction. Domestic discourses personified the now privatized values of religion, morality, and class distinction in a naturalized, essentialized, transcendent feminine. Domestic femininity at once embodied and utterly sentimentalized the values and privileges of private property.

Domesticity and Democratic Peculiars

Returning to the question of what forces nineteenth-century discourses of domesticity served, I want to summarize the ground covered so far and then propose the possible role that domesticity played in the construction of racial difference in America. Many feminist historians have identified the complex and ambiguous ways domestic discourses served middle-class white women in America.[48] My reading of Beecher has demonstrated how these discourses shaped the contours, values, and sociospatial limitations of a sentimentalized feminine identity and existence for these women. Striking paradoxes concerning women's labor and their apparent lack of self-interest structure or motivate Beecher's domestic economy; they provide the mechanisms whereby this economy transforms certain class issues into gender issues through its articulation of the housewife's body and agency. Domestic economy disciplines the domestic body so that it labors to produce itself as a body that appears not to labor; it formulates a housewife's agency as a will to appear not to will, an agency directed toward the cultivation of an absolutely selfless subjectivity. The effectivity of this discipline lies in its production of a being diametrically opposed to, and thus the symmetrical complement of, the universal white male subject being concurrently constructed within the legal, political, and public sphere. Not only does this symmetry reorganize class differences under the rubric of gender difference; it also establishes the terms whereby racial difference would be constructed and understood in the nineteenth century.

Whereas the American colonial and revolutionary periods integrated religious, civic, and economic systems of value in, and therefore *as*, the "property" of a prosperous landowner class, the principles of democracy necessitated a dismantling and privatization of these systems. Universal white manhood suffrage eradicated property-based civic status and replaced it with privilege based exclusively on whiteness and manhood. By denying suffrage to free African Americans and all women, the law now explicitly constructed the "states" of whiteness and manhood as constitutive of civic merit and privilege and as determining the set of people entitled to equality under the law. The shift in the franchise from rights based on property to rights predicated on identity universalized the legal subjectivity of white men; by legislative tautology, their subjectivity became identical to those properties that now defined the legal construction of equality. Concurrently, those who fell outside the construction of this self-evidential truth—women, slaves, free blacks, children, the mentally ill—were no longer disenfranchised because of their lack of access to property ownership. Rather, the law marked them as lacking whiteness, maleness, or both, and therefore as dispossessed of the privilege of equality.

While early nineteenth-century American legal discourse did not, of course, invent the notion of manhood or of whiteness, it did propose these qualities as equivalent to the civic and political privilege once accorded to property owners. That is to say, legal and civic exclusions to equality based on race and gender are constructed from, while they also obscure and displace, those based on wealth and class. To borrow terms from Hortense Spillers, the new suffrage laws disengaged values that were once contingent on *property* and now located them in the *personality* of those who were entitled to equality. Thus the self-possession and economic disinterestedness of the propertied and therefore properly individuated man became the inherent characteristics or properties of white men per se.

With universal white manhood suffrage, social hierarchies predicated on possession ostensibly lost public state sanction and became privatized. Yet the category of those now entitled to equality—white men—retained a proprietary foundation in part because of the very differently compromised relations of white women, slaves, and free African American men and women to property, and therefore to autonomous individuality. From the start, American women's legal rights were severely compromised by the principle of *coverture*, inherited from British common law, whereby a wife's legal subjectivity, her right to own property, and so on were completely absorbed by her husband. That is, as a legal subject, the woman, upon her marriage, ceased to exist. Beginning in the 1830s, this legal principle would be contested and incrementally reformed throughout the century.[49] As the criterion of property ownership was removed from the constraints on women's rights, womanhood in and of itself became a legal disposition to inequality. The lack of autonomous individuation and independence inferred by this legal disposition was concurrently celebrated and idealized in domestic discourses as women's innate delicacy, dependence, and selflessness. In other words, the cult of domesticity fabricated a sentimentalized personality from women's propertyless state. Complementing the civic individuation of white men accomplished by universal white manhood suffrage, domestic femininity, consisting of, among other things, the sediments of Christian values, attempted to invent women's power precisely as and within confinement, selflessness, and dependence.

The perfect symmetry of the white man/white woman, public man/private woman, and economic man/spiritual woman binaries imagined in nineteenth-century America can be read as a neat conceptual veil or grid formed from events that it then subsumes or obscures from view. Of all the shifting property relations and transformed and transforming social identities riddling the cohesion of America in its first hundred years, none is more profound or dramatic than the defense and dismantling of the institution of slavery and the correlative formulation of racialized identities in the United States.

The legal, social, and political construction of African Americans as a separate and distinct race is inextricable from the institution of slavery, whose codes, as Hortense Spillers puts it, attempted to "transform personality into property."[50] If we bring slavery into the picture of significant social and ideological relations between property and subjects in the nineteenth century, we find that slavery is the picture, its frame, its context, and its foundation. The horror of this peculiar institution was that it lined human beings up on either side of a great divide that was articulated as the very determination of humanity itself: either being or having property.[51] In its attempt to legislate subjects into objects, slavery turns the social contract inside out and turns the agency of the law (and the fantasy of Enlightenment reason) against its own fundamental humanist suppositions. In the relation it establishes between personality and property, we can readily see that the person diametrically opposed to the propertied or unpropertied self-possessed white male citizen was actually not his healthy and happy wife whose interests he always protected at the ballot box. It was instead the slave of either gender, fundamentally deprived of all rights, of all human properties, of any possible claim to agency or "self-possession."

Nowhere does slavery reveal its dangerous truths more readily than in its effects on kinship relations. Remarking that the slave exists in an economy "where 'kinship' loses meaning, *since it can be invaded at any given and arbitrary moment by the property relations,*" Spillers observes that "under conditions of captivity, the offspring of the female does not 'belong' to the Mother, nor is s/he 'related' to the 'owner,' though the latter 'possesses' it, and in the African-American instance, often fathered it."[52] As Spillers's vocabulary makes evident, metaphors of possession dominate the expression of affectional and dependent familial relations and resonate eerily with the slave's status as property.

We can also hear this eerie resonance in nineteenth-century domesticity's sentimental canonization of white motherhood, a transformation that humanized childhood socialization, emphasizing nurturance and love rather than discipline, hard work, and the breaking of children's will. As midcentury approached, the cult focused increasingly on the figure of the mother and less on religion and conversion during the same years that saw an intensification of public discourse about slavery.

In the Northeast a cult of sentimentalized domesticity, ever more popular throughout the country; in the South a peculiar institution of human property predicated on the decimation of kinship relations: the coincidence is uncanny, suggesting how domesticity influenced and was influenced by the construction of race in this same period.[53]

Slavery precedes and provides the concrete and ideological basis for the construction of racial difference in America. In an essay titled "Slavery, Race, and Ideology in the United States of America," the historian Barbara Jeanne Fields incisively argues that race is a racist ideology that came into being "at a discernible historical moment. During the revolutionary era, people who favored slavery and people who opposed it collaborated in identifying the racial incapacity of Afro-Americans as the explanation for enslavement."[54] She notes that in the U.S. Constitution, a distinction is made between "free Persons" and "other Persons," a distinction reiterated in a contemporary and "widely used textbook of American history" as being that between "whites" and "blacks."[55] The frank statement of unequal legal states (persons who have the status of persons versus persons who have the status of property) is thus superseded by (erroneously cited) racial distinctions. Recounting the history of indentured servitude in the context of slavery, Fields notes that the decline of this servitude greatly enhanced the importance of race as a rationalization for slavery:

> Race explained why some people could rightly be denied what others took for granted: namely, liberty, supposedly a self-evident gift of nature's God. But there was nothing to explain until most people could . . . take liberty for granted—as the indentured servants and disfranchised freedmen of colonial America could not. Nor was there anything calling for a radical explanation where everyone stood in a relation of inherited subordination to someone else.[56]

Fields's argument explains the reasons for the rash of laws denying suffrage to free African American men, even or especially in the North, at the same time the franchise was extended to all white men. The expansion of freedoms for some made ever more explicit the profound contradiction slavery posed to the ideals that shaped America. As this contradiction was most pointed in the free bourgeois states of the North, it was there, Fields observes, that "racial ideology assumed its greatest importance."[57]

The relationship Fields articulates between slavery and race repeats the pattern I have noted persisting across an array of social positions in the early nineteenth century; this relationship generates the particulars of a social identity or personality from within discourses involving changing or transformed property relations. In the case of slavery, however, the distinction that underpins the very notion of property relations, that between subjectivity and property, between subjects and objects, upon which myriad legal (as well as ontological and epistemological) presumptions are based, has been utterly collapsed. Race ideology ensures that the inhumanity of this system redounds to the account not of the slaveowner but of the slave. Within these terms, racism or racial ideology or discourse must rationalize the slave (a person existing as property) becoming black man or black woman (a person marked by racial difference) as an entity *becoming human.* Racial stereotypes certainly bear this out. The point I would like to pursue here concerns the influence of domestic discourses on the formation of these stereotypes.

We need look no farther than Catharine Beecher's philosophical formulation of women's place in American democracy to see the terms through which the simultaneous construction and collapse of gender and racial differences were effected and mystified. In her chapter "The Peculiar Responsibilities of American Women," Beecher argues that the ideal of equality can be sustained only by laws that maintain "certain relations and dependencies in social and civil life." Noting the "duties of subordination" necessary to any endeavor or social relation, Beecher lists the unequal relation between "husband and wife" as primary and exemplary in her series of examples: "parent and child, teacher and pupil, employer and employed" (2). Beecher's articulation, like the cult of domesticity overall, converts what Fields refers to as "relations of inherited subordination" to duties of subordination that mark the special place of women in American democracy. What emerges as American women's "peculiar responsibility" is the responsibility to embody the necessity of the inequality of equality as *their* place, that place being the domestic sphere. Any nineteenth-century historian or literary critic would agree that the discourses of the cult of domesticity formulate the differences of the "private sphere" in feminine terms. Yet if we align the late eighteenth- and early nineteenth-century discursive evolution of domesticity with concurrent legal and political transformations that affected constructions of class and race, it seems legitimate to assert that the cult of domesticity operates to feminize, privatize, and domesticate the entire set of the disenfranchised and, thus, the question of inequality itself. Beecher's assertion that the equality that democracy ensures is that everyone can choose the superior to whom they will be subordinate inflates the affectively nuanced power relations of courtship, marriage, and family to constitute all power relations. Equating the nation with the bourgeois Northern family, Beecher blatantly omits the institution of slavery (because slaves cannot choose their masters) and marks her perspective as regionally limited despite its national address. Yet in these Northern and Southern peculiarities, the one silencing the import of the other, in the uncanny and unsettling resonances in domesticity's idealizations of motherhood and slavery's absolute debasement of it, one nevertheless can discern a significant and profound relation.

Domestic Fictions: *Uncle Tom's Cabin* and Sentimental Rights

Catharine Beecher's sister Harriet Beecher Stowe takes the principles of the cult of domesticity and places them in a fictional narrative that explicitly combines motherhood and slavery. Attributed with turning public sentiments definitively against the South's peculiar institution, Stowe's text clearly positions domesticity and maternity as the heart and moral center of American democracy. *Uncle Tom's Cabin* extends a fairly regionally specific vision of domesticity to encompass and resolve the needs and problems of an increasingly incoherent and divided nation. Yet it does so through the conventions of melodrama, sentimentality, and allegory which personalize and privatize what were otherwise legal questions about rights, citizenship, and travesties of justice.

As its title, contents, and critics indicate, the novel is first, last, and foremost about domesticity.[58] "Snowy" cloths, drapery, and spreads abound in a series of domestic arrangements and settings; maternity is enshrined, both as a force that can protect ("white" maternity) and as one that needs to be protected (the slave's maternity). Using various domestic sites—the Shelby, St. Clare, and Legree plantations, the Quaker settlement, Legree's slave quarters, Uncle Tom's cabin, and the Birds' house—and characters with different opinions about and procedures for the proper functioning of a household, Stowe allegorizes the conflicts between the North and South within the framework of domesticity.

In the novel, Stowe includes a character strikingly like her sister Catharine. Ophelia St. Clare, an efficient, intellectual spinster from the North, organizes and cleans so effectively that her status as a "lady" is put into question. Yet Ophelia must learn from her Southern slaveholding kin to have affection for "negroes"; it is through her character that Stowe inveighs against the racism of the North. Yet, tellingly, she uses Ophelia's pragmatism and efficiency in her household management to locate the character flaws that are the source of her racism. The housekeeping expert from the Northeast lacks warmth, sentiment, and a maternal sensibility, while white Southern women suffer an array of defects from slavery's influence, ranging from total moral depravity (Marie St. Clare) to genteel and ineffectual helplessness (Mrs. Shelby).[59]

In the household of Senator Bird and his wife, Mary, Stowe articulates the necessary symmetry that, by wedding home and nation, man and woman, overrides all other divisive social differences. The narrator expresses Senator Bird's shock at his wife's inquiry about what has been happening in the Senate by observing, "Now, it was a very unusual thing for the gentle little Mrs. Bird ever to trouble her head with what was going on in the house of the state, very wisely considering that she had enough to do to mind her own."[60] Mrs. Bird proceeds to engage her husband in a heated debate about the Fugitive Slave Act, countering his argument that it will keep the peace with "our brethren in Kentucky" with Scripture and the higher laws of Christian charity. Speaking on behalf of the "poor homeless, houseless creatures," she insists that she will break this law the first chance she gets. Just then, the fugitive slave Eliza and her son arrive at the Birds' house. Though denying that she has been treated unkindly by her master and mistress, Eliza reduces the entire Bird family to tears by recounting her loss of two of her children and the threat of losing her young son. Mrs. Bird's position on the Fugitive Slave Act is vindicated when Eliza's story prompts Senator Bird to break the very law he voted for that day in the Senate.

The narrator's contrast of the two houses (state and domicile, his and hers) seemingly endorses Beecher's and the cult's separate but equal policy of gender relations. Yet slavery is clearly an issue that the state cannot effectively address. Emboldened by the higher powers of God and maternity, little Mrs. Bird undercuts the importance of "great public interests" with the truth of "private feeling." Stowe narratively subordinates the political and economic issues that divide North and South to a conflict between public interests and private feeling, between senator-husband and Christian-mother. Mrs. Bird never takes a political stand; rather she asserts her Christian and maternal duty to care for "oppressed and abused creatures." The effectivity of her maternal ministry is affirmed; sentiment and pathos override the law.

Stowe returns again and again to the horrors of treating people as property, but that horror is consistently written to, and contained within, the account of the family and domesticity. When George, also a fugitive ex-slave, is reunited with his wife, Eliza, and their son, he exclaims to her, "Oh, Eliza, if these people only knew what a blessing it is for a man to feel that his wife and child belong to *him*! I've often wondered to see men that could call their wives and children *their own* fretting and worrying about anything else."[61] George, as Stowe conceives him, wants nothing more than his rights to kinship, to affective property relations whose gendered terms have been established and sentimentalized by the cult of domesticity. The limits to his aspirations, to his characterization, to the construction of the "negro" race or racial difference overall are presaged in the title Stowe gives to her book. *Uncle Tom's Cabin* is about slavery, gross transgressions of civil rights, persecution, antipathy between North and South, inhumanity, and the "negro" race, all brought together and contained under a figure of diminutive domesticity—a cabin.

Like her sister, like the cult overall, Harriet Beecher Stowe positions domesticity at the heart of American democracy. The overwhelming, astounding success of her novel indicates that her construction of racial difference within an overarching frame of domesticity effectively served and organized diverse and powerful social forces in the discursive milieu in which it was produced. The dynamics of Stowe's text reveal functions of the cult of domesticity obscured at the time by the sociopolitical divisions of North and South, and both then and now by valuable historical inquiry which is nevertheless limited by the gendered terms of difference the cult enshrined. These functions mark one of the paths whereby the inhumane property relations constituted by the institution of slavery are transformed into the racial and racist "becoming human" identity of free African Americans.

While *Uncle Tom's Cabin* vehemently objects to slavery, it replaces it with a formulation of racial difference contained within and subjected to strictures of femininity and domesticity. Stowe invokes true Christian motherhood in her narrative as the force that both unites the different races within a common humanity and also configures enlightened white women (Mrs. Bird, Rachel Halliday) as the mothers to the nation, to all its children and its beleaguered, childlike peoples. Her novel nationalizes sentimental domesticity by domesticating the most salient national problem of her time. Either literally (Topsy) or figuratively (Uncle Tom) rendering "negroes" as children, as childlike or childish (the mature mixed-race couple Eliza and George leave the country), the narrative transforms the actual inequality of slavery into the developmental inequality of African Americans as a race. Assimilating the necessary inequality of equality with and through the maternal metaphor, Stowe's text indicates how the sentimental imperatives of compassion, benevolence, and pity relocate hierarchical power and property relations in the racialized and infantilized identity of the freedman. The construction of racial difference effected by *Uncle Tom's Cabin* shores up the power, status, and effectivity of white women's gender identity. It ensconces a racialized, but Christian and compassionate, hierarchy within the dynamics of gender difference in such a way that the relationship between the two is marginalized and obscured by the gendered division of public and private spheres.

The Legacy of Domestic Femininity

Domestic femininity emerges from an array of social interests, changes, and forces that construct and secure social identities within mystifying networks of power and place. This discursive entity mobilizes and anchors a social imaginary wherein economic and social inequities are naturalized, sentimentalized, and personified as features of racial, class, and gender difference. Both structurally and historically, domestic femininity functions as a classist and racist discourse. But its implications and effects with regard to slavery and race are as paradoxical as Child's market-resistant notions of American domesticity. Taking *Uncle Tom's Cabin* as the exemplary instance, we see that its protest against slavery had very diverse consequences. Credited with garnering and unifying support for abolition and the war to overthrow slavery, the novel nevertheless functions conservatively. Like Beecher's domestic economy, *Uncle Tom's Cabin* accommodates democracy's inequities by finding a place and constructing an identity for those subjected to these inequities, converting the terms of subjection to the features of a particular social subjectivity.

The importance of the cult of domesticity or of true womanhood cannot be overestimated. This discursive formation provided for the invention via triangulation of a sentimentalized relation to property (domesticity), a gender identity (womanhood), and a moralized authenticity ("true") as the measure of both. Domestic femininity feminized and sentimentalized the civic inequality that was privatized by universal white male suffrage. This displacement of property or class privilege from the "public" to the "private" sphere makes industrial capitalism possible in the United States by allowing it to exist alongside, but not in blatantly obvious contradiction to, democratic public discourse. In addition, this displacement repositions individual subjects in relation to the law, converting what had been legally sanctioned and acknowledged states of privilege and inequality to legal inclusions and exclusions to civic life predicated on newly emerging social identities conditioned by these very laws. Thus these identities themselves embody privatized instances of various types of legal exclusions and inequalities. These social identities operate, as does domesticity, in ways that paradoxically both resist and accommodate the status quo. Ultimately, the resistance mustered in the name of such social identities usually function conservatively, because these identities themselves function to rationalize and mystify material inequities. For example, capitalism obviously benefits from a social identity (domestic femininity) that allows privileged individuals a sentimentalized moral relationship to their property.

Even in the face of second wave feminism, the triangle wherein womanhood or femininity, private property, and moral authenticity are imbricated has proved particularly powerful and resilient. We are still wrestling with its discursive legacy today. Contemporary feminism, attempting to define its political and epistemological object (women's or woman's identity) has had to grapple with, and has sometimes necessarily fallen prey to, all the elements of female specificity constructed in the nineteenth century: a sentimentalized and morally based sexuality and maternal function, an innate affiliation with the domestic, a subjectivity limited to "personal" life, a sense of power constrained to interpersonal influence, and finally a tendency for the object "woman" to override other social and material differences.[62] Similarly, identity politics, of which feminism is the exemplar, reveals its roots in the early nineteenth century and the legal transformations I have discussed in this chapter by approaching legal inequalities and injustices from within privatized and personified positions of exclusion, that is, identities. Such politics are thus necessarily, if unfortunately, vested in the symptoms of their own legal malaise—the ideological and conservative structures of social distinction that displace the consequences of unequal property relations onto the personalities of the excluded.

By the end of the nineteenth century, technology was sounding the death knell of the cult of domesticity. It did so largely by once again recoding the private as a place of deprivation rather than as a complement or opposition to the public sphere. In the next chapter I discuss Frederick Winslow Taylor's efficiency principles, a scientific cult that displaced true womanhood as the basis for the exemplary American home. Nevertheless, as I have just suggested, the ideological structure of the cult of domesticity is still very much with us.

Tayloring the Home

The Fantasy of Domestic Engineering

The suburban house is a type of progress.

The House Beautiful (July 1903)[1]

Turn-of-the-century domestic discourses represent the domicile and its significance in markedly different terms from those of their Victorian predecessors. The prevailing social ethos shifted from an emphasis on a superior, feminized otherworldliness and sentimentality to one that espoused the values of science, objectivity, and progress. Instead of public and private spheres being constructed and neatly opposed by gender, purpose, and value, as they were in the hands of the Beecher sisters and the cult of domesticity, the American turn toward technology, invention, and science resulted in representations of the private sphere as permeable, receptive, accommodating to or demonstrative of new "progressive" ideas. The ascension of science secularized the discursive distinctions between the spheres and, consequently, altered the predominant constructions of appropriate femininity. The ethos of appearance so crucial to Catharine Beecher and the cult of domesticity's constructions of a class-based, moralized femininity persisted but assumed a differently nuanced ideological character and function.

The many technological, chemical, medical, and hygienic discoveries of the late nineteenth century culminated in a discursive transformation whereby the moral power of sentiment gave way to the moral power of science. One of the founding fantasies of twentieth-century America was that science, technology, and progress could cure all social ills.[2] Domestic discourses shaped and were shaped by this fantasy; they provided the means whereby scientific values and technological paradigms infused and altered middle-class American domesticity, femininity, and morality.

Discursive overlays between *Americanism*, a term that European intellectuals used to describe the explosive success and influence of twentieth-century American production methods, inventions, and technology, and contemporaneous American domesticity include the professionalization of home economics in universities; the affiliation of such departments with the nascent disciplines of sociology, political science, and urban studies, as well as with architecture; the merging of social reform and domestic design; and, more generally, the overall societal convergence of scientific standardization and morality.[3] Conceptions of appropriate domesticity were generated and circulated within a cluster of institutional practices and locations, most notably connected to education, social reform, and industry, all of which were linked to a distinctly American identity. This public-*cum*-institutional reconfiguration of domesticity was engineered by, addressed to, consumed by, and created for the benefit of white middle-class women.

To get to the ideological pith of the domestic engineering movement, I intend to focus on two specific texts that mediate between Catharine Beecher's domestic legacy (education for women, women's special authority, the home as women's place of expertise) and the ideas of Frederick Winslow Taylor about industry and efficiency. Such texts demonstrate how Americanism and Fordism inflected domestic discourses and, more important, domestic femininity in the early decades of the twentieth century. Several questions direct my reading of these texts: What happens to the moralization of femininity and the class and racial distinctions that proceed "naturally" from it in an age that invests so much value in science and standardization? What now marks the specificity and importance of private space and the domicile, heretofore the moral sphere, when middle-class white women begin to conceive of their housework in terms of factory efficiency and time management? How do writers on domestic engineering treat issues of racial and economic differentiation, if at all?

Seventy years passed between the publication of Catharine Beecher's *Treatise on Domestic Economy* and a group of books by various authors—among them Christine Frederick, Lillian Gilbreth, and Mary Pattison—who proselytized a scientific approach to housekeeping.[4] Referred to as "domestic engineering" or "household management," this new approach applied Frederick Winslow Taylor's efficiency methods and Frank Gilbreth's time and motion studies to the performance of housework. In this way Beecher's spatial formulation of the home and its physical, cultural, and metaphysical functions was replaced by the concept of a home organized by an emphasis on time, schedules, and the increases of efficiency available with the use of proper tools and disciplined bodily movement. Beecher and the cult of domesticity had constructed domestic values as precisely subjective, emotional, and spiritual—values assured and perpetuated by feminine and maternal authority. Domestic engineers, by contrast, promoted the objective authority of science, of the expert, and of rational, calculated housekeeping methods that guaranteed results for all.

The new domestic engineers imported ideas generated in the "public" sphere by outside experts and applied them to their own "private" housekeeping. Rather than distinguishing a uniquely feminine from a masculine authority, they envisioned themselves as efficiency acolytes, following in the footsteps of experts on whose reputation the housewife-engineer's own expertise was then asserted. The most influential expert was Frederick Winslow Taylor, whose *Principles of Scientific Management*

(1911) had a direct and immediate impact on domesticity despite its explicit concern with efficiency in factory management. Christine Frederick recounts in *The New Housekeeping: Efficiency Studies in Home Management* (1912) that after overhearing her husband's conversation with a business associate who was explaining Taylor's ideas to him, she decided, despite some doubts, to apply "that efficiency gospel . . . to *my* factory, *my* business, *my* home."[5] In her book, *The Principles of Domestic Engineering: Or the What, Why, and How of the Home* (1915), Mary Pattison describes the receipt of Taylor's book in the mail. In reading it, she found his ideas "an answer from above" to the housework problems she had been pondering.[6] Gone are the moral authority and special spirituality that the cult of domesticity appropriated for women, although they symptomatically reappear in Frederick's and Pattison's perspectives on Taylor's methods as an "answer from above" and an efficiency "gospel." Domestic engineers domesticated a positivist belief in reason and science, and thereby secularized the impulses to social reform generated by the domesticity cult in the nineteenth century. Their movement brought women back into the home with the same *social* impulse that had brought them into the public sphere earlier (to educate future American citizens), only now their "public" moral authority was replaced by a "private" professional code.

In the interval between Beecher and the domestic engineers, the conditions that influenced Beecher's construction of a domestic economy as the complement of the developing market economy continued to transform social and economic life. A consumer revolution occurred in the latter half of the nineteenth century that significantly influenced turn-of-the-century constructions of bourgeois housekeepers and the private sphere. Spawned by increases in discretionary income in both the working and middle classes, this economic phenomenon was bolstered by technological advances and inventions that lowered commodity costs while also expanding the market with many new products. Whereas the technological inventions of early industrialization had furnished apparatuses of production, inventions in the second half of the nineteenth century resulted in consumer products such as automobiles, bicycles, the telephone, and chemical dyes.[7]

In America the gap between production and consumption that had opened up in the antebellum period widened considerably. The mass market became increasingly standardized, new products proliferated, and the advertising business was born. The private individual became a consumer—or, rather, the middle-class housewife did. As the anecdotes of both Frederick and Pattison indicate, constructions of the private sphere now emphasized its receptivity to and its dependence on resources— material and discursive—coming in from outside the home. The task of the bourgeois housewife was increasingly represented as one of mediation. In her role as consumer she had to negotiate material interactions between the home and the market. She also had to mediate or manage the profound contradictions to which the consumer economy gave rise. In short, white middle-class housekeepers now presided over a "private" sphere constructed as a place of autonomy and individuality in contradistinction to the workplace, while at the same time this place was positioned as necessarily reliant on externally produced goods, methods, and technologies. Domestic engineers wrote books that were in immediate dialogue with new industrial discourses that synthesized the contradictory imperatives of autonomous individuality and passive, dependent consumption in a modernized type of domestic femininity. I trace the evolution and contours of the paradoxical persona of the domestic engineer in the remainder of this chapter.

Discipline and Relaxation

The program of the domestic engineers realized to the fullest possible extent the disciplining of domesticity begun by Catharine Beecher and her contemporaries. But reading domestic engineering in terms of Foucauldian disciplinary techniques produces the same contradictory or problematic effects that the reading of Beecher's domestic economy as a discipline produces. As we will see yet again, the home is consistently constructed by disciplinary forces and discourses as *other* to the workplace. The contradictions this distinction provokes in the texts of the domestic engineers is at once more pronounced and more subtle than in Beecher insofar as the domestic engineers advocate homes modeled precisely on factory spaces and techniques. Both Christine Frederick and Mary Pattison instruct housewives to acquire stopwatches and notepads, to analyze carefully and plan their every movement, to fashion their homes and kitchens according to "the route of material" through domestic space, to establish "auto-operative" houses. They thereby implement the set of disciplinary techniques related to time, precise bodily movement, and the control of objects that Beecher's domestic economy lacked. Still, domestic engineering must be approached through the legacy of Beecher's domestic economy and the crucial ideological transformations it underwent in the years that separate their work. For this reason it is worth comparing Beecher's domestic economy with that of the domestic engineers.

The function of education is a particularly telling place to look for the changes between Beecher and the domestic engineers, especially because it establishes a two-way conduit between the university and the home, public and private. Beecher's *Treatise on Domestic Economy* emphasizes the need for women's domestic education strictly within the context of the private sphere. Yet the consequences of her advocacy resulted in domestic education's completely bypassing the notion of separate spheres and instead stressing the interrelations between the household and society.[8] Beecher uses the idea of a discrete domestic sphere to indicate the importance of the home to society; the "new emphasis" of her successors stresses a significantly different connection between public and private spheres. Social reformers in the Progressive Era used domestic education to try to improve the habits and standard of living of impoverished immigrants. "Public school cooking classes offered a way to teach thrift, nutrition and cleanliness, and American ways to the poor through their children," notes Susan Strasser. Domestic education here figures within an ideology that pervaded the Progressive Era: "Social progress depended on public attention to matters formerly considered private."[9]

The "benevolent" domestic hierarchies articulated in a work such as *Uncle Tom's Cabin* persist here, but in a somewhat altered form. Whereas the ideology of separate spheres located affective moral power in the home and the domestic woman, the Progressives and the domestic engineers construct the home as the proper *object* of benevolent reform ministrations. In their texts the home, the private sphere, becomes explicitly a place of deprivation, a place lacking in knowledge and resources: for the white middle class, it lacks the rational techniques necessary to any efficient and properly modern enterprise, as domesticity is hopelessly fixed in tradition; the domesticity of the poor and the working class is unsafe, unsanitary, dangerous to public health and morals, and in need of expert guidance.[10] The rhetoric of domestic education now inverts the expertise of public and private, constructing and promoting public scientific experts as rescuers of the benighted private sphere.

In Christine Frederick's introduction to *The New Housekeeping*, we can see how this inversion organizes and then overrides differences among classes and peoples. It does so by finally endorsing the universality of reason and science that now characterized the American nation.[11] Outlining her reasons for writing her book, Frederick recounts the desperate straits of housekeepers, asserting finally that middle-class homemakers are the most in need of relief. The wealthy do not have "the problem of housekeeping" because they can always "buy service." Poor women also avoid this problem because, first, they "come from the class of servants," and second, "their home making is far less complex, their tastes simple, and society demands no appearance-standard from them." Philanthropic efforts assist the poor in efficient housekeeping:

> Settlements, domestic science classes, model kitchens and tenements, nursing stations, slum depots, charity boards, health boards, visiting nurses, night schools and mission classes are teaching, *free*, the women of the poor how to transmute their old-world ignorance into the shining knowledge of the new hemisphere. (11)

Within the space of a page, Frederick subsumes the distinctions among social classes within those that distinguish U.S. citizens from immigrants. All the poor become immigrants, suggesting that all proper Americans are middle class and native born. Tradition is both European and impoverished, discounted as "old-world ignorance," while domestic engineering represents the "shining knowledge" of the new world.[12]

Frederick's articulation of America's national identity does not rest on democracy, as Child's and Beecher's had, but rather touts the superior efficiency and knowledge of the American nation. Mechanization, the assembly line, the power of science and engineering put to the service of capitalism all presumably guaranteed America's workers higher wages and greater leisure.[13] Frederick identifies her own lack of leisure time and the impossibility of doing all her chores efficiently and well, along with the "servant problem," as the reasons for her investigation of scientific management in the home. Time, not space, organizes both the problems addressed and the solutions offered by domestic engineering. Time itself is differentiated in a way that was not at all evident in Child nor pronounced in Beecher. The distinction between public and private spheres is now overlaid with an increasingly important temporal difference—that between work time and leisure time.[14]

Thus, ironically, Beecher's emphasis on education leads to a generalized degradation of housekeepers' traditional skills. The expertise of tradition, of the domestic, and of the housewife is overridden in the transformations that render the home utterly reliant on the market for its functioning. In 1900, at the Lake Placid conference where the discipline acquired the name "home economics," Henrietta Goodrich argued that "professionalism required the creation of a hierarchy within the home economics movement."[15] Glenna Matthews writes, "The birth of home economics as a discipline . . . is part of the larger pattern of the development of the culture of professionalism in the late nineteenth century." By definition, a profession requires a lengthy tenure of hierarchical education and training which ideally results in the trainee's acquisition of a certain level of proficiency in a given field. Professionalism in home economics therefore necessitated the standardization of household procedures in order to determine what constitutes proficiency with regard to actual practices. More significantly, professional home economists had to "distance themselves from that lowly amateur, the housewife."[16] The discipline of home economics established its authority in opposition to that of the housekeeper's traditional skills. To justify their profession, home economists asserted the ineptitude and inefficiency of untrained amateur housekeepers, who needed to learn their craft from educated domestic professionals. Matthews summarizes the home economists' position in words that capture the impetus for both Frederick's and Pattison's texts: "Therefore, the only way that beneficent change could come to the home was through the instrumentality of the outside expert."[17]

The depreciation of housekeepers and domestic traditions was a seemingly unavoidable effect of the development of home economics. Yet this development created and was created by new opportunities for women. In this historical period (1900–1930), women could do graduate work in the sciences only if they directed their studies to domestic concerns.[18] This cultural constraint accorded with the character of the nascent discipline and the Taylorized mood of the culture overall; although home economics would eventually come to emphasize psychology and human development, in this period the objective sciences dominated its perspective and enshrined the values of standardization, controlled experimentation, and scientific method to the detriment of experience, craft, and tradition.

Some women were nevertheless able to use the home and domesticity to gain access to educational institutions and opportunities that otherwise would have been forbidden to them. They parlayed their culturally imposed specialization (domesticity) into educational departments and professional positions, creating in effect a domestic enclave within the university system.[19] This maneuver had negative results, however. It segregated home economists from housewives and instituted a hierarchical relation between them based both on the progressive accumulation of institutional knowledge and, frequently, on disparate material resources; and it compelled domestic professionals in academia and later in commerce to found not just their professions but their very identity on the presumed incompetence of housewives, the poor, immigrants, and racial minorities. While the home remained a woman's place (in the academy and commerce as well as in the actual domestic site), the professionalization of home economics wrested from housewives the meager authority that had been constructed by Beecher and the cult of domesticity. This ideological transformation placed the housekeeper in the same relation to domestic knowledge in which she was increasingly being positioned in relation to products at this time—that is, as simply a consumer. Pattison's housekeeper paces the floor and loses sleep, bereft not only of the necessary machines and commodities to perform her tasks properly, but also of the requisite knowledge and expertise to manage her own sphere professionally—until she comes upon Frederick Winslow Taylor's management principles.

Managing Schisms: Autonomy and Automation

Frederick Winslow Taylor's *Principles of Scientific Management* (1911) operates within an economy and set of values decidedly alien to the ideals of domesticity perpetrated by the "separate spheres" ideology. Taylor seeks to ameliorate the hostility between factory management and workers by reformulating their relationship in cooperative terms. He argues that his system of scientific management can give both parties what they want—higher wages for workers and lower labor costs for management—by instituting an efficiency program that elicits maximum labor output. In his schema management provides the brains to complement labor's brawn; he designates their functions in such a way that the two are compelled to work together. Rather than relying on workers to devise their own methods of completing a given task, Taylor asserts that management must scientifically determine the optimal procedure, the best way to do it, through careful experiments. This experimentation should include a detailed analysis of every movement, tool, and variable involved in the task as well as the selection of the proper worker for the job. When the tested procedure is implemented, workers who perform the task correctly should be rewarded with higher wages. Management will realize greatly increased profits from production rates that double or triple as a result of these efficient procedures.[20]

Taylor also recommends that management collect all of the traditional job knowledge possessed by the workers and record and store it in a central planning office. But he repeatedly makes the point that a worker's or user's experience can never equal the insight and expertise of the scientist in discerning overarching laws of efficient operation through careful calculations and experiments.[21] This type of cooperation between labor and management crucially depends on the distinction between workers' public and private lives. A worker participates in the automation of his body, thus acceding to the increased rationalization of his labor in return for compensations that improve the quality of his private life. In other words, Taylor's system, predicated on a hierarchical division of labor, a series of wage incentives, and a functional distribution of mechanized bodies, relies for its success on its opposition to a hypostatized private sphere. At home, the mechanized, automated laborer, whom Taylor refers to as a "high-priced man," becomes once again an individual, a person possessing the agency, ability, and will necessary for autonomous, self-motivated action.[22] His skill as an automaton on the job improves the quality of his and his family's leisure. The saving of time in one place increases the value of time in another. Yet this hypostatized private sphere constitutes the women who inhabit it, by implication, as "high-priced" within the home and invisible in public—except as students about to return to the home. Pattison, Frederick, and the rest of the domestic engineers explicitly investigate and articulate the differences in this model as it applies to women.

Both Pattison and Frederick believe in the (gendered) distinctions between the public and private spheres. Pattison fervently touts the values and importance of the domestic sphere, of the single-family private dwelling. For her, "the marked difference between the private home and the public institution" is that "the former gives freedom to the individual and the motive; the latter is opposed to individualism, giving authority to a pledge or order." While she allows that the private home is not the most economical or efficient form of social organization, the "great values that accrue" from it more than compensate for its drawbacks (32). Frederick, much less florid in her rhetoric, notes the distinctions in more pragmatic terms. She initially resists the application of scientific management to the home because the home-maker, unlike the factory worker, does all jobs all day, rather than one specific task over and over again. Unlike the factory worker's job, the homemaker's various roles also interrupt the timely and efficient performance of tasks—the baby cries while she is ironing or water boils while she cleans the floor. Each writer carefully delineates the ways in which the home is necessarily different from and superior to the market in terms of hierarchies, wages as reward, and the intricate divisions of labor necessary to Taylor's efficiency procedures. Their overarching reason for adopting his principles is therefore very telling.

Both women find in Taylor's little book a solution to the so-called servant problem, as well as to the problem of housewives' leisure and professionalism. Domestic activists from Beecher on decry the use of domestic labor, claiming that such servitude does not accord with democratic principles. Less publicly voiced reasons involve the repugnance bourgeois housewives felt in having their homes invaded by poor, illiterate immigrants and blacks, the only household help readily available after the rise of the factory system.[23] Scientific management, by offering the housewife methods for doing more work in less time with less wear and tear on her body, alleviates the need for servants, or so the domestic engineers argue. Reiterating Beecher's concern with white middle-class women's health and appearance—a concern that, as we have seen, both masks and maintains class difference—the domestic engineers similarly locate their anxieties about domestic labor in relation to racialized class issues. To rid the home of what were perceived to be foreign elements—wage labor and servile, impoverished, un-American bodies that had to be managed—the domestic engineers look to an industrial model alien to the domestic sphere in another way. They select a system that depends on a mechanized body, on movements timed, spaced, and planned for efficiency, and finally on rewards realized in the private sphere for alienation experienced in the workplace.

Domestic engineering, by necessity, focuses on the housekeeper and her body, on the ways she can be trained and managed to effect more scientific housekeeping. Its approach to this body is much more alienated, in that sense, than is Beecher's concern with health. Yet the representation of this housewife must also extend beyond the authority of Taylor's discourse, directed as it is to the management of factory workers. The housewife must represent in some way the values of the private sphere—individuality, freedom, autonomy—against which the disciplinary regimes of the workplace are defined. Their housekeeping must engineer a fit between Taylorism and domesticity, between the public and private spheres; it must accommodate the oppositional values of automation and autonomy.

Consequently, one motif that traverses these texts involves a persistent focus on the actual and potential relations between public and private spheres in terms of time, space, and laboring bodies. In relation to work, the two spheres can be equated. Yet in their articulations of leisure, style, and love, the private sphere remains distinct, based on the fundamental character of femininity and the domicile. While the procedures the domestic engineers suggest render the housewife replaceable and expendable, her uniqueness and value as a wife are securely located elsewhere.

Pattison aligns the workplace and the home in the opening of her book by discussing a room modeled on a factory location, a place she refers to as the "home office." The chapter titled "An Auto-Operative House" opens with the observation that every home should have a system of organization that would allow a newcomer to enter and take charge immediately, because the truly efficient housewife does not allow herself to become indispensible to her household. The location, use, and contents of every room in the house should be referenced in "a small card index" in the office. In addition, every room should have a number on its door, with a card on the inside indicating the contents of the room. The housekeeper's cataloguing system should also include all information about "the home and the family"; Pattison suggests a color-coding arrangement combined with a tree-branch-twig chart to place every element and occupant in the home in relation to "the economic arrangement of the whole" (63). The housekeeper's first task involves making herself expendable by objectifying and recording all things familial, by defamiliarizing domestic space and everything it contains. Indexes and charts catalogue her expertise, rendering it abstract and transferable so "that not even a word *need* be spoken between the outgoing and incoming manager; a mere gesture of the hand as to where to find the central desk, or starting point, being sufficient" (61).

"In close touch with the market"

Beyond the household manager's fundamental quality of replaceability, the domestic engineers' attention to what is incoming and outgoing finds a pronounced focus in the housewife's role as a "purchasing agent." Significantly, shopping is one of the first specific housekeeping chores that both Pattison and Frederick discuss. The priority of this task reflects the most telling change between their principles of housekeeping and Beecher's. Owing to the drastic separation effected between production and consumption by the "second" industrial revolution, the housekeeper is now first and foremost a consumer. Scientific consumption requires a housewife to be well informed about value and—as Pattison says—"in close touch with the market" (70). Both writers suggest that women organize consumer groups, try to eliminate middlemen who distribute goods, and patronize shops that stock reliable products. They also argue that women need substantial knowledge of chemistry, hygiene, and nutrition in order to evaluate consumer products. Pattison asserts that it is as important to know "the effect of cold storage upon foods and the very great part it plays in the economic and health problems of the day, as to know the science of cookery." The housewife's skill in purchasing should equal her skill in producing a meal. Because the family no longer controls food production, women must *police* the foodstuffs that come into the home. They should regard the "fight for proper inspection of our food supply, and the unadulterated and reliable or staple form of all material that goes to make a home," as necessary and as important as the "fight for suffrage" (72).

Both writers detail public systems and goods that permeate or affect the domestic sphere. The increased trade with a public market requires the housekeeper to regulate what enters and leaves her domain in order to guard against both contamination (by bad products) and economic exploitation. For housewives, consumption becomes a form of gender/knowledge aimed at the market economy. In this respect, domestic engineering is similar in form to Child's frugality, which supplements the market, and to Beecher's home economy, which provides a spiritual (and invisible material) counterweight within the market. The terms change, but the housewife's knowledge consistently mediates between two presumably distinct worlds.

Thus, according to Pattison, the proper training for a domestic engineer should therefore include "knowledge of and acquaintance with materials of every sort that enter the home, and their use, with comparative worth" (194). Frederick's advice to consumers includes an entire chapter, titled "Business and Economics," that cautions the housewife always to patronize name brands but never to buy them on sale. Her reasoning is that sales destabilize the profits of companies that stand behind their products with their name, and thus imperil their continued existence (204–10). Domestic engineering also emphasizes the importance of the new appliances in efficient housekeeping. Pattison celebrates technological developments that lighten a housewife's load, but cautions that various brands and models should be scrupulously tried and tested for efficiency and quality.[24]

The domestic engineers do not advocate the vote for women, but they do see women's role as extending into public affairs, specifically in relation to the supervision and regulation of public services. Building regulations control the home's physical construction and appearance; public utilities connect it to supplies of gas, electricity, and water. Necessities for sustenance are now usually acquired by purchase rather than by domestic production. Pattison concludes, "In truth, home-making can no longer be said to be a private undertaking. It is a public function, regulated and formulated by local and State authorities" (248). Because women "prepare and distribute food" (while men grow and store it or earn the money to buy it), they should act as a "guard over the market" to ensure against "dietetic pollution." As nurturers and mothers, housewives should "raise" standards, while men must make these standards work. Whereas, earlier, women produced or recycled to make up for the lack of money or products in an emerging market economy, now they regulate production passively through informed consumption.

This ability to raise the standards of the private home can be acquired only by means of rigorous higher education. Domestic engineers, Pattison writes, should acquire "all the scientific information possible, included under the general head of physics, of the science of energy, together with chemistry, sanitation, hygiene, culinics, dietetics etc." (194). Going beyond Beecher, neither Frederick nor Pattison promotes the maternal, mimetic mode of learning. Frederick argues that the home is "less and less a place where you can teach the things every woman should know." Education ensures that daughters will know more than their mothers. She concludes:

> Last, by dignifying home economics as a *science*, and placing it on a level with other cultural studies, your daughter will learn . . . the dignity of housework and home-making as she would never have learned it or accepted it in your own home kitchen. It is a fine antidote against the unnatural craving for 'careers' and the reluctance to give attention to and take pride in those things which a woman's part in life makes it imperative for her to know, sooner or later. (233)

The class blindness (some women *must* work outside the home) and gender role conservatism evidenced in this passage are articulated and justified in relation to science and education. Woman's proper role is no longer dictated by her innate spirituality and place but is rather seen as natural or unnatural within a scientific schema that will become manifest in all women's lives "sooner or later." The domestic engineer must be trained not in the home but at the university; thus both writers outline a comprehensive four-year course of study for a degree program in domestic engineering.[25] Ironically their advocacy itself attenuates women's demands for access to the public sphere proper: the vote, work, politics.

The housewife exploits the consumer's freedom of choice. With this freedom she can (supposedly) regulate or even control the market. No longer a producer or creator, the well-educated domestic engineer applies the methods and systems she learns in the classroom and laboratory to her own home. In this way, as Pattison argues, she raises societal standards, producing better citizens and providing an example of "a more perfect form of government." Unlike their predecessors, Frederick's and Pattison's housekeepers inhabit a home that the authors represent as infiltrated at all levels by "public" technologies, products, and discourses. These incursions give rise to new roles for the housekeeper to perform. In the diverse interactions between public and private spheres, the domestic engineer acts as a moderator, a filter, and a negotiator between them, whereas for Child and Beecher the housewife represented and created an alternative to the market.

A Particular Efficiency

Within the home, the housewife's primary concern is efficiency, the path to eliminating wear and tear on her body. In "The Route of Material," Pattison traces the path of commodities as they enter the home to be used or stored. At a "receiving station" they are weighed, recorded, and routed to their proper storage area. The location and arrangement of this receiving station, she instructs, should be planned in terms of the necessary movements the housekeeper will have to perform to clean, store, or prepare the food or dry goods she is receiving. Several rules should be strictly followed as she plots this or any housekeeping process. "No travel in a backward direction is allowed in a properly routed task," and all the necessary equipment and material required for a job should be kept "as near the point of use as can be arranged" (77). Furniture should be placed in accordance with the sequence of a task and spaced so as to entail the minimum number of steps and movements between work stations. Minute plans are crucial to efficiency, plans that precisely dictate the movements of the housewife's body as well as the space through which she moves. Similarly, Frederick's text applies Frank Gilbreth's famous time and motion experiment with bricklaying to her own dishwashing. She analyzes every movement it takes to wash a dish and ultimately rearranges the entire layout of her kitchen to eliminate two unnecessary gestures from her washing procedure.

Her reward? Fifteen minutes cut from the overall performance time for the chore. Scientific management, efficiency, and tools in the home can provide the housewife with only one reward: leisure time. Her work results in not working, and little else, thus making the domestic engineer's injunctions about homemaking as a "career" ironic at best. Unlike Gilbreth's bricklayers, whose elimination of wasteful movements results in significantly increased profits and wages, the housewife gets no monetary reward for increased automation. Like Child's housekeeper, she "saves" time; like Beecher's, she finds that her new housekeeping methods improve "the state" and result in "public progress." Rather than valuing the housekeeper's frugality, as does Child, or her special spirituality, as does Beecher, the domestic engineers envision the housewife as a college-educated expert in the most challenging career of all: homemaking. Frederick argues that "far from being dull drudgery, homemaking . . . is fascinating and stimulating if a woman applies to it her best intelligence and culture" (186). But this application requires a special sort of splitting for the housewife.

The Woman Who Is Her Own Servant

Beyond her function as consumer watchdog and efficiency expert, the domestic engineer must also get her housework done, and it is in this area that the discrepancies between home and factory become most pronounced. In "The Instruction Bureau," Pattison discusses the nature and function of the housekeeping library. Intended to replace the hand-me-downs of traditional knowledge, the bureau should contain all the information the housewife possesses or collects about housekeeping, indexed and systematized. The home office and the instruction bureau take their model from the planning office in Taylor's factory. These rooms designate spatially the mental, managerial component of housekeeping. They delimit one role the housekeeper plays, that of manager, to one of her other roles as laborer. In domestic engineering, the mental and manual hierarchy, the planning and performing functions distributed among groups of workers in Taylor's factory, must be contained, played out within the singular person of the housewife.

Both authors manage to fit this aspect of Taylor's system to the domestic situation by literalizing his distinction between manual and mental labor. Frederick refers to the "woman who is her own servant" (153), while in a chapter titled "Time and Motion Study," Pattison rationalizes the functions of planning and performing in relation to the housekeeper's head and hand. Planning involves careful analysis of and repeated experiments with the movements constituting any and all household tasks. This procedure demands, at every stage, that different functions be performed by the head and hand:

> The hand learns just where to move in the dispatching of each subject, and the head goes its own way in planning and co-ordinating the different parts, for they should work together by never interfering with each other. In the study of time and motion experiments, both head and hand should be keenly alive to every phase of detail that can be grasped and analyzed; the head *thinking* them out, and the hand *feeling* them out through close concentration. . . . [W]hen practice has shown the best way, the head and hand should separate somewhat, the head looking beyond or ahead of the hand to properly plan the next step. (108)

Neither Pattison nor Frederick questions the logic of applying Taylor's mental work–manual work distinction to the singular personage of the housewife, but the implications of their move are profound in terms of female subjectivity. While Taylor's scientific management splits male subjectivity across space—home and work—

the housekeeper subject is split within the home, as manager, servant, and sign of leisure. Domestic engineering multiplies the housewife's functions and distributes their representation across fragments of her body. This Cartesian housekeeper self-simulates her own authority and position as manager-master by taking her own body as laborer-slave. She objectifies herself and her knowledge, performs elaborate experiments on her every gesture, times herself, counts her own steps, subjects her body to detailed training. She charts passages through her home, running from position to position on her own auto-assembly line. Taking herself in hand, she standardizes her housework and supervises her own automation, making herself into a phantasm of efficiency, a completely Taylorized housekeeper.[26]

Yet she also exceeds this robotic representation insofar as her image inhabits another discourse that disguises her mechanization. Each book features a photograph of its female author on the title page. Frederick's housekeeping book includes a photo of the author in a flowing white floor-length lab coat in her experimental kitchen. Pattison's example is even more dramatically symptomatic. The title page of *Domestic Engineering* faces a full-page frontispiece showing the author, her hair up and elegantly coiffed, a lace drape falling off her bare white shoulders. Beneath her photograph rests her signature in flowing script, and beneath her title the modest disclaimer "An Attempt." The title page proclaims the author's intention "to evolve a solution of the 'domestic labor and capital' problem; to standardize and professionalize housework; to reorganize the home upon 'scientific management' principles and to point out the public and personal element therein as well as the practical." Despite these blatant pretensions to science, both authors' portraits reassure the reader that science and standardization have not altered a delicate, feminine appearance or character.

Domesticity, the ideology of the private sphere, apparently cannot tolerate the idea of a mechanized housewife. No less an expert than Taylor himself doubted the benefits of applying his own efficiency principles to the home. In his introduction to Pattison's text, Taylor expresses anxiety at the prospect of mixing women and machines:

> We are accustomed to associate the use of machinery with the matter-of-fact side of life. As eminent an authority as Ruskin has taught us that its presence acts as a blight to all our artistic instincts. It may, therefore, be a question in the minds of many whether its daily use might now tend to diminish the interest of the wife in the aesthetic side of her surroundings; cause her to neglect her personal appearance and to care less for the . . . distinctly feminine things that give a home its greatest attraction. If this were true then the introduction of machinery in the household might indeed prove to be a doubtful blessing. (16)

Taylor, however, reassures the reader that not only is Pattison a pioneering scientist, but also she is "always . . . well and artistically dressed" (16–17). These remarks sit oddly in the larger context of Taylor's introduction, which traces the fluctuating relationship between machinery and the home. At the beginning of the industrial revolution, the removal of machines, specifically the spinning wheel, from the home to the factory lessened women's workload. Now, says Taylor, "the return of machinery to the household" will again lighten the housewife's burden (15). Given his own assertions about the liberating effects of machinery, Taylor's concerns for women's appearance and aesthetic sense seem contradictory; by his own argument, machines should give wives more time to attend to aesthetics and their appearance. Taylor's real concern seems to be that machines in the home will verify that *work* occurs there. His argument emphasizes the new terms that characterize public and private spheres, where home-female-*leisure* opposes factory-male-*work*. Machines inhabit the matter-of-fact side of life, the workplace, the factory; wives, agreeable in their personal appearance, belong in a feminized, aestheticized vision of the (bourgeois) home. Pattison, however, allays his fears. In her text she manages not only to bring the factory home but to disguise its presence there as well. Her physical appearance, her clothing, and her "good taste" in home styling dissipate the threat to domesticity posed by her advocacy of engineering and machinery.

In Pattison's text, as well as in Taylor's introduction, the ideal domestic engineer, the worker best suited to implement scientific management effectively in the home, emerges as an excessively feminine housekeeper. Unlike her factory counterparts, the mechanized home manager-worker must attend always to the question of beauty. In domestic engineering, the mechanized body must be hidden within a beautiful, well-dressed body, and scientific discourse must be "artistically," sentimentally appointed. Throughout her book, Pattison's style very noticeably slips from the pragmatic tones and diction of "scientific" discourse to florid, sentimentalized platitudes that aestheticize or ornament her argument. The contradictions between Taylorism and domesticity surface under the competing rubrics of "science" and "art." For example, Pattison describes her housewife hanging out the laundry:

> The effort of hanging up the clothes [is] perhaps the greatest one, but what sensible and appreciative woman should object to the healthy and exhilarating exercise of properly reaching up to place in the fresh delightful air of Heaven, the newly washed and sweet smelling clothes of her own household—a charming study in motion when properly performed. (90)[27]

In another instance Pattison attempts to define the ideal home, suggesting that it "is the constant production of an atmosphere, or a state of organized existence for the purpose of providing proper shelter, comfort, nourishment and encouragement for the development of each individual member. A re-creation center, fertilized by the heart and mind of all within, and ever pregnant with life's best joys" (30).

What is at stake in this discursive maneuvering between science and art for domestic engineering, for "domesticity"? Both texts, but particularly Pattison's, are symptomatic of a transformation whereby the home is increasingly deprived of productive functions in culture. It no longer generates products (Child) or valid knowledge forms (Beecher); it consumes them, bringing them into the home. The private home comes to serve capitalist economy both as a consumer of its products and as the benevolent ideological and structural other to its alienating, dehumanizing practices in the workplace. Though interdependent with this economy and its values, the home must appear to be distinct from it by representing values of individuality and freedom. Thus the fit that these writers engineer between Taylor's authoritative method of scientific management and domesticity cannot, must not, be a perfect one.

Even if Taylor's method is the best available, the home cannot be an efficient factory workplace, nor can the housekeeper be a mechanized worker without both losing their proper domestic identity. Thus the primary negotiation that the domestic engineers effect between Taylorism and domesticity occurs at the level of aesthetics and appearance. Taylor's liberatory discourse about the "high-priced man," the factory worker who realizes the benefits of his own automation in increased leisure time and a more affluent private life, depends on this man's domicile and family being distinct from his workplace. Taylor's anxiety about the housewife's proper feminine appearance again masks class issues within a discourse about femininity and domesticity. What Taylorism and Fordism both promised American workers was the possibility of a middle-class lifestyle for everyone—at home. Taylor obviously believes a properly feminine housewife to be a necessary part of that package. Faced with the domestic engineer's project to implement his scientific management in the home, he resolves the looming contradictions by asserting that the housewife and home cannot *appear* to be a mechanized worker and workplace. In the face of generalized scientific "truths," aesthetics, style, and appearance become the only avenues of expression left to a privatized, consumptive discourse of individuality.[28]

"A Better Dress": The Morality of Feminine Appearance

In the work of the domestic engineers, the middle-class housewife's pleasing appearance is a moral imperative, as it was in Beecher, but that imperative has been secularized. I conclude the discussion of domestic engineering with one of Pattison's stories that illustrates the effect of this morality on home and housewife. She opens her first chapter, "What Is a Home?," by relating a tailor's parable. To illustrate the method of scientific management, she gives two examples of ways to make a dress:

> Where the work is all mechanical, with no particular understanding as to the relation of the seams and "lines" to the human form in general . . . the work proceeds in parts, probably from pattern suggestions, that even if perfect in themselves, fail in developing either the best talent of the individual worker, or in bringing out the personal charms of the wearer, because of there being no clear perception of the unity of parts, in relation to the object for which they are intended. . . . The other way is to consider well at the start, the composition of the dress in general, its significance, why certain colors, textures, and designs suggest certain people, the occasions and the personality for which the particular dress is desired and the utmost that can be done with the material at hand. As the work proceeds, there will be constant improvement upon the original thought and the dress and the worker will *grow* under the operation. In the latter, all the study possible will be put upon the idea or object of the dress before it is begun. . . . This method requires more thought and headwork, but there is less waste and fewer failures . . . in carrying out the plan. (29–30)

Pattison applies Taylor's management to the making of the second dress, putting science to an aesthetic, individuated purpose; the choice of task implicitly feminizes the procedure. In her version, Taylor's method necessitates cooperation not between the worker and management but between the worker and the wearer, the producer and the consumer. Where Taylor's case studies evaluate efficiency in terms of variables such as speed, manpower units, profits, and rates of production, Pattison's example asserts that scientific management produces a better product, a better dress.

She concentrates on aesthetic improvements in composition, design, color, and texture, variables that concern surfaces and appearance. She emphasizes Taylorism's attention to context and detail but avoids its interest in monetary gain.

Pattison's example of tailoring a dress provides a nice figure for the work of the domestic engineers in general, as it involves managing a fit between an ideal pattern and an actual individual model, who in this case is female. Domestic engineering pins and cuts the home to the measure of Taylor's pattern of scientific management. This tailoring operation can express the values of domesticity only in the aesthetic variables of the text, in its style, its sentimental color and tone. Similarly, the Taylored, mechanized domestic engineer must also be well tailored. If she works like a machine and runs her home like a factory manager, she must also be able to disguise these "matter-of-fact" aspects of her life under an inordinately delicate feminine appearance and manner. In this paradigm, codes of femininity in the private sphere emerge and operate as the discourse of individuality's defense against Ford's, Taylor's, and Gilbreth's mechanization of the (male) laboring body in the public sphere. This housekeeping differs from Beecher's in that the home is no longer a woman's place so much as it is a feminized place, its domesticity signified in ornament, platitude, and frill.

Both Frederick's and Pattison's texts produce exaggerated codes of femininity in the context of an ideological conflict between two presumably oppositional economies that are in reality crucially dependent on each other. These codes hide, manage, and ameliorate the ideological contradictions of the texts. In the work of the domestic engineers, codes of a defensive femininity and reactive consumerism colonize the housekeeper's body, her home, and her text as simulated professionalism transports domestic expertise from the kitchen to the academic laboratory.

Labor as the Appearance of Leisure

Housekeepers' writings about housework conjoin a symbolic practice—writing— with a socially and historically inflected experience related to female gender construction and domestic labor in America over the last two centuries. In the writings I have considered, housekeepers in different historical moments enter into complex discursive negotiations with the ideologies attendant upon a developing market and consumer economy. Increasingly, that economy attempts to exclude the contributions of housekeepers, to render their work invisible, and this invisibility serves an array of powerful social forces and discourses. While the writers participate in and contribute to the evolving hegemonic construction of women's place in a consumer economy, their basic motivation, to write about housework, puts them at odds with the ideology which asserts that women do not work and that the private sphere is a place of leisure. The contradictions and distortions evident in Beecher's, Frederick's, and Pattison's texts illustrate how central the idea of housework as non-labor has been to class, race, and gender constructions in the nineteenth and twentieth centuries, becoming crucial to formulations of American nationalism and democracy. It is no coincidence that these writers are white middle-class women. In Child we see the germs of both gender and class identities, but they are not yet self-conscious, not yet engaged, as they are in Beecher, in the fabrication of universal male and female subjects based on bourgeois norms and values. In Frederick and Pattison, femininity and domesticity become definitively associated with consumerism, leisure, style, and individualism in a way that serves to locate appropriately "feminine" women outside work, production, and the market, whatever the material realities of the home and the workplace.

In describing the evolution of domestic femininity in the nineteenth and early twentieth centuries, I want to argue for a materially based trajectory involving successive formulations of women's household labor. In Child, domestic labor has material value in and of itself, albeit of a negative kind. Housework prevents expenditures of money for all women, no matter what their class. Beecher's domestic economy locates the value of housework in its spiritual, social, and political effects, not in the labor itself. Indeed, labor's traces on the bodies and appearance of white middle-class housekeepers become the problem her domestic economy sets out to solve. Thus a class-based appearance standard, infused and mystified with spiritual and nationalist values, becomes integral to understandings of women's domestic work. Crucially, that work should appear not to be work. In the writings of the domestic engineers, women's work becomes a secularized attention to "a pleasing and delicate appearance." Both dependent on and fashioned as resistant to the alienation of the market and the workplace, domestic femininity bears the burden of representing all that one works for: leisure, unalienated pleasure, a place that is one's own outside the purview of the market. Thus domestic handbooks of the nineteenth and early twentieth centuries reveal that many of capitalism's most provocative and seductive phantasms rely on the appearances represented by a particularly gendered and presumably leisured body, and on the class privilege of that body absorbed into its feminine and feminized biology.

In the early twentieth century, women's increasingly significant role as consumers was emphasized by all the writers on domestic engineering and was in fact the very rationale for the name "home economics," which was chosen to represent both the overall movement and the academic discipline that was being invented during these same years.[29] These consumer duties required middle-class white women to be socially and publicly more visible at the same time that new visual technologies and industries, of which the cinema is a prime example, were making this class of women much more representationally visible. The trajectory of women's domestic work, and the increasing insistence on its invisibility by the very women who initially approached domestic labor *as* labor, provide a very different context for the most prevalent mass cultural representations of domestic femininity in this century—that of the housewife and mother in commercial cinema. While feminist film theory in particular has rigorously addressed the function of female spectacle and appearance in relation to psychoanalytic constructions of the psyche, the gaze, subjectivity, and spectators, other approaches have taken into consideration women's image within a history of visual representation. To a certain extent these different approaches have assumed gender difference as a distinction that is outside historical, national, and social influences and differences, and certainly outside all considerations of labor and work.

My foray into the nineteenth-century antecedents for certain representations of women in film has been meant to investigate the social and historical underpinnings of a particular type of femininity—the domestic variant—and thereby place it in a context of women's work. The image of woman in feminist film theory has always been understood in terms of sexuality; it has not been approached within a history of representations of women's domestic labor. It is the invisibility of this labor, this lack—as much as an abstracted sexuality—that underlies what has been a dominant premise about visual representation: that men act and women are to be looked at. The pedagogical texts on domestic femininity indicate the moral, ideological, and social functions that have shaped considerations of women's labor, a labor that becomes increasingly about appearance and morality. It is this genealogy, the socio-historical construction of this invisibility, that I propose as a way to reconsider women's appearance in the cinema. As this genealogy indicates, the moral and fetishistic value of white middle-class women's appearance is always also about normative constructions of race (whiteness) and class (middle) that effectively mask the representational absence of other differences.

In the public world of entertainment and consumption, as we will see, the housewife learns very little about how to perform her tasks. She is, however, being taught a great deal about her domestic roles and social functions.

• PART II •

HOUSEKEEPING IN HOLLYWOOD

FOUR

Silent Film, Silent Work

Early Cinema and the Domestic Melodramas of D. W. Griffith

> The spectacle presents itself as something enormously positive, indisputable and inaccessible. It says nothing more than "that which appears is good, that which is good appears."
>
> GUY DEBORD, Society of the Spectacle (1967)

The fully Taylorized housekeeper described by Christine Frederick and Mary Pattison hides her mechanized industrial housekeeping practices and labor behind an inordinately feminine and pleasing appearance. This appearance, as Taylor himself points out, is the necessary value and condition of her efficiency. Thus the evolution of pedagogical housekeeping texts in America, written to and for a specific group of women, culminates in a secularized standard of appearances that locates affective moral virtue in the erasure of domestic labor. In this manner the domestic sphere becomes a performative space treasured precisely because it allegorizes a class position on female labor, which is that it should not appear to be what it is.

Any film scholar can discern the striking similarities between this paradigm of housekeeping and the "invisible style" that would come to dominate the cinema— that is, that all the work and technology that go into producing a lush image and coherent narrative are rendered invisible by being kept off-camera. The pedagogical literature on housekeeping thus provides a necessary context for the cinema, not only because of the cinema's symptomatic representations of domestic femininity, but also because these texts indicate clearly that domesticity sets the terms for its own representation. The cinema did not create the appearance standard levied on middle-class white American women. It invented neither deceptive narrative spectacles from which all traces of labor have been removed nor a gaze trained to find beauty and desire only in a leisured, delicate appearance. As the domestic housekeeping manuals demonstrate, these structures already existed in the middle-class home by the end of the nineteenth century, forming the essence of good housekeeping. It is obvious why and how the cinema drew on previous aesthetic and entertainment forms such as theater and photography. Yet in its developing and insistent focus on private life and on the spectacle and performativity located there, the cinema also drew on the model of middle-class American domesticity, in which an invisible style, articulated by and around the spectacle of leisured white womanhood, had already been perfected. Significantly, this tradition of performance and spectacle was predicated entirely on values related to the suppression of domestic labor.

While the question of "the woman's image" has dominated feminist film studies, that image has usually been understood as wholly related to female sexuality and consequently to gender inequity and representation. The national political and cultural circumstances that attended the nineteenth-century development of a morally inflected appearance standard for middle-class white American women indicates that the significance of these women's appearance, both in and out of the cinema, extends far beyond gender. Thus these domestic housekeeping texts provide a necessary context for fully understanding representations of domesticity in the first and most enduring form of mass culture in the United States. Related to the privatization of class and racial privilege, the visual and ideological suppression of women's domestic labor historicizes the sexual and aesthetic iconography of femininity in Hollywood cinema. The crucial point that I would like to register at the outset of this part of my book is that domestic femininity and domesticity entered the cinema not only as narrative content and preferred mise-en-scène, respectively, but also and more important as forms of representation laden with social meanings from which the cinema drew heavily.[1]

In this section I approach individual films as illustrative of the fact that the cinema, in its representations of domesticity, is always representing what itself has already become a performance. Taking up Guy Debord's assertion that that which appears is good and that which is good appears, I review films that have been of particular interest to feminists because of their focus on melodrama, domesticity, and female protagonists. I have limited this study to melodrama because of feminist film theory and criticism's persistent interest in this genre, and because of the melodramatic structure of nineteenth-century domesticity, increasingly predicated as it was on the spectacle of feminine delicacy, the mystification of class difference, and structures of dissembling related to virtue. I show that in all of these melodramatic films, representations of housework, which domestic pedagogy has established as that which, however good, should *not* appear, trouble the narrative and thematic coherence of the texts. Furthermore, as I argue, that troubling has as much to do with race, class, and the structuring absence of housework as female labor as it does with sexuality and gender inequities.

Scenic Housekeeping

From its earliest days the cinema turned its fascinated and fascinating gaze on the bourgeois home and the activities that transpired there. As the Lumières' first cinematic programs demonstrate, scenes depicting bourgeois domesticity (*Le repas de bébé*, 1895, for example) and the labor of everyday life provided early filmmakers with a wealth of subject material. In America, after the initial technological novelty of moving images dissipated, documentary films, including scenics—"family views from everyday life"—greatly outnumbered fiction films before 1903.[2] Whether in the scenics or in fiction films, however, the early cinema transformed housekeeping from an activity to be performed as quickly and discreetly as possible to a phenomenon to be observed and consumed as pleasurable entertainment. Yet the nature of and emphasis on domesticity in the cinema changed dramatically in its first three decades; narrative films increasingly moved away from representations of housework that explicitly acknowledged it as labor. Using the work of D. W. Griffith, I consider the social and ideological nuances of these changes as they relate to constructions of appropriate femininity and domesticity in early twentieth-century popular visual culture.

Film melodrama and advertising, particularly for domestic products, interpellated female spectators and consumers with related, if contradictory, messages that significantly inflected social constructions of appropriate femininity. The early decades of the twentieth century saw the development of both mass cultural entertainment (with the film industry as the exemplary institution for the first half century) and the culture of consumption. New notions of the female spectator and the female consumer arose from these developments and, in very different ways, altered prevailing notions of the middle-class housewife.[3] Similarly, nineteenth-century conceptions of the appropriate wife also shaped notions of the spectator and consumer. In early melodramatic film texts, the middle-class home became the site of mass public spectacle, wherein the nuclear family was idealized for its presumably "natural" universality.[4] This transformation in domesticity arose from a synthesis of diverse working- and middle-class entertainment forms wedded to Progressive middle-class values. Cinematic narrative joined an aesthetic of sensationalism and voyeurism, made possible by new visual technologies and an evolving film rhetoric, to highly moralized conventions of melodrama. Thus, while women's work was initially valued in both films and advertising, social and economic forces involving labor, leisure, class and racial identity, and appropriate gender roles eventually resulted in its virtual erasure from film melodrama. Nowhere are the particulars of this process more evident than in the melodramas of D. W. Griffith. The southern sensibilities and antiquated Victorianism that informed his films also made manifest the interrelated particulars of racialized and class-based gender construction and performative domesticity. Unlike many film narratives that assumed public and private spheres that were racially homogenous (e.g., white), Griffith's films frequently presented racially mixed and class-mixed social milieux.[5]

Registering the moral and social contradictions that riddled women's lives at the turn of the century, Griffith's films also participated in constructing and enhancing those contradictions. In an astute commentary analyzing Griffith's role in developing the genre of the woman's film, Scott Simmon notes, "To the extent, then, that Griffith's woman's films argue that American society is best served by maintaining women in private, family spaces, those films, almost by the very nature of their being films, are divided against themselves."[6] Griffith made a public spectacle of "private, family spaces" and the women who should be maintained or contained therein. At issue were questions of women's proper place, questions that in the early twentieth century were inseparable from issues of women's visibility. The cinema challenged

Victorian notions of women's place and visibility in two salient respects. As representation, early films depicted "private life" for mass consumption, thus publicizing scenes from that life as entertainment. In its conditions of exhibition, the cinema participated in the changing relation of all women to the public sphere. While overt gender and tacit class distinctions in the nineteeth century were rationalized by the social and economic geography of separate spheres, women's increasing involvement in business, leisure, and reform activities in the "male" public sphere generated considerable social anxiety.[7] Many of these issues surfaced as sexual and racial paranoia provoked in part by the question of what the new social visibility of (middle-class white) women, domesticity, and maternity, both on and off the screen, might mean.[8] As in the nineteenth century, cultural narratives treating proper femininity and domesticity functioned to organize and contain other social distinctions. In the twentieth century, however, the pressure of visuality and new forms of leisure and commodity culture imbued highly moralized constructions of femininity and domesticity with hedonist and exhibitionist tendencies. While literary and pedagogical representations of women's domestic labor provided the material basis for femininity's spiritual function in the nineteenth century, in the twentieth century, the culture industry came to obviate both the material and spiritual functions of such labor in promoting the difference between the spheres in terms of leisure, commodities, and personal fulfillment for all. Cinematic constructions of domesticity and femininity were crucial in this transformation.

Representations of domesticity in the early cinema ultimately resulted in a paradox. While the explicit, realistic, and widely disseminated visual images of housework available in the cinema might be expected to register forcefully the fact of women's domestic labor, instead the cinema followed the path of nineteenth-century domestic housekeeping manuals. That is, these representations chronicle how visual depictions of housework ultimately continue to mystify and dehistoricize "women's work." This mystification is the result of the coincidence and interaction of two very different phenomenal axes, involving new visual technologies and the vestiges of nineteenth-century morality, respectively. In making publicly visible the details of everyday domestic life, a life emphatically constructed in the nineteenth century as private, the cinema altered the social construction of that life, prompting a complex cultural revaluation of the notion of "visibility" itself. This revaluation of visibility necessitated a transformation in the understanding of hegemonic Victorian virtues concerning gentility, class, domesticity, and femininity, precisely because these values had been based on what was not visible, what should not be seen. The increasing importance of an unlabored feminine appearance for middle-class white women, registered in the housekeeping texts written throughout the nineteenth and early twentieth centuries, attests to what was at stake in the profound relationship that developed between visibility and morality in the social valuation of domestic femininity and labor. The invisibility of such women's work mystified class difference by constructing appropriate femininity as apparently unlabored, affective, and spiritual—a passive and moralized gender identity that contrasted with active, libidinized masculinity. The twentieth-century visual technologies that "colonized" entertainment and commodity experience paradoxically document and obscure this invisible labor within narratives that intensify the relation between moral and appearance standards subtending ideals of appropriate domestic femininity.[9]

In the silent cinema, the filming of private life in the early "actualités" and "scenics" gave way, as the classical style took shape, to representations of the domestic as the preferred mise-en-scène for fictional melodramatic narratives.[10] Documentary genres, which greatly outnumbered fiction films before 1903, were gradually superseded by the classical fictional narratives that would dominate the industry. Scholars date the years of this transformation around 1908–9, with the classical Hollywood narrative in place by 1913.[11] Yet this fictional mode incorporated film's documentary capacity. Thus, while the ever-increasing verisimilitude of setting, acting, and narrative participated in changing the status and character of the private sphere and its primary occupant, this process actually began in the earliest years of the film industry with the "cinema of attractions."[12] This cinema blended fantasy, narrative, and documentary modes of representation as display. It positioned housework as an object of this public, multigeneric, mass-reproduced show. Thus it began to alter the character of that labor.

Airing the Family Laundry

Films within the cinema of attractions readily demonstrate how the explicit visual documentation of a housekeeping task results in erasing its identity as labor. They also indicate how the cinema's gaze changes the character of everyday life by making the private public precisely in terms of display, consumption, and entertainment. In "Scenarios of Exposure in the Practice of Everyday Life," Constance Balides addresses the implications of the new cinematic visibility as it relates to women. She focuses primarily on comic films made in the United States before 1907 that depicted sexualized images of women in everyday life. "That women should be constructed as sexual spectacles . . . is not in itself surprising," she observes; it is instead the *nontheatrical setting* of their sexual objectification that renders these films significant. Because they use everyday events to stage the exposure of women's bodies or to depict titillating sexual situations, they transform everyday space from an area where daily activities are performed to "a locus of display." This transformation infers a spectator for whom the display has been arranged; it also subordinates whatever activity is being performed (by the woman) to the relations of looking that now determine the significance of the scene.[13]

In *A Windy Day on the Roof* (1907), that activity is housework. A housewife, her back to the camera, is hanging laundry (knickers and a camisole) on a rooftop clothesline. As she bends over to pick up the wet clothes, a painter working on the side of the building looks up her skirt. Discovering him, the housewife dumps water on his head, and he falls out of the frame. Balides asserts that the film enacts "a conflict over the legitimate use of space (looking or domestic labour) and who will have the authority to define this use (the painter or the housewife)." From the painter's point of view, the woman is sexualized; his look isolates and abstracts her from her environment and her work. Thus, "the space of everyday operations is made invisible." Yet the film's ending, with the woman alone on the roof, reasserts "the visibility of . . . the space of everyday life."[14] I would argue that the meaning of the rooftop and the chore for the housewife is overridden not only by the painter's looks but also by those of the filmmaker and the spectator. If, as Roland Barthes argues, representation is "the practice which calculates the place of things *as they are observed*," then the gaze of filmmaker and spectator calculate both the rooftop and the hanging of the laundry as components in an eroticized conflict of looks.[15] The rooftop becomes a sexualized scene, the domestic task a backdrop to an erotic transaction that completely subsumes the significance of the labor being performed. That labor and the narrative for which it provides the "scene" are fashioned as a entertainment product to be consumed.

Balides discusses an array of films, many involving women in the workplace, in which women's dignity or privacy is accidently compromised in a public place. As with *A Windy Day on the Roof*, the films' narrative structures generate tension between women's everyday activities, often their *work*, and their status as erotic objects. She relates this phenomenon to contemporaneous social discourses concerning prostitution and sexual harassment and to generalized concerns about women's presence in the public sphere. But what interests me is the way in which these films visually publicize and eroticize formerly "insignificant" spaces and activities. Although writers on housework certainly publicize housework, they formulate it as a problem, as labor, as drudgery to be streamlined and hidden behind a pleasing and leisured appearance. *A Windy Day on the Roof* both sexualizes and commodifies the act of hanging laundry by rendering it as public display for leisured consumption. Thus it doubly obfuscates the status of hanging laundry as work, instead rendering it narrative act and erotic play for the painter, the laundress, and especially for spectator-consumers of both genders.

A Windy Day on the Roof presents a comic conflict between a decidedly working-class pair that transpires not in the backyard of a private home but in a public place to which strangers of both genders have access. The narrative it presents plays in a darkened theater, a public place to which strangers of both genders have access. In both its content and its context of display, the cinema reorganizes public space as it relates to gender, class, and women's domestic labor both visually and materially. The playful attitude of the cinema of attractions toward sexuality is bereft of any overt moralizing; it therefore predates the changes that render the cinema a mass entertainment medium, palatable to the middle and upper classes as well as to working-class spectators. The cinema of attractions makes a playful farce of airing the family laundry; such a narrative must acquire weighty moral significance for the industry's status as mass entertainment to be realized.

A Moral Tale

As many film historians point out, after an initial experimental stage in the late 1890s, the cinema established itself primarily, but not exclusively, as a leisure activity for the working class and immigrants.[16] Lary May notes: "In these realms [nickelodeons, saloons], immigrants and workers found amusements which catered to men and women of all ethnic groups. Here film makers began to find a market for their films

of low life: boxing, girlie shows, and stories that reflected much of this atmosphere."[17] The cinema of attractions drew its spectators from the immigrant population and the working class for reasons both social and economic. As films were silent,
there was no language barrier to prevent non–English-speaking immigrants from
understanding and enjoying them. For both generally impoverished populations, the
price was another appeal. Initially incorporated into other forms of working- and
mixed-class entertainment, such as vaudeville, burlesque, and so on, the cinema was
cheap, convenient, and free of the moral constraints that characterized proper bourgeois leisure activities.

For the middle and upper classes and, according to their values, for women of all
classes, the conditions of exhibition, the subject material, and the clientele of the
early cinema rendered it completely inappropriate as a leisure activity. May writes:

> When film makers tried to reach into middle-class markets, they found themselves
> thwarted by the continuing strength of Victorian assumptions about amusements.
> Despite the . . . increasing affluence . . . [and] expansion of leisure time and pursuits
> for the bourgeois, the movies at the turn of the century faced an almost insurmount-
> able barrier in the class and sexual divisions of respectable entertainment. A popular
> literature of books and mass magazines that could be *enjoyed in private* had spread over
> the nation; but it was limited by price and subject matter to the tastes of the affluent.
> . . . [P]ublic amusements for the Victorians remained in exclusive neighborhoods, usu-
> ally revolving around the church. . . . Here, above all, women could be protected, far
> removed from the wide-open amusements of the lower orders.[18]

Middle-class resistance to the cinema stemmed from a matrix of ideas on which
crucial class and gender constructions depended. Chief among these were distinctions between public and private worlds and behaviors, culturally appropriate domesticity, gentility, and femininity—in short, the gender–social space bifurcation that
remains the most persistent legacy of the cult of domesticity. Many of the ways in
which the cinema violates this ideology have to do with visibility—not just in terms
of inappropriate subject matter on the screen (*Windy Day on the Roof*), but also, and
more important, in the inappropriate public visibility and consequent vulnerability
of women in an unlit, unsupervised, undifferentiated audience. This ideology, contested by many developments of the late nineteenth and early twentieth centuries
(the department store, the office, the cinema, and mass culture, among others), provoked several reactions with regard to the cinema.[19] The middle class's passive resistance to the box office was coupled with active Progressive measures to censor the
new institution. Immigrant entertainments spurred the moral outrage of the Progressives because they were beginning to attract "respectable women" and "working
women of all classes," who were thus "drawn to arenas that had previously been the
preserve of prostitutes."[20]

Significantly, reformers articulated the problem the cinema posed in terms of
domesticity and, thus, of the overall health of the nation. Jane Addams wrote:

> We cannot expect the fathers and mothers who have come to the city from the farms
> or have immigrated from foreign lands to rectify these dangers, we cannot expect that
> youth themselves will understand this emotional force which seizes them, and when it
> does not find the traditional line of domesticity, serves as a cancer in the very tissues of
> society.[21]

The historian Glenna Matthews notes the alliance between the Progressives and the home economics movement that grew out of the separate spheres ideology. Both shared in the dubious classist, ethnocentric attitudes that Lary May also sees in Victorian biases against mass culture and the cinema. May writes, "The Progressive movement was in part a reaction to the millions of immigrants from southern and eastern Europe in the late nineteenth century—men and women who clustered in the cities and seemed less assimilable than earlier waves of immigrants."[22] Chief among the Progressives' concerns were the domestic habits and organization of immigrants' homes and families.[23]

The Progressives seized upon domesticity and the family as the embodiment of all that modern life and the new industrial corporate world threatened to tear asunder.[24] May writes, "Given that modern industry disrupted the family with the dual forces of exploitation and mass production, the values of the good home had to permeate the entire city."[25] Yet, as both Matthews and May assert, the good home is a white Anglo-Saxon Protestant middle-class home; this home includes parents (the government and reformers) who will rescue the beleaguered children (immigrants, the working class, and the poor) who could not establish a proper bourgeois home without help and instruction. The Progressives sponsored an array of undeniably valuable and necessary reforms to regulate and control exploitive business practices. All of these reforms were promoted in terms of their benefit to the family.[26] Yet because the Progressives and the home economists both assumed some version of the separate spheres ideology and idealized the white bourgeois family, the ethnocentrism revealed in their social policy perpetuated the same assimilative pattern as that articulated by the "benevolent" abolitionist racism of the nineteenth century: blacks and immigrants are children who need to be guided and trained, and thereby brought into the American "family." This model, which obfuscates questions of rights with a rhetoric of white bourgeois generosity and benevolence, rests on the gender–social sphere distinctions that continued to mystify its ethnocentric, racist, and classist strains precisely around the issues of visibility, publicity, and women's labor.

The cinema's increasing focus on the family related economic, social, and industrial forces to the rise and ultimate dominance of the narrative film. The move to classical narrative cinema involved the redirection of cinematic attractions to the interests of more complex, character-centered narratives that had a salient moral message. In "From the Opium Den to the Theatre of Morality," Tom Gunning underscores the importance of morality in coordinating and synthesizing powerful but diverse economic, social, and aesthetic interests in the cinema. The years 1908–9 witnessed significant transformations in the film industry, its social identity, and its aesthetic form. Gunning notes two crucial developments that occurred at the end of 1908. First, "the formation of the Motion Picture Patents Company (MPPC) . . . was a move to consolidate the film industry on an economic basis and to raise the social status of film as a form of entertainment." While the MPPC fashioned movie ads that promoted the "Moral, Educational and Cleanly Amusing" qualities of their product to uplift its image, Mayor George B. McClellan Jr. ordered all the nickelodeons in New York City to be closed at the behest of Progressive reformers and clergy. At issue was both the risqué content of the films and, more important, the circumstances of their exhibition—darkened venues where classes and genders could mix freely. The possibly beneficial moral influence of the cinema established a common ground where the MPPC's financial interests in a middle-class audience (and consequently increased revenues) could readily blend with the social and religious concerns of Progressive reformers.[27] Thus, rather than "beating" Progressive reform, at least initially, the cinema in some ways "joined" the movement and thus participated in changing the social understanding of the separate spheres and gender differences perpetuated by the Progressives themselves.

Directly descended from the cult of domesticity, the programs that Progressive reformers promoted were based on family- and home-centered values. The well-educated middle-class women active in this reform movement did not trangress the separate spheres so much as they extended the definition of what was considered domestic, becoming, in a certain sense, "angels" of the city, the state, and other people's homes. As the writings of Christine Frederick and Mary Pattison indicate, these women saw their appropriate feminine influence as reaching into all areas of public works, resources, and systems that affected domesticity. In an urban milieu, these diverse concerns included garbage removal, the cleaning of city streets, and urban design, as well as poverty, prostitution, the domestic habits of immigrants, and the control of nefarious social influences, including the cinema. The process whereby the cinema was transformed from "a realm of darkness" into "a means of illumination and instruction" involved this institution's repositioning itself not only in terms of class and status but also in terms of its function.[28] To avert identification as a public problem, the cinema assumed the role of a morally uplifting social influence. In so doing it became aligned both with a middle-class perspective and with what the culture identified as a feminine function—to provide moral vision and uplift.

Yet it seems very telling that this social function frequently addressed itself to little more than the cinema's dangers to women, in terms of both women's inherent vulnerability in dark and "democratic" public spaces and their susceptibility to entertainment not disciplined by a moral message. Historians agree that the price of middle-class respectability for the film industry was ultimately that its exhibition venues and its product had to become appropriate for middle-class white women. These seemingly diverse interests—moral and economic—found apt aesthetic application in the work of one filmmaker in particular. Gunning notes, "The sort of transformations in narrative style which we associate with the work of D. W. Griffith at Biograph . . . were wedded to film accreditation as a form of moral discourse."[29]

D. W. Griffith's particular significance rests not with his moral outlook per se but in his ability to articulate this perspective with the formal means and economic and social ends afforded him by the cinematic apparatus. Critics note how Griffith practices ethical intercutting and imbues the oppositions he articulates through parallel editing with moral judgments.[30] In fact, Griffith explicitly saw himself as a reformer and publicly promoted himself and his films as such.[31] His films interest me because they explicitly enact anxieties and conflicts about women's appropriate role—their sexuality, their labor, their social visibility, and their proper place—within the moral spectacular of the evolving narrative film in early twentieth-century culture.

As in the nineteenth century, middle-class white women, their moral sensibilities, and their relation to home and domesticity operated discursively to contain, situate, and in a certain sense override the other significant cultural differences and anxieties that critics have identified as salient in this period. In this instance respectable (read: white middle-class domestic) women's supposed interests provided a moral standard whereby the entire culture's interests in the cinema and its product were measured and served.

In the remainder of this chapter I consider the confluence of issues of visibility, morality, and women's work in Griffith's domestic melodramas. In addition to analyzing how Griffith's representations of women both generate and mystify class, ethnic, and racial anxieties, I am also interested in how female sexuality as moral spectacle functioned to assimilate the attractions of the early cinema to the narrative coherence of the classical model. Griffith's anachronistic constructions of femininity were both profoundly influential and relatively short-lived in the cinema's history, indicating, among other things, the degree to which nineteenth-century constructions of domesticity and femininity retained their efficacy and power in the early twentieth century.[32] His films essentially recapitulate, in spectacular melodramatic narrative form, the same sort of social, political, and moral displacements that are accomplished in very different ways in housekeepers' texts of the nineteenth and early twentieth centuries. In his films the physical delicacy that signified (white middle-class) femininity's superior moral role in the nineteenth century is visually reinvoked to both moral and sensational ends in the cinema. The class-coded importance of feminine appearance in constructions of appropriate domesticity are diffused in mass media entertainment texts that initially (e.g., *Windy Day on the Roof*) publicized and eroticized private everyday spaces and activities, particularly the home, housework, and decent working- and middle-class women. Griffith reinscribed Victorian ethical codes within his film narratives such that their functions as entertainment and uplift were neatly and cleanly blended. These films warrant discussion, however, precisely because of the medium and the narrative form through which he represented these nineteenth-century values.

D. W. Griffith's Domestic Imaginary

To begin, while my focus is on cinema as a mass medium, some of Griffith's success undoubtedly derived from his astute application of melodramatic stage conventions in his cinematic narratives. This dramatic form had already been successfully Americanized in nineteenth-century theater, and so spoke to a particularly American sensibility. Christine Gledhill explains:

> Melodrama's adaptation to the different socio-political conditions of American culture was transformative. First there was no already situated landed aristocracy against which a rising bourgeoisie had to struggle. The dominant ideology was republican and democratic, the evils of class inequality and injustice associated with a European yoke recently thrown off. American drama's national specificity was initially confined to expression of a democratic sensibility. The compatibility of melodrama with this form of nationalism was a major reason . . . for its centrality to the nineteenth-century American stage. American adaptation of melodrama began to dismantle the class oppositions of European melodrama. In the first instance, melodrama's stress on unpremeditated feeling as an index of moral status and social value functioned for American

nationalism as a 'great equaliser,' bypassing inequalities of class and education. Secondly, the expression of class oppositions in European melodrama were, in American versions, often transposed into country/city oppositions.[33]

Representational emphasis on "unpremeditated feeling as an index of moral status and social value" is, of course, naturalized as a feminine function, an aspect of feminine gender identity.

In Griffith's cinema this melodramatic ethos becomes embedded in relays of gazes, in themes concerned with appropriate and inappropriate appearances, and, most important, in oppositions involving women's work and sexuality. All are construed within a specularized moral field that differs in crucial ways from theatrical representation. Through the use of editing, close-ups, and point-of-view shots, the cinema encourages an individualized reception very different from theater's public one. The critical focus on women in film has consisted almost exclusively, as has the cinema's predominant focus, on women's sexuality. I would supplement that account by suggesting that that emphatic sexual visibility is based partly on the invisibility of women's domestic labor, an invisibility that allows for the noncontradictory perpetuation of a host of crucial social binaries. I wend my way through Griffith's oeuvre, paying close attention to those films that specifically address morally imbued constructions of the domestic feminine. Griffith, unlike his successors, gives women's domestic labor considerable narrative weight and moral importance. He therefore provides a starting point from which to measure the significance of the classical cinema's later avoidance of any extended representation of this kind of labor.

Far from presenting spectacles of the home and domesticity as completely positive, Griffith represents the family and domicile in highly ambivalent terms, threatened from both within and without.[34] Developing and exploiting to the fullest extent the pathos generated by spectacles of delicate white women or girls in peril, Griffith subjects his heroines to overwhelmingly cruel fathers and husbands (*The Sealed Room*, 1909; *The New York Hat*, 1912; *Broken Blossoms*, 1919; *Way Down East*, 1921), inadequate husbands or fathers (*The Mothering Heart*, 1913; *Death's Marathon, The Birth of a Nation*, 1915; *True Heart Susie*, 1919), reprehensible seducers and rapists (*Way Down East, The Birth of a Nation*), vicious gossips (*The New York Hat, Way Down East*), criminals and malevolent servants (*The Lonely Villa, An Unseen Enemy*, 1912), and the machinations of idle, rich, seductive women (*The Mothering Heart, True Heart Susie, Way Down East*).[35] Often the cruelty or evil involves the performance of domestic work. In *The New York Hat*, a dying mother passes a note to her clergyman which explains that her husband "worked her to death" and requests that he look after her daughter. *An Unseen Enemy* presents a slatternly housekeeper who solicits criminal assistance in robbing the sweet young sisters for whom she works.

Compelled by the demands of melodramatic narrative and the twists of his own psyche, Griffith positions the home, the family, and most especially the young, beautiful white woman as never really safe, whether from other family members or even within her own home.[36] While his heroines are often thrown out of their houses, Griffith also frequently shapes his dramas around the sudden conversion of domestic spaces from places of happiness and safety to death traps assailed by murderous predators from whom there is no escape (*The Lonely Villa, An Unseen Enemy, The Birth of a Nation, Broken Blossoms*).[37] Although he constantly uses flowers, gardens, and nature in the mise-en-scène to characterize the sweetness and innocence of his heroines, the pastoral outdoor scene also menaces, whether because of the "evil" men who lurk there (*The Birth of a Nation*) or because of the terrors of nature itself (*Way Down East*).

Thus Griffith depicts domestic scenes from everyday life, but he infuses them with danger, heartbreak, and loss, as well as with all the virtues that he considers valuable: domesticity, maternity, and their embodiment in chaste, delicate white femininity. The fierce stoic virtue of his heroines contrasts sharply with the fragile, childlike beauty of the actresses who play them and the helplessness their roles compel them to represent. Although men are attracted to them, these heroines do not display any overt signs of sexuality. Unlike the films Balides discusses, Griffith's films frequently pose sexuality (male or female) as a threat to marriage, motherhood, and the bourgeois home—or, in other words, to the proper white girl-woman. Invariably placed "in distress," his "respectable" heroines mark the place where Griffith most effectively blends sensational attractions and uplifting moral concerns. The kinetic charge of images of speeding trains, cars, and horses mobilized in last-minute rescues are intercut with images that constitute their motivation and moral justification: images of the frail heroine in peril. In addition to creating suspense and articulating a moral judgment in the pointed contrast between two situations or characters, the formal device of parallel editing also subsumes the visual and action-oriented sensations of early cinema within the moral, psychological motivations characteristic of classical narrative.[38]

What I would add to this analysis is simply to observe the profoundly socially marked character of Griffith's heroine-driven melodramas. The heroine's gender-coded physical helplessness effectively masks the power of the racial and class privilege and the bourgeois morality she represents. While she embodies universal values that must be protected and saved, she is customarily assaulted by a man marked by very particular differences; he is either nonwhite or non–middle class. Thus these differences become isolated as outside and deviant from a humane and virtuous norm. With very few exceptions (e.g., *Broken Blossoms*; *His Trust*, 1911; *His Trust Fulfilled*, 1911), her rescuers are also white and middle class, but they are, of course, men. The heroine's formal position in the narrative, as both character and value that must be saved, effectively places the class-marked pleasures of the early cinema, its sensational attractions, in the service of the entity that embodies the moral values and privilege of the white middle-class while also transcending them in her universalized feminine identity: the imperiled (white) woman.[39]

As my analysis of nineteenth-century women's texts on domestic economy in part I makes clear, the evidence of physical labor on women's bodies became increasingly more important in domestic discourses as an implicit signifier of class difference. White middle-class women's position as moral guardians of the culture became associated with a certain kind of appearance—delicate and angelic rather than hardy— that would be besmirched by signs of heavy physical labor. Needless to say, such an appearance fed the sensational visual dynamics of film melodrama.[40] It would seem, then, that cinematic representations of women's labor, as well as their sexuality, would have problematic implications related to class identity. But Griffith uses significations of domestic labor to critique forms of public leisure and entertainment that he, as well as Progressive reformers, saw as threatening to the family, to public morals, and especially to the safety and chastity of young white women. Ironically, his narrative program to reform the cinema and its product involved critiquing visual displays of women's sexuality, forms of public entertainment that brought together mass audiences, and leisure time and pursuits in general, all of which were or became crucial to the cinema's and his own success. I want to look at Griffith's domestic melodramas for how he attempts to counteract or subsume the representational attractions of feminine sexuality within narratives that promote women's domestic and reproductive labor as their fundamental natural and moral destiny.

In his melodramas that focus on the home, Griffith frequently uses representations of domestic labor to depict the authenticity and moral value of the heroine's emotions, her "unpremeditated feeling." *The Mothering Heart* (1913), for example, sets up a number of contrasts that affirm the moral values of maternal domestic womanhood while deriding a sexualized and leisured femininity. It articulates these contrasts through the characters of the "good wife" (played by Lillian Gish) and her nemesis, the "idle woman," who has designs on Gish's husband. In the titles he gives these two characters, Griffith imputes an immoral sexuality to a woman who is "idle." He visualizes the moral contrasts between the two women by means of gazes and appearances.

The film renders the relative merits of all the characters in terms of whom they look at, what their looking leads to, how they themselves look (that is, appear), and last, the places where we see them. The opening scene, which introduces Gish, clearly demonstrates these visual-moral dynamics. The film begins with a tight iris on her face and shoulders, a halo of light around her hair, surrounded by the leaves on a branch.[41] The frame opens to reveal her admiring a tree in a garden. An intertitle, "The Mothering Spirit," introduces a shot series depicting two puppies playing, as one gets his head stuck in a can. A shot of Gish watching follows, then another of her rescuing the puppy whose head was stuck, then picking both puppies up and embracing them. Her beau arrives and proposes marriage. With a shake of the head, she refuses him. He looks terribly dejected, and she changes her mind.

The looks Gish gives in this opening sequence indicate her regard for beauty (the tree branch) and her care and concern for the helpless (the puppy) and the dejected (her suitor). She looks at and out for beauty and people and things that need her nurturance. The film cues its audience to assess her character and her value in terms of her looks, both her appearance and her gaze; the moral quality of the latter (she sees, then rescues, the puppy) infuses the sentimental framing of the former (the iris shot of Gish's delicate beauty). The film literally equates appearance standards (looking good) with cinematically conceived moral standards (good or benevolently intended looking), an equation realized in the spectator's identification of (and possibly with) the beauty and goodness of Gish's character. At another level the sequence indicates how the cinema resolves its problematic access to character interiority or psychology, especially in the silent cinema. Gish's gaze gives the audience access to her feelings, which then become the indicators of her moral status and social value. She responds to and acts upon the needs of others, accepting a marriage proposal because of her "mothering heart."

From the garden, the film moves to the early days of the marriage, where it again makes use of gazes and appearances, now involving Gish's domestic labor, to further elaborate the value of her character type. Introduced by the title "The Path of the Struggling Young Husband Made Smooth," the first several shots show Gish sending her husband off in the morning with playful kisses and then retiring to her adjacent workroom. Clad in an apron, she irons in the foreground, while in the background we see the laundry she takes in to earn money. The work is hard and her customers are mean, but the shot that ends this sequence depicts Gish holding a coin up in front of her, delighted with the economic contribution she can make to her household.

The space of the home is split in a parallel editing sequence when the husband returns home, dejected and depressed. He enters the front room. The next shot depicts Gish holding her head, her body drooping in exhaustion, in the back room. In a series of shots switching back and forth between the two rooms, Gish catches sight of her husband. We see him hanging his head, then we see her rearranging her hair, straightening up, smiling, altering her appearance before entering the other room to cheer him up. She includes giving him the money she has earned among her ministrations to him (hugging him, setting out tea), but she keeps her exertions and exhaustions a secret from him. As many critics have pointed out, melodrama grants its audience greater knowledge than its characters possess, and this disparity produces pathos. We see the effects of Gish's labor on her body and appearance, but her husband does not. This disparity of visual knowledge displays for the audience Gish's uncomplaining and self-sacrificing nature, her value as a good wife. It also articulates her visual knowledge as equal to the audience's and greater than her husband's within the home space. Altogether the sequence imbues both an "unlabored" feminine appearance and a certain kind of dissembling or deception (about the arduousness of housework and femininity) with very positive moral significance.

The film builds the conflicts and moral message that structure its narrative by comparing Gish's looks (both meanings intended) with those of the "idle woman." Introduced in a bar filled with a wealthy and elegantly attired clientele, the "idle woman" (as she is explicitly called in an intertitle) sits at the table next to the young couple and flagrantly makes eyes at the husband. Dressed in a low-cut sleeveless gown, she displays herself and her sexuality boldly through her appearance and her active, desiring gaze. Later in the narrative, the film uses her character to give us another, very negative example of feminine dissembling. The "idle woman," seeing the young husband walking down the street, feigns helplessness at opening the door of her automobile. He, of course, jumps to help her. Her damsel in distress act precipitates the affair that temporarily wrecks the young man's marriage.

The Mothering Heart organizes many other issues about gender, the public sphere, entertainment, and women's appropriate place precisely in relation to women's labor or leisure. Griffith enhances the implications of the work/leisure opposition in the film's use of space and the motivations of other characters. The young husband's inclination to have a good time, to enjoy his prosperity once he has found a job, leads, via the cabaret where he initially takes his wife, to his illicit entanglement with the idle woman. Public leisure activities, the allure of spending rather than an earlier historical ethos based on accumulating, seduce men away from their familial responsibilities.[42] Griffith suggests the dangers of public entertainments in the visual contrasts he constructs between domestic space and the attractions and visual pleasures of the cabaret featured in this narrative.

Both the editing and the mise-en-scène are much more complex in *The Mothering Heart*'s cabaret scenes than in the domestic or garden scenes. The establishing shots emphasize the crowd's frenetic and chaotic activity. The women are all seductively, if elegantly, dressed. Griffith intercuts shots of the stage, the entire space of the cabaret, and medium shots of the tables where the protagonists sit. On stage, first a campy bacchanal and then an apache dance performed by a working-class couple titillate the crowd. The dance alternates between close and highly sexualized dancing and implications of violence; the man, a dead ringer for Battlin' Burrows in the later *Broken Blossoms* (1919), raises his hand to his female partner as if to hit her. Originating in the Parisian underworld, the apache dance was a semiacrobatic, violent duet dance developed from the underworld's imaginings of Native American men's presumably brutal treatment of women. The dance was popular in vaudeville and burlesque shows and, in Griffith's film, inferentially links working-class and Native American men in their mistreatment of women.[43] Griffith's compressed visual repertoire manages to refer explicitly to the indiscriminate mixtures and dangers of public entertainment venues: classes, genders, good women and bad; the free and open use of alcohol and smoking; explicit displays of sexuality; and, finally, the seduction and violence that are possible consequences of this public mixing.

In each of the sequences set in the cabaret, Griffith articulates these threats in relation to Gish's character. The first sequence in which she accompanies her husband, reluctantly, to the cabaret depicts her registering her discomfort visually in her gestures, her facial expressions, and her refusal, despite her husband's repeated injunctions, to have a drink. Her clothing, her demeanor, and her relation to the crowd (a woman glares at her when she trips and runs into her chair) indicate that she is out of place. The two subsequent cabaret sequences refer to the implicit effects of irresponsible leisure on upstanding middle-class private life. In the first, the ruin of the marriage is suggested as Griffith punctuates shots of the husband and the idle woman flirting and drinking in the bar with shots of the young wife waiting and growing more and more agitated at home. The second implies the terrible threat to motherhood itself, as shots of the cabaret and the ending of the husband's illicit relationship are intercut with shots of the young wife, now living with her mother and attending to her dying baby.

Within the specular mechanics of the cinema (gazes, looks), Griffith triangulates a morally appropriate femininity with a certain place (the home) and with certain activities (maternity, nurture, and housework). Through the character of the idle woman, evil femininity is seen to reside in cabarets and on the street and to engage in risqué forms of public leisure and active sexual desire. The intimate mise-en-scène of the home, organized by the good wife's activities and maternal, nurturing gazes, is contrasted with the chaos and danger, the indiscriminate character of public places and the uncontrolled visual congress that transpires there. All of these threats are embodied in the figure of a woman who is idle, who does not perform the work for which she was intended—maternity and domesticity.

Through the character and looks of the "idle woman," Griffith visually critiques active feminine sexuality, a leisured, affluent class who do not appear to have to work, women's autonomy in the public sphere, and certain leisure activities per se—drinking, smoking, and crude forms of entertainment. The idle woman's "come-hither" glances are calculated, her helplessness is a sham; measured by the melodramatic ethos of unpremeditated feeling, she is evil. Yet, significantly, Griffith condenses all her negative qualities—her nefarious looks, her deceptive helplessness, her active sexuality—in the descriptor "idle." He visually and narratively equates feminine sexuality with a lack of industrious activity. Thus he allays or mutes the class-oriented critique that his characterization and mise-en-scène suggest by referring to an overarching moral opposition between domestic work and leisure that specifically applies to women. Images of affluence and wealth signify the potent dangers of active feminine sexuality not contained by the home, marriage, and maternity, rather than the unjust distribution of resources indicated by similar images in *A Corner in Wheat*. Griffith frequently uses images of domestic labor to suggest the industry, productivity, and value of maternity. His idealized maternal iconography, however, positions domestic work and the home as women's designated function and place in a spiritual and natural reproductive order. Yet this order applies only to some women.

"Good" women may be wealthy, and they may have others do work for them. Even though the plantation wife in *His Trust* and *His Trust Fulfilled* (both 1911) and the aggrieved upper-class wife in *Death's Marathon* (1913) do not do any housework, both are married and have children. The *Trust* films displace domestic responsibility from the wife to the faithful slave; they are particularly interesting for the way they handle race and domesticity, a topic I discuss later.[44] In *Death's Marathon* the wife tends to her child while her wealthy husband gambles away the family money, becomes more and more abusive, and finally commits suicide. The suitor she had earlier turned aside (her husband's best friend) steps in to take his place. Her character embodies the traditional Victorian "angel in the house" in that her role involves raising the children and being a good moral influence on her husband, while servants do the housework. Wealth in and of itself is not negatively valued in Griffith so long as affluent women are married and reproductively active.

Writing on Griffith's role in the development of the women's film, Scott Simmon connects Griffith's frequent injunctions against leisured women precisely to reproductive issues: "Only an idle woman has leisure unoccupied by procreation or other domestic work." He relates the pointedly maternal ethos of Griffith's women's films to social admonitions by Theodore Roosevelt concerning "the 'wilful sterility' or 'race suicide' among the upper class," a problem exacerbated at the time by rising rates of divorce instigated by women.[45] Significantly, Roosevelt's concern with "race suicide" formulates the behavior of a certain class (the "upper" class) as a threat to a certain race (the white Anglo-Saxon "race") possessed of a certain degree of affluence. Griffith's films demonstrate these same concerns; although Griffith is obsessed with women and reproduction, he limits the idealized category "woman" in a number of obvious and not so obvious ways. The classist and racist implications of this idealized category are signified in the relations of "other" characters to maternity and labor, implications I explore in the next section.

The Color of Maternity

Two secondary characters in *The Birth of a Nation* (1915) repeat in many ways the oppositions embodied by the good wife and the idle woman in *The Mothering Heart*.[46] While the mulatta character Lydia Brown, housekeeper and mistress to the Northern Senator Stoneman, displays both her distaste for her housework and a scheming and ambitious sexuality, the much more positively depicted (and unnamed) "mammy" in the Camerons' Southern household does her work, looks on delightedly at the white folks' doings, and refuses to be emancipated after the war. Mammy frequents the margins of the Southern sequences, her gaze directed toward her white masters and their narrative actions. In one of the porch scenes, young Ben plays a game of hide-and-seek with his sister Flora in the center of the frame, while in the left corner Mammy looks on, laughing and clapping. She is a delighted audience; her gaze directs the spectator's back to Flora and Ben.

In one brief scene, however, Mammy transgresses in her housekeeping duties. When a black associate of Senator Stoneman's accompanies him to the Cameron estate after the end of the war, Mammy refuses to take his bag, looks him up and down, and scolds him for his arrogance. Here her look has force, agency, and visual and narrative centrality: the interaction between the two characters takes place, albeit in long shot, in the center of the frame, as she defends the white social order, the status quo to which she is subject.

This scene parallels an earlier one in which Lydia Brown is introduced. Senator Sumner has taken his leave of Senator Stoneman in the library and encounters Lydia in the hallway. He demands his hat. She, having heard he is a Southern sympathizer, refuses to get it. When he takes umbrage at her behavior, she hands the hat to him but drops it on the floor instead of giving it to him. After he leaves, she sinks to the ground and tears her clothes, mad with rage. When Senator Stoneman later joins her, she uses her torn clothing seductively with him. Unlike the scene with Mammy, Griffith films Lydia in medium shot and puts her in the center of the frame; she faces the camera, looking almost directly at it with a wild, crazed expression. Mary Alden, the actress playing Lydia in "light" blackface, exaggerates her character's gestures and performs grotesque facial expressions for the camera, staring off at nothing. Griffith frequently used this framing—of a character gazing in the direction of the camera, eyes uplifted—to signify that character's fantasy or absorption in thought. Lydia's gaze, as well as her appearance and demeanor, though prompted by her rage at her unequal social positioning and ambitions for equality, are visually represented as demented, monstrous, and *sexually* motivated. By contrast, Mammy's *maternal* rejection of her emancipation (so she can take care of the white folks) is lauded by the film.

Unlike the good wife and the idle woman, both the black woman's and the mulatta's representational spaces are restricted to the Northern and Southern homes of their white masters or employers. The public/private dichotomy that conditions Griffith's evaluation of white women's sexuality does not apply to their completely familialized, private presentation. The sexual/asexual opposition he articulates between Lydia and the mammy visualizes and contains their own sexual and reproductive capacities or lack thereof strictly within the context of the white family. Mammy functions as a nonreproductive, asexual maternalized entity toward her white folks. Lydia exists, both genealogically (as a mulatta) and narratively (as Stoneman's actively seductive mistress), within the sexual economy of the white family. Significantly, the film transforms the historical aggression of white men against enslaved black women (one possible narrative of Lydia's parentage) into *her* active, dangerous sexuality.[47] The narrative further proposes that her interracial sexual congress with Senator Stoneman wreaks political havoc on a national level: the miscegenational relationship that the film depicts her as instigating, and to which Stoneman weakly succumbs, destroys his ability to govern wisely.

In contradistinction to this situation, which the film represents as the Northern mode of incorporating the races to produce a national family, Mammy and the faithful manservant-slave represent the Southern version. Cohabiting with the white family as abject, asexual workers, performers, and audiences to their white folk, they know their place. No black families are presented in *The Birth of a Nation*, and not only is Mammy asexual, but her maternity, converted into asexual, but nurturing service, is also completely contained within the white family. Mammy's femininity does not exist; the film "mammarizes" her maternity in a rotund appearance, visualized solely in reference to masters to whom she defers. Her gaze never wanders beyond the master's narrative in the ways Lydia's does. The melodramatic distribution of good and evil that covers these two characters articulates two alternatives for blacks in the visual field: unnamed, complicit, yet utterly marginal abjection as "good," and a completely sexualized articulation of character and agency as "evil."

In the perverse "birth" of a nation which this film attempts to convey, the two mulatto characters (Lydia and Silas Lynch) constitute its most profound impediment. Although the film should be about the conflict between the North and the South, the relations between the white Southerners and Northerners it depicts are remarkably loving and amicable, in fraternal, sororal, and sexual dimensions. The reproductive problem, as James Baldwin points out, is embodied instead in characters whose "type" is signified by the word that white men fix upon to describe the product of their own interracial coercions: mulatto, "from mulo, a mule . . . *mules are usually sterile.* And a further definition: in biology, a hybrid, *especially a sterile hybrid.*"[48] The mule is a product of inter-species intercourse and does not merit the biological designation of species itself because it is incapable of producing fertile offspring. The two characters, Lydia and Silas Lynch, embody and manifest an array of paranoic displacements as condensed, virulent, and horrifying as any return of the repressed. The historical lust and violence that produced them and the guilt over these acts become cinematically *their* lust, their impunity, their violence, their "acts," which then sanction the vindictive violence that will be exercised to maintain the purity of the (white) race. Flora's "pure" blood which ultimately spawns the Klan justifies racial imperialism through the "virtue" of white women's chastity.

While maternity and/or a chaste feminine appearance orient the significance of domestic labor for white women in Griffith's films, for women of color neither is relevant. Either possessed of a monstrous, crazed sexuality that is so potent it threatens U.S. nationhood or rendered utterly asexual, a household drone, women of color are not *women* in the way Griffith defines this idealized category. Differentiated not in terms of their acceptance or denial of their necessary and natural reproductive role but strictly in terms of sexuality, good black women have no sexuality, and therefore are not women but docile laborers; bad black or mulatta women do have it, but their "sterile" and dangerous desires exceed the bounds of the human species itself. Significantly, Griffith locates both characters within the white family, a trope of containment that dominates classical Hollywood narratives and still persists in some representations of African American women.[49]

Griffith's earlier two-part film *His Trust* and *His Trust Fulfilled* (1911) depicts this same representational matrix in relation to a black man.[50] As *The Birth of a Nation* articulates and contributes to the profound paranoia about difference and reproduction that inhabits our history and our national imaginary, so do these two films—Griffith's first two-reeler, released under two separate titles—inadvertently reveal the machinations and paradoxes relating to the "trust" which helps maintain the white man's house. The film begins as a slaveholding Confederate colonel goes off to war, taking his faithful slave George aside to give him his sword and the responsibility of protecting his wife and daughter. The colonel is killed in battle, and, in the first film, George saves both the young daughter and the sword from the burning plantation house. He takes his master's family to live in his own home, a small rustic cabin, where he hangs the sword over the fireplace and sleeps outdoors on the doorstep to protect his precious trust.

In the second film, *His Trust Fulfilled*, the first title sets the scene: "The Emancipation, but George remains faithful to his Trust." George is depicted doing all the caretaking for the family, both inside and outside the house. Without her husband the plantation wife cannot function, and she dies, "giving" the sword to George for a second time. The next title, "The Little Orphan," introduces a series of sequences wherein George secretly pays for all the daughter's expenses of attending a fancy boarding school. She thinks that the money comes from her estate (which, in a certain way, it does, coming from her emancipated property). All George's savings are depleted. Finally, the daughter marries a prosperous young man, while outside the picket fence surrounding the yard where the wedding takes place, George looks on with great pleasure. The setup of this sequence resembles the finale of King Vidor's *Stella Dallas* (1939) and works in a similar fashion. Deprived of all material reward and recognition, save that of the solicitor who conveyed his money to the girl and of course the film viewer, George is idealized precisely and only as an emasculated father figure. In the final sequence George takes down the sword, receives a handshake from the solicitor, and grins broadly. The transfer of the sword from father to slave imparts phallic power to the latter only in economic, not in sexual terms; furthermore, that power is subject to "his trust."

Like the good wife in *The Mothering Heart*, George keeps his labor a secret; his sacrifice contributes to the pathos of his trust. Unlike her, however, George deteriorates in appearance throughout the film; his clothing becomes more and more tattered, his back more and more bent. The marks of his labor are not hidden, though his financial contribution to the girl and her dependency on him are. Instead of expressing a visual affiliation with natural beauty, George is associated with servility and animality; at one point he gets down on his hands and knees so the young daughter can ride him, and his protective gesture of sleeping on the doorstep allegorizes his liminal humanity while celebrating his loyalty. George performs both maternal and paternal functions for the girl while appearing to be her servant and her pet. He publicly carries her suitcases and scrapes and bows before her, while privately he uses all his savings to support her. Both housekeeper and wage earner, he carries the responsibilities of both parents without any of the power, recognition, or sexuality. As with the mammy figure in *The Birth of a Nation*, Griffith visualizes George's value in his work for his master's family and in his refusal to be recognized or honored for it.

Thus, the two-part film *His Trust* and *His Trust Fulfilled* visualizes and sentimentalizes the "charge or duty imposed in faith" on George by his master. Yet because the colonel owns George at the time of this investiture, other senses of the word *trust* also apply to this interaction. Meaning both "reliance on future payment for property or credit" and "a property interest held by one person for the benefit of another," George's "trust" can refer not only to the execution of his duty, but also to his life and very being as the inheritance, credit, or property interest owed to this slaveholder's child. He is the executor of himself as property. Griffith's film articulates the same conversion of "property to personality" that underwrote determinations of identity in the nineteenth century. George's loyalty, his trust, personifies his status as property on the threshold of humanity, as his abject labor, sexlessness, and selflessness inscribe his place and function, even in his own home. Like Mammy's, his reproductive agency is utterly desexualized and dedicated to the white family, which he serves as both mother and father, housekeeper and field slave. Those very few of Griffith's films that do represent blacks (most often with white actors in blackface) use domestic labor and the home to indicate their proper place and function within white homes. In Griffith's world, however, "good" black people do not reproduce, they are not sexual, and they have no public independent existence outside of what he envisages as a white home in a white nation organized solely around the feminine and maternal capacities and frailties of white women.

Domestic labor helps organize class and racial difference in relation to representations of transcendent white femininity in Griffith's *Broken Blossoms* (1919). Several stunning sequences delimit the life choices available to the impoverished, illegitimate Lucy, played by Lillian Gish. Following the intertitle "A married friend has told her—'Don't ever get married,'" we see Lucy's friend, harried, unkempt, and exhausted, scrubbing laundry in a tub, surrounded by dirty, needy children. A second shot depicts Gish receiving this information as she brushes the hair of one of the daughters, watched by the husband, complaining and irascible, positioned in the middle of the frame. The ladies of the street also advise Lucy against their profession. The film represents these grimly visualized alternatives—impoverished reproduction or sexual traffic—as Lucy's only options. In Griffith's imaginary, poverty deprives maternity of its spiritual, transcendent character, primarily on a temporal axis. If futurity is the temporality of the middle class and tradition that of the aristocracy, for the poor, the limitations of the present override the significance of familial reproduction. Lucy and her friend's many children have no value, just as her friend's maternity has no value, because her offspring have no significant future and therefore no reproductive relevance (and vice versa).

Images of Lucy cooking and sewing isolate her in meditative vignettes or depict the accidental or imagined mistakes in her housewifery that precipitate increasingly brutal and iconographically sexualized beatings by her father.[51] The "Yellow Man,"

Cheng Huan, who befriends Lucy, is a disappointed missionary in this counter-colonization narrative. While Griffith renders the "Yellow Man" much more sympathetically than Thomas Burke does in the short story "The Chink and the Child" on which the film is based, he retains Burke's London setting, thus avoiding the resonances his film would have had if set in the United States as a result of the Chinese Exclusion Act.[52] Cheng Huan's commercial work as a merchant represents the failure of his spiritual visions—visions he has replaced with a vacuous, opiated gaze. The puritanical but essentially optimistic (future-oriented, reproductively oriented) work-versus-leisure motif that secures the gazes, appearance, and overall visual field of a film such as *The Mothering Heart* and the later *Way Down East* does not operate in this narrative. Unlike the gaze of the good wife or Mammy or Lydia, Lucy's gaze has no narrative agency. Her eyes are usually downcast or restricted to desiring glances at "pathetic" objects: the flower she cannot afford, the gifts her unknown mother has left her, the doll that Cheng Huan gives her.

While Lucy looks at these objects, a variety of other gazes are directed at her: the sadistic and threatening looks of her father, the leering, lascivious glances of Evil Eye, and the longing gaze of Cheng Huan, as well as the gaze of the spectators. Dudley Andrew argues that through the looks at and of Lucy/Gish, Griffith displaces spectatorial desire from the narrative to "static portraits of Lillian Gish." This displacement occurs as a result of the hostile, threatening, and lacivious gazes insistently directed at Lucy (by Battlin' Burrows and Evil Eye) and her reaction:

> Her own gaze in response buries itself in a series of self-reflections and the narrative energy they contain. Thus all visual and dramatic power is focused on her where it is held tight within the narcissism of her own perception. In a cruel world she dares not lift her eyes as a prelude to action or defense, instead latching on to fragile mirrors of herself.[53]

The objects that she contemplates "are in every case figures of her, and in the final case, her own reflection," with the consequence that everyone's eyes—spectators', characters', even and most especially Lucy's own—are on her. This "hermetic" circuit of visual desire, culminating in Lucy's delighted contemplation of her own image in the hand mirror, locates "art" in her image. As Andrew argues, "Art, conceived here as timeless, self-absorbed pictorial value, has used and transcended the 'prop' of narrative to achieve this 'higher' goal."[54]

Construed in terms of art rather than sexuality, Andrew's argument nevertheless invokes one of the primary oppositions that shape Laura Mulvey's argument in "Visual Pleasure and Narrative Cinema": the female form, isolated, spectacularized, fetishized, threatens the narrative flow by freezing it in moments of erotic contemplation. Griffith here fetishizes and feminizes "art" through the image of Lillian Gish. The value of her image transcends that of the bourgeois narrative; Lucy's reproductive capacity—valueless in terms of narrative maternity—is located solely in her image. Through the ostensible agency of Cheng Huan, that image is spiritualized and desexualized; he puts her on an altar, adores her from afar.[55] His gaze operates as a narrative conduit, referring the spectatorial gaze to the innocent Gish.

In *Broken Blossoms*, family, work, and love lead nowhere. The destitution of Lucy's situation is ultimately represented not by her poverty but by her father's violence and

brutality. Building from Andrew's argument that only Lillian Gish's beauty, an analogue for the beauty of Griffith's film practice, emerges as value from this doomed
narrative, another value emerges from the fact that that beauty is marked. When
Cheng Huan moves to kiss Lucy at one point, she draws back in terror. The reasons
are overdetermined by the film: both her youth and her whiteness make her
untouchable, the two literally confused in the image. Thus Lucy's innocence is seen
to emanate from both her youth and her race. As a vision, the white girl-woman is a
value in and of herself, not to be touched, but to be visually revered by (racial) others. Cheng Huan distinguishes himself by the denial of his desire, something of
which none of the other characters, especially Lucy's father, is capable. In *Broken
Blossoms*, the specularization of the white heroine transcends her class status (Griffith explicitly refers to her as "BEAUTY" in an intertitle), though she and her domesticity are doomed narratively. Lucy's beauty and her poverty organize the male
relations among the poor and dissipated according to racial and national backgrounds; both class and colonial motifs are subsumed by her appearance and her
death. Griffith uses race in this film to abstract and aestheticize the nationalist vision
of *The Birth of a Nation*: beautiful helpless white women, of no matter what social
class, can and should be revered by all.

Griffith's *Way Down East* (1920) explores the paradoxical implications of knowledge, seeing, and helplessness for intensely moral female heroines whose bodies figure prominently in the attractions and allure of his films. The Manichaean social
geography (public/private) constructed in *The Mothering Heart* and the disingenuous North-South division in *The Birth of a Nation* is construed as a city-country
distinction in the later, much more elaborate film *Way Down East* (1920).[56] Here
Lillian Gish (again!) plays the character Anna Moore, but as an opening title
informs us, "She might as well be called 'Woman.'" We know from *The Birth of a
Nation* that "Woman" is white. *Way Down East* locates her in an agrarian setting
and focuses on the dangers of courtship and seduction, telling the story of Anna's
betrayal in a false marriage and its aftermath. The narrative begins when, strapped
by financial difficulties, Anna's mother sends her to their wealthy relatives in
Boston, Cousin Emma Tremont and her two daughters. All of the events, sets, and
characters of the urban sequences emphasize the city's leisured snobbery. When
Anna arrives, she gives Cousin Emma a knit hug-me-tight that Anna's mother made
"with her own hands." Out of Anna's view, Emma holds the garment between
thumb and forefinger in disgust, immediately handing it off to the butler. Her gesture associates women's homespun handiwork with defilement, an insult to her
character and class. As she is in the middle of hosting an afternoon bridge party, she
shoos Anna off to a deserted parlor.

Leisure events make up the city sequences—the bridge party, the Tremont ball
("the social event of the season"), Anna's visit to the lavish apartment of Lennox
Sanderson, and her false honeymoon. Anna's downfall is precipitated by an aunt who,
to pique her sister Emma and her arrogant nieces, dresses Anna up and brings her
to the ball in an elegant and provocative gown. Anna protests its immodesty ("But
Auntie, it has no top!") and veils her shoulders in a gauze wrap to make her entrance.
As she walks down the stairs with her aunt, she pauses to take in the scene before her,
her face wide-eyed and childlike with fascination. Griffith's framing takes in the stair-

case, some of the crowd below stage left, and Lennox Sanderson stage right looking up and seeing young Anna contemplating the crowd. An intertitle has informed us that Lennox is a wealthy and notorious ladies' man; his gaze at Anna indicates the nature of his interest in her. Quickly maneuvering her away from other suitors, he regales her with fantastic compliments, inviting her to see herself (as the audience does in a cutaway coded as Lennox's fantasy) as "Elaine, Lily Maid of Astolat."

The moral-visual matrix of gazes and appearances that Griffith articulates here is much more complicated and paradoxical than in any of the earlier films for several reasons. Unlike *The Birth of a Nation*, with its epic scale, this film focuses on an intimate story of a young girl. In this film Gish's character must represent both goodness and alluring feminine sexuality, qualities divided between the good wife and the idle woman in *The Mothering Heart*. Significantly, Gish as the good wife sees more, knows more, and demonstrates a much greater degree of narrative agency than she does as Anna Moore. In the cabaret, when her gaze intercepts the desiring look of the idle woman intended for her husband, the wife immediately understands and objects to its import. She leaves the bar, as she will ultimately leave the marriage. Earlier, when her husband cast a disparaging glance at the staid outfit she planned to wear to the cabaret, the good wife displayed irritation with him. Anna Moore, by contrast, allows herself to be provocatively dressed, then eyed and fantasized as a sexualized and desirable object of the gaze, although Gish's performance clearly registers Anna's ignorance of her sexual effect. In several of the city sequences, we see Anna, left alone in a parlor or with a maid in a bedroom, imitating the elegant, affected walk and gestures of her cousins, and then laughing, clapping, or skipping in childish amusement. Her play-acting is limited to these private moments, however. In her short but fateful stint at the ball, the elegance of her gown and her appearance is counteracted by her guileless and childlike gestures and conversation with Lennox.

In order to maintain the morally charged oppositions that shape his Victorian construction of white middle-class femininity (sexuality/maternity, leisure/work, public/private) and yet to narrate this tale of seduction, Griffith must resort to a host of visual and ethical ironies that continue to haunt morally conceived notions of white femininity today. Ethically, Anna's sexual allure must be separated from her own agency and knowledge. Thus her appearance (again in both senses) at the ball is a special "dress-up" and treat for her, arranged by her aunt. Griffith uses the scenes of Anna's performing her cousins' grown-up, sophisticated gestures precisely to demonstrate her childlike innocence. Her playful artifice certifies the pure and unpremeditated authenticity of her feelings, in effect, her incapacity for "real" dissembling and feminine pretense. She can only play at such feminine wiles.

Anna's gaze in the city sequences, unlike that of her predecessor in *The Mothering Heart*, demonstrates her naïveté rather than any degree of perceptive or affirmative agency. Initial shots depicting her with a broom emphasize her familiarity with housework, and her knit gloves are visually "homey" enough to undercut her admiring assertion to her mother that they are all the rage in the city. Arriving at the very tall door of her relatives' home, Anna, her back to the camera, leans way back to try to see the top of the house. Inside the Tremont home everyone—the butler, the maid, Cousin Emma and her daughters, Lennox Sanderson and the other swains at the ball, the eccentric aunt—looks Anna up and down, whether with lust, disgust, scrutiny, disdain, admiration, or adventurous pleasure at the transformation in her appearance. While they knowingly look at and assess her, Griffith consistently manipulates the mise-en-scène, the framing, and the information given in intertitles to highlight what Anna does *not* see. Rushing to embrace Cousin Emma when she first arrives and giving her the hug-me-tight, Anna misses her cousin's scornful once-over and her handing off the gift in disgust. Engrossed in displaying her "fashionable" gloves to the daughters, she misses their exchange of sneering glances.

Anna's looks—at the door, at her cousin, at her gloves—display her childlike character and her spontaneous feelings of wonder and affection. Griffith frames these looks in such a way that they simultaneously indicate what she cannot see: the insincerity and putting-on of appearances of everyone around her. She is taken in, literally and figuratively, by attractive facades, fine manners, and fine clothes. Visually Griffith renders her innocence inextricable from her ignorance (what she cannot see), and thus infuses that ignorance—of her own sexuality and beauty, for example—with positive moral value. Yet because of what her gaze does not discern —false appearances, sexual desire, the emptiness of grandiose compliments—Anna will fall.

In the hotel scene depicting that fall, Anna's sincere and loving looks at Lennox give him pause; yet a chance glimpse of her comely ankle (rendered in close-up) sets him again on his evil course. The battle between the (moral) power of Anna's face and gaze, which register her unpremeditated and spontaneous innocence, and the (sexual) power of her physical appearance, registered in Lennox's calculated and desiring gaze at her, is waged and lost without Anna, or "Woman," even knowing it. Indeed, her lack of knowledge is precisely the point. Yet, if we consider the degree of knowledge and agency the heroine in *The Mothering Heart* has, we can see that Griffith's solution to the problem of visually merging virtuous morality and sexuality in the same feminine body was to infantilize, to blind the gaze and alienate the visage of this character from her own body and its effects, and to fragment this body and its sensibilities for the viewer. She does not see or know or possess any effective agency until after her fall.

Sanderson seduces Anna by a false marriage, then abandons her completely when he finds she is pregnant. Anna's mother dies, and shortly after she gives birth, her baby dies as well. Thrown out of the rooming house where she has had the child because she does not have a husband, Anna walks the countryside looking for work. She is taken in at the Bartlett farm, Mother Bartlett's scriptural admonitions over-riding Squire Bartlett's reservations about taking in a girl with no family. The Bartlett farm and village contrast with the Tremonts' urban Boston in almost all respects. Whereas all the sets, clothing, and action in the earlier sequences focus on leisure events (we never see a kitchen, for example, or anyone doing any work), here the focus is on the preparation of food, mealtimes, farmwork, visits from family and townspeople, in short, events from everyday working life. The city sequences exclusively feature a wealthy urban class among whom Anna is depicted as clearly out of place. In Bartlett Village, by contrast, Griffith manages to convey a sense of community among the Bartletts and an array of secondary and sometimes very eccentric characters. Even Lennox Sanderson, whose country estate adjoins the Bartletts' farm, fits in, though his attentions to the Bartletts' cousin Kate are always closely supervised.

Throughout this part of the film, Anna is continually associated with domestic labor, whether she is churning butter, baking, setting the table, fetching water, sewing, taking visitors' coats, or preparing Squire Bartlett's pipe. Her hard work endears her to the family, a title informs us, but it also demonstrates the nurturing agency that her gaze and her character have in this environment. Seeing the squire asleep in the sun, Anna covers his face; when Mrs. Bartlett picks up a heavy bucket, Anna takes it from her. While she is initially subjected to an array of appraising looks when she arrives, Squire and Mrs. Bartlett, son David, and spinster-neighbor Martha assess her, albeit with very different levels of accuracy and perception, for the moral quality of her character, not for her lack of fine clothes and social sophistication. Whereas Mrs. Bartlett's and David's gazes recognize Anna and her value immediately, Squire Bartlett's and Martha's register lingering suspicions.

The visual ironies that shape the earlier part of the film (Anna's playful airs that demonstrate her character's sincerity and lack of pretense, her looks that do not see) lead to the substantial moral and narrative ironies that structure the second part: her eyes now open, her gaze both knowing and capable of perception and agency, Anna cannot speak or express herself. Sanderson moves about freely while she lives in fear of exposure. Whereas the city sequences are articulated around her inability to see, here the film concerns itself with other characters' inability to see or understand the truth about her. Anna cannot explain to David why she cannot marry him. Squire Bartlett cannot grasp her value when that value is challenged. He throws her out when he learns of her past. Although his compassionate wife and son see Anna's value much more clearly, they cannot prevent the squire's actions. They, like Anna at this point, have some knowledge and vision but only limited agency and power.

Cinematic melodrama turns precisely on characters' varied misinterpretations or misrecognitions of information in the visual field. Unlike in the novel, where descriptions of characters' feelings and interiority can provide a measure against which to assess the veracity of appearances, in the cinema, especially the silent cinema, appearances provide the only standard. Thus aberrations of seeing, misrecognitions, and acts of dissembling are distributed across all characters, whether they are good or evil. The individual character's relative knowledge and varying intentions determine the value of his or her acts. Given, then, that characters' appearances, their gazes and the objects of those gazes, and the narrative milieux in which they act indicate their level of knowledge, interiority, affect, agency, and moral value, a comparison between the two protagonists in *The Mothering Heart* and *Way Down East* indicates the representational price that must be paid to locate sexual and cinematic "attractions" in and on the bodies of respectable white heroines. We can see that Griffith's rendering of Anna Moore's sexuality as visual spectacle in the later film compelled him to deprive her correspondingly of both knowledge and agency, deprivations that did not characterize the heroine of the earlier film.

Furthermore, the consequences of Anna's inadvertent sexual display, of her being looked at, are deadly in terms of the false marriage and tragic maternity that result.[57] Taken in by and engaging in an ethos dictated by fine appearances, Anna receives a proposal and marriage commitment that are also just a show. But given the medium in which this drama occurs (the cinema is, in a sense, only "fine appearances," also "just a show"), Griffith's critique risks reflexively impugning the cinema itself. In the second half of the film, however, appearances have a truth value that supersedes that of the law (the comic constable who is completely ineffectual), academia (the earnest and awkward professor), the spoken word (Martha's gossip and the story of Anna's past), and moral rules (the squire's) that adhere to the letter but do not respect the spirit of the law. Anna's appearance and her visually represented actions (her nurturing looks, her domestic labor) depict the truth of her character, as Mrs. Bartlett, David, and especially the audience realize. As I read it, this film allegorizes and evaluates the potential visual and moral appeals of the cinema, condemning appearances that relate only to sexuality and leisure as false and deceiving, but endorsing a moralized visual and narrative field wherein representations of domestic labor and nurturing maternal gazes buttress the age-old equation of beauty and goodness in the persona of Anna Moore/Lillian Gish. In this distinction between true and false appearances, domestic work functions as a signifier of moral authenticity while leisure signals duplicity and moral callousness.

Many critics argue that Griffith's saccharine perspective and anachronistic view of women signal the doom of his later films and their overly sentimental outlook. Writing on the fall of Griffith's popularity in the 1920s, a critic notes: "But times and taste alike were changing. From now on Griffith's films were often criticized even by the trade press as melodramatic."[58] In 1924 James Quirk boldly admonished Griffith in an editorial in *Photoplay*: "Your refusal to face the world is making you more and more a sentimentalist. You see passion in terms of cooing doves or the falling of a rose petal . . . your lack of contact with life makes you deficient in humor. In other words, your splendid unsophistication is a menace to you—and to pictures."[59] Yet it is important to distinguish exactly what survived of the nineteenth-century ethos Griffith subscribed to and what was jettisoned. While representations of women in melodrama continued to be laden with moral concerns related to their maternity and sexuality, leisure was no longer criticized per se. Nor did subsequent directors and films tend to juxtapose leisure to domestic work as a means of certifying the moral integrity of a white character in any kind of straightforward way.

In Griffith's visual and moral field, leisure, active sexuality (male or female), the city, and public entertainments are negatively valued in contradistinction to what he holds dear: maternity, domesticity and domestic labor, private family life, nature, the country, and simple, community pleasures. Yet his very effectiveness in developing a moral-specular cinematic rhetoric and visualizing these threats to domesticity ironically, yet very predictably, superseded the limitations of his own anachronistic sensibilities. Within the context of the argument I am constructing here, Griffith's commercially successful visual mapping of a virtuously moral but helpless character onto a sexualized white feminine body was one part of a highly effective synthesis of disparate political, social, aesthetic, and economic interests. The delicate white woman defiled or in distress provided a lucrative opportunity for combining highly moralistic narratives with riveting cinematic shocks and attractions. The conflicted class interests converging on this icon are veiled by Griffith's emphasis on gender and his propensity to distribute positively valued images of work and negatively valued images of leisure onto female characters marked by maternity and sexuality, respectively. Appropriate femininity is always maternal and industrious, universalized by woman's helpless morality, no matter how white and how unlabored her appearance.

In the evolution of the culture industry, advertising and film industry discourses, among others, positively construct the value of leisure and emphatically associate it with femininity. The adage of an economic and commercial order that the working class must become more self-indulgent certainly extended in this period to women. As many historians of advertising note, in the twenties women were identified as the primary target of commercial rhetoric. For both the culture industry and consumer culture, the sexual woman had to be merged with the moral woman in some way. In the long run, Griffith's focus on a buttoned-up, chaste femininity, his relentless critique of public leisure activities, and his devotion to domesticity ultimately did not serve the economic and social discourses that achieved primacy in this era. Molly Haskell notes that while Griffith was the most important director of the period 1915–25, he was superseded by a "trend towards a more sophisticated view of the world."[60] What is overridden in Griffith's viewpoint is a moralistic condemnation of leisure, of spectacle, of women outside the home. In the next chapter I discuss several films that act out, in precise detail, the cultural and representational transformations that convert domestic labor from a form of physical work to something other than labor.

Lessons in Labor and Love

The Melodramatic Imperatives of Hollywood Housekeeping

> There was no dust in her house but she knew now that that was not the thing of vital importance.
>
> LOIS WEBER, *Too Wise Wives* (1921)

Griffith's domestic melodramas illustrate with particular clarity the representational conventions that the cinema inherited from nineteenth-century domesticity. Yet his Victorian vision of a highly moralized performative femininity was not only anachronistic and excessively sentimental, it was also represented as opposed to leisure and overt displays of sexuality, two crucial attractions of the nascent film industry. Griffith's sensibility was quickly supplanted by more sophisticated renderings of "appropriate" domestic life that tended to validate leisure and commodity acquisition and suppress the fact of domestic labor. Furthermore, even during Griffith's heyday, an array of films took on the question of women's work and its value within the home and marriage from a much more modern viewpoint. Many of these films were comedies, such as *A Windy Day on the Roof* and Alice Guy Blaché's *A House Divided* (1913), though others adopted didactic formats that, while lacking the sensations and extreme moral polarities of melodramas like Griffith's, nevertheless recounted implicitly pedagogical stories about proper domesticity. These films reveal the explicitly moral and implicitly political standards that now defined the "goodness" of home and wife within a secular commodity culture. Their narratives foreground the values that constituted the success and competence of domestic femininity as it was disengaged from images of useful labor.

A striking example is Blaché's *Making of an American Citizen* (1912). Blaché, who shares with Georges Meliès credit for being the first narrative film director, was also the first woman to direct films. Beginning work with Gaumont in France in 1896, she moved to America in 1910, starting her own film company, Solax, in Fort Lee,

New Jersey.[1] With the uncannily accurate eye of an outsider, Blaché captures the crucial relationship between appropriate domestic femininity and U.S. citizenship in her film *Making of an American Citizen*.[2] An opening intertitle introduces the Orloffs, "an unhappy couple" from eastern Europe, who decide to come to America when encouraged by other emigrants. The visuals depict Ivan Orloff, swarthy and heavyset, in a cart drawn by his mule and his wife, upon whose back he liberally applies his whip. The rest of the film depicts Ivan's four lessons in citizenship, each of which involves his learning proper gender role behaviors and interactions in America.

The Orloffs' arrival in America is signaled by the intertitle "In the land of freedom. His first lesson in Americanism." This sequence sets up a visual epistemology that directly relates male behavior and U.S. citizenship to the iconic status of women. Coming off the boat, Ivan's wife, who is carrying all their belongings on her back, sits down to rest. Blaché positions her in the shot with the Statue of Liberty directly behind her.[3] As Ivan prods his wife with his walking stick, the couple is accosted by a very affluent-looking gentleman in a suit and tie, who takes the heavy bag away from the wife and gives it to Ivan. Ivan initially struggles, protesting that his wife is his property to do with as he will, but finally he succumbs.

As the affluent gentleman and Ivan struggle, they are aligned horizontally in the shot, while the Statue of Liberty rises up behind Ivan's wife in a vertical relation to her. The relationship between citizen and aspiring citizen (the two men) is conditioned by the iconic and monumental relationship women bear to the nation (Ivan's wife and the statue). This shot and its narrative pit Ivan's "Old World" notion of women as property against their symbolic American embodiment as national icon. Articulating an emphatic visual relationship between the literal woman and the iconic woman in this shot—suggesting that while the man aspires to citizenship, the woman is now invested with iconic status—Blaché also brilliantly allegorizes a transformation in class and gender relations that is crucial to American citizenship. In this and in all Ivan's subsequent lessons in Americanism, what he must learn is that women are not property, not beasts of burden, and not appropriate objects of violence for lower-class men who have no one below them but their wives. Rather, women in America are symbolically elevated; objectified within that position, they function to organize and legitimate violence between men as citizens. In the figuration of the nation as female, (male) citizens must place themselves at the service of women. Thus the affluent gentleman intervenes and corrects Ivan not because of his superior class position, but because Ivan is mistreating a woman—a woman visually aligned with the icon of the nation.

The film emphasizes this point in Ivan's second and third lessons, which are administered respectively by a working-class Irish bloke in the city and a farmer in the country, both of whom also witness Ivan abusing his wife. In each case Ivan has reacted violently when his wife either does not effectively perform an act of labor (she has trouble pulling his boots off for him) or when she takes what is portrayed as a well-deserved rest from some backbreaking chore, as in Ivan's third lesson, which takes place in their new home in the country. While Ivan sits in a rocker on the porch, his wife labors in their vegetable garden. Overcome with the heat, she sits down to rest and Ivan rushes down, picking up a hoe to hit her. A passing farmer stops him and, holding his whip aloft, makes Ivan carry his wife to the rocker and get a wet cloth for her head. The farmer explains to Ivan that *he* should work in the field, not his wife, and tells Ivan to pick up the hoe himself, threatening to whip him if he does not.

The affluent gentleman, the working-class urban man, and the farmer all forcefully and violently correct Ivan's violent behavior; their intervention is morally justified because they are acting in the interests of Ivan's wife. When Ivan is ultimately arrested, tried, and sentenced to six months' forced labor for beating his wife (his fourth lesson), the state legally intrudes into his home and private life precisely on his wife's account. Thus, although women are not themselves citizens (female suffrage is eight years away), the film asserts that violent action among American citizens and between the state and its citizens is legitimated by women and by the respect and service that should be accorded them in their symbolic and iconic role as representative of the nation.

Introducing his term of forced labor, an intertitle informs us that "Ivan begins to profit from all the good advice he has received." As the word "profit" indicates, the register of Ivan's lessons in Americanism shifts from the moral-legal to the economic. In the sequences depicting Ivan's return home "Completely Americanized," he becomes productive, a change denoted by images of him laboring in the fields and bringing home a melon and other vegetables he has grown to show and offer to his wife. In the final scene he comes in for dinner as she arranges flowers on a neatly set table. She wears an attractive dress and a flowing white apron. He caresses her as he puts on his jacket for dinner, prays with her, and then holds out her chair for her. He presents the meal to her, literalizing his service to her in the food "he has put on the table." This high point of his immigration marks a shift from his former sense of brute domestic mastery to his identity as a worker. His wife ceases to be his property, and he becomes productive, his service to her and his productive labor denoting the realization of his citizenship.

The film's narrative proposes that "Americanism" and American citizenship derive, first and foremost, from appropriate domesticity and the proper treatment of women, a view depicted as shared and consensual across social and ethnic classes and throughout different geographic locations (urban and rural). For Ivan, adapting to the laws and customs of his new country consists entirely in his learning and conforming to bourgeois norms of gender behavior, where propriety rather than property relations govern his relationship with his wife. Although the lessons of citizenship do not pertain specifically to Ivan's wife (as she is not a citizen), her living in "the American Way" requires her to forgo labor in the fields, to refuse to be treated as a beast of burden, and to adopt performative conventions of feminine behavior—evidenced by her attention, in the final scene, to both her own appearance and that of her home. Most important, the final sequence *withholds* any image of Ivan's wife visibly working. Her activities in the final sequences are all symbolic—arranging the flowers, admiring the vegetables Ivan has brought in from the fields, looking pretty within a home space that is itself attractive. In that we repeatedly see her labor in the earlier parts of the film and we do not after Ivan's conversion, the film associates the *visibility* of women's labor with Ivan's un-American, animalistic, and unacceptable lifestyle. In the final scene the film makes an emphatic and striking connection between the regulation of male violence and the invisibility of women's labor, associating both with the highest possible values—appropriate citizenship and domesticity. In other words, the nation requires that his violence and her labor disappear under appropriate gender roles.

In the United States, then, gender rather than class, ethnic affiliation, or geography dictates proper behavior and, hence, citizenship. As Blaché's film astutely illustrates, it is the law of the land to "protect" women from visible displays of exploitation or even labor, but to do so for the sake of defining and regulating *male* citizenship. Ivan's unruly and uncivilized behavior (in addition to mistreating his wife, he does not take his hat off in court and shows no understanding of proper public behavior), his appearance (dark, heavy-set), and his facial expressions and reactions (crude and volatile) are all associated with the identity "eastern European." Thus the film visually interprets Ivan's ethnic, cultural, and national differences in relation to his behavior toward his wife, designating their collective embodiment as uncivilized (and un-American). As he subsequently makes himself subject to "American" norms of gender behavior, Ivan's other cultural differences and their significance are wholly privatized, subsumed within the domestic sphere and the universal difference between men and women. As the only difference that ostensibly matters, Ivan's treatment of his wife becomes the basis of his relation to the state, and to the violence and control it can wield over him in mediating between the domestic and the economic as emphatically separate and gendered spheres.

D. W. Griffith's *Birth of a Nation* tells a very similar story, depicting the racialized violence of the Ku Klux Klan as both motivated and sanctioned precisely in relation to virtuous white womanhood and domesticity. Yet for Griffith racial difference precludes assimilation, a stance he indicates, as I discussed in chapter 4, by refusing to represent African American women within the conventions of domestic femininity. Griffith imagines a domestic sphere, allegorical of the nation, dominated by the luminous authority of white women, with all racial others assembled in servile and reverential relation to her. Taken together, Blaché's and Griffith's visions of the nation, both located in the private sphere and concerned with the positioning and containment of difference, presage the classical cinema's treatment of these issues. Basically classical cinema tends to represent racial difference in the register of ethnicity (as marginalized characters, usually servants in films about women and the home) and articulates norms or transgressions of assimilation within the ethos of appropriate domesticity and gender relations. Thus ethnic, racial, and class difference *along with* domestic labor are rendered invisible under the aegis of appropriate white domestic femininity.[4]

Classical Hollywood Domesticity by and for Women

Envisioning the domestic woman as transcendently and morally valuable within a secular and increasingly commodity-oriented culture industry raises some significant problems. While "good" femininity in cinematic domesticity must bear the burden of representing all that is worthwhile and positive about private life, it must also be leisured, narcissistic, and performative, an embodied yet *moralized* promotion of commodity acquisition.[5] While Blaché's film explicitly relates the invisibility of women's domestic labor to the gender-driven machinations of American citizenship—including its fundamental fantasy that the difference between men and women can stand in for, organize, and mystify all other social differences—other women-directed films tell moral tales about appropriate domestic behavior among the affluent bourgeois themselves, although these films generally contain lessons for wives, not for their husbands. Feminist film theorists have recovered and researched the oeuvres of the women who directed films during the classical period.[6] These directors produced work on many different topics; yet two of the more prominent, Lois Weber and Dorothy Arzner, each directed films that explicitly narrativized considerations of appropriate domesticity and the role of women's housework within it. While Arzner's *Craig's Wife* (1936) explicates the melodramatic imperative that ultimately dictates the place of housework in all dramatic accounts of domesticity in the classical Hollywood cinema, Weber's *Too Wise Wives* (1921) provides an earlier look at the transformation in domesticity fully realized in the later film. Both films register changes in appropriate domestic femininity by dramatizing them as moral conflicts.

Lois Weber's *Too Wise Wives* explores the appropriate character of domestic femininity within the affluent bourgeois lifestyle whose values Ivan and his wife are taught to emulate. It addresses the question of where one locates competence and merit in the now wholly performative and symbolic conception of successful femininity. As the pun in the title *Too Wise Wives* indicates, the film's narrative is not concerned with absolute binaries regarding good and bad domesticity so much as with establishing the general boundaries within which appropriate domesticity takes place.

The film opens on Mrs. David Graham, her head bowed over her sewing, as a title explains that she is "the martyred kind of wife who lives only for her husband." Her behavior is contrasted with that of her husband's old flame, Mrs. John Daly, who married a richer man. Sara Daly, though "wholly selfish and a poor housekeeper," has nevertheless "through study and calculation made a very successful wife." While Mrs. Daly knows how to perform to please her husband, Mrs. Graham, "through a very excess of adoring, unselfish love is unable to reason calmly about how to please" hers.

Tellingly, all Mrs. Graham's excessive and misguided attentions have to do with domestic labor. She kneels at her husband's feet as she cleans up the ashes from his "dirty smelly pipe." She knits him a pair of slippers ("his pet abomination") and insists on cooking breakfast for him herself because their cook cannot possibly get it right. Because she is at the stove, she is not at the table waiting to greet her husband when he comes down to breakfast; she rushes in with a plate to serve him, her face all sweaty, and then forgets to take off her apron. Since fried chicken is his favorite food, she has cooked it for him every day for breakfast. His reaction to too much of a good thing—fried chicken again?!—locates the film's message about effective housekeeping not in moral absolutes but in nuance and judgment.

In contrast, Mrs. Daly never enters the kitchen. She is arranging flowers at the breakfast table when her husband comes down, and she has placed a rosebud for his buttonhole next to his newspaper. At breakfast she flirts with her husband, rushing over to kiss him and making eyes at him when he looks up from his paper. Noting that he is visibly disconcerted over the taste of his breakfast, she tells him, "Don't eat anything you don't want, darling." She is a terrible housekeeper, but her husband feels himself "lucky" and is at pains to compliment her on everything she does. When she was dating David Graham and he dropped pipe ashes, she would laugh and say, "Good for the moths, old darling. Do it again!" David appreciated her ability to make a fellow comfortable and thought her "broadminded."

The plot of *Too Wise Wives* involves Sara Daly's ongoing attraction to David Graham. Although she married for money and sees her identity as a loving wife as a "role"—one the film gives ample evidence that she performs very well—she still yearns for David. When she writes him a letter proposing an assignation, it is delivered to Mrs. Graham, who does not open it but fears it portends the worst for her marriage. In the end, David realizes his wife's value when Sara Daly's plans for him come to light; Sara understands that her own husband's love, faith, and pride in her are very dear; and Mrs. Graham has the profound revelation that pleasing her husband has much more to do with attention, flirtation, and femininity than with being a good housekeeper.

In *Too Wise Wives*, questions of the wives' respective housekeeping talents quickly drop out of the picture. The film emphasizes that the husbands' affective needs for their wives exceed their material needs for their wives' housekeeping skills. Although sexual desire is vaguely suggested as a problem, it is subordinated to issues of the men's "comfort" and the women's "broadmindedness." The film's comparison of the two wives ultimately promotes the value of seductive attention and coy feminine performance that is *not* dishonest. The successful wife, rather than producing desire or service, produces seduction and a rapt attention to her husband's ego. Thus the film recounts a morality tale about newly conceived ideas regarding companionate marriage. Arising in the 1920s, this marital model stressed a more encompassing relationship between husbands and wives, in which emotional support, friendship, and companionship were emphasized, rather than the more homosocial, separate sphere arrangements of Victorian marriages. In the context of this transformation, *Too Wise Wives* clearly promotes the value of feminine attention, companionship, and performance in marriage over competency in domestic labor.

Both Blaché's and Weber's films exemplify the tendency of an emergent classical Hollywood style that not only avoids representing housework as a valued type of labor, but also, when domestic labor is an explicit narrative issue, asserts that it is actually *detrimental* to successful domestic life. When housework is not itself a narrative issue, classical films tend to use images of domestic labor for their emotional, symbolic, or moral resonance. In this way the cinema marks a transition similar to that in the nineteenth century between Child's and Beecher's texts and those of the domestic engineers in the early part of the twentieth. But while Weber's *Too Wise Wives* illustrates some of these changes, it lacks the considerations of sexuality and social difference that inform subsequent melodramas. Focusing more specifically on housework than any other classical Hollywood melodrama that I have found, Dorothy Arzner's *Craig's Wife* makes a narrative out of what happens to the housewife in the classical Hollywood cinema.

Griffith's domestic melodramas, saturated with populist notions of the cult of domesticity, and Blaché's and Weber's morality tales about the necessary invisibility of domestic labor provide an important context for *Craig's Wife* (1936), the film I discuss in the remainder of this chapter. During the period in which the play version, written by George Kelly in 1926, then a silent film (1928), and finally Arzner's film were produced, ideas about marriage and domesticity underwent significant transformations as a result of reconceptualizations of women's domestic role.[7] Whereas the perfect woman and wife in Griffith's work forgoes sexuality and leisure for the spiritual, emotional, and material labors of marriage and maternity, and Blaché's and Weber's wives develop symbolic and affective domestic skills, respectively, the condemnation of housekeeping in *Craig's Wife* fully clarifies the paradoxical moral imperatives levied on housewives in commodity culture.

In this respect, Dorothy Arzner as an auteur provides a dramatic contrast with D. W. Griffith. Whereas his prominence in the history of cinema has always been asserted, Arzner's fame derives primarily from her being one of the few women directors in the classical Hollywood cinema.[8] Critical work on both directors tends to read them in relation to their sexual lives, and Arzner is seen to subvert the narrative system Griffith put in place.[9] Certainly her representations of women deviate considerably from his shivering virgins. The primary texts of her oeuvre—*Christopher Strong* (1933), *Craig's Wife* (1936), and *Dance, Girl, Dance* (1940)—have served as the starting points for critical speculations on female authorship,[10] for the problem of recuperation and feminine discourse,[11] and for a reconsideration of the problem of fetishism.[12] I take a somewhat different approach to *Craig's Wife*, seeing Arzner's work and that of Blaché and Weber not in subversive contradistinction to a particular history that excludes them, but as providing a particularly cogent perspective which participates in that history. Thus I consider Arzner's representation of appropriate housekeeping in its specific social-historical context, noting the visual and psychic priorities of domestic femininity endorsed by both this film and its social environment.

The text of *Craig's Wife* actually suggests such a reading by promoting itself as documentation of a certain type of wife. In a scene that presages the film's crisis, Walter Craig's aunt, Miss Austen, attempts to convince him that his wife, Harriet, is dangerous to him. Despite his aunt's many assertions of Harriet's flaws, Walter remains skeptical. Finally she tells him about a conversation she accidentally overheard at a restaurant: "I was lunching in town last week when a man you used to know came in with his wife. They didn't see me. The woman proceeded to tell the man how he should sit down and what to do when he was down and so on. Finally the man said to her, 'Say, who do you think you are, Craig's Wife?'"

Citing the film's title as well as alluding to its protagonist, this incident pointedly gestures to a social world beyond the boundaries of the text it names. From the particular instance of Walter Craig's wife, the film identifies a generalized type—a domineering woman obsessively attached to her home—and proposes its own title as an appropriate label for such women. Reviews written on the film's release acknowledged its extratextual significance and suggested that its social resonance would heighten the film's appeal. The *Variety* critic wrote:

> Every neighborhood has its Mrs. Craig whose husband is a sympathetic concern for other women, and the picture is bound on this score to get considerable box office stimulating chatter. Men will secretly hope that overly meticulous wifes [sic] will see the show and that also should nudge the gate.[13]

The *Motion Picture Herald* reviewer concurred: "Some who witness it see in its principal character a composite portrayal of women they know."[14]

The *Variety* review indicates that the industry trades *explicitly* theorized the relationship between gender roles, representation, and box office draw. The demonization of Harriet Craig and "women like her" provokes social chatter about a certain kind of inappropriate domestic femininity. The paradox of a woman's proper place shapes the narrative's overarching conflict: Harriet Craig's belief that she should be the dominant force in her home is challenged and overturned by the narratively sanctioned view that a wife's place is to love and to be subject to her husband in *his* home. The narrative uses Harriet's obsessive housekeeping to structure this conflict. But if placed and analyzed within the historical context of 1920s and 1930s America, *Craig's Wife* tells a very different story. In my reading the film uses the moral structures of melodrama to stage a "fixed" debate between two historically distinct visions of marriage and domesticity. The historical relationship between past and present visions of domesticity is thereby mystified and effaced; the earlier version, represented by Harriet Craig, becomes an immoral alternative to, rather than the historical antecedent of, the more modern version.

My reading of *Craig's Wife* links the psychic implications of its images of housekeeping and its use of narrative structure and melodrama with images and ideas concerning domesticity drawn from a wider social context. I begin by making some generalizations about Hollywood's visualizations of housework in the classical period. Unlike the early silents and the transitional texts of Griffith, Blaché, and Weber, classical Hollywood films do not present images of housekeeping as a type of work, but instead use these images for their moral, emotional, or symbolic resonance. The examples that follow span six decades and include both studio and independent productions, indicating the prevalence and persistence of this phenomenon. In *The Public Enemy* (1931), director William Wellman heightens the pathos of the finale by cross-cutting between shots of Ma Powers (Beryl Mercer) upstairs, shaking out the sheets and making up the bed for her son, Tom (James Cagney), and shots of Mike Powers (Donald Cook) downstairs, waiting for and finally receiving not his brother but his brother's corpse. The editing underscores the futility of Ma Powers's act and symbolically converts the bedsheet into a winding sheet. In *All That Heaven Allows* (1955), Jane Wyman's character pensively dries a coffee cup as she discusses her romantic troubles with her close friend, played by Agnes Moorehead. Her action, wiping round and round the cup, serves as both a realistic detail and an apt visual metaphor for the trapped, circular movement of her feelings and thoughts. Wyman uses the cup as an "expressive object," turning it into what James Naremore calls a "signifier of feeling."[15] The contemporary film *Sex, Lies, and Videotape* (1989) exploits the stereotype of the sexually frustrated housewife's proclivity for cleaning by depicting Anne (Andie McDowell), who has problems with sex, shining her kitchen faucet with sharp, whiplike gestures and furiously vacuuming her rugs.

In each of these examples, the representation of a housekeeping task serves to convey the emotional state of a character or helps to foster more generally expressive effects in a scene. Classical Hollywood films usually transform images of *any* type of labor into vehicles for emotional or symbolic expression. This kind of transformation, which takes the objective social, political, or economic fact and converts it into an emotional, personal, subjective experience, is, as many film critics and theorists have argued, a fundamental operation of Hollywood films derived from their melodramatic lineage.[16] Images of housekeeping present an exemplary case of the phenomenon, because their iconographic conversion from productive to expressive labor mirrors and reinforces the historical fate of housework: since the industrial revolutions, this labor has been incrementally deprived of any productive economic functions or exchange value. *Craig's Wife* converts this historical change into a moral issue, transforming the value of the housewife's productivity into imperatives about her personality and emotions.

The Importance of Being Affective

The studio press release for Columbia's 1936 version of *Craig's Wife* summarized the film as follows:

> Harriet Craig is a selfish, suave, iron minded wife whose only love is her house which she keeps in meticulous show window fashion. It is her warped idea of respectability and security. Her husband must go outside to smoke. In one way or another, she alienates the affection and devotion of the aunt, her servants, her neighbors and niece. Willful, self-centered, lying and suspicious, she puts her husband into crime that her idea of respectibility might be maintained. Finally she drives her husband from her side to be left a lonely woman in a cold empty house.[17]

This press release articulates a stunning set of equivalences that reveals the industry's part in the paradox of reconciling women to a home into which men and commodity culture have been inserted. Harriet keeps her only love, her home, like a department store window where her husband is not allowed to smoke or relax. Oriented in a particular way toward commodity culture, she makes her home in that image to such an extent that familial and patriarchal relations are alienated.

As the synopsis indicates, the film is explicitly concerned with the role of emotion in marriage. It announces this theme in the opening scene, where we see Harriet (Rosalind Russell) visiting her ailing sister in an out-of-town hospital. Accompanying Harriet is her niece, Ethel, who has abruptly left college and her boyfriend to be by her mother's side. In a highly melodramatic establishing shot, Harriet sits some distance from her sister's bed while Ethel kneels beside it, embracing her mother and weeping. As Ethel enthuses about her upcoming commencement and how proud her mother will be of her in her cap and gown, a close-up reveals the sick woman's eyes filling with tears. Concerned that Ethel is upsetting her mother, Harriet consults a nurse in the corridor: "I'm afraid all this emotion will set her back. . . . Don't you think she'd make a quicker recovery if she didn't have visitors?" The nurse is in complete agreement: "Well, Mrs. Craig, if you'll excuse my saying so, visitors always set patients back." Harriet resolves to leave for home and take her niece with her.

On the train ride back, a conversation reveals that Harriet opposes emotion outside the sickroom as well. Her still considerably distraught niece reveals that she is engaged and very much in love. Harriet remarks that romantic love may be a liability in marriage, a notion Ethel finds appalling. When Ethel remonstrates, "You married Uncle Walter because you loved him, didn't you?" Harriet responds, "Not with any romantic illusions, dear." She tells Ethel that she married "to be independent." Astutely, if inadvertently, suggesting the precariousness of women's economic position in society, she says, "I had no private fortune, no special training. The only road to emancipation for me was through the man I married." For Harriet, romance is absurd and trust of her spouse unnecessary because she discreetly watches over and controls everything her husband does: "It doesn't bother him if he doesn't know." She believes that the destiny of a home should be in a woman's hands rather than her husband's. Ethel finds Harriet's marital management scheme "not quite honest."

The film then introduces Walter Craig. With his wife out of town, Walter goes to play poker with a friend, Fergus Passmore. He finds Fergus slightly drunk and very depressed about his wife, Adelaide, whom he suspects is having an affair. Walter dismisses these suspicions out of hand and suggests to his friend that he get away for a while to clear his head. A cut immediately takes us to a nightclub scene, where we see Adelaide entering arm in arm with another man, a scene that demonstrates Walter's innocence and naïveté. The two conversations—Harriet's with Ethel and Walter's with Fergus—introduce Harriet's and Walter's very different ideas about emotion and marriage. While Walter advocates blind love and trust, Harriet's attitude is much more calculating and businesslike: a woman must protect herself and secure her home, avoiding the caprice of romantic love. The conflicts in the ensuing narrative all revolve around these two very different approaches to domestic relationships.

Images of housekeeping function in the film both to characterize and to criticize Harriet Craig; the narrative sets up an implicit comparison between her skills at managing a house and her abilities as a wife. As a housekeeper, Harriet excels to a fault. An obsessive household manager, she keeps an immaculate home by supervising her servants closely. Her cool detached personality is expressed by the polished surfaces of her home. Although Dorothy Arzner adheres fairly closely to the dialogue of George Kelly's play, she envisions the movie set very differently.[18] Kelly's stage directions call for dark greens and deep browns enlivened by canary yellows and golds, all against "dark, highly polished wood," but Arzner stresses Harriet's fastidiousness by decorating the Craig home primarily in white.[19] White rugs cover the floor, white curtains hang in most of the windows. All of the walls of the interior and exterior of the house are beige or white. White Grecian statues sit on pedestals and atop the telephone table. The woman of the house matches her home; she is always meticulously groomed, and at one point she even dons a gown and styles her hair in a manner that suggests the Grecian motif that dominates her decor.[20] Costume designer Lon Anthony dresses Russell in nothing but beige and white for the duration of the film. The house and the wife both gleam, immaculate, spotless, without visible blemish.

Yet the film renders Harriet's housekeeping skills as pathological and her marriage as a fraud. When she returns home, she walks through rooms and surveys them like a military inspector. She sharply upbraids the housekeeper, Mrs. Harold, for bringing roses into the living room ("There'll be petals all over"), and she scolds the Irish maid for using the front stairs instead of the back. Frowning, she makes a minute adjustment in the position of an urn on the mantle and runs her hand over the top of a table, checking her two extended fingers carefully for dust. When she finds a phone number on a slip of paper next to the phone, she complains of the clutter and grills the housekeeper as to its significance. Learning that her husband went out the night before and left the number where he could be reached, she goes upstairs and surreptitiously calls the telephone company to try to find out where he was. The company will not release the information but relays a record of Harriet's call to the police. This call initiates the film's crisis, for Fergus Passmore has murdered his wife, Adelaide, and killed himself, and Harriet's call potentially implicates Walter in the crime. She later lies to Walter about it, and his discovery of her deceit instigates a confrontation between them that ends their marriage.

Harriet's gaze, as this synopsis suggests, is evaluative, critical. She looks for mistakes, dust, disarray. Although her appearance is very elegant, her authoritative, active gaze aggressively commandeers the space and all the people in her home, positioning them as objects not of her desire or nurturance but of her clinical assessment or disapproval. The film represents Harriet's obsession with her home and her fanatical housekeeping exclusively through tasks of cleaning and straightening. Harriet's concern with cleanliness extends to social matters as well. She fires her Irish maid, Mazie, after finding out that Mazie's boyfriend has stopped in the kitchen for a moment, telling her that she will not stand for having tramps in her home. She threatens to leave Walter if he tells the police that he was at the Passmore residence the night of the murder because she refuses to have her name "dirtied by scandal."

What comes in and goes out of her home is of supreme importance to Harriet. While she has no apparent problem with having female relatives or servants live in or visit, she accuses Walter's aunt of turning her home into a public thoroughfare when the aunt invites a widowed neighbor, Mrs. Frazier, in for a visit. We also learn that she has subtly put an end to visits from Walter's friends. In addition to indicating her need to control and monitor her environment, Harriet's obsessive-compulsive cleanliness signifies a repressed and frigid sexuality. When Walter Craig comes rushing into her bedroom to welcome her home, Harriet is perfunctorily affectionate and playful, but she rebuffs or interrupts her husband's more ardent advances by pointing out that he's mussing the bedspread, wrinkling her clothes, interfering with her unpacking. She practically *sweeps* him out of the room.

The Demonization of Separate Spheres

The visual and dramatic use of cleaning in *Craig's Wife*, juxtaposed with Harriet's lack of emotion and warmth, allows for two related interpretations of its significance within the historical and cultural contexts in which the play and film were produced. The Freudian implications of Harriet's fastidiousness indicate a fear of dirt and contamination related to an abhorrence of sexual contact and intimacy. For audiences in the twenties and thirties, the condemnation of a rigid, controlling, compulsive housewife would resonate with new cultural priorities stressing the importance of sex and romance in marriage. Writing of the attitudinal changes in early twentieth-century American discourses about sex, Beth Bailey asserts that "a celebratory current began to gain strength by the 1920's. Some of the more accepting attitudes toward sex stemmed from the doctrines of popular Freudianism, which seemed to insist that a freer expression of sexuality was necessary for mental health."[21] In looking at marriage during the same period, historian Elaine Tyler May sees a new cultural emphasis on enhancing "domesticity with excitement" in order that the home "revitalize" the man. She finds the new attention to sexuality part of a larger societal shift that increasingly stressed romantic love as the only proper incentive for marriage.[22] *Craig's Wife* deftly uses Harriet's exemplary cleanliness to render her character unsympathetic to an audience, to indicate her sexual and emotional inadequacies as a wife, and to imply that she is mentally unhealthy or "crazy" about her house. The *Variety* review, noting Harriet's "abnormal passion for house-holding at the expense of every other homely and affectionate relationship between man and wife," suggests her pathological sexual character by calling her a "married spinster."[23]

Harriet's cold, controlling behavior is explained, if not forgiven, when she tells Walter that her mother went to an early grave, left penniless and broken-hearted by an unfaithful, improvident husband whom she loved dearly. This anecdote attempts to render Harriet's values and behavior intelligible within the moral universe assumed by the film. Harriet behaves the way she does because she has been emotionally damaged. It is her idiosyncratic family history, not social history, that makes her calculating. Yet prior to this revelation from Harriet's past, Arzner has made her seem genuinely confused by or oblivious to the values held by other characters. When she and Walter confront each other, she tells him quite unabashedly that he has gotten his "share of the bargain" in their marriage. Mortified, he replies that he never considered marriage a bargain and did not know she did. Harriet counters, "You didn't expect me to go into something as important as marriage with my eyes shut, did you?" While the prevailing ethos of the film indicates that a rational, calculating approach to marriage is a dishonest approach, at an earlier moment in American history, what now is seen as Harriet's overriding sin of making a dispassionate decision about her marriage partner would have been difficult for an audience to appreciate as evil or immoral. In making Harriet's attitude evil, the film dehistoricizes pragmatic approaches to marriage, enshrining romantic love as the only possible motivation for it.

Harriet's cleaning can be viewed from another perspective that depersonalizes or politicizes the conflicts I have been describing. Mary Douglas offers an interpretive model that elucidates some of the cultural and symbolic implications of cleaning. Her book *Purity and Danger* investigates notions of pollution, contamination, and dirt as they function in modern as well as primitive societies. She argues that the ritual, productive, symbolic aspects of pollution taboos are obscured in our culture by a scientifically authorized discourse of hygiene and health:

> As we know it, dirt is essentially disorder. There is no such thing as absolute dirt: it exists in the eye of the beholder. If we shun dirt, it is not because of craven fear, still less dread or holy terror. Nor do our ideas about disease account for the range of our behavior in cleaning or avoiding dirt. Dirt offends against order. Eliminating it is not a negative movement, but a positive effort to organize the environment.[24]

Specifically referring to housewives, Douglas observes that the activities of "scrubbing and cleaning" are not performed primarily "to avoid disease." Rather, the housewife in performing these tasks is "separating, placing boundaries, making visible statements about the home" she is creating from "a material house."[25]

Cleaning is a productive process in Douglas's view, a fact that can be discerned from the significance of dirt: "Where there is dirt there is system. Dirt is the by-product of a systematic ordering and classification of matter, in so far as ordering involves rejecting inappropriate elements."[26] These ideas afford another, more socially oriented interpretation of Harriet's cleaning and her regulatory policies concerning who enters her home and who does not and what behaviors are permitted of those allowed entry. If cleaning is a mode of instituting system and order, then Harriet's fastidiousness can be seen not only as an expression of sexual frigidity but also as the means by which she establishes the boundaries and rules of her domain. The system she institutes is based on strict discriminations between what should remain outside her house, what is dirty or dangerous (flowers or organic material, scandal or social dirt, men—excepting her husband—and women who are not related to her and are not servants), and what she allows in it. Her cleaning and her notions of dirt articulate a domestic sphere that is almost exclusively female and familial; its extremity indicates the extremity of her social aspirations: to be left to herself, to have her own world. The character obtains her desire, as in the end she is in possession of her home. But the moral framework of the film depicts her triumph as hollow, defusing the social and political import of her material independence by presenting its attainment in the context of emotional loneliness and suffering. While Harriet's view of domesticity contains the remnants of a different social milieu from that assumed by the film, the narrative uses the character to personalize and condemn, rather than historicize, this alternative point of view. This condemnation hinges on Harriet's inability to feel emotion.

Harriet Craig's abilities to keep or manage a house do not compare in importance to her moral responsibility to care sincerely for her husband, relatives, neighbors, and servants and to maintain a healthy emotional environment in her home. The film uses images of a well-kept house, a paragon of cleanliness and meticulous order, to suggest the cold, barren sterility of Harriet and her home—a home explicitly compared in the narrative to a hospital, a morgue, and, in the press release for the film, a department store. The message of the film is that even though Harriet is a superlative housekeeper, she is no homemaker. Her belief that the destiny of a home should rest in a woman's hands recalls the ideology of separate spheres, but the film condemns this belief by representing her character as territorial, selfish, dishonest, and presumptuous, interested in possessions but not emotions. Yet, if we strip aside these moralistic trappings, the character transgresses in regarding her home as a workplace and her marriage as a contract or bargain. Thus, in certain respects, she embodies the values and attitudes of a prior social era which has now been successfully displaced by a more expressive vision of the home and domesticity. Harriet's view of domesticity, like her Grecian decor, is antiquated, a thing of the past.

By framing its moral in terms of domestic labor, *Craig's Wife* tells the story of what has happened to the middle-class home and its keeper in consumer culture since the 1920s—in the wake of the domestic engineering movement of the previous two decades. For that reason it is worth recounting these socioeconomic changes in greater detail. In the early decades of the twentieth century, the increased emphasis on consumption coincided with and in some ways participated in the shift I noted earlier in the character of marriage and the home. "Into the twentieth century, marriage remained a life goal and domesticity a center of women's existence, but ideals focused more on man than God," as historian Phyllis Palmer observes. By then "women were encouraged to be beautiful (and youthful), sexually alive (but not immodest), and intelligently charming (but not overly intellectual)." Whereas the nineteenth-century housewife lived in and managed "a female world" that operated as a counterpart to her husband's, "the modern woman organized her life much more around men and heterosexual relations."[27] In the 1920s the phrase "companionate marriage" came into common use to describe marriages sustained not by the rigid constraints of moral social codes or religious dictates, but by the more personal bonds of "mutual affection, sexual attraction." Couples married and, more important, stayed together for love. "The goal of marriage was no longer financial security or a nice home," write Stephen Mintz and Susan Kellogg, "but emotional and sexual fulfillment and compatibility."[28]

Public discourse and speculation on the properties of a good wife signified the widespread acceptance of the ideal of the companionate marriage. The twenties saw a dramatic inflation of public interest in women's emotional role in the home while at the same time the importance ascribed to their actual labor waned. As Glenna Matthews observes, "Recognizing that the home was no longer a center of production, experts argued that it was uniquely suited to foster emotional health in an industrial society. . . . The housewife thus became the party in charge of psychological adjustment."[29] Magazine articles and advertising focused on the emotional components of woman's role as mother and wife. Matthews remarks that the 1920s revealed "an ever-increasing self-consciousness about the home's expressive function."[30] In cultural representations the housewife's responsibilities shifted from tangible domestic chores to intangible emotional tasks. Her job was now expressed in terms of her ability to love and nurture her husband and family.

Advertising, the rhetorical voice of consumer culture, played a large part in promoting and publicizing the emotional role of the wife, home, and private life. The message advertisers sold reflected changes in the notions of the individual and the self that arose from profound economic changes. T. J. Jackson Lears argues that the social transformations of the nineteenth century resulted in a crisis of the self that was endemic to the early twentieth century. This crisis stemmed from the secularization of Protestantism, from urbanization, and from technological development, all of which led to a pervasive sense of unreality among the American bourgeoisie.[31] The new bureaucracies that dominated business exacerbated this "decline of autonomous selfhood" because "an interdependent and increasingly corporate economy circumscribed autonomous will and choice."[32] As traditional institutions and social structures such as religion and community lost their ability to apprehend the position of the self in the modern world, an emphasis arose on the authenticity of the individual's private life and on self-realization and fulfillment. A "therapeutic ethos" articulated private life as a healthy escape from a completely rationalized and oppressive workplace by focusing on the importance of intense personal and emotional experiences.[33]

Lears asserts that advertisers quickly assimilated and perpetuated this cultural discourse, which shaped their new, non-rational advertising strategies. Historian Susan Strasser concurs. Whereas ads were initially designed to inform consumers about products, in the early decades of the twentieth century they were increasingly intended to solicit and manipulate the consumer's desires and fears.[34] Lears notes that the shift in tactics reflected a change in advertisers' perceptions of the public. They came to view—or, better, to interpellate—their audiences not as "strong-willed, rational beings, but as impulsive and susceptible to suggestion." Ads offered audiences "not information but feeling."[35] While Lears points out that irrational, emotional appeals were used to advertise products for everyone, he also notes that women's cultural position let them in for a substantial share of emotional manipulation. Advertisers increasingly invoked the private sphere and the quality of private life in order "to promise the maintenance of domestic harmony through intelligent consumption." They went so far as to create and promote maternal or wifely guilt by threatening dire consequences to the family of the housewife who did not use a particular product.[36] The "therapeutic ethos" used by advertisers thus articulated private life, and specifically housekeeping tasks, in terms of *emotional* rewards and threats, suggesting to the housewife that her choice of crackers or soap was a measure of her love and concern for her family.

Through the example of advertising, Lears illustrates the cultural character of the therapeutic ethos and suggests one means by which it spread. He details how the social and economic changes implicit in the consumer revolution instigated the development of a secular morality predicated on concerns about psychic, emotional, and physical health and the achievement of personal fulfillment.

What gets left out of Lears's account is the different ways his therapeutic ethos affected men and women and members of different social classes. The changes taking place in the economy in relation to middle-class men compensated them with an increased patriarchal presence in the home (their therapeutic ethos). Their wives were compensated for the loss of their own sphere and its authority through a public commodity culture (their therapeutic ethos). In both instances the private was penetrated by the public, making the personal and emotional experiences occurring in the home into a mass public spectacle. This exchange explains how the epochal changes taking place in the male-dominated business sector ended up setting the terms for *women's* films—that is, how the loss of *male* self in the world led to an overinvestment in the *female* self in the home. *Craig's Wife* acts out the effects of these transformations by condemning a housewife who refuses emotional spectacle in her cold, controlling attitude toward her home and her commodities.

Harriet Craig is a descendent of the Victorian "angel in the house," the protector of a domain articulated as separate and aloof from an outside world that threatens it. She herself does not do housework; she manages the home, its atmosphere, and those who work within it. Time, however, has robbed the angel of her spiritual and material functions, and, as an upper-middle-class housewife, she has little real work to do. Borrowing an image from the past, the film manages a thinly veiled class critique through the depiction of Harriet's inordinate privilege and her haughty attitude toward those who are subordinate to her. The film's screenwriter sharpens the critique and gives it a very timely resonance in one of the changes she makes to the plot of Kelly's play.[37] In Kelly's version, Harriet fires Mazie because she leaves raffle tickets on the mantle. In the film, Harriet fires the maid because her boyfriend has visited the kitchen to say hello. Harriet proclaims that she "can't have every *tramp* that comes along in her kitchen." The allusion to the depression is unmistakable. In populist America in the 1930s, Harriet's affluence and her attitude would have been particularly vulnerable to criticism; thus Harriet's autonomy, her belief that a home is a woman's place, is wedded to a selfish isolationism and a sense of class privilege at a time when that privilege would have been viewed as especially offensive and obnoxious. Of course, the critique is very limited in scope. It is not a class critique but a critique of a certain type of woman in that class. Harriet is evil because of her manner, not because of her money; by contrast, Walter Craig is represented as the soul of generosity and benevolence. In addition, the maid and her boyfriend are obviously in love; they kiss and are affectionate with each other. Harriet's derision at the boyfriend's intrusion into her home expresses her inability to sanction romantic affection for anyone, especially her servants.

The Melodramatic Imperative

Though ultimately a very problematic example of the form, *Craig's Wife* adheres to certain obvious conventions of melodrama. It tells a tale whose conflict and resolution involve the struggle, vindication, and recognition of a moral principle. Peter Brooks asserts that this revelation of the "moral occult" is especially important to the melodramatic form because such narratives are "about virtue made visible and acknowledged."[38] Yet *Craig's Wife* makes visible and celebrates something more often associated with melodramatic expression than with specifically moral or ethical issues. The measure by which all the characters in *Craig's Wife* are judged is their ability to feel emotions and to care about others, and by this measure only Harriet fails. The extent to which the film supports emotion or sentiment as a value regardless of the moral actions of individual characters becomes clear in its comparative assessment of Adelaide and Harriet. Despite her adultery, despite the fact that she "drives" her husband to murder her and kill himself, Adelaide holds a more secure moral position in the film than Harriet does. Walter tells Harriet reprovingly, "There was one thing about Adelaide. She wrecked herself and Fergus because she loved somebody."

Cast in a melodramatic narrative, the pragmatic, contractually based notion of marriage and domesticity represented through Harriet's character is immoral and dishonest; Harriet plays the villain of the piece. Yet she is not a typical villain by any means, nor is *Craig's Wife* a typical melodrama. Harriet neither kills nor harms anyone, and if she is a harsh employer, she still pays her servants "better than anyone in town." The plot structure of the film is also unique in that typically melodramatic events and situations—the Passmore murder-suicide, the victimization of Harriet's mother—occur off-screen and figure only marginally in the comparatively undramatic and benign story of the Craig marriage. The most dramatic moments in their narrative occur when Walter smashes a vase, scattering shards everywhere, or when he dirties an ashtray. The marital struggles in *Craig's Wife* are waged not over adultery or betrayal but at the level of propriety, order, and cleanliness. Inverting the proclivity of melodramatic sets to express the inexpressible through pronounced excess in the mise-en-scène, the Craig home is excessively spare, austere, rigid, and bland. Love, passion, and devotion, the film suggests, are both messy and moral. To be clean and untouchable is to be sick or dead.

Craig's Wife, in indicting its heroine for not loving, feeling, and suffering, indicts her for not partaking of a melodramatic sensibility. Harriet views her private life in professional, economic, "public" terms; she considers her marriage and housekeeping pragmatically, in relation to her financial situation and her lack of any other employment opportunities. In the end she errs not because of her actions or fastidious household management—which might be more adequately critiqued in the character of a comic shrew—but because she seems incapable of "unpremeditated feeling." While, as Christine Gledhill observes, melodrama has always stressed "unpremeditated feeling as an index of moral status and social value,"[39] in *Craig's Wife* that index is dissociated from any substantive moral questions and becomes a social value in and of itself. Thomas Elsaesser remarks that melodrama, whether employed to conservative or subversive political ends, always tends to interiorize and personalize "what are primarily ideological conflicts."[40] He finds this tendency endemic to popular culture's approach to social problems. What is personalized in Harriet Craig is her inability to capitulate to this process. Thus *Craig's Wife* illustrates the extent to which the melodramatic imagination, and, by inference, popular culture, is complicit with an exclusively expressive view of the home and housekeeping.

Industrial and consumer revolutions restructure social geography such that the home becomes the primary, private context in opposition to the public market. The cultural sensibilities described by Brooks's notion of the melodramatic imagination and by Lears's idea of the therapeutic ethos derive from this opposition, promoting and perpetuating a moralistic worldview that can see the family, housewives, and the home only in privative, emotional terms. Such sensibilities highlight the primacy of personal experience and the private individual, the everyday and the emotional, positioning these aspects of life as an antidote, either moral or therapeutic, to the vapidity and amorality of the workplace. Lears connects the therapeutic ethos to the rise of the culture of consumption, while Elsaesser finds melodrama to be a pervasive mode in popular culture texts. The similarities in their work point to the close conceptual and dramatic affinities that persist between the commodity rhetoric of the marketplace and culture industry narratives. In the purview of both, housekeeping becomes, must become, a moral and emotional rather than a practical issue. Any other perspective on domesticity is comprehensible only as a moral transgression or as a form of mental or emotional sickness.

Although many of these tendencies are exhibited in D. W. Griffith's work, *Craig's Wife* indicates how affirmative expressions of feminine sexuality become visually insinuated in the moralistic discourses that shape social notions of appropriate womanhood. Whereas Griffith keeps the expression of unpremeditated feelings strictly segregated from those of a knowing feminine sexuality, *Craig's Wife* collapses the two: feminine sexuality *is* emotion. Furthermore, and most significantly, these values are explicitly contrasted with good housekeeping. Harriet Craig's "professionalism" is negatively imaged. Domesticity, explicitly assessed as work, is condemned as cold and unfeeling. This film explicates how women's housekeeping duties are completely subsumed and masked by gender imperatives to be emotional, moral, and (not too) sexual—imperatives vitally linked to the economic necessity that women be nonproductive consumers. Both generically and as a specific text, *Craig's Wife* participates in changing cultural discourses concerning marriage, sex, and romance by perpetuating an ethos wherein emotion and sexuality have assumed moral proportions and romantic love has become the only honest incentive for marriage.

The Servant Problem

The moralized imperatives of maintaining a pleasing appearance, affect, and sexuality levied on middle-class white housewives serve other purposes than just those of consumer culture. Tellingly, *Craig's Wife* organizes its allegory of feminine failure in relation to issues of social difference. The white sets, appointments, and wardrobe of Harriet Craig inadvertently if astutely literalize the pervasive bourgeois whiteness of classical Hollywood domesticity. Yet that whiteness results not from the exclusion of other differences so much as from their placement within and in relation to a "white" household. As with most Hollywood domiciles, the Craig home includes members marked by economic, ethnic, and, inferentially, religious difference: the servants. Both the maid, Mazie, and the housekeeper, Mrs. Harold, are Irish, and both live in. The Irish servant, like the African American one, is a stereotype served up with regularity in Hollywood. Yet the servants in *Craig's Wife* are not representationally normative in either a historical or a narrative sense. Thus the film's use of them clearly subordinates social difference (class, ethnicity, religion) to a "universalized" gender morality nevertheless bounded by race.

In America by the 1920s the majority of domestic servants everywhere but in the South were African American women, and they tended to do day work rather than live in. The reasons were twofold. First, Americans who employed servants were suspicious of the eastern Europeans who now provided the largest pool of immigrants seeking work as domestic laborers. Second, many more non-service jobs (in factories, businesses, and so on) were now open to women who had previously done housework (Irish, Swedish, and German immigrants and native white women) but were not available to African American women.[41] Thus the live-in Irish servants in *Craig's Wife* are not expressive of normative experience during the period in which the play was written and adapted to film.[42] Yet rather than fault the play and the film for their failure to "reflect" their times, I prefer to draw attention to the particular effects the narrative generates in its use of Irish live-in servants: basically, it addresses and reconciles gender norms to difference within an all-white household. These effects emerge in relation to the role the servants play in the narrative of *Craig's Wife*.

Unlike the nameless and featureless servants in so many films who take coats, serve dinner, open doors, and disappear, Mrs. Harold and Mazie play particularly important roles in this narrative. Their importance is signaled by the fact that the film begins with them: the opening shot is a close-up of Mrs. Harold shouting "Mazie!" in horrified outrage as she sees the maid touching one of her mistress's treasured vases. Later in the film, Harriet's dismissal of Mazie for visiting with her boyfriend in the kitchen is a crucial plot event that leads to Mrs. Harold's resigning her post in the household as well. Significantly, Mrs. Harold leaves with Miss Austen,

Mr. Craig's aunt, to travel with her on a trip around the world. Thus the housekeeper is assimilated into the family at the same time that Harriet loses all her familial connections, to be left alone in an empty house. The moral that the film delivers through this turn of events has to do with the way it articulates differences among women and designates which of these differences matter.

Harriet, like her niece Ethel, Miss Austen, and her neighbor Mrs. Frazier, is financially comfortable, if not downright well-to-do. Her similarity with these women can be contrasted with her difference from her servants. The mistress-servant relationship distinguishes these women socially and economically, and is undergirded by ethnic and religious differences as well. Yet the film works very hard to negate the significance of these differences and to promote another standard of differentiation altogether. In that Harriet Craig pays her servants exceptionally well, the film shifts the location of her villainy from her economic relationship with her servants (her class difference) to her affective treatment of them (her failure as a woman). While all the other women in the film, whether of the servant or the mistress class, are cordial, affectionate, and emotional, Harriet is cold, pragmatic, and controlling. She therefore does not possess the symbolic affective domestic virtues that secure social and economic hierarchies even as they privatize and efface them. Thus the film's denouement, as Mrs. Harold is assimilated into the extended family and Harriet is excommunicated from it, teaches that for women it is emotion, not property or money, that is the distinction that counts.

Within the film's narrative structure, the servants' identity as Irish rather than African American, as live-in rather than as day workers, serves a variety of functions. With live-in servants, different social classes can be represented as living under the same roof; the home therefore effectively allegorizes the nation pulling together in times of economic duress (the depression). More significantly, the assimilation of the Irish housekeeper into the family marks one position among the oscillating variables that define racial difference in America. Whereas at various earlier moments in American history the German, the Irish, the Italian, and the Russian "races" were sufficiently distinct from "native whites" to be the objects of discriminatory racialized violence, here the film imagines the home/nation within the bounds of a generalized whiteness whose internal differences (class, ethnicity, religion) are related and subordinated to a presumably universalized gender morality. Mrs. Harold's assimilation into the family/nation because she is a better companion, friend, and woman than Harriet denotes that Irishness is no longer sufficiently distinct from whiteness to preclude Mrs. Harold from being favorably compared with Mrs. Craig.

While *Too Wise Wives* generates moral standards for appropriate domestic femininity by comparing two women within a homogeneous socioeconomic milieu (bourgeois, white), *Making of an American Citizen* measures the domestic behavior of a male immigrant against that of American men of all classes. *Craig's Wife* is the female corollary to *Making of an American Citizen*. It uses emotion, which it identifies as something all women must have, to construct commonality or horizontal relations among women of all classes in the same way that the earlier film uses citizenship to construct horizontal relations among men of all classes.[43] *Craig's Wife* establishes this commonality by comparing the emotional competency of a white upper-middle-class housewife with that of her working-class servants, a measure by which the housewife fails. Thus, unlike Ivan, who aspires to citizenship but is always represented as lacking in relation to all the other American citizens he encounters, Mrs. Harold and Mazie already belong to a group (women) within which they are identified as superior to Mrs. Craig, even though she obviously outranks them in terms of class and ethnicity.

Specifically, Mazie, Mrs. Harold, Miss Austen, and Mrs. Frazier, to a greater or lesser degree, all understand more about Walter Craig's needs and behave more affectionately toward him than his wife does. Thus feminine emotion, besides being morally imperative for women, also constitutes a kind of knowledge or affective wisdom that only Harriet lacks. Within this representational context one has only to think of the characterizations of African American mammies and maids in the classical cinema, the rote insistence on their naïveté and ignorance, to imagine the radical implications of casting an African American housekeeper or maid in this film or play.[44] The problem would derive not from the housekeeper's being familialized per se, but rather from the portrayal of maid and housekeeper as both wiser than and morally superior to a white woman. *That* narrative would not be told in Hollywood cinema until Douglas Sirk's *Imitation of Life* in 1959, simultaneous with the civil rights movement. *Craig's Wife* demonstrates that, in 1936, the range of differences across which gender remained constant constructed whiteness as a limit. The racialized other, though positioned as relative and subject to universalized gender norms, nevertheless remained outside the differences these norms contained—outside the "white" family and, hence, socially sanctioned and recognized sexual relations.[45]

As in the pedagogical housekeeping texts of the nineteenth century after Child, the servant problem looms large among the significant concerns of Hollywood domesticity, whether it is narratively emphasized or not. In each case the problem of the servant in the home provides a ready allegory for the problem of difference in the nation, whether that difference is economic, ethnic, racial, or religious. The role of the white middle- or upper-class mistress in the master-servant dyad is to ameliorate the absolutely hierarchical economic and social relations of servitude by familializing them, giving them a personal and affectionate dimension. *Craig's Wife* indicates that the stakes involved in white bourgeois women's affective domestic femininity could not be higher. Not only does this gender construction organize the significance of marked and unmarked social differences, but also it does so by sentimentalizing unequal property and economic relations around a universal gender norm that makes affect a precondition, and therefore a moral rather than material justification, for consumption and class rise.

The films I have discussed in this chapter demonstrate how cinematic representations of a sentimentalized and/or symbolic domestic femininity organize relations among male American citizens, dictate affective priorities between bourgeois husbands and wives, and establish gender norms as the implicit basis for the construction of "whiteness" as a racial category that suppresses its own internal differences. Each film generates these effects by promoting the suppression of women's domestic labor as a *moral value* related to the housewife's identity as a leisured creature who pleases her husband, who both serves and performs his affective needs, and who looks lovely as she effects her "sincere" performances.

Significantly, each of these films was directed by a woman; each marks a moment (short silent, feature silent, feature sound) in the development of the classical film form; and together they chart the representation of domestic femininity before and after women achieved citizenship. *Making of an American Citizen*'s representation of domestic femininity is concerned solely with dictating the symbolic means by which every male citizen in America stands in the same relation to the nation and the state, figured through his domestic relations with his wife. In contrast, the latter two films, one coming a year after women achieved suffrage, the other sixteen years later, are both concerned with domesticity as a means of establishing homogeneity among women. Weber's *Two Wise Wives* limits its gender homogenization by class, as she considers only two women of the upper-middle class who have sufficient economic means to effect a leisured, emotive femininity. Yet that femininity explicitly overrides these women's public activities. Although both women attend the same "Women's Social and Political Club" lecture, their interests there are depicted as wholly personal—assessing each other's appearance and engaging in small talk, which of course reveals an utter naïveté about politics. Thus the relevant similarities among affluent women are limited, significantly, to their affective capacities, whether at home or in the public sphere. *Craig's Wife* extends the gender franchise and the right, as well as the imperative, to emote much farther, encompassing all social classes, while remaining within the expanded boundaries of "whiteness."

Blaché's, Weber's, and Arzner's films about domesticity are significant not just because of the films themselves, but in relation to their directors' careers within the industry. Ironically, my point is not that, as women directors, they were different, but that they were part and parcel of the transformations in the industry precisely through its representation of women and domesticity. And because they were highly successful, if also later overlooked, they provide a template with which to measure different periods in film history between 1896 and 1943. Blaché first owned her own company and then shared ownership of two subsequent companies with her husband until the demise of their enterprises and most other independents in 1919.[46] Lois Weber wrote, directed, and sometimes starred in highly successful silents for Gaumont and then for Universal, where she was "the top salaried director of the silent era," until her didactic style lost popularity in the mid-twenties. If her success was considered "unprecedented," her decline was somewhat like that of Griffith himself.[47] Dorothy Arzner was also successful and prolific, directing seventeen features, most box office successes, for four major studios—Columbia, Paramount, RKO, and MGM—in the heyday of the studio era.[48]

Although film criticism initially identified female directors for their "difference" and exclusion, these three directors are notable for a high degree of autonomy and gendered self-consciousness during the period leading up to and through the consolidation of the studio system. While Blaché ran her own companies for most of her career, Universal "sponsored, built, and provided Weber with her own studio far from the bustling lot."[49] Though Arzner never had her own studio, she once remarked, in relation to her belief that the director of a film had to have total control, "I threatened to quit each time I didn't get my way, but no one ever let me walk out."[50] Each director noted during her career how her gender contributed in significant ways to her filmmaking abilities. For example, Blaché believed that women's superior knowledge of the emotions made them better film directors than men. Arzner felt that a male director could not bring a woman's viewpoint to the screen.[51] The three films I have examined reveal the extent to which these women participated in bringing domestic discourses into relation with seemingly more "public" ones. But it is the fact that they were successful and somewhat autonomous within the industry that matters most insofar as it positions female authorship within pivotal moments in public discourse. It is important to note, then, that at every moment in the discourse on domesticity—from the nineteenth-century domestic housekeeping manuals to the feminist films I discuss in part III—women have been both authors and objects of knowledge.

Thus Hollywood housekeeping was not just a man's job; but the differences that women directors brought to this topic and system, while telling, were also part of the same system. D. W. Griffith's populist valorization of women's labor presents Lillian Gish, comely with a broom, sweeping up a homey barnyard. *Craig's Wife* signals emphatically that a housewife's cultural duties are less involved with sweeping than with being swept away, as romantic love provides the aura that mystifies even as it stimulates relations between home and market. If women are to be consumers, they must do so passionately, selflessly, with no trace of avarice in their choice of or affection for their husbands. The test of or excuse for this system lies in the result of being swept away: maternity. In the next chapter I consider the inherent paradox of maternal melodramas insofar as their family discourse places the mother between husband and daughter, between money and love.

SIX

The Labor of Maternal Melodramas

Converting Angels to Icons

> It has come about that obviously productive labour is in a peculiar degree derogatory to respectable women. . . .
>
> THORSTEIN VEBLEN

The Hollywood maternal melodrama flourished in a period of sustained economic crisis beginning with the depression and persisting through the national deprivation for the war effort in the forties. At the outset of this period, the genre acquired a specifically American character, eliminating the European influence that had dominated it in the twenties.[1] Reflecting the increasing nationalism and isolationism pervasive in Hollywood overall, maternal melodramas also registered changing or problematic relations among gender, labor, and national identity precipitated by these economic crises. Unlike the melodramas I have considered thus far, which either assume or participate in constructing a homogeneous notion of "woman," these maternal melodramas locate significant social differences within that relationship where we would least expect to find them: between mothers and daughters. In each instance these differences, of class and race specifically, are structured through the mother's and daughter's very different relationships to household labor.

Just as Lydia Child and other nineteenth-century female authors prescribed nationalist, market-resistant tactics of accumulation for the American housewife as the United States adopted and adapted to a market economy, so the maternal melodramas I examine in this chapter prescribe their version of the role women, mothers, and the domicile should play in another epochal moment: the economic crises of late capitalism. This chapter thus signals a major transformation in the predominant cultural view of women. The nineteenth-century construction of women as angels changed to one featuring their central role as icons in the twentieth century. The domestic discourses I have examined indicate how the class-based attention to white housewives' ethereal, quasi-religious identity and appearance in the earlier period laid the groundwork for their morally inflected iconic function in the twentieth. While the earlier vision of women was promulgated in a body of knowledge produced by and for women, the latter arose from within the first and most predominant form of mass entertainment. Iconic domestic femininity linked mass entertainment to the emerging commodity culture, as is evident in the connections that developed in the first several decades of the twentieth century between the cosmetics, clothing, and housewares industries and the movies.[2] We have seen how the housekeeping manuals of the nineteenth century indicate the ways in which distinctions between public and private spheres and class and racial demarcations were generated and organized around the benevolent white middle-class housewife. The chapters in this section chronicle how the same figure organized a primarily visual reorientation of public and private that was amenable to the needs and social organization of late capitalism.

D. W. Griffith's films exemplify the issues and problems at stake in representations of women in the transformation of angels to icons. Both domestic labor and overt sexuality were key representational problems for the movies, the former because it did not accord with the pace and pleasure of an entertainment medium and the latter because it challenged prevalent Victorian morality with regard to women. The films of Alice Guy Blaché, Lois Weber, and Dorothy Arzner show how moral imperatives concerning affect and appearance replaced domestic labor in determining the melodramatic housewife's function. In each narrative, that function is finally to organize and subsume all other social differences under that of gender. Arzner's *Craig's Wife* also demonstrates how emotion was used to moralize women's sexuality at the same time that sexuality and emotion were first tied in crucial ways to women's roles as consumers.

Whereas *Craig's Wife* expresses ambivalence about women's domestic labor and isolation in the home, the films I discuss in this chapter are ambivalent about women's position as mothers instead of wives, as producers instead of consumers. They resolve their ambivalence about women's productivity in the direction of women's function as images or icons—for one another, for male admirers, for the film audience, and within the commodity scene. Produced in the classical mode of film narrative, these texts make use of the mother-daughter relation to cathect intensely and sentimentalize their economic meditations. Although all the films I discuss have been the subject of much feminist scholarship, the signficance of domestic and paid labor within them has been held secondary to considerations of gender.[3] My analysis attempts to invert that hierarchy.

John Stahl's *Imitation of Life* (1934), King Vidor's *Stella Dallas* (1937), and Michael Curtiz's *Mildred Pierce* (1945) all make salient use of household skills within melodramatic narratives of female class rise. A staple of melodrama, the tale of class rise usually involves a man entering a set of relations in the public sphere; the backwardness associated with the home he leaves behind is productive of intense pathos. Where women are the protagonists, class rise occurs *through* the home and privatized affective relations rather than by getting out of and beyond them. Such narratives explicitly engage modern cultural beliefs concerning gender and labor by bringing women and their love into explicit relation with what are characterized as public and masculine concerns: work, money, ambition, and success. The moral structure of melodrama renders these narratives prescriptive; they dictate what sorts of behaviors, beliefs, and motivations are and are not acceptable for women in a cultural moment marked by dire economic straits.

In all of these films, for example, female ambition for economic improvement, in and of itself, is anathema to notions of appropriate femininity. As *Craig's Wife* indicates, changing social mores concerning romantic love subjected women to strict moral censure if they acknowledged and tried to exploit romantic love for financial security, even if marriage was, as Harriet Craig describes it, their "only road to financial independence." In *Stella Dallas* the heroine marries up, consciously manipulating her sexuality and feigning domestic skills to improve her social position, tactics that presage her unsuitability for the class to which she aspires. Although marriage is specifically related to class for women, both *Craig's Wife* and *Stella Dallas* indicate the paradox at the heart of the bourgeois woman's proper relation to financial well-being: she can have no explicit ambition or desire for it, though her femininity absolutely depends upon it. Recounting feminized Horatio Alger stories, whether failed or not, each of the films I discuss in this chapter uses maternity and housekeeping to justify the heroine's ambition, the former serving as motivation and the latter as the labor that leads to success. In each, an absent or inadequate husband and father compels the maternal protagonist either to parlay her skills into a cash-producing enterprise or to displace her own social ambitions onto her daughter. Thus each narrative distributes activities of production and consumption, ambition and self-sacrifice, labor and love—activities usually divided by gender and public versus private spheres, at least for the middle class—through or across the mother-daughter couple. All of the films manipulate this couple to negotiate the vexed ideological terrain of women as economic agents in this particular historical moment.

Unlike maternal melodramas involving a son (for example, *Blonde Venus*, 1932; *Madame X*, 1920, 1937, 1966; *Letter from an Unknown Woman*, 1948), in which a social fall, a separation, or a death divides mother and child before the middle of the film, those involving daughters often examine the problems of pathological closeness and lack of separation. Many critics have explored the psychoanalytic implications of such narratives. But the questions that animate my discussions involve how and why these films formulate a split between the mother and daughter. In each case the answers involve appropriate social roles for women of different classes and races, their relationships to consumption and work, and the social and economic function of the home. The mother-daughter trope organizes other uneasy proximities treated by the narrative; that is to say, the inevitable separations that occur at the culmination of these stories put a safe distance between these other issues figured in and around the biological and social closeness of mothers and daughters. By invoking household skills that then become income-generating activities, the films split hairs; housework becomes "not work" in relation to the "work" that earns a living. And earning a living for all of these mothers has a tremendous affective price. Juxtaposed to mothers' ability to work is their ability both to love and to consume, activities the films frequently align.

The role of domestic labor, especially its relation to maternity, functions very differently in these melodramas than it did in Griffith's films. Rather than hard work visually signifying the integrity, virtue, and maternal ability of the female characters, in these films women's expertise at sewing, cooking, and cleaning is represented much more ambivalently. The dichotomies that Griffith employs, whereby labor is opposed to leisure, maternity to sexuality, and chaste looks and appearances to glamorous, highly sexualized gazes and display, suggest the reason for this ambivalence. Hollywood promotes its obvious commitment to leisure, sexuality, voyeuristic looking, and spectacular display and appearance by using maternity and sentimentalized looks and appearances to imbue leisure, sexuality, and spectacle with positive moral value.

The binary element celebrated by Griffith but not present in these later melodramas is domestic labor as an inherently moral and laudable activity. Instead these films make use of the equation between benevolent looking and looking good in relation to women characters, but in a considerably altered form. Now these visual positions are distributed across a melodramatic field shaped by very different values from those that animated Griffith, one of which is the belief that women must be relatively self-indulgent consumers. These maternal melodramas are particularly interesting for the ways in which they manipulate the value of the image and the look within narratives ostensibly concerned with women's economic agency as wage earners or domestic producers of some kind. While motherhood serves to motivate the heroines' ambition and success, the self-sacrifice and denial of desire inherent in the maternal ideal potentially threatens the consumer impulse. These films attempt to resolve the paradox of women's economic agency and the problematic differences between women by evaluating women's production and consumption within an overarching ethics of the visual. In the end, the films promote themselves and the commodity scene in general by suggesting that sometimes women must be satisfied with just being or having an image.

In this chapter I examine how and to what purpose three films enact the split between mother and daughter: as class difference in *Stella Dallas*; as racialized role and locational distinctions in *Imitation of Life*; and as genre difference in *Mildred Pierce*. Each particular split prescribes values for mothers that involve irresolvable paradoxes in relation to financial necessity: that appearances should be valued over industry and ambition, but only if these appearances are genuine (*Stella Dallas* and *Imitation of Life*); that in gaining the public world as producers, women risk losing their families, their homes, their lovers, and their daughters, even if they would have lost them to financial ruin anyway (all three films); that women cannot be wives, mothers, and workers, they cannot have it all, even if historical circumstances seem to demand that they do (all three films).

The economic crises of this particular period posed a significant challenge to the gendered social geography and roles that had heretofore functioned so efficiently. Maternal melodramas express and contain the implications of this duress in the pathos of mothers and daughters torn apart by conflicts between love and money. In a vale of tears, these conflicts are resolved in a very self-reflexive direction: for women, success lies in affect, consumption, and a thrall to images.

Taste Tests: Stella Dallas's Clever Maternity

What we learned . . . was how the goods of that world of privilege might be appropriated, with the cut and fall of a skirt, a good winter coat, with leather shoes, a certain voice; but above all with clothes, the best boundary between you and a cold world.

CAROLYN STEEDMAN, *Landscape for a Good Woman* (1986)

That's not a woman, it's a Christmas tree.

Stella Dallas

King Vidor's *Stella Dallas* (1937), adapted from Olive Higgins Prouty's 1923 novel of the same name, tells several stories of class rise and fall, that of the eponymous heroine constituting the heart of the narrative. Written in the prosperous twenties, the novel (like the film later adapted from it) imbues Stella Dallas's character with an outspoken, fun-loving sexuality which she flagrantly exploits to snare a husband of a much higher class position than her own. Thus the narrative embeds new social attitudes and feminine behaviors characteristic of all social classes in the twenties — a more hedonistic and explicit female sexuality oriented toward the use of cosmetics and other self-marketing skills — in an ambitious, explicitly working-class character.[4] Stella indirectly refers to these aspects of her character by frequently mentioning the fact that she has "stacks of style." The film explores the connections between class and femininity precisely in the register of appearance, clothing, and "style" in ways that ultimately equate women's domestic skills with bad taste.

The film opens with young Stella Martin (Barbara Stanwyck) standing in front of the dilapidated worker's cottage where she lives with her family, trying to catch Stephen Dallas's (John Boles's) eye by posing with a book of love poems. Although this ploy fails, ambitious Stella does manage to marry the very well heeled but down-on-his-luck Dallas. The film then focuses on Stella's relationship with her daughter, Laurel, after her marriage to Stephen falls apart. Trouble arises in Laurel and Stella's relationship because of their distinct differences in taste, manner, and appearance. Stella's attempts to promote Laurel's social standing by sending her to the best schools and taking her to fancy resorts are continually hampered by her own inability to fit in with refined society. Stella's garish clothing and brash manner alienate the cultivated set that Laurel moves in quite comfortably. When Stella finally realizes that she is the greatest obstacle to Laurel's social success — specifically, her social manner and behavior threaten Laurel's blossoming romance with a very wealthy young man — she feigns a romantic interest in a dissipated old friend whom Laurel despises and tells her daughter that she wants her to go live with her father. Heartbroken, Laurel falls for this subterfuge. The film ends with Laurel's marriage to her beau; outside on the street Stella watches through a large picture window as Laurel says her vows and her husband kisses her. In the last shot of the film, Stella walks off down the street in triumph.

Viewed from within its central conceit, *Stella Dallas* appears to be a film about maternity, idealization, and loss. Linda Williams notes Stella and Laurel's ultimate separation from each other in exactly these terms: "It is as if the task of the narrative has been to find a 'happy' ending that will exalt an abstract ideal of motherhood even while stripping the actual mother of the human connection on which that ideal is based."[5] Yet from the vantage point of labor and gender, the film uses mother and daughter to represent different class positions, values, and skills; it registers their fundamental incompatibility through a series of tragic misrecognitions between the two women that are ultimately resolved through Stella's aspiration to and satisfaction with an image. The film plays out the class-inflected relationship between mother and daughter through a particularly appropriate figure for the intersection of labor, gender, and appearance: clothes.

To gloss briefly the appropriate historical resonances: the removal of textile production from the home to the factory inaugurated social and economic distinctions integral to the shaping of modern class and gender distinctions. Marx's *Capital* begins with an analysis of the textile industry and the different use values of two commodities it produces: linen and coats. Feminism distinguishes itself from critical theory in part by locating what Marxism cannot explain: differential relations to desire, commodities, and power based on gender. Marx could not figure the symbolic value of the "cut and fall of a skirt" or "a good winter coat" in women's liminal and increasingly visual role in signifying and embodying class difference. *Stella Dallas* locates this problem within a particular historical moment by finally representing the tragic difference, the split between mother Stella and daughter Laurel, as that between low and high fashion. The film develops this visual motif in the context of three family narratives of class rise and fall.

Stella Martin comes from a family of mill hands. After trying and failing to catch Stephen Dallas's attention by making herself into a pretty picture at her front gate, she goes inside the drab, ugly little cottage and talks to her mother in the kitchen. The film presents Stella's mother as a wreck of a woman, hunched, old, dragging herself from task to task in her run-down kitchen. The image equates her appearance with her labor; she has been broken down by a hard life of domestic work. In order to make a better life for herself, Stella sews fine clothes, contrives a meeting, and puts on an act for the fastidious Stephen Dallas. She insists on wiping his glass clean before he drinks from it. She has, unbeknownst to him, already observed him doing the same thing. She also tells him that she made the deli lunch that she shares with him on this occasion. Her exertions pay off. They marry.

Daughter Laurel is the product of this mixed-class marriage that quickly runs aground. Stephen takes a job in New York. Laurel, though separated from her father and raised primarily by her mother, nevertheless takes after him. The film gives us this information by depicting Laurel, as a toddler in her highchair, wiping her tray clean with her bib. Stella laughs and says, "She's the spit of her old man." Laurel becomes the genuine article of which her mother is only a copy; she *instinctively* exhibits the behavior (fastidious cleanliness) that her mother affected and performed to snare her father.

The film compares mother and daughter in very class-coded terms which subtly align cultural refinement with leisure and passivity. Laurel is a good student; she likes books. She is charming and personable, but she does nothing except to practice very good leisure skills—Ping-Pong, biking, tennis, taking in museums, reading literature, and dancing. Stella's desires and talents are much more focused, pragmatic, and goal-oriented. Her early ambitions for herself in cultured society fade after her husband leaves her, and she focuses them on her daughter instead. She studies the clothes in shop windows and sews excellent copies of them for her daughter. Stella's aspiration to become middle class through marriage fails. Her daughter does not fail—not because she has ambitions for class rise, but precisely because she does not. Laurel is characterologically middle class; she is the spit of her old man.[6]

Stella's efforts to improve herself can be compared with those of her husband, who, at the opening of the film, has experienced a precipitous class fall. His very wealthy father, saddled by debts, commits suicide. Stephen is left to fend for himself, his inheritance gone, his marriage to an aristocratic fiancée, Helen Morrison, now impossible, his good family name ruined. He works his way up through the company at whose factory Stella's brother is employed. By the time he is reunited with the very wealthy, elegant, and saintly Helen, Stephen has put his life together sufficiently to be an adequate suitor for her. He reassumes an upper-class position, having proven himself to deserve it by what are decidedly middle-class standards: ambition, hard work, and industry. But if hard work ensures success and class ascendancy for a man, the narrative construes women's work and drive in decidedly different terms.

While in Stephen's story the film lauds a man who makes it on his own, Stella's attempts to better herself, to make (of) herself something more than a working-class drudge, produce pathos when compared with her daughter's extremely passive refinement and successful class ascension. The film works this comparison around Stella's and Laurel's very different taste in clothes. Whereas Laurel always dresses very tastefully in tailored suits or gowns with simple and elegant lines, Stella's creations for herself are baroque sensations of fur, loud pattern, and frill. Stella, by covering her arms with bracelets and her neck with ropes of pearls, by sewing dresses with loud polka dots and flounces of lace and ruffles, monstrously overdoes femininity's ornamental function. As the film progresses, it repeatedly places her in public venues (a train, an expensive resort) where the very tailored, sedate, and simple clothing of all the other women in the mise-en-scène foreground Stella's fashion excesses as anomalous and grotesque. She stands out; she is a public spectacle. At the resort where Stella and Laurel go on vacation, Stella gets all decked out and flamboyantly perambulates the grounds. One of Laurel's male friends comments after Stella walks past, "That's not a woman, it's a Christmas tree."

For Stella, class is something one puts on, the more the better. Whether with her clothes, her feigned performances (her interest in love poetry and very clean glasses), or her exaggerated, affected gestures, Stella produces spectacle in place of class. She insists that her African American maid, who is young and inexperienced, put on airs when answering the door or the telephone, making her deliver lines which she invariably confuses. The narrative sentimentalizes class difference by rendering it pathetic; it contrasts the exaggerated and comic airs of Stella's maid and of Stella herself to the gliding, vaguely aristocratic men in morning coats who attend Helen Morrison and her household. The film's very pointed and duplicitous visual conceit is an inverted version of the emperor's new clothes: it represents the distinction that Stella so desperately seeks to put on as precisely invisible.

Stella Dallas locates itself squarely within the problematics of class distinctions as they relate to women as opposed to men. In the self-consciously heart-wrenching contrast the film presents between Stella and Laurel, it juxtaposes an array of values delimiting failed versus successful femininity: bad versus good taste, production versus consumption, agency versus passivity. Stella's clothing, her appearance, her ambition, her love of dancing, nightclubs, and fun, and, much more subtly, her skill with a needle, destine her for failure, not ultimately as a social climber but as a woman. She is *not* a woman, the film asserts, thus transforming questions that really concern class into issues of successful as opposed to failed femininity.

But beyond this story, which is one the Hollywood cinema tells over and over again, *Stella Dallas* makes specific statements about women sewing their way into the middle class in the waning years of the depression. Although a tradition of housewifery dating back to Lydia Child suggests that in times of economic duress, housewives sew and make do for themselves, resisting the market, *Stella Dallas* emphatically weighs in against that option.[7] The film's disingenuous message—that even if Stella's hideous taste bars her entry to any refined home, she is still a very good mother—veils another, more historically apt truism: that Stella's ability to sew the appropriate clothing for the class to which her daughter is destined simultaneously identifies her as someone who could never be assimilated to that class. Women of that class *never* make their own clothes. The film explicitly articulates this point in the scene in which Helen Morrison helps Laurel, come to visit with her father and his new wife, unpack her trunk. Helen admires Laurel's clothing, remarking that she and her mother must have had such a wonderful time shopping for clothes. Laurel corrects her: "Oh, no, my mother *makes* all my clothes." Helen sits back on her heels and says, "Oh, how clever!" The elegant, rich, beautiful, and saintly Helen Morrison shops; she does not sew.

But the film valorizes consumption in other ways as well. Film critics have noted the narrative's basic incongruity—that Stella can make beautiful clothes for her daughter but cannot apply such taste to herself, that she cannot, as *Time's* critic quipped, just "wear quieter costumes" instead of "sending her daughter to live with her father and his new well-bred wife."[8] Yet looked at from the standpoint of production and consumption, this incongruity makes ideological if not narrative sense. Stella can sew, can make clothes, can produce; she just cannot successfully consume. She can make beautiful clothes, but only her daughter can recognize them as such, want them, and wear them. In the split the film describes between Stella and Laurel, middle and working class become distinctions in high and low fashion, between following the crowd and fitting in or making it on one's own. Stella's independent autonomous spirit—she can pull herself up through her own ingenuity and fashion sense; she does not have to buy, she can sew; she can produce her own image—is roundly condemned by the film not as immoral but as pathetic. From a more distanced vantage point, the film notes that the classes cannot mix, they cannot socialize or successfully marry. Yet the narrative does clearly imagine how the class conflict it represents may be resolved.

Stella Dallas appeared during the period when the film, fashion, and cosmetics industries were first coming together; the film articulates this relation in an extensive meditation on seeing and appearance which ultimately construes class (in the sense of refinement) as having a certain relationship to images. Stella and Laurel's relationship is predicated on profound misrecognitions: neither of them can see herself or each other and the differences in their appearance and manners until Laurel's friends cruelly point them out. Their relationship with each other is imbricated within their own respective relationships to images, and the status of images within the film. Stella Martin initially conceives an interest in Stephen when she sees his photo in the newspaper. She arranges herself as in a tableau to attract his attention. When she and Stephen go to the movies, Stella expresses the wish that she could be just like the people on the screen. She yearns to be "in the picture," to be a photo in the newspaper, to be something that she is not. She tries to make herself up, to meet the right people, to draw attention to herself—and this trying, this ambition, marks the unbridgeable distance between who she is and who she wants to be. At the end of the film Stella gazes up at a daughter-become-image—for her, for passersby on the street, for the film audience. In the window frame, so like both film screen and shop window, the text refers to the place where the interests of the culture industry and commodity culture coalesce. In this story of class struggle turned sentimental, heart-wrenching maternal melodrama, the text resolves its conflict by making Laurel an image screened, boxed, held up to be aspired to and admired, her (m)other an enraptured spectator. Even if Stella cannot finally inhabit Laurel's world and her refinement, at the end of the film she can recognize and appreciate it. Dressed much more sedately than she has been before, Stella walks off triumphant, satisfied with just an image.

Maternal Couples: Labor Segregation and Commodity Integration in John Stahl's *Imitation of Life*

Why can't I be white?

Peola in *Imitation of Life*

John Stahl's *Imitation of Life* (1934) approaches the problem of women's domestic and paid labor through two mothers and their daughters, one maternal couple white, the other black. It explicitly confronts the limits of feminine gender homogeneity that implicitly shapes the narrative of *Craig's Wife*. Adapted from Fanny Hurst's very successful 1933 novel of the same name, the film examines how women of different classes and races exist, and must exist, differently in public and private spheres and in relation to labor, sexuality, and leisure. Like *Stella Dallas*, the film severely limits the options open to women, emphatically signifying these contraints through the mise-en-scène. *Imitation of Life* ultimately demonstrates that women, black or white, cannot have it all—they cannot exist simultaneously in public and private spheres, enjoying successful marriages and careers.[9] The film relays these messages by what it refuses to image or imagine. By carefully limiting the locations in which the action takes place, the narrative confines its protagonists to very distinct roles and social spheres.

The ending of the film does not resolve the fates of all its characters with the closure characteristic of the classical Hollywood mode of production. The futures of the affluent white mother, Bea Pullman (Claudette Colbert), and her daughter, Jessie (Rochelle Hudson), are arrested and suspended by their intense love for the same man, Stephen Archer (Warren William). Bea's maid and cook cum reluctant business partner cum companion Delilah (Louise Beavers) has died, and her daughter, Peola (Fredi Washington), is on her way back to the "high-toned" school in the South that her mother had wanted her to attend. Without a specific career or husband or imminent marriage in sight for any of its characters, the film ends as it began with Bea and Jessie, much older but still coupled, walking out of the garden and into their New York townhouse. The lack of closure about the ultimate fates of Bea, Jessie, and Peola enhances the importance of place rather than action; the narrative's resolution involves the spaces these women end up in rather than what happens to them.

In keeping with the claustrophobic, static quality of most melodramas, *Imitation of Life* conveys its conflicts about social locations not through action and plot but through its mise-en-scène. It restricts these locations, with very few exceptions, to domestic space. The film begins in Bea Pullman's home; it moves to the pancake house–domestic residence where Bea and Delilah both work and live with their daughters. It ends in Bea's townhouse and Delilah's basement apartment. The only other locations depicted in the film are Peola's classroom, the restaurant where Peola works as a cashier, Stephen Archer's apartment-laboratory, where Jessie, not knowing his relationship with her mother, flirts with and declares her love for him, and finally the church and street scenes of Delilah's funeral.

Unlike Bea and Jessie, Peola and, to an even greater degree, Delilah have a public existence. Delilah is a public domestic icon.[10] The neon Aunt Delilah pancakes sign graces the New York skyline, and a montage sequence depicts her image being reproduced on hundreds of boxes of pancake flour. Delilah, utterly and apparently only domestic (she repeatedly affirms her aspirations just to cook and take care of Miss Bea and Jessie), becomes a sign and product that can potentially enter anyone's home. From Delilah's first appearance in the film, the narrative tacitly articulates and approves a paradigm of racial relations as blacks looking into, getting into, white homes—as servants and domestics. Aunt Delilah's pancake flour is an abstraction of that process. Her role as a consumer icon is to signify not sexuality but service. She is a servant in a box—what Aunt Delilah makes, the white housewife serves—producing better food with less toil in economically strapped times. The convenience and support of a black cook is available for all; if people can not afford the cook herself, they can purchase her facsimile in a box. Delilah's role as commodity icon is predicated on her absence: she is *not* where her image is (in every white home, assisting white women in their domestic work). The *commodity* fantasy of Aunt Delilah signals in some sense the breakdown of the nineteenth-century *abolitionist* fantasy of a familial, domestic assimilation of the races under the aegis of enlightened white womanhood. *Imitation of Life* underscores the passing away of this fantasy in two important respects.

The masses of people who attend and participate in Delilah's funeral are predominantly African American. The clergy and the uniformed members of the various lodges who attend her coffin suggest Delilah's considerable presence in a civic, community, and church life that greatly exceeds the white domestic life at Miss Bea's in which we have seen her ensconced.[11] The funeral scene forcefully registers a public and an African American context for the drama of *Imitation of Life* that throws into striking relief the limitations of its heretofore privatized, claustrophobic, and racially retrograde vision. Prior to this scene, the only other African American characters in the film besides Delilah and Peola have been other maids and butlers in Miss Bea's employ. Significantly, Delilah has no interaction with them. Posthumously, her community emerges as a world utterly separate from and not contained by the white household whose location has controlled the narrative.

Peola also cannot be contained by the white household and is depicted as exiled, unable to be assimilated to it, precisely because she appears to be white. The question of Peola's appearance and identity is framed both publicly and privately—in her classroom and her workplace, and in front of the living room mirror, where she addresses to her own reflection the dilemma of looking white and being black.[12] When Peola is caught "passing" by her mother at school and later in the restaurant where she works, the film locates the truth of racial identity in Delilah's rather than Peola's face and body, thus framing the daughter's difference from her mother, her very appearance, as false.[13]

Peola cannot be assimilated into the appearance standard, the image repertoire, of white femininity because she is not different enough; she is not a mammy or a domestic. Thus mirrors and images lie in Peola's case. The film completely displaces the question of her feminine beauty and sexuality onto its obsession with her racial identity. Her appearance, her relation to mirrors, is about where she can learn, where she can work, fit in, find a place, and never remotely about her femininity, her desire, or her sexuality—all aspects of women's domesticity from which Peola is excluded. Although Delilah is eminently satisfied with her own lot in life, she wants her daughter to go to school so that she will not end up having to clean someone else's house. The only domestic future the film can imagine for Peola is that of a maid; her life problems are limited to those of finding appropriate employment. She is "smarter than Jessie," is an excellent student, and is destined for some kind of service work, as a cashier or teacher. Being a wife or mother (sexuality or maternity) is *never* imagined for her. The "enlightened" perspective of this film asserts that progress for black women comes not in wanting to be white, but in accepting more advanced but always asexual service roles in segregated public environments.

A very different image standard exists for white women, one that is resolutely personal and highly sexualized. The film frames Bea from the outset as a beautiful woman, sought after by the businessmen she flirts with to obtain equipment and loans to start her business. She has no interest in them, however, and cares only about her daughter Jessie. Yet despite Bea's very successful business career, the film never depicts her in her office. The only two scenes in the pancake house that actually show her working are scenes in which either her business cohorts are flirting with her or passersby on the boardwalk are "windowshopping" captivated by her appearance as she makes pancakes. Jessie has no function in the film other than to shop, go out at night, take her boarding school classes very lightly, and fall in love with the wrong man. Her image is utterly sentimentalized; a childhood photograph of her is referred to in the film so that Stephen can comment on what "a grown-up young woman" she has become when he meets her. Her entire characterization, bland and banal, confines her strictly to leisure pursuits, courtship, and heartbreak. Her mother, highly successful in business, is nevertheless punished for her success by having love forbidden her, except within a household constituted around maternal love. But the real narrative crux of the film lies elsewhere.

As Delilah is dying, she asks for Peola's picture, which we never see. Looking at it, she says, "It never did her justice." While Jessie's photograph signifies her sexual maturation, Peola's raises the question of justice in relation to her image. The photograph cannot apprehend Peola's beauty because the racial inscrutability of her appearance completely invalidates her femininity. Though possibly a throwaway line, the metaphor nevertheless gestures toward the impossible conjuncture/conjecture that haunts and ruptures the narrative of this film: that of an image of femininity that all women can inhabit, can fit, that does all women justice. *Imitation of Life* indicates that there is no such universal image by allotting its characters very different relations to images and to themselves as images. When Delilah dies, her magnificent funeral brings together a community whose presence overwhelms the domestic scope of the film up to that point. Yet her identity as a commodity icon recuperates her image and her community to that domesticity; Aunt Delilah lives on, without a patronym, but with a familial role, as a stereotype animating both urban skylines and white kitchens as a reassuring domestic icon. Her daughter Peola, whom no image or reflection can adequately apprehend, literally disappears from the visual register of the film and from its domestic sphere after her mother's funeral.

The segue from the funeral to the film's final scene occurs by way of the neon sign of Aunt Delilah flipping pancakes. In the shadow of this sign, which now relocates "democratic" representation from benevolent white domesticity to the commodity scene, Bea and Jessie linger in a garden, dressed in flowing, elegant gowns. Isolated from the public sphere, economic industry (Bea may quit her job), and domesticity, they nevertheless remain the ostensible and, in the end, ornamental focus of the narrative. Because of Peola, the film represents the white maternal couple as dominating the narrative without at the same time being able to offer them as universal images of femininity. Delilah, moral but naive, maternal but asexual, and thoroughly assimilated to white domesticity, poses no threat to this standard; Peola, beautiful, young, and smart, marks the limit of its capacity for representation or assimilation. She must be banished both from the image repertoire of the film and from any narrative prospects of a personal domestic life. Thus the film's class- and race-based image of domesticity depends on distributing racialized roles and social spaces among its characters.

Bereft of domestic duties, marriage prospects, and gainful employment, Bea retains her maternal function, giving up her suitor for and sharing her dressmaker with her daughter. Having no relation to utility, drive, or desire, a mother and not a wife, she nevertheless looks very comely, posing with her daughter in their garden tableau. Behind them, Delilah's image publicly represents the smiling domestic, racializing service and housework and promising them both in a box. The African American community represented in the film locates its civic pride in Delilah's face and fame. Peola, by far the most interesting character, knows better and leaves the domestic scene to find intellectual, if anonymous, employments elsewhere. Finally, Jessie and Bea are sitting pretty in the shadow of a particularly compelling, if (because) class-based and racialized, consumer fantasy: that housework will always be someone else's labor, even if that laborer can be acquired only as an image stamped on the form of an inert commodity.

A Total Girl Economy: Maternity and Murder in Michael Curtiz's *Mildred Pierce*

> My mother, a waitress!
>
> Veda in *Mildred Pierce*

Unlike Peola and Delilah, whose apparent differences underwrite one of the maternal tragedies in *Imitation of Life*, in *Mildred Pierce* (1945), mother Mildred (Joan Crawford) and daughter Veda (Ann Blyth) appear to be mirror images of each other. From that point in the narrative when Veda becomes a woman, the film dresses and coifs the two actresses very similarly, doubling their image to split their function: Mildred, an excessively maternal and successful producer, and Veda, an excessively greedy and cold-hearted consumer. In correlating mother and daughter in these terms, the film measures Mildred's extraordinary business sense (she tells a detective, "Everything I touched turned to money") by its maternal motivation and its marital consequence: her intense devotion to her viperous daughter Veda gets one husband killed and another unjustly framed for murder.

In some respects *Mildred Pierce* retells the story of *Stella Dallas* in that Mildred's class rise affects her daughter's social positioning. Yet in the earlier film Laurel and Stella are distinguished by character and taste, while in the later one Mildred and Veda assume opposite but complementary economic roles. That is, the film's class narrative is embedded not in a narrative of tragic individual differences, but rather in one where money and economic concerns are pointedly foregrounded. Tellingly, unlike in *Stella Dallas* and *Imitation of Life*, whose narratives culminate in heart-wrenching maternal sacrifices, in *Mildred Pierce*, a generic hybrid of maternal melodrama and film noir, the daughter is ultimately sacrificed so that the marital couple can be reconstituted. In the doubling and splitting that animate the drama of this maternal couple, anxieties about women's roles as producers and consumers are duplicitously interrelated; that is, the perfect and closed economic unit constituted by Mildred's production and Veda's consumption, by Mildred's maternity and Veda's greed, results in incest and murder. In the end, which is also the film's beginning, both the law and Mildred's first husband must intervene to restore order.

Mildred Pierce is a housewife's Horatio Alger story gone awry. Its plot seems to satirize the American dream by suggesting that economic wealth and success are incompatible with personal happiness. But because Mildred is a woman, the reasons for both her success and her downfall are related to her gender and her maternity rather than to any Faustian ambitions in and of themselves.[14] Initially the fault does not seem to be Mildred's. Her weak and unambitious husband, Bert, loses his job and leaves her for another woman, forcing Mildred to seek employment to support their two daughters. Their younger daughter, Kay, succumbs to pneumonia while on an outing with her father and his mistress on a day when Mildred is seeing her own new love interest, Monte Beregon. Mildred redoubles her efforts to provide for her remaining daughter, yet her commitment to Veda and to their fatherless family clearly provokes the rest of the narrative catastrophes.

Critical readings of *Mildred Pierce* tend to relate its narrative and thematic contradictions, many generated by the splitting and doubling characterizations of Mildred and Veda, to its formal generic blend of the maternal melodrama and film noir.[15] The film's locations, however, indicate that even within those "evenly lit" scenes that make up its maternal melodrama, *Mildred Pierce* differs dramatically from its counterparts in the thirties. While *Stella Dallas* and *Imitation of Life* restrict their mise-en-scène primarily to domestic locations, despite the obvious narrative motivation for workplace scenes in the latter film, *Mildred Pierce*'s locations emphasize employment and work: a real estate office, a lawyer's office, the first restaurant that Mildred works in, its waitresses' dressing room, and, repeatedly, Mildred's restaurants and her offices. Indeed, even in Mildred's own kitchen, we see her harried in her domestic labors as her voiceover emphasizes the home as workplace: "I feel as if I had been born in the kitchen and worked there all my life. . . . I married Bert when I was seventeen. I never knew any other kind of life, just cooking, washing, and having children."

Mildred's description equates maternity with housework, the home with the workplace; the Pierce residence does not conform to the myths or the structure of the sentimentalized and private domestic sphere. Rather, the family's maternal and sexual interactions take place within a predominantly commercial sphere (from restaurants to racetracks) radically bifurcated by work (production) and leisure (consumption). All of the personal relationships in the film, whether successful (Mildred and her friend Ida, Mildred and her maid Lotty) or troubled, (all the other relationships) are resolutely economic. Mildred's "purchase" of Monte as a marriage partner may pale in comparison to Veda's avaricious and false marriage and pregnancy, both "settled" in a lawyer's office, yet in both instances money contaminates or completely replaces emotion as the basis of maternal and sexual relations. Though for very different reasons, both Mildred and Veda confuse money with love, even as the narrative itself insistently fuses home and workplace.

Within the very muddled spaces and economy of this maternal melodrama, the film noir sequences depict the corrective interventions of the law. The legal investigation of Monte Beregon's murder pursues the link between the dissolution of Mildred's first marriage and the crime. In the interview that constitutes the frame narrative of the film, the first flashback recounts Bert Pierce's irritation both at Mildred's baking pies to bring in extra money to spoil their daughters and her nagging him to look for a job. James M. Cain's novel, from which the story was taken, was published in 1941, a time when public sentiment ran very much against married women who also worked outside their homes.[16] Beth Bailey writes:

> Before World War II, Americans assumed that if a woman took a job, it meant that her husband had failed as a provider (and thus as a man). Confession-style articles detailing the misguided attempts of married women to hold paying jobs were staple fare in women's magazines during this period. These articles dealt not only with the woman's waking to the error of her ways but also with her husband's attempts to deal with this public challenge to his masculinity.[17]

But the narrative launches its most profound critique of Mildred through the character of her rapacious and amoral daughter. As literary critic Paul Skenazy notes, "a strong association . . . between food, finance, and mothering" runs through much of Cain's fiction.[18] Rather than taking the connection between food, finance, and mothering in a psychological or psychoanalytic direction, as Skenazy does, I prefer to examine it in more economic terms. In his analysis of *Mildred Pierce*, Skenazy considers these associations as they relate to the perverse incestuous relationship between Mildred and Veda—of which only traces remain in the plot of the film. Yet in terms of narrative logic, the trope of incestuousness remains central. The film transforms the sexual attraction between the two in the novel to an oral-economic relationship that structures the film.

Mildred Pierce develops a bleak scenario from a situation in which women's work—cooking, mothering, tending the home—becomes confused with wage labor. The pervasive anxiety or fear that the film expresses through Veda's character involves the protection of certain activities—love, marriage, and maternity, those functions that define the private sphere—from the incursion of fiscal considerations. The film also provides a particularly dramatic and acute example of cultural ambivalence about women's roles as consumers, an ambivalence that seems to arise as a consequence of the gendered and economic codings of public and private space in the wake of industrial and consumer revolutions. Whereas a film such as *Stella Dallas* clearly wants to encourage women to consume in lieu of an individualist impulse to make their own style and their own clothes, *Mildred Pierce* inveighs against the specter posed by Veda of women's consumer desire uninflected by any interest in marriage, maternity, or men other than that motivated by economic gain for immediate consumption.[19] Thus the basic dichotomies dealt with in all these maternal films—public/private, male/female, producer/consumer—change in relation to different historical conditions and prevailing socioeconomic forces.[20]

The incestuous relation the film constructs between Mildred and Veda as a closed familial and economic unit depends on the inadequacy of the male characters as producers and consumers. Whereas Bert is a bad producer, Monte is a bad consumer; he joins with Veda in spending all of Mildred's money. The film brokers Mildred from her murdered husband Monte back to where she belongs with Bert through the agency of the law, and in doing so recodes this transaction within a *moral* economy. For order to be restored, Mildred must exchange Veda for Bert; she is denied even the ability to sacrifice herself for her daughter. *Mildred Pierce* signals the end of the maternal melodrama and its function during the period from 1930 to 1945: to formulate and nostalgically resolve the successive economic crises from the depression to World War II through cultural ambivalence directed at women's new economic roles.[21] Both *Imitation of Life* and *Mildred Pierce* frame the economic crises facing their maternal protagonists as exceptional, impossible to resolve adequately (with women as successful businesswomen, wives, and mothers), and above all short-term. As the denouements of all these narratives suggest, the need for white middle-class women to work was never supposed to be permanent, and it always resulted in these women losing out or being punished in some way narratively. (The irony, of course, is that economic transformations made their participation in the work force necessary at precisely the same time—and ever since.)

In addition to its pointedly commercial settings, *Mildred Pierce* has a very democratic cast. Lotty the African American maid, Ida the unmarried (lesbian) career
woman, the many working-class waitresses, the Asian American valet who keeps
Monte Beregon's beach house, along with the three types of white men (aristocratic Monte, entrepreneur Wally, wage slave Bert) and two types of white women
(producer-mother Mildred, consumer-daughter Veda), allegorize a social order characterized by ethnic-racial, sexual, and economic diversity. Yet from the first flashback,
the film depicts that the center, the white heterosexual couple and family, is not holding, and as a result all other social relations become confused, lacking necessary distinctions in place and role. For example, after working as a waitress for six weeks,
Mildred recounts that "I felt like I had worked in a restaurant all my life," her words
exactly echoing her earlier description of cooking in her own kitchen. This collapse
of distinctions between public and private is underscored again when Veda insists
that Lotty wear her mother's waitress uniform, in case Lotty has to answer the door-
bell. The uniform conflates and aligns maid and mother, appearance standards (Lotty
answering the door) and economic necessity (Mildred paying the bills), domestic
work in and out of the home, alignments that leave Veda hissing in derision, "My
mother, a waitress!" Her vehemence speaks to a racist and classist cultural fantasy that
finds these two roles absolutely contradictory, mutually exclusive. Yet the film's anxiety about the collapse of conventional social distinctions, undercut when voiced by
Veda, is affirmed in what appear to be comedic throwaway lines delivered by the
maid Lotty.

Lotty's fortunes follow those of her mistress, Mildred. She initially helps Mildred
bake pies at night and keeps the Pierce home during the day while Mildred waitresses. But when Mildred opens her own restaurant, Lotty is in the kitchen helping
out. She remarks on opening night, "This is just like my wedding night, so exciting!"
and tells Mildred's partner Wally, to his chagrin, "You look very pretty in your apron,
Mr. Fay." Her initial comment equates a highly significant personal milestone with
a business accomplishment, while her second scrambles appropriate gender roles,
both in her enunciation and in its object. These gag lines resonate with the gender
trouble evidenced by Mildred's handing Monte a load of cash under the table at a
fancy restaurant, sorting through and paying his exorbitant bills for an array of commodities, and finally "buying" his hand in marriage. That is, Mildred's business acu-
men, her mixing of maternal affect and money, upsets and thoroughly throws into
question the clarity of what the film depicts as crucial differences: between public
and private, business and family, male and female, middle and working classes, and
differences relating to sexuality, race, and generations.

Unlike its predecessors, *Mildred Pierce* works particularly hard to get its protagonist back together with her husband, finding its femme fatale not in some sultry
urban setting but in the suburbs, in the heart of the nuclear family. Unlike Laurel
Dallas, Jessie Pullman, and Peola, whose lack of a father merely results in, at least for
the first two, an insipid and banal sweetness, Veda's lack of father and excess of
mother makes her a homicidal femme fatale in the tradition of film noir. The culture of the forties was rife with concerns about excessive mothering, as evidenced by
Philip Wylie's vitriolic *A Generation of Vipers*, published in 1942. But the larger point
concerns the economic mystifications accomplished through references to domes-

ticity and the mother-daughter dyad. In films before *Mildred Pierce*, preservation of the daughters served as narrative motivation; in *Mildred Pierce*, both daughters are sacrificed in favor of the husband's reinstatement. In this narrative, the ambitions that usually provoke the protagonist's downfall are displaced from mother to daughter. Significantly, Veda conflates the class conflict between herself and her mother with a sexual competition when she goes after Mildred's husband, Monte. Coincident with the collapse of Mildred's fortune, this collapse of the generational difference between Mildred and Veda instigates the murder with which the film begins and rearticulates this mother-daughter relationship in incestuous terms. Unlike maternal melodramas, in which moral transgressions have emotional consequences, in film noir they have legal consequences. Thus, *Mildred Pierce* locates a splitting of genres in its mother-daughter coupling, mother meeting femme fatale over the body of her dead second husband. The law must be called in to break up this total girl economy. The war is nearly over; Mildred must give up her daughter and go home to her first husband.

In one of the film's final images, all of its confusions are implicitly resolved. Screen left, Mildred and Bert, the white middle-class heterosexual couple, stand bathed in morning light, while in the shadows, screen right, two working-class women scrub the floor on their hands and knees, their faces and identities obscured. Feminist critics have alternately read this scene as a metaphor of Mildred, and women in general, being put back "in their place," or, more literally, as depicting specifically working-class women "in their place" in a narrative that is not about them.[22] As I read it, the film and the image assert quite directly that the two cannot be separated. That is, the image positions a now correctly normative and generalized domestic femininity (represented by Mildred) against intragender difference (working-class women), the former romantically lit and narratively foregrounded, the latter in the shadows, keeping the margins clean. The "new dawn" for Mildred and Bert—their reunion made mythic, made metaphoric of all men, all women, all couples, by the lighting and composition of the set—is literally just the end of the workday for the cleaning women on the night shift. The narrative, which culminates in this image, insists that white middle-class married women cannot work in public but must be returned to their homes and husbands, must serve as identificatory icons for all women, while at the same time it registers, quite concretely, that *other* women do work, must work, have always worked in public. As with Peola in *Imitation of Life*, *Mildred Pierce* distributes appropriate places and roles among women whose differences of race, class, and sexuality are visually and narratively related to their appearance, their affective capabilities, and thus their suitability to star in the spectacles and dramas of private life. Like Peola, other women are relegated to the public obscurity of service jobs or labor, while the white woman must inhabit the familialized and domesticated place of woman as wife, mother, sister, and Woman; her place secures everyone else's. All the maternal melodramas I have discussed attempt to work out the problem of other women, and of differences between women, each concluding that they exist but are difficult to image or imagine.

The film's denouement, illuminated by brilliant sunlight, signifies the triumph of justice, truth, and propriety. The skewed social, monetary, marital, and familial priorities that have led finally to violence, deceit, and death have been corrected by the

Law. Husband and wife, ex-mother and ex-father, depart, arm in arm, restored to their proper place. The last shot of *Mildred Pierce* depicts the couple, reunited, walking out into the celestial beams of morning sunlight from the Halls of Justice. And in the darkened foreground of the shot, in its margins, the cleaning women vigorously scrub the floor of the state, an ironic final image in a film so concerned with women and their place in work, love, and family.

The Iconic Labor of White Femininity

In both *Stella Dallas* and *Imitation of Life*, images take the place of character aspirations or "resolve" irresolvable dilemmas: Laurel Dallas becomes the image to which her mother once aspired; Aunt Delilah provides a safe alternative public and domestic icon for women who are not white. *Mildred Pierce*, locating its mother-daughter coupling between the two genres of melodrama and film noir, does not, cannot, resolve its conflicts with just an image because Mildred's and especially Veda's desires are too active, too venal, too public. Maternal sacrifice cannot solve or allay the threat of active feminine desire; the law must be called in to wind up the dilemmas posed in the genre of film noir. Yet a melodrama made in the late fifties readily exhibits the intimate relation between the logic of maternal melodrama and the iconic, if morally vapid, femininity this genre ends by purveying.

Douglas Sirk's acclaimed 1959 remake of *Imitation of Life* changes Bea Pullman to Lora Meredith, a struggling actress who becomes a star. The motif of domestic labor for white women is dropped in favor of the iconic self-reflexivity Sirk articulates around Lora's new profession. Tellingly, femininity itself becomes labor, and that labor is very, very white. Lana Turner plays Lora, setting a seal on a decade when impossibly blonde blondes dominated the movies and the definition of stardom — "sex bombs" Lana Turner, Marilyn Monroe, Jayne Mansfield, Dorothy Malone, and domestic icons Donna Reed and Doris Day. *Imitation of Life* becomes a narrative of a star being a star, her maternity utterly eclipsed by her iconic function; in a climactic confrontation scene between Lora and her daughter Susie (Sandra Dee), Susie says, "Oh, Mother, stop acting!" Sirk's *Imitation of Life* sets the symbolic bankruptcy of white femininity and its affect-laden appearance standard against the quiet altruism and dignity of Annie Johnson (Juanita Moore). At Annie's funeral, Lora is amazed by the number of people who attend. Sirk underscores Annie's public and private good works and, in the character of Mahalia Jackson, introduces the only real person in the very false world of *Imitation of Life*.[23] His film signals the end of the maternal melodrama, the end of a fantasy of white beauty and white morality blended in the same iconic maternal feminine entity. Presaged in Stahl's 1934 version, Sirk's staging of the funeral scene implies that the woman off-screen, the black woman who has died, is much more important than the blonde woman, her employer, who weeps for her, and who might only be acting as she does.

While nineteenth-century domestic manuals articulate a universalized womanhood congruent with ideas of nation, the Hollywood cinema's various suppressions and representations of domestic labor initially promote an iconic version of that gender universal. As the films discussed in this chapter demonstrate, however, the kindred mystifications of domestic labor and social difference secured by white domestic femininity break down, fragmenting that womanhood and using differences in generation to conceive differences in race and class. Maternal melodramas of this period highlight the notion that not all women belong in the same place, nor can they all be imaged in the same way. Through the splitting of mothers and daughters, they indicate how women are and must be split among themselves. Significantly, these divisions, articulated as they are across the mother-daughter couple, are a cause for pathos, not political engagement. In choosing to deal with mothers and wives and simply using daughters as the motivation for their mothers' ambition, the films select roles about which women have considerable and increasing choice (whether to become wives or mothers) and make these roles seem inevitable. This inevitability then haunts the social distinctions treated by the films through its mothers and daughters.

Within the iconic regime of the Hollywood cinema, universal womanhood breaks down into a series of particulars and expresses a new foundation of nation: that no one woman can be metonymic of all women. Rather, these films encourage complex forms of identification: on the one hand, pathos for the vibrant yet ultimately failed or unrepresentable characters marked by class and racial difference (Stella, Peola); on the other hand, the mothers who cannot have it all and who are ultimately forced into an ornamental and banal role (Bea Pullman, Mildred Pierce). Tellingly, the most insipid roles (Laurel Dallas, Jessie Pullman) are saved for white daughters who presumably will face none of the hardships their mothers had to overcome, and will be required only to be happy, pretty wives and mothers. Veda Pierce foretells what will become of this fantasy.

Each of these films suppresses the connection between daughters and fathers in favor of the maternal connection. Yet the paternal function is vigorously reasserted in very different ways in the culmination of each narrative. In *Stella Dallas*, Laurel leaves her mother first to live with her father and then to marry a facsimile of him; her sojourn with her mother is envisaged as an unfortunate and heartbreaking aberration of a romance out of synch with the social and economic order. *Imitation of Life* ultimately denies a heterosexual union to any of its foursome because it cannot reconcile racial, generational, and gender differences within the same narrative. *Mildred Pierce* makes the most dramatic statement about absent fathers, turning Veda into a monster who must consume everything her mother produces. This hunger extends even to her mother's second husband and justifies the sacrifice of Veda, necessary to convert Mildred from maternal producer to docile and domesticated wife.

Feminist filmmakers speak from the position of the daughter, about which no woman has a choice, and deconstruct the inevitability of the roles (wife and mother) about which every woman can choose. Engaging the economic, emotional, and moral mystifications that have underpinned constructions of domestic femininity, these filmmakers use images to dismantle the appearance standard by which women are measured and discerned. In the next section I return to texts authored by women in a very different context from that of the nineteenth-century writers on domesticity or of twentieth-century film directors who produce film narratives for a mass audience. These feminist filmmakers address women's iconic function in relation to the private sphere. Yet they do so from within an alternative rather than a popular discursive position. Whereas Catharine Beecher spoke to a substantial portion of the U.S. population, and classical film entertainment garnered very large audiences, feminist filmmakers of the 1970s and 1980s articulated their ideas from within an international but increasingly constrained and embattled sector of the private sphere: that allotted to the circulation of knowledge. Thus in the final section of this book I consider the most self-reflexive and knowledgeable texts about domesticity, which are, at the same time, the least popular. This paradox is another that haunts American domesticity: it must remain the most highly visible of all that we cannot see.

• PART III •

HOUSEKEEPING AGAINST THE GRAIN

SEVEN

Housekeeping against the Grain

Feminist Domesticity's Visible Style

What if we turned recipes into poetry?

SILVIA BOVENSCHEN

Introduction: Visible and Invisible Work

In a series of superimposed stills, a broom moves back and forth, sweeping dirt off the bricks of a patio. No hand is visible; the camera frames the bristles of the broom. Beneath the dirt, a word emerges—a brand name engraved on the brick. The word is "SAVAGE," a term that also describes the character of the surface that the brick covers and civilizes. The image, from Patricia Gruben's experimental film *The Central Character* (1977), captures the salient motif of the work, the role housekeeping plays in articulating and maintaining the oppositions between surface and depth, inside and outside, nature and culture. Yet, as the paradoxical image-inscription suggests, these apparently separate categories overlap, imbricated in a pattern of distinct but interdependent surfaces.

Gruben's film implicates another surface, that of the celluloid itself, in this pattern of interdependence. The film aestheticizes housework, allows it to move from what Silvia Bovenschen calls the "pre-aesthetic realm" of the household and private life to the "artistic realm." Bovenschen makes use of these distinctions to discuss the ways in which women's "creative impulses" were stunted "by [their] exclusion . . . from the artistic realm" and "evaporated under the strain of women's daily routine."[1] For her, art must circulate publicly, must communicate, and must possess the quality of disinterestedness. Given this notion of art, both the home and housework seem antithetical to aesthetic activity, the home because of its isolated, privatized character, and housework because even its more decorative endeavors are ultimately functional and performed for emotional reasons or rewards. Yet, in a utopian flour-ish, Bovenschen speculates on a time when women might clear out this "realm," opening it up to a future when they might turn "recipes into poetry."[2]

The feminist filmmakers that I discuss in this section do exactly that; by aes-theticizing housework and rendering its labor visible, they make cogent conceptual and political interventions in the hegemonic vision of domestic femininity perpetu-ated by the American culture industry. Their films refuse accepted ideologies about women's place, appropriating domesticity and femininity at the level of cinematic images, narrative structure, and genre conventions. In this way these films tell a story and make connections that Hollywood films will not or cannot. Of course, Holly-wood housekeeping did not end with maternal melodramas. In the fifties and beyond, domestic melodramas have continued to register threats posed to the white bourgeois family by divorce, class and racial difference, imperiled masculinity, feminism, war, alchoholism, drug addiction, and economic hardships of various kinds.[3] What did end with the maternal melodramas, however, was the cultural fantasy that white bourgeois domestic femininity can stand for, can provide an image for, all women. The fraying or breakdown of this fantasy signaled the larger cultural erosion of a master narrative (a transcendent gender binary) crucial to the U.S. cultural and national imaginary since the beginning of the nineteenth century.[4] Second wave fem-inism figures within this breakdown in a particularly complex and paradoxical man-ner. While self-reflexively attacking the social, economic, and political position of women as embodying the "inequality of equality" touted by Catharine Beecher more than a century before, the culturally dominant modes of U.S. feminism nevertheless presumed a universalized woman as their object. That woman, by default, was white, middle-class, and heterosexual.

As my own initial readings of my family photograph indicate, the generalized research object "woman" both produces and occludes theoretical and political knowl-edge about women. In all the theorizing about the difference *of* woman, differences *among* women often could not be seen. Keeping in mind domesticity's crucial and persistent role in the hegemonic construction of a universal femininity in the United States, I examine its role in the construction of academic feminist film theory in the 1970s and 1980s. My interest is not to dismiss or supplant this theory but to histori-cize it relative to concurrent feminist film production that specifically addressed domesticity. At the same time I review these feminist films for their specific contri-bution to the discursive trajectory I have attempted to trace in this book.

In part I, I considered how the science of housekeeping, invented from discur-sive models such as recipes which housewives had available to them, synthesized an array of contradictory social forces, producing crucial political effects. The con-struction of male public and female private spheres instituted gender as the primary social difference and forged a coherent nationalism around the mystification of class distinctions and the articulation and domestication of hierarchical racial identities. Significantly, a nascent feminism—developing out of modernity's construction of domesticity, gender identity, and woman's place—is also a legacy of nineteenth-century domestic femininity.

Though not as obvious a couple as domesticity and femininity, yet a considerably more troubled one, domesticity and feminism have been inextricably linked throughout the last two centuries. I considered some of the historical underpinnings of this connection in part I. In the twentieth century this link persisted in different manifestations and forms. While the Progressives' attempts to domesticate social and public spheres included both feminine and feminist impulses, Betty Friedan's publication of *The Feminine Mystique* in 1963 instigated, at least in part, feminism's second wave. Her book exposed the stultifying effects of domesticity on well-educated middle- and upper-class women. Spawned by reactions against and critiques of domesticity and housework, feminism's second wave initially focused on the political implications of domestic arrangements, including birth control, child care, reproductive rights, equal opportunities for women outside the home, and so on. The women's work that I look at in this section grows out of these concerns, approaching the links between domesticity and feminism as both material and representational.

The argument of this part of the book develops from the histories and concerns of the previous two. Like the texts I discuss in part I, these films are produced by women about an issue of concern to women: the construction and experience of domesticity. Though engaged with political and aesthetic polemics, and therefore having pedagogical effects, these feminist films differ in starting from and reacting to mainstream industry narratives and representational conventions related to women. In part II, I discussed well-known Hollywood films whose treatment of domesticity, maternity, and femininity typifies a culturally and commercially sanctioned view of women's housework as completely affective and appearance-based in both morally and sexually inflected ways. Foregrounding white middle-class women against backgrounds of intragender difference, domestic melodramas articulate a series of displacements wherein women's relation to money, labor, and social difference is visually and morally construed or overridden by their (presumably natural) feminine allegiance to love, pathos, maternity, and sexuality. The feminist filmmakers discussed in this part of the book share a reaction to this tradition of filmmaking defined by Hollywood and American commercial culture.

The chapters in this section sample experimental, independent women's cinema of the last twenty-five or thirty years. While this sample is meant to be more provocative than comprehensive, these films represent the end point of the discursive trajectory on domesticity that I have examined to this point. Speaking to and against this tradition, these films also participate in it, exploring the insights and limitations of their own feminist intervention. Women's experimental and avant-garde cinema of the seventies and early eighties registers a crucial shift in the women's movement overall from materially based concerns about equal pay, child care, and wages for housework to issues, such as pornography, that are focused on sexuality and representation.[5] The films I discuss here mark a very special place in this transition, as they blend concerns about women's labor and representation, taking up housekeeping as an aspect of both women's material history and their symbolic existence as sexual and domestic icons.

Arranged generically rather than chronologically, the films are Chantal Akerman's *Jeanne Dielman* (1975), Marleen Gorris's *A Question of Silence* (1982), Patricia Gruben's *The Central Character* (1977), and Zeinabu Davis's *Cycles* (1988). Of the four filmmakers, only Davis is American. Though born in Texas, Patricia Gruben relocated to Canada. Marleen Gorris is Dutch, and Chantal Akerman is Belgian.

While I am deviating from my focus on *American*-authored texts, the films all share a feminist reaction to mainstream Hollywood filmmaking, whose conventions and gender norms became globalized throughout the twentieth century. Indeed, if the films I discussed in part II taught women all over the world the precepts of a commercially primed affective domesticity (Housewives "R" U.S.), the films I discuss here speak back to that tradition, both from within a Eurocentric context (Gruben, Akerman, and Gorris) and from a position that directly contests that context for its ostensible universalism (Davis).

But the selection of films and their international, predominantly Eurocentric character also illustrate important features about feminism and U.S. feminist film theory in the seventies and eighties. These films, particularly *Jeanne Dielman* and *A Question of Silence*, represent canonical texts within U.S. feminist film theory, reflecting *its* Eurocentric, international character in U.S. film studies. Feminism of this period assumed the preeminence and autonomy of the gender binary over other social distinctions, ultimately making its contestations against gender discrimination implicitly class and race based. This assumption surfaces in the both the films and the contemporaneous criticism in certain ways; unlike the Hollywood domestic melodramas, almost all of the films discussed here assume a homogenous domestic sphere, that is, one *not* marked by differences of race and class within the family unit. Still, films produced in the 1980s, as I will point out, became more ironic and informed about such universality.

Collectively these films refigure what is still a substantial component of female gender construction in Western culture: images of women as housewives. They demonstrate the very diverse ways in which feminists have reappropriated, remotivated, and recycled various aspects of housekeeping. Certain thematic repetitions emerge from the films themselves. While culture industry narratives and commodity discourses tend to obfuscate the actual labor involved in housekeeping and subsume it within the emotional roles demanded of mothers and wives—roles determined by familial relations and expressive ties—the films I discuss foreground housekeeping as a kind of work. They defamiliarize housework by defamilializing it, stripping it of the emotional connotations that usually attend images or narratives of cooking, cleaning, and shopping. Yet these filmmakers do not simply condemn housework as drudgery. While Gorris's *A Question of Silence* uses the figure of the housewife in a critique of women's oppressive social roles and the fallacious representation of those roles, Gruben, Davis, and Akerman, in very different ways, find beauty and humor in images of housework. The four films also address different social-spatial divisions which the home and housekeeping assist in figuring or maintaining. *Jeanne Dielman* minutely details a housewife's routine and her psychological and physical relation to domestic space. *A Question of Silence* uses a shopping incident to explore how working-class women's association with the home and private life has so silenced them that they cannot be heard by the law or other public institutions. *The Central Character* considers the role of housekeeping in creating and sustaining the distinction between "nature" and "culture," while *Cycles* explores social distinctions between the ritual and the banal, the spiritual and the everyday, which operate in the service of dominant cultural arrangements.

Reflecting the formal debates within feminist film theory itself, the films I have selected include both narrative and experimental alternatives to Hollywood. Chantal Akerman's *Jeanne Dielman* and Marleen Gorris's *A Question of Silence* are feature films directly engaged with challenging conventions of narrative filmmaking—both formal and content based—as they relate to mainstream representations of domestic femininity. *Jeanne Dielman* makes use of the rhythms and repetitions of housework to construct a film whose aesthetic form mimes structural features of this specific type of oppressive labor. *A Question of Silence*, which involves a catatonic housewife, addresses ideological questions about women's ability to speak and be heard in cultural institutions and representational genres dominated by classist and sexist points of view.

Patricia Gruben's *The Central Character* and Zeinabu Davis's *Cycles*, by contrast, both represent a distinct moment in two different phases of women's avant-garde film production. Gruben's film presents a poetic experimental meditation on order and dirt, chaos and play, through the activities of a housewife, its "central" character. Part of the feminist ascension that attended the eclipse of other alternative cinemas in the United States in the seventies, Gruben received state support for her filmmaking from the National Film Board of Canada.[6] In the United States, her film circulated within the independent social network established by the classical avant-garde, wherein films were produced, distributed, and seen. The classical avant-garde constituted a predominantly nonnarrative aesthetic and political alternative to the mass-produced spectacles of mainstream narrative cinema. It stressed the cinematic experience as a transcendental expression that would take individual viewers out of themselves. Zeinabu Davis's *Cycles*, produced within the subsequent media arts movement, uses an array of allusive tactics to challenge any universalized conception of domesticity, locating social and historical differences precisely in the home. The media arts movement arose from a different alternative network comprising the state, corporate foundations, and the university. These social institutions supported a sphere within which films were made and seen that articulated and advocated alternative social identities (based on race, ethnicity, sexuality, and gender).

While Gruben's and Davis's experimental films have not accrued a great deal of commentary (as with most feminist avant-garde films), many feminist critics have written on both *Jeanne Dielman* and *A Question of Silence*. These films are usually posed as "other" to Hollywood's classical cinema. The influence of psychoanalytic and semiotic theory on feminism led to the argument that "in order to counter the aesthetic of realism, which was hopelessly compromised with bourgeois ideology, as well as Hollywood cinema, . . . feminist filmmakers must take an oppositional stance against narrative 'illusionism' and in favor of formalism."[7] Thus critics often apply problems articulated by feminist critical theory to feminist narratives, investigating questions of female spectatorship and subjectivity or the possibility of a feminine or feminist aesthetic, largely from a prescriptive, proscriptive position. Although the insights of other critics have been very helpful to me, my interest in the filmmakers' use of housework necessitated a slightly different approach.

Because a certain kind of privatized housekeeping emerged from the same social and economic circumstances that produced psychoanalysis—and because those circumstances, augmented by psychoanalytic knowledge, also produced an understanding of the home as the site of the personal, the emotional, and the sexual—

psychoanalysis, as it was initially taken up by feminist film theory, participated in the ideological process whereby housework became invisible. Feminist psychoanalytic film theory developed an approach to cinema that cohered around questions of spectatorship to the point where other crucial questions were foreclosed: How are cultural constructions of gender, race, class, and labor related? In what material and discursive ways have theories of gender construction predetermined the approach to and understanding of other social differences? How have certain feminist approaches and interpretations repeated the ameliorative social and discursive functions of femininity itself in the structural privatization of questions of difference? I want to make clear that I am not critiquing psychoanalysis per se, but rather questioning how its application to the problem of spectatorship and subjectivity functioned within feminist film theory and its understanding of the meaning of feminist film texts. Thus, in order to *look* at feminist renderings of domesticity and reconsider their project and import, I read *Jeanne Dielman* and *A Question of Silence* by inverting the usual relation between theory and text. Rather than determine what feminist psychoanalytic theory can say or has said about domesticity and women's subjectivity within these texts, I attempt instead to determine what these filmmakers' reconstructions of housework tell us about the scope and assertions of feminist psychoanalytic film theory.[8]

Interestingly, all four of the films I discuss in these chapters render housekeeping dramatically visible; moreover, by specifically alluding to Freud, *A Question of Silence* and *Jeanne Dielman* engage psychoanalytic theory in relation to housekeeping and women's labor. In the two narrative films, concerns with affect, subjectivity, and psychoanalytic narratives and interpretations are emphatically correlated with the labor that produces and maintains the mise-en-scène of the (universalized) bourgeois family and its libidinal conflicts. Such a context implicitly questions the limits, the efficacy, and the comprehensiveness of feminist psychoanalytic theory's explanatory power. It calls into question the emphasis of film theory, but particularly *feminist* film theory, on subjectivity and spectatorship as understood through psychoanalytic theory. Such an emphasis necessitates a focus on the formal aspects of the film to the exclusion of its specific subject or context. The suppression of the material substance and context of specific films in favor of theorization predicated on universal norms of perception and subjectivity results in the loss of the film's particularity and in the reproduction of an ahistorical theoretical model; it produces a privatized, universalized reading, if you will. If one reads psychoanalytic theory in light of these films, their content, materiality, and specificity, as well as their form, give nuance to and historicize a valuable but necessarily limited theoretical model. Thus, in addition to reading all four of these films for their vision of housework, for what they can say or show about housework that has perhaps not been shown before, I read them for how they demonstrate the limitations of the idealizations (domesticity) or theoretical models (psychoanalysis) that this labor and its invisibility have helped produce. In reading these films, I looked finally for what these women did with an aesthetic surface, how they transformed a cultural imposition into an aesthetic inscription. In the remainder of this chapter, I discuss Chantal Akerman's *Jeanne Dielman*.

Narrative to the Time of Housekeeping:
Chantal Akerman's *Jeanne Dielman*

Somewhere every culture has an imaginary zone for what it excludes, and
it is that zone we must try to remember *today*.

CATHERINE CLÉMENT

Now, as always, the most automated appliance in a household is the
mother.

BEVERLY JONES

The full title of Chantal Akerman's film—*Jeanne Dielman, 23, Quai du Commerce,
1080 Bruxelles* (1975)—identifies its protagonist by a domestic mailing address
(metaphorically associated with commerce), locating her within a particular city,
nation, and language. Thus the film limits its scope to a specific household in a very
specific place, examining the housewife's existence within it. It also employs a realistic narrative format.[9] Yet because Akerman uses housework as both the film's subject
and an aesthetic model for its formal structure, the resulting text is anything but conventional. The comparatively lengthy film (its running time is over three hours)
minutely details Jeanne's daily housekeeping routine over the course of three days.
On the afternoon of the third day, Jeanne murders a man, her afternoon sex client,
an event that takes perhaps thirty seconds of screen time, and the film ends as she
sits motionless for seven long minutes at her dining room table in the darkness.

In the relationship between its relatively undramatic, minimal subject material
(three days of housework) and its protracted length, *Jeanne Dielman* challenges the
conventions of narrative cinema in somewhat the same terms in which James Joyce's
Ulysses challenged those of the novel. Yet where *Ulysses* is a stylistic tour de force, the
day in Dublin rendered so as to chronicle the history of Western letters and styles,
Jeanne Dielman overwhelms us with its austerity and formal simplicity. And while
Ulysses details a father and son's journey through Dublin and their return home to a
modernized Penelope, *Jeanne Dielman* tells the tale of a housewife who, like many
real as well as fictional housewives before her, never really seems to leave home at all.

In interviews Chantal Akerman has been quite clear about her intentions in making the film and about the aesthetic and narrative respect she accords to housework.
Talking with Marsha Kinder, she remarks that "the attention I show to this woman's
gestures is very positive, to show that someone doing the dishes can also be used for
art."[10] She also sees her focus on housework in political terms, as an attempt to document something that is usually invisible. In an interview with Janet Bergstrom, she
identifies *Jeanne Dielman* as a feminist film precisely in its relation to the standard
practices of film narration: "I *do* think it's a feminist film because I give space to
things which were never, almost never, shown in that way, like the daily gestures of a
woman. They are the lowest in the hierarchy of film images. A kiss or a car crash
come higher, and I don't think that's an accident."[11] Akerman's interest in housework
leads her to create a film whose formal strategies derive from this aspect of many
women's social experience. While not articulating *the* position of female subjectivity

(universal, ahistorical), *Jeanne Dielman* does something more practical, more provocative, more replicable. It takes a concrete, historically class-bound and gendered experience within a specific national culture and uses it as an aesthetic formula, a model for generating a film narrative. Thus Akerman makes the personal political via aesthetic invention.

In so doing she enacts what Rachel Blau DuPlessis calls for in her experimental theoretical piece concerning the debate over a female aesthetic:

> For the woman finds she is two irreconcilable things: an outsider by her sexual position, by her relation to power; an insider (if middle class)(but how? on her own terms? attached to husband) by her social position. . . . How then could she neglect to invent a form which produces this incessant, critical, splitting movements. To invent this form. To invent the theory for this form.[12]

DuPlessis goes on to quote Joan Scott, who explicitly relates this doubling to the problem of labor: "From this perspective, our personal, social and historical experience is seen to be shaped by *the simultaneous operation* of relations of work and sex." DuPlessis concludes, "Following this, the female aesthetic will produce art works that incorporate contradiction and nonlinear movement in the heart of a text."[13] Likewise, the aesthetic objectification of housework that constitutes the formal structure of *Jeanne Dielman* resonates with its narrative content to produce an ambivalence that cannot be fully apprehended by any ideological statement or determination.[14] For this reason I want to examine the film's formal structure in some detail.

This ambivalence is captured in the opening minutes of *Jeanne Dielman*, which typify the rhythm and style of the rest of the film. It opens with a medium long shot of Jeanne, in profile, standing in her kitchen in front of the stove. Despite our visual distance from the action, we can clearly hear the hiss of the gas jet, the raspy scratch of the match, as we watch Jeanne light the burner under a pot on the stove. A bell rings, and Jeanne very slowly, very deliberately, begins to unbutton her blue housecoat, turning to walk across and off-camera to the left. The frame remains empty while we hear footsteps, water running, and the sounds of Jeanne rinsing her hands. She walks back into view and again partly off-screen to the left to dry her hands. During this action we can see only the middle of her body, as her head and lower torso are cut out of the frame by her proximity to the camera. She turns off the light and leaves both the room and the shot. While the camera remains fixed in darkness in the kitchen, we hear her footsteps, the sounds of a door opening, her greeting, and a male voice responding "Bonjour." As the door closes, the camera cuts to a shot of Jeanne in the hallway, taking a hat and coat from a man we cannot see. She walks off-camera, and we hear the sound of hangers. Coming back into the frame, Jeanne leads and the man follows her down the hallway to a door at the back of the frame. Jeanne opens the door, and the two enter. The door closes, and the camera holds the shot for a full ten seconds. Then Akerman cuts to the same space in darkness. The door opens, and the next sequence begins.

As I hope this example indicates, the sound track greatly enhances the visual emphasis on housekeeping tasks. The film encourages us to look at the home and the chores that occur within it while deemphasizing characterization, plot, and dialogue. The banal, everyday noises of burners lighting and meatloaf being squashed and kneaded are miked so that we hear them with particular clarity, as if we were much closer to their source than we actually are. In a conventional narrative such sounds, if we heard them at all, would serve as background noise for the much more narratively important dialogue. Ambient sounds are everywhere foregrounded in *Jeanne Dielman*, a film that contains very little dialogue and no nondiegetic sound at all.[15] Akerman also makes atypical use of off-screen sound. In conventional films, out-of-frame noises are intended to generate suspense or to prepare for a character's entry into the frame; but in *Jeanne Dielman* we hear only the continuous, monotonous noises of everyday housework. As is the case with the opening sequence, such off-screen sound does not compete with the sound of other, more important activities occurring in the frame.

Akerman often leaves the screen empty, photographing rooms that Jeanne has vacated. Throughout, Akerman's use of off-screen sound and space requires viewers to identify aurally actions that are routinely performed at home but are usually invisible. As spectators we readily infer hand-washing and answering the door from the sound cues provided in the opening sequence, just as, in our familiar domestic experience, we often locate household members and determine their activities from such noises. Thus we simulate familiar domestic activity in listening to and looking at this film. Significantly, these cues are not integrated within a narrative in which a character's passions or a cause-and-effect sequence completely overrides the depiction of labor. Here the labor *is* the narrative.

The cinematography in *Jeanne Dielman* is equally striking, chiefly because of the static use of the camera, which does not move and follow its subject. Repeatedly Jeanne enters and leaves our field of vision in the course of her tasks. Despite her movement within and outside the frame, Akerman keeps the framing stationary and level. There are no close-ups, nor are there any point-of-view shots; the camera visually remains at the distance of a medium long shot, as if it were an inanimate eye regarding Jeanne at her tasks. Because Akerman repeats camera setups and matches them with specific tasks, we come to expect a specific vantage point in each room. Janet Bergstrom observes that Akerman's cinematography emulates the precision and predictability of Jeanne's housekeeping.[16] It also, as Akerman states, emphatically identifies the point of view: "You *know* who is looking; you always know what the point of view is, all the time. It's always the same."[17]

The two other stylistic systems, editing and mise-en-scène, are similarly geared exclusively to Jeanne and her work. The editing in this film is minimal. Jeanne's movement in and out of rooms, shops, and other locations prompt the cuts. Within a given location there are very few edits, and these again are motivated by Jeanne's actions, specifically by her performance of housekeeping tasks. Akerman's stylistic choices consistently mime the monotonous rhythms, patterns, and routines of everyday work. The film's locations are all dictated by the exigencies of Jeanne's routine and tasks. Even the lighting within her apartment emphasizes her work routes and patterns and, consequently, the length of shots. Like Child's frugal housewife who vigilantly conserves energy and money, Jeanne turns lights on and off, hence dictating cuts or fades or our very ability to see the image as she moves from room to room. In a similar fashion, the real duration of a chore in a room or shop determines the length of a given sequence or shot, rather than the length being determined by a dramatic event for which such chores would usually serve as a momentary back-drop or a realistic effect.

As with Lydia Child's book format, Akerman patterns all aspects of her film on housework. The cause-and-effect pattern usually emphasized in film narrative is here replaced by the structure of a housewife's daily routine, an inexorably repetitive, habitual pattern of activity that caters not to dramatic excitation and release, but to the more mundane servicing of basic bodily needs—housework. Rather than being determined by an overarching linear plot, the events that occur in *Jeanne Dielman* are motivated by a housewife's concerns. One determinant of these events is social convention—the arrangement of the day according to mealtimes, bedtime, times when shops are open and school is in session. Another involves personal needs, though notably not Jeanne's; for example, she gets up early enough to shine her son's shoes so they will be ready when he dresses for school. Finally, the efficiency charac-teristic of housework impels Jeanne to plan her work so that, whenever possible, more than one task can be accomplished at the same time. In the opening sequence Jeanne carefully arranges the cooking time for that evening's dinner to coincide with the duration of her afternoon sex work.

In the end, however, certain events cause the disruption of Jeanne's schedule, lead-ing to the disorder that terminates her routine. Miscalculating the time on the sec-ond afternoon, perhaps because she begins to experience some pleasure with her client, she burns dinner and forgets to comb her hair neatly. Interestingly, the causes and effects that interrupt this routine are themselves depicted in the rhetoric of housekeeping, an aspect of the film I discuss in more detail later on. In structuring her plot to conform to a housekeeper's routine rather than to the cause-and-effect pattern of classical film narrative, Akerman demonstrates in concrete detail that housework entails fitting things in, scheduling around, taking into account *others'* needs. The only thing Jeanne could be said to do for herself is to sit and have coffee, either at home or in a café, in the course of doing her chores. Yet even this activity is depicted as completely habitual and ritualistic. When Jeanne finds her usual table at the café occupied, she sits elsewhere, but it is evident that this change ruins her pleasure, and she quickly leaves without finishing her coffee.

Housework is a mode of activity that institutes ritualized behavior; it is both pro-foundly isolating and redundant. Akerman emphasizes these perceptions by record-ing Jeanne's chores in real time, which, as Marsha Kinder observes, "forces us to see how many steps are involved in each simple task. It also accentuates the central prob-lem of boredom."[18] Jeanne performs most of her work alone, in silence, the static camera stressing the fact that in many of the sequences Jeanne is the only animate, animating entity we see. The obsessive attention that Akerman accords to Jeanne's daily labor also makes concrete the Sisyphean character of housework, the constant doing and undoing, the erasure of all effects and products that it produces. To make veal cutlets, Jeanne takes out all the necessary bowls, implements, and ingredients: she dips the meat and breads it, and then she cleans up, leaving the kitchen looking exactly as it was when she (and the viewer) entered it fifteen or so minutes earlier.

Using the idiom of domestic work as her model, Akerman challenges the con-ventions of linear film narrative. Yet her film does not adopt the aggressive tactics of anti-narrative, shocking spectators out of their complacency by systematically violating their expectations of a film text.[19] Rather, the film replaces the logic of causality characteristic of narrative with a highly ritualized pattern of repetition. As a corollary, the spatiotemporal relations typical in film narratives are also changed. Here time and space are not subsumed to narrative aims but rather replace them. The duration of Jeanne's tasks, the endlessness of her days, and her solitary relationship to the space of her home are the very substance of this narrative. Jeanne's home, the primary space or location in this story, does not, as in classical narrative, simply serve to characterize her, to emphasize the features of her construction that then motivate and rationalize narrative action. Instead, as her comings and goings illustrate, she animates her domestic space, articulates it in relation to her work. Her interaction with the space of her home is accorded much more screen time than her relation to any other character in the film. Similarly, her relationship to time becomes dramatic on the third day, when, as a result of her being ahead of schedule, the excess of time throws her (and us) into a panic.

Jeanne cannot be said to have any goals beyond those of maintaining her space and her schedule, and we are certainly not given insight into what her desires might be. Although there are events in *Jeanne Dielman* that might fall under the rubric of "complicating action," these events could not be said to be obstacles to be overcome in the same way that Mildred Pierce's problems with money or Harriet Craig's problems with company function in their respective narratives. In *Mildred Pierce*, money problems provoke a dramatic change in Mildred's life. She gets a divorce and a job, becomes a waitress and then a restaurant owner. In *Jeanne Dielman* there is no change. When the potatoes are burned or the post office is closed, the character simply has to repeat actions until her tasks are completed successfully. Dramatic tensions arise in *Jeanne Dielman* when Jeanne's routine or manner of performing her tasks is disturbed in some way. The narrative of *Jeanne Dielman*, in its precise and obsessive attention to Jeanne's chores, cues audience expectations and assumptions in a way that inverts conventional narrative expectations. The first time I saw this film, I jumped when Jeanne left the lid off the bowl on the dining room table. She does not notice her oversight for a while, and the sight of the uncovered bowl generated tremendous anxiety in me, as did certain later details, such as an unbuttoned blouse or mussed hair. The fifteen minutes that Jeanne spends making meatloaf, the ritualistic precision of her schedule, lures us into expecting a manner of performance and presentation that will *not* change. Indeed, if the narrative generates any strong feeling initially, it is perhaps the fear that nothing *but* housework will happen, interminably. Akerman, after painstakingly constructing such an undramatic context and set of expectations, can then convey shock, drama, and malaise with the most insignificant of gestures, the most subtle slips.

Jeanne Dielman alters women's conventional cinematic function as spectacle by unearthing and foregrounding another feminine social role whose narrative representation has been almost completely repressed: that of woman as housekeeper, as laborer. One of the effects of this process is that *Jeanne Dielman* takes the stereotype of the "mad housewife" and renders that madness in a manner suitable not to the spectacular conventions of melodramatic narrative, but according to the practices and conventions of housework itself. Broadly speaking, the representational structure of *Jeanne Dielman* uses the figure of the obsessive and frigid housewife to engage and challenge certain truisms, most compellingly articulated by psychoanalytic theory, concerning the representation of women in film narratives. As Jeanne, an agent of scrupulous domestic order, becomes disordered and deranged, she does not weep, scream, or tear her clothes; instead, Akerman expresses that disorder in the idiom of housework. Thus an uncovered pot or a button left unbuttoned becomes an expression of madness that is much more menacing and frightening than a temper tantrum or some other kind of affective display. The film refuses to subsume Jeanne's character within convenient categories such as "woman" or "mother" that would override or contain her role as a housekeeper by emphasizing more "emotional" female roles.

Jeanne's positioning in the frame and Delphine Seyrig's performance of the character depict a female body in ways not often seen in films. In conventional films, representations of women's bodies signify, stylize, and reify sexual and emotional functions culturally taken to be feminine. This performance of "woman," of the feminine, presents the female body as defined by a relationship to an other, either by means of provocative, inviting poses or in soft-focus close-ups that capture an openness, an emotional exposure, particularly through the eyes. Jeanne, by contrast, is not open to the gaze, and does not receive or reciprocate it with her body or expression. She averts and avoids it. Frequently Seyrig/Jeanne's back is to the camera while she washes the dishes or cleans the bathtub, and when she faces us, her eyes are downcast, her features and facial expressions closed. Camera placement enhances this effect. We usually observe Jeanne from a distance; thus her face and any emotional expression are doubly inscrutable. Instead of focusing on the actor's face and gestures to convey interior emotions, the images highlight the movement of Jeanne's body as a *working* body, engaged in labors that are fundamental but invisible to bourgeois domestic culture. Her schedule, her labors, the exigencies of her relationship to domestic space as her work space all dictate her movements. Her solitude is everywhere emphasized. Men do not look at her; her body does not pose. Rather, she cleans the bathtub or washes her own body, completely self-absorbed by routine tasks and the need for order. As she washes the tub with her back to us, her elbow raised, the depiction of the event in real time allows the spectator to contemplate her balance, the procedure she follows, the movements of scrubbing stabilized by an elbow raised and frozen.

By watching Jeanne scrub the bathtub, wash the dishes, set the table, and make the coffee, the unchanging gaze of Akerman's camera introduces an alternative erotics of the domestic to that conventionally purveyed by melodramatic film texts. Film theories of narration and spectatorship that address the issue of desire have little if anything to say about the kinds of visual and narrative pleasure afforded by this film, perhaps because most of these theories revolve around representations of the sexualized rather than laboring female body. *Jeanne Dielman* proposes a different set of narrative interactions between spectator and text, and, as a consequence, it construes the psychoanalytic, Oedipal version of the family somewhat differently. Akerman's camera and narrative present us with a woman to be watched rather than looked at. Jeanne is not positioned as a fetishized sexual icon or as the victim of narrative sadism and punishment. She works and we watch her work. She is usually engaged in some activity, her actions deflecting our attention away from her body as a specifically gendered or sexual object. Even when she is nude, Jeanne does not function as a conventionally erotic spectacle. Akerman alters the eroticism that usually attends a woman bathing by showing Jeanne systematically, with an almost clinical precision, scrubbing every inch of her body, cleansing herself (we find out later) after sex work.

At least one critic (and several spectators I know) has compared the camera's perspective of Jeanne to that of a young child watching its mother go about her chores.[20] Akerman claims in an interview that the perspective in this film is always hers. She wanted to avoid manipulating viewers, so she did not use the son's point of view nor did she interject the camera more intrusively into the action. She decided to hold back, to respect the woman "in her space."[21] Yet Akerman lends some support to the opinion that there is something of a child's point of view in the representation of Jeanne when she asserts that the film "came from my memories of all the women in my childhood."[22] There does seem to be something reminiscent of an infant's domestic experience in the repeated views of Jeanne's back, in the camera that remains still and immobile as she briskly enters and leaves its field of vision. Some of the pleasure of *Jeanne Dielman* perhaps derives from its re-creation of this very primitive familiarity with housework. It represents the perspective of an infant witnessing not the primal scene but the movements and postures of its mother engaged in housekeeping.

In her commentary on the film, Mary Ann Doane also makes a reference to the mother-infant relation. She argues that *Jeanne Dielman* "elaborates a new syntax" that allows for a different "speaking" of the female body. In its syntax, *Jeanne Dielman* "undoes the structure of the classical narrative" through a prolonged parody that emphasizes what conventional narrative represses.[23] Doane's full argument is too complex to recount here, but one of her salient points concerns the integration of symbolic and social forces in the formation of infantile drives by means of the mother's care of the baby's body. The psychosexual development of the infant occurs by way of his or her orifices, which the (external) agency of maternal care, together with other internal factors, converts to erotogenic zones. As Jean Laplanche points out, these zones of care are also zones of exchange and sexual excitation, the latter of which the infant experiences as an "alien internal entity." Doane makes the point that these exchanges implicate the social from the outset in the body's investment with sexuality. Recognition of this social element allows us to move away from the essentialist and antiessentialist positions vis-à-vis the female body that have stifled feminist film theory in recent years, and to acknowledge the "body [as] a condition of discursive practices."[24]

I recount Doane's argument in some detail because it connects the construction of *Jeanne Dielman*'s plot to important questions in psychoanalytic film theory. She stops short of the argument I will make in regard to this film, but the comments she and Laplanche make about maternal care warrant further discussion that ultimately will bear on my examination of domesticity and labor. First, the major activities or tasks involved in housework (feeding, cleaning) are literally embodied in the infant's needs for its mother's care. While Laplanche states that the zones of exchange that constitute these needs function to "focalize . . . maternal fantasies," it bears mentioning that this erotic exchange between mother and child involves a component of labor for the mother as well. More important, the cultural positioning of the woman and mother as the agent of feeding and cleaning makes her an important determinant of infantile eroticism; but that eroticism and consequent subjectivity, given Doane's argument, must be inflected and shaped by culture and class-specific standards of cleanliness and child care, norms and modes of feeding, and so forth.

In Doane's discussion of this film, she does not mention the fact that Akerman herself very pointedly invokes psychoanalytic theory in ways that challenge the usual psychoanalytic narrative of the family. The film makes this challenge explicit by reducing the Oedipal narrative in *Jeanne Dielman* to two conversations that take place between Jeanne and her son on successive nights. In one of the very few dialogues in this film, Jeanne's son reveals the horror he feels when thinking about his (now deceased) father having had sex with Jeanne. She refuses to respond to his very baldly articulated Oedipal anger (he refers to a "sword plunging into her"), shuts off the lights, and goes to bed. Given that Jeanne and her son hardly speak to each other at all, these conversations, with their violence and intensity, sound very odd and out of place. But there is a certain logic to the inclusion of such material. In her film Akerman does not do away with psychoanalysis, with the Oedipal drama of the bourgeois family, with questions of desire in the familial matrix; she simply contextualizes this metanarrative by inserting it, as a story, within the everyday experiences of bourgeois housekeeping. By this means she fills in what Freud, unquestionably a bourgeois gentleman ensconced in a bourgeois household, left out of his imaginings. Whereas he freely looked back to myth, transformed it to speak the truth of the family (all families, for all times) and the (male) subject, he ignored the real material conditions of his own family and his own time, nation, and race, all of which shaped the context of his vision. Thus bourgeois women's work, their housekeeping, can be seen as the foundational structuring absence of an aesthetic, a theory of narrative, and a subject all purported to be universal. This absence facilitates others, such as nation and race—material contingencies that become irrelevant in the construction of a trancendent human subjectivity.

Akerman, as Doane observes, makes a narrative from this structuring absence. And, in Teresa de Lauretis's terms, she constructs a social vision of something heretofore perhaps unrepresentable. Rather than acceding to the cultural view that housework is simply a part of motherhood (and an invisible part at that), her film depicts motherhood, libidinal tensions, sexuality, and Oedipal anxieties as facets of bourgeois housekeeping. For Jeanne, "making love is merely a detail," an assertion that collapses a phallic economy. Akerman literally renders sexual intercourse as part of bourgeois women's work for Jeanne, a widow who has bills to pay. Ever the scrupulous housekeeper, Jeanne prepares for and cleans up after her afternoon clients in the same way she prepares the kitchen and cleans up after making meatloaf. She places and then removes the towel that protects the bedspread from stains, she airs the bedroom, she cleans her body. Despite her precautions, however, her afternoon chores themselves introduce an element of disorder into her schedule that she cannot easily rectify, clean up, or do away with.

The culmination of *Jeanne Dielman*'s narrative, the protagonist's tortured orgasm and then murder of her client, derives from the same vexed relationship between sexuality and cleaning or orderliness that often characterizes mad housewife narratives. Jeanne is similar to Harriet Craig in that she is fanatical, repressed, and obsessed with cleanliness. Yet whereas *Craig's Wife* "explains" Harriet's anality as being emotional and sexual in origin, and also punishes her for being a bad wife, Akerman refuses to motivate Jeanne's madness by recourse to any explanation other than her life, her profession as a housewife. Harriet's fastidiousness works narratively as a symptom or sign of her sexual frigidity. Jeanne's madness is more complexly rendered as existentially, materially based. Deriving from her experience of pleasure at work, it is signified in the film by disorder, by ruptures and mistakes in Jeanne's obsessive routine and scrupulously professional job performance. Pleasure disturbs her; it messes up her hair and her orderly life.

Akerman's film enacts in Jeanne's character what the visual dichotomy constructed by *The Central Character* suggests: housework comprises very contradictory imperatives that, embodied in a single individual who is committed to doing all aspects of her job well, might easily drive someone mad. Akerman does not simply throw out pop Freudian notions of the crazed, compulsive, and frigid housewife; she borrows that story to tell it from within the housekeeper's experience of the home as a workplace. It is the same story, told without the presumption that a strictly libidinal economy defines and structures domesticity and everything that happens within it. Such an economy is posed as the antithesis of housework, a threat to its order, perhaps *its* structuring absence.

Jeanne Dielman supplements a pervasive and particularly Eurocentric bourgeois vision of both narrative and domesticity. That vision stresses the association of private life with leisure, consumption, and familial, affective experience. It generally excludes any acknowledgment of women's household labors. Akerman's film contains a very specific address to the worker who has maintained the milieu, the mise-en-scène, of that private life. Her film succeeds as an aesthetic tribute to a tradition of housekeeping that began as a supplement to an emerging market economy and became coextensive with it. That is, in *Jeanne Dielman* Akerman invents a compelling cinematic aesthetic from the experience of housework while at the same time she documents both its horror and its historical end point—the complete saturation of the domestic by market relations. The film also offers a critique of both conventional film narratives and psychoanalysis. It concretely locates the origins, context, and construction of the often grandiose illusions of their fictions in the trivial and mundane practices of a bourgeois housewife in Brussels. It makes art out of the antithesis of art, narrative out of the most nonnarrative acts one could imagine—housework and its particular labors.

Conventional narrative attracts viewers, draws them in, by structuring lacunae in their knowledge, by depicting a causal event and provoking speculation on what its effects will be, encouraging audiences to wonder what will happen next or why an event has occurred or why a character acted in a certain way and so on. The term *narration* describes the consequent interaction between spectators and texts, the process whereby textual cues prompt spectators to ask such questions, to make assumptions, to have expectations or make inferences about the ongoing story. David Bordwell finds these interactions to be the foundational impulse of narrative: "Narratives are composed in order to reward, modify, frustrate, or defeat the perceiver's search for coherence."[25] If we consider these various factors with respect to *Jeanne Dielman*, we can see that this film transforms them in ways that demonstrate the alterity of housekeeping to conventional narrative, from Hollywood to the Oedipal myth that explains subject formation.

Jeanne Dielman is predicated on a different logic of narration and address. It captures what Althusser theorized but whose ambivalence he could not adequately express: the beauty and the horror of how different interpellations are historically inhabited. Between the subject and the nation is a place that is both a home and the "quai du commerce." It is the noncommercial and its entry point, a home and not a home—in short, the uncanny, economically rendered.[26] If Freud recuperates the uncanny into castration anxiety, here his own example of the automaton best points to the conjuncture of history and the aesthetic figured in this housewife as an alternative not to her subjectivity but to the profound ambivalence of her address: *Jeanne Dielman, 23, Quai du Commerce, 1080 Bruxelles.*

EIGHT

Converting Melodrama to Manifesto

A Question of Silence

All laughter is allied with the monstrous.

CATHERINE CLÉMENT

Marleen Gorris's *De Stilte rond Christine M.* or *A Question of Silence* (1982) does not focus exclusively on the work of housekeeping. Rather, as the Dutch title (literal translation, "The silence around Christine M.") indicates more clearly than the English, the film is centered on the catatonic silence of an enigmatic woman named Christine M. Gorris takes up the figure of the silent (silenced) housewife in order to transform various generic (in all senses of the word) accounts of women's silence.

Reputedly developed from a newspaper account of a housewife who bludgeoned a shopkeeper to death,[1] the narrative of *A Question of Silence* recounts the crime, arrest, psychiatric evaluation, and trial of three women who kill the male shopkeeper of a women's clothing boutique. Unlike *The Central Character, Cycles,* and even *Jeanne Dielman, Question* embodies the norms of classical narrative filmmaking. Despite its controversial plot, the film does not deviate formally from the standard conventions of film narration. It employs a causal logic to link story events, and considerations of time and space are clearly subsumed to narrative demands. There are no violations of the invisible style, save perhaps for the odd electronic music and sounds that make up the nondiegetic part of the sound track. The film relays its story information by means of a counterpoint constructed between the flashbacks that reveal the actual commission and contextual circumstances of the murder and the primary action that propels the narrative forward—the investigation of the three women's sanity.

The three murderers—Christine, a housewife; Ann, a waitress; and Andrea, a secretary—do not know one another before the murder. They meet at the boutique by coincidence. Christine's attempted theft of a skirt precipitates the incident. The shopkeeper sees her put the skirt in her bag and walks over to her; when he pulls the item out and looks at her with his brows raised, she takes it away from him and stuffs it back in her bag. Ann and Andrea, looking on along with four other women, proceed to imitate Christine, brazenly putting clothing in their bags. When the shopkeeper steps back in amazement, the three women surround him and, with the housewife delivering the first blow, methodically beat him to death. The four other women, two very young white women and two middle-aged women, one white, one black, stand and silently witness the act.

We learn about the crime in retrospect through the investigation conducted by Dr. Janine Van den Bos, a court-appointed psychiatrist. When, at the film's conclusion, Janine argues to the court that the women are sane, the lawyers and judges are shocked. She upsets them further by suggesting that the crime was motivated by gender inequities. A pugnacious prosecutor retorts that he does not see how the crime would be in any way different if three men had killed a female shopkeeper. The women in the courtroom—defendants, witnesses, and finally Janine herself—explode into laughter at this comment. They are expelled from the court as the film ends without a verdict.

As this plot summary indicates, *A Question of Silence* tells a shocking story, one that defies an array of cultural-legal beliefs about women and violence, the most notable being that women resort to violence only in personal contexts.[2] Jeannette Murphy observes that, given our social taboos about women and violent behavior, "for three women to murder, arbitrarily and with no good reason, an unknown, unthreatening and ineffectual man is unthinkable."[3] The film generated considerable controversy upon its release, with many male and some female reviewers decrying what they saw as the film's advocacy of retributive violence against men. Stanley Kauffmann called it "vile" and "loathesome," grounding his criticism in what he regarded as the film's underlying premise: "that any woman has the right to kill any man because of the history of male domination and selfishness." (Interestingly, in the same review he referred to Akerman's *Jeanne Dielman* as a film whose violence was acceptable because "we had a long journey through social pressure and disintegration before the act and a view of collapse after it.") *A Question of Silence* seemed a "shocking perversion" to him because the three women were "unremorsefully prepared for punishment."[4] Stanley Kauffmann is certainly not a knee-jerk critic of cold-blooded violence, repented or not (he loved Sam Peckinpah's *The Wild Bunch*), but he was made extremely uncomfortable by the impersonal violence perpetrated by women in *A Question of Silence*. The discomfort and anger the film arouses derives both from its dispassionate murderesses *and* from the explanations and the context it gives for their violent act.

Although many critics have written on the theme of violence in *A Question of Silence*, the film interests me because it illustrates how generic constructions of "private" life and domesticity effectively constrain and silence women.[5] The film, which locates a housewife at the heart of that silence, opens with a scene that introduces us to the psychiatrist-investigator, Janine, and her attorney husband, Ruud. They are sitting on their couch reading and watching television. Janine attempts to initiate sex with her husband, but he rebuffs her, telling her, "I'm working." Janine responds, "I am too," and with mock aggression takes a pen and runs it down the length of his torso as if she were cutting him open. (Her gesture is identical to one that we see Andrea make later in earnest in the murder of the shopkeeper.) When she reaches his genitals, he jumps up, laughs, and rolls on top of her, embracing her. The scene ends with this playful resolution of domestic conflict. Mary Gentile observes that this event sets up from the beginning the "muffled, yet competitive power struggle . . . that characterizes Janine's relationship with her husband," a relationship that deteriorates as her involvement with her three clients grows.[6] While playful, Janine's desire requires a mock aggression predicated on invoking a phallic signifier from her profession (pen) in order then to renounce it for her husband's penis.

Immediately afterward we are introduced to the subjects of Janine's investigation—Christine, Ann, and Andrea—in three separate sequences that depict their lives and activities just prior to their arrest. Significantly, while Ann and Andrea are shown working in the "public" sphere, Christine, like Janine, is depicted at home, though Christine sits on a couch in a cluttered and chaotic living room that is quite small in comparison with Janine's. The film then depicts the process whereby Janine is brought into the case and begins working with the three women. As Gentile remarks, "Block by block, the film is constructed of symmetrical, balanced sequences. We listen as Janine interrogates each of the women, in turn and repeatedly, and gradually she comes not only to understand their actions, but to identify with them as women."[7] While I agree with her characterization of the plot construction, I disagree with her comment about Janine. She comes to understand the three as women whose life experiences exceed the class and racial norms with which she is familiar and which inform her psychiatric practice, which are depicted as woefully inadequate to understand their crime.

Although *A Question of Silence* is ostensibly a crime drama, it is not about a search for a criminal: "Contrary to the classical thriller, the 'whodunnit' question is not the issue, and the 'whydunnit' soon begins to unfold from the clues we get about the lives of the women we see on screen."[8] Gorris makes Janine analogous to the medical investigators who routinely diagnose and sometimes cure women's insanity in film melodramas or so-called women's films.[9] In her professional capacity she is entrusted with answering the very questions that engage us as spectators in the film's hermeneutic structure: Why did these women commit this crime? Are they crazy? She bears our questions and, as a psychiatrist, is presumably an expert source of the answers to them. It is through her and "her progressive enlightenment within the course of the narrative" that a strong position for audience identification is established.[10] Yet although psychiatry is posed as the mode of our enlightenment, Gorris uses the figure of Janine and the questions and expectations generated by the narrative structure to illustrate the inadequacy of psychoanalysis as a method of understanding these women and their crime.

A Question of Silence operates in a tradition of narrative filmmaking from which it differentiates itself, not formally as *Jeanne Dielman* does, but in terms of what the narrative reveals as the causes of certain events and in the way it elicits the spectators' participation in its hermeneutic structure. It is in the answers that Gorris's narrative provides to the question "Why did these women kill this man?" that the film transgresses the typical conventions of classical narrative and, specifically, as I shall argue, the conventions of the melodrama or women's film. As Robert Ray has pointed out, the "formal paradigm" of Hollywood cinema depended on "consciously established rules for shooting and editing." Correlatively, "Hollywood's thematic conventions rested on an industry-wide consensus defining commercially acceptable filmmaking. This consensus's underlying premise dictated the conversion of all political, sociological, and economic dilemmas into personal melodramas."[11] *A Question of Silence* exactly reverses this premise, refusing to understand or explain the three women's actions in personal, moral, or psychological terms at all. Rather, in very schematic, objective flashbacks and in the sequences that depict Janine's fieldwork (interviewing Andrea's boss and Christine's husband), Gorris systematically makes manifest the indignities, the daily oppressions, and the trivial but relentless instances of sexism that these women experience.

Her examples are not subtle. One sequence depicts a board meeting where Andrea is the only woman present. She makes an analysis of a potential market and suggests a course of action. Her boss dismisses her recommendation and a few moments later praises the same idea when it is voiced by one of his male business associates. This same associate then physically silences Andrea, putting his hand over hers to stop her from stirring her coffee and clinking her spoon against the cup. Ann is subjected to a constant barrage of sexual joking and insults at the café where she works, and, in her role as mother and wife, is shown to have been ill treated by both her husband and her daughter. In an interview with Janine, Christine's husband dismisses the significance of his wife's silence by referring to her as "the quiet type." He grumbles that he provided for her and worked hard while she had nothing to do all day. Called "three very ordinary women" at least once in the film, Christine, Ann, and Andrea function to a certain extent as types. Furthermore, by distributing various experiences of sexism through these characters and by *not* depicting any character's emotional or personal response to them, the film effectively generalizes these experiences and renders them typical.[12] Lucy Fischer sees the three as standing for "Everywoman."[13] Gorris very carefully distinguishes Christine, Ann, and Andrea from Janine as part of the class-based critique at work within this film. The three murderessess collectively represent Everywoman as a class of women whose voices and needs have been occluded or silenced by the dominant means of representing and understanding women primarily as middle class.

Despite the fact that *A Question of Silence* includes very few depictions of actual housework, its critique is structured and developed around the character of the housewife Christine. I have chosen to discuss this film because the figure of the silent housewife and Gorris's use of her engage and challenge the way women and women's work have been represented in film narratives addressed to women and also in feminist and other film theory. In certain ways Gorris's film mimics features of the women's picture or melodrama. The character of Christine, mute and trapped, seems a pointed allusion to the conventional protagonists of women's films—women usually confined to the domestic sphere who suffer but, for any number of reasons, cannot speak.[14] This particular character's lineage includes the heroines of eighteenth-century sentimental novels and melodramas, a tradition that is one precursor of the classical Hollywood cinema.[15] Christine is also related to Freud's hysterics, bourgeois women ensnared in familial seductions, whose disorders and silences influenced and shaped psychoanalytic theory, one important precursor of contemporary film theory. All these mute women share three related characteristics, albeit characteristics which in the case of Christine are consistently transformed: they have an intensely cathected relationship to the home and family; they suffer from an inability to speak; and finally, both hysterics and melodramatic heroines, with the obvious exception of Christine, are associated with narrative discourses (melodrama and psychoanalysis) that construct, explicate, and resolve conflicts or problems in terms of characters' moral or psychological interiority.[16] These discourses are historically affiliated with the rise and perpetuation of bourgeois consciousness.

As Griffith's heroines and characters such as Stella Dallas and Bea Pullman indicate, the silent, suffering domestic woman is endemic to the bourgeois imagination—an imagination whose fantasies and positioning of women *A Question of Silence* consistently rejects. In particular, the film refuses to participate in melodramatic conventions of interiority and emotion which infuse and shape the melodramatic heroine. Interiority, as Thomas Elsaesser notes, derives historically from an ideologically motivated emphasis on "private feelings and interiorised codes of morality and conscience associated with emergent bourgeois consciousness." Thus melodrama involves the "interiorisation and personalisation of what are primarily ideological conflicts." But the cultural work effected by the melodramatic imagination is not gender neutral. The etiology of the genre lends it to articulate class and, later, racial conflict through scenes of rape and sexual aggression.[17]

Elsaesser's comments explain the peculiar nature of melodramatic interiority—that the personal and emotional self is a moral rather than a psychological self—and they historicize the melodramatic conversion of social dilemmas into personal problems. More important, Elsaesser indicates the proclivity of melodramatic narratives to transform class issues, derived from materially based distinctions, into issues based on gender and sexuality ("sexual exploitation and rape"), a transformation that implies a switch from "public" to "private" concerns. Women thus become ideal melodramatic victim-protagonists by means of this displacement, which not only implicates gender and sexuality in the mystification of class conflict and other social problems but also positions women as the privileged signifiers of interiority and the personal.

The gendered realms of public and private override or supersede other materially based social distinctions. In this process women come to assume a burden of signification at least as cumbersome as that of castration.[18] They also bear, fairly exclusively, the burden of representing the personal, the private, and, most important, the emotional self. Correlatively, gender and sexuality, encoded and represented through and by women, also become privatized, enmeshed in the moral, emotional, familial criteria that figure "private life." In this representational paradigm, then, it becomes difficult, if not impossible, to conceive of gender issues impersonally, without emotions, as functions of public societal dynamics that override the affective experience of the individual.

A Question of Silence agitated Stanley Kauffmann and other critics by refusing to locate the women's violence within this gendered narrative matrix. I have noted how the film typifies experiences of misogyny by generalizing these experiences through the characters of Christine, Andrea, and Ann. The film further tempers our identification with them as private, personal individuals in its treatment of their emotions. The three are depicted as strikingly dispassionate, most notably during the murder scene, but also throughout Janine's investigation and in the courtroom as well. The only emotion they express, albeit infrequently, is anger. They do not weep, nor do they express any kind of angst over the killing of the shopkeeper. Similarly, we are not privy to their emotional responses to the incidents of sexism they encounter. The narrative reinforces this distanced view of their lives by consistently giving external social evidence for their anger and their violence.

Through the character of Janine, the narrative also systematically discounts the legitimacy of psychological explanations for the women's actions. Because of her class position, Janine greatly enhances the comprehensive character of *A Question of Silence*'s critique of both melodramatic and psychoanalytic accounts of women's silence. Janine is a bourgeois professional woman who is (initially) insensitive to the real conditions of her clients' lives (as when she suggests to Ann that she simply remarry or get another job). A court-appointed psychiatrist, she demonstrates the affiliation (certainly historically accurate) between the state, class privilege, and psychoanalysis. Thus Andrea is contemptuous when Janine asks her questions with a clearly psychoanalytic agenda, especially questions concerning her childhood or her sex life. Armed with her professional expertise and her tape recorder, Janine gets nowhere when she approaches the murderous catatonic housewife. The film makes quite clear that, listening with Freud's ear, Janine will never be able to understand Christine's story. As Andrea explains, Christine has stopped talking because no one was listening to her.

The "question of silence" or "the silence around Christine M." concerns finally not only the capacity to speak, but also the ability of others to listen. Significantly, the film presents psychoanalysis and the law as two institutions that can neither hear Christine nor understand the motivation for her crimes. Both are invested in ascribing the murder committed by the three women to interior, personal disorders. To acknowledge that these women had material reasons to kill would compel members of the court to realize what Janine (and the spectator) realizes in the course of the film: that women have public, political lives conditioned by material exigencies that are not and have never been fully apprehended by the emotional or the "personal." Gorris strikes at one of the most pervasive social stereotypes about women, statistically supported—that they are capable only of crimes of passion—to indicate how fundamental our gender stereotypes are. This crime was unthinkable: *A Question of Silence* investigates why. Thus, even in the trial scenes (a familiar device of melodramas), Gorris brackets moral issues of guilt and innocence, good and evil, and focuses instead on attempts by the court and psychiatry to relieve these women of the responsibility and agency they very much want to claim for their actions.[19]

Gorris indicates the degree to which Janine changes by having her deliver to the court the explanation for the women's crime. In response to the prosecutor's assertion that the murder was completely irrational, Janine argues that the women's motive can be discerned in the particulars of the crime: three women murdered a man who was the proprietor of an expensive women's clothing store. Her comments expose the class and gender bias implicit in the prosecutor's offhand characterization of shopping as a "harmless pastime." Gorris's housewife is provoked to kill while shopping, an activity that is part of her work, and one that brings the gross disjunction between the economy of the home and that of the market into sharp focus.[20] The fact that the boutique sells expensive women's clothes heightens the irony of the prosecutor's misunderstanding. What is socially coded as a "harmless pastime" is also culturally promoted as necessary and important business for women: maintaining their clothing and their appearance. What the prosecutor, the judges, and Janine's husband cannot understand is perfectly clear to all the women involved. As Janine remarks, "It really is quite funny" that the prosecutor does not understand that it would not be the same thing at all for three men to kill the female owner of a shop.

Gorris deals melodramatic conventions one last blow when her characters, including the four silent witnesses who attend the trial, laugh uproariously at the culmination of the film, soliciting laughter from audiences as well. One reviewer comments, "Rather than weep as cinema has so often asked of women in the past, we too cannot help but laugh."[21] *A Question of Silence* delivers its strongest charge by introducing a third term into the (gendered) opposition between silence and speech, a term rich with potential associations for feminism and feminist theory: laughter. Rather than solicit women's identification with the suffering and pathos of melodramatic heroines, an identification marked by tears and wet hankies, *A Question of Silence* prompts at least some of its audience to feel a comic response.

The film concludes not with a verdict but with a punch line; indeed, one way of reading *A Question of Silence* would be to consider it a jocular manifesto. In order to "get" the meaning, in order to participate in the outbreak of hilarity that provides the narrative with its resolution, a spectator must carefully follow and accept the terms of the "joke" Gorris painstakingly constructs. This joke involves making women's issues public, manifest in the dynamics of the narrative, thereby invoking an identification in stark contrast to that solicited by melodrama. The beauty of the film lies in its demonstration that a woman's point of view or spectator position, contrary to psychoanalytic film theory's pronouncements, *can* be constructed.[22] Gorris locates that position in an instance of humor, as the j/ocular character of the film hides a place of seeing, of spectating for women, lodged in the construction of a joke. If laughter is the best medicine, it tellingly places the film's women outside the law (literally: the courtroom) and the home, which psychoanalysis and melodrama so effectively wed.

Marleen Gorris does not use housework as an aesthetic influence in the construction of her film. Rather, she takes up various cultural mystifications of the silent housewife, most notably those produced by psychoanalysis and melodrama, and systematically inverts both the story they tell and the way they tell it. She demonstrates the ways in which cultural systems and representations frame the three women such that their anger and the reasons for it can be understood only as madness. Christine is indeed a "mad" housewife, and Gorris's film constructs a context where her rage, if not its consequences, seems completely sane.

Despite their radical differences in approach and style, *Jeanne Dielman* and *A Question of Silence* tell very similar stories, each featuring housewives and murder. Each film poses a challenge to melodramatic representations of women, in terms of formal structures (*Jeanne Dielman*), narrative construction (both films), and character-ization (both films have dispassionate and affectless female protagonists). In both narratives the female protagonists kill men with whom they have economic relations: in *Jeanne Dielman* a man who is a consumer and in *A Question of Silence* a man who sells women's clothes. In their common focus on economics and labor, both films insist on an understanding of gender that exceeds sexuality per se. Thus each regis-ters socialist feminist concerns that characterized European, primarily anglophone, feminism but did not figure prominently in U.S. feminist psychoanalytic film the-ory in the seventies and early eighties.

Contemporaneous reviews and critical articles by U.S. academic film feminists, especially on *Jeanne Dielman*, tend not to emphasize, if they note at all, these films' pointed contextualizations and critiques of psychoanalytic theory as it relates to both conventional film narrative and the representation of women. Akerman's film locates itself specifically by a mailing address, and situates psychoanalysis within an exchange between mother and son, both of whom exist within overarching national, political, and economic structures that ultimately condition the narrative of *Jeanne Dielman*. *A Question of Silence*, by contrast, insists on marking the class biases that character-ize both psychoanalytic understandings of women and the relations between mid-dle- and working-class women. It deserves comment that the films' reworkings of domestic femininity and its significance differ from academic film feminists' theo-rization of this femininity, and that their respective uses of psychoanalysis are cru-cial to their differences. While the films position psychoanalysis as one of several contending discourses within a set of material relations, U.S. feminist film theory took up psychoanalysis as a coherent methodology that provided an understanding of both the medium (apparatus theory) and its spectator. Whereas this theoretical orientation understands history through the filter of spectatorship or technology, the films, in their respective aesthetic and ideological renderings of women's domestic labor, gesture at more complex apprehensions of the aesthetic and the historical, the economic and the subjective.

The gap between film theory and feminist films' respective visions of domesticity serves to historicize the treatment of domestic labor within hegemonic psychoana-lytic feminist film theory; like differences among women (race, class, sexuality), this labor was not really seen or theorized as labor during this period, even if feminist narrative films were representing both the labor and the differences among women. In any case, neither the films nor the theory had extensive cultural circulation in the United States. *Jeanne Dielman*'s U.S. release and reception speaks to the types of con-tainment that have characterized both feminist film production and academic fem-inist discourse in this country. Writing on the film in the *Village Voice*, B. Ruby Rich asserts, "When *Jeanne Dielman* became Akerman's breakthrough film in 1975, it seemed to speak directly to all of us engaged in feminist theory and film criticism."[23] The international and universal homogeneity of this profession expressed in Rich's statement sits squarely in the context of this feminism's own marginalization. Rich's column celebrates the limited United States commercial release of the film eight long years after it entered the feminist film canon in the United States and abroad. Thus the most cogent and accessible aesthetic reconsiderations of domestic femininity never reached any kind of mass audience because of the commercial constraints endemic to the U.S. film industry. In addition, their critical reception was conditioned and contained by a theoretical apparatus that understood gender as wholly apprehended by sexuality and subjectivity. The consequence was that women's work and women's labor, both domestic and aesthetic, were once again subsumed in considerations of their affect and appearance, however sophisticated and theoretically informed the understanding of those terms came to be.

As narrative features, *Jeanne Dielman* and *A Question of Silence* were conceived in relation to and in competition with mainstream narrative cinema, however limited their U.S. and international distribution. The experimental films I consider in the next and final chapter, unlike these two feminist features, were never fashioned for commercial or theatrical release, but instead explore domestic labor as the occasion for avant-garde imaginings.

NINE

Experimental Domesticities

Patricia Gruben's The Central Character
and Zeinabu Davis's Cycles

And therefore there is a female aesthetic, but not a female aesthetic, not
one single constellation of strategies.

RACHEL BLAU DuPLESSIS

In 1960 Yoko Ono wrote *Kitchen Piece* as part of her *Instruction Paintings* series:
"Hang a canvas on a wall. Throw all the leftovers you have in the kitchen that day
on the canvas. You may prepare special food for the piece."[1] Just as Lydia Child
appropriated the recipe to serve as the basis for a system of knowledge about domesticity, so Ono takes it up to fashion a stunning piece of conceptual art that con-
founds instructions and experience, print and image, art concept and art object.
Kitchen Piece also solicits an entirely different public and orientation for the recipe,
the kitchen, and the home-cooked meal. She transforms what has been understood
as the antithesis of art into its very mode and substance. Before her time in this, as
in many other aspects of her work, Ono anticipates U.S. feminist artists' intense
interest in the domestic from the 1970s onward.[2]

Betye Saar's 1972 artwork *The Liberation of Aunt Jemima* brilliantly appropriates
the pernicious modes of historical and commodity integration figured in the trademark of Aunt Jemima and the happy, benevolent mammy character she supposedly
represents. Against a backdrop of the mass-produced trademark, the liberated (and
three-dimensional) Aunt Jemima holds a broom, a rifle, and a pistol on either side
of a picture which forms the front of her floral print dress. The picture depicts a
smiling mammy holding a white baby behind a picket fence, a white sheet thrown
over it. The Black Power fist rises up in the middle of this image, utterly disrupting
the fantasy that informs it—that of the servile domestic assimilation of racial difference. Astutely capturing and contesting both the cultural and commodity manifestations of this national fantasy, Saar presents her multiple Aunt Jemimas (as

trademark, fantasy image, and revolutionary) in a box that mimics the "servant in a box" purveyed by the trademark and narrativized in the 1930s versions of *Imitation of Life*. Finally, the title of the piece invokes "women's liberation" and reminds white feminists that the metaphor of their domestic slavery has literal, embodied, and commodified nonwhite antecedents.

Ono and Saar are notable for foregrounding domesticity within works that challenge the conventional object of art itself, and for doing so in advance of the theoretical treatises that promoted formal innovation as an essential component of feminist aesthetics and politics (for example, Laura Mulvey's call for avant-garde feminist film in *Visual Pleasure and Narrative Cinema*). Their challenge to the object of (conceptual, multimedia) art relates to wider activities involving performance, social activism, and political movements "in the streets" that characterized the American avant-garde of this period.

Martha Rosler's 1975 film *Semiotics of the Kitchen* brings film and theory into the multiple valences of this aesthetic work on domesticity. The title of the piece refers to Ferdinand de Saussure's and Charles Sanders Peirce's science of signs. This reference signals a larger professionalization of feminism that occurred during this period. Like the domestic engineers before them, some feminists adopted and adapted theoretical systems, such as semiotics and psychoanalysis, within academic discourses and disciplines, one of the most notable examples of which was film studies and film theory. Rosler's film, illustrative of this moment, is didactic, formalist, and antiaesthetic. It depicts a young woman, who frequently looks at the camera in the style of documentary rather than fiction, as she works her way through an alphabet of kitchen utensils—apron, bowl, chopper, dish—demonstrating their use. Her gestures, however, are exaggerated and violent, abstractly expressing the rage generated by housework that Akerman and Gorris render as experience in their films. Rosler provides an example of avant-garde feminist film on domesticity generated from within the context of feminist theory. The two films I consider in the remainder of this chapter transform aspects of domesticity into an occasion for experimental film practices. Yet their very different historical moments and modes of production reflect significant changes in the emphasis of feminist or women's aesthetic work on domesticity.

The Metaphysics of Housework:
Patricia Gruben's *The Central Character*

Patricia Gruben's experimental film *The Central Character* (1977) works with an aspect of housekeeping that I have not had occasion to mention until now: its symbolic function in maintaining the liminal social space of the home. As a cultural border or boundary, the home constitutes a margin between culture and its traditional other, the natural world. Sometimes this "border" is literally represented in the form of a wooded backyard or garden, requiring an attention to landscaping that solicits the natural while taking care to cultivate it. But the increasingly infrequent spatial placement of the home in between nature and culture supports more ideologically based distinctions between these two realms. How, exactly, is the home a liminal social space? The activities that cultural convention dictates should be performed in the home relate to the body and to the provision of physical necessities. As the place where we presumably eat, drink, defecate, rest, have sex, and seek shelter, the home is linked with activities coded as physical and "natural." Yet it also figures as a sign of civilization and its distance from nature; as Oscar Wilde remarked, "If Nature had been comfortable, mankind would never have invented architecture. . . . I prefer houses to the open air."[3] Thus one task that the home—or, better, the idea of the home—performs is a transformative one: as an interstitial space, it delimits an area in which specific practices create the distinctions between two territories, the natural and the cultural or the physical and the social. Articulating elements of both, the home is neither. Rather it figures as a place of paradox, connoting at once a refuge or area outside the frantic public world and a shelter inside, protected from the natural elements. Housework manages these conflicting significations. Thus, women—as housekeepers, as homemakers, as the agents of this semiotic operation—become identified with its contradictions and effects. Like the home, women are neither nature nor culture; their liminal functions make both them and their work invisible. *The Central Character* literalizes and demonstrates these paradoxes.

In the film, an amorphous protagonist—initially a housewife—is transformed as her voice and persona move from the emphatically organized environment of the kitchen to the organic profusion of the woods. The film sets up an ambiguous relation between its central character, her activities, and the locations through which she moves. While highlighting the ways in which housekeeping practices construct and maintain a domestic environment, Gruben also illustrates the effects this environment has on the highly ambiguous identity of its protagonist. Focusing attention on food, its raising, acquisition, and preparation, the film aligns two functionally similar yet structurally distinct spaces—the kitchen and the garden. It then traces changes in its protagonist as she moves from the kitchen to the garden to the woods. This protagonist never assumes a distinct identity; instead she takes on the "character" of her surroundings. In the kitchen and the garden she concerns herself with order and cleanliness. Once in the woods, however, she becomes diffuse and wild; she literally revels in dirt.

Gruben uses primarily verbal and architectural texts to render the domestic space of the kitchen. The film opens with a woman tonelessly reciting a grocery list on the sound track as a text scrolling up a black screen describes her struggle with two bulky grocery bags on her way into the house. The format of a scrolling text recurs, intercut with images, giving us fragmentary descriptions of the events and chores that structure a housewife's domestic existence. All these chores involve a struggle between food and dirt, cleanliness and disorder. Over a floor plan of the kitchen's layout, superimposed titles tell us:

> Entropy is the main problem in the modern kitchen, regulating traffic flow, keeping fingerprints, food particles and other unhygienic particles out. A nucleus of order must be maintained. A kitchen is white steel and chrome for earlier detection. Why is it that disorder is more contagious?

A subsequent text notes that as the woman prepares to fix herself a meal, she must be very careful "to remove all the grit"; a recipe scrolls up the screen, followed by instructions for sprouting potatoes. Utilizing a poetic logic, Gruben plays off the organic implications of the word *cultivation* (as vegetal growth) against its culturally oriented meaning of refinement and polish. But the woman's proclivity for cultivation proves to be her undoing. The next text informs us that the potatoes exhibited "phenomenal growth" and "overtook the kitchen." To get to her dishes, the woman "had to pull roots off the cupboard door." The last written text in the film has the character of a fairy tale: needing to find more containers for her plants, it announces, the woman ventures into the woods, sprinkling seeds behind her to mark her way home. But the birds eat the seeds.

The printed passages that punctuate these initial sequences of *The Central Character* mark the film's movement toward disorder. Beginning with the straightforward description of the grocery list, the clinical treatise on the horrors of entropy, and the recipe, the superimposed texts gradually become a fantastic narration detailing the transformation of a certain milieu and of the character who inhabits and maintains it. Initially the images illustrate the texts. After the passage on entropy and fingerprints, we see a hand scrubbing a dirty footprint off a floor. The early sequences of the film use still images to depict the housewife as an unseen agent of order: we see a broom sweeping a patio then a hand scrubbing a floor, we hear a voice observing that the patio must be swept "every day." Time-lapse photography of wildly growing roots accompanies her remark that "the natural world takes dictation from science." The first visual representation of "the central character" depicts her lying in a bathtub, a fern frond dangling down toward her floating hair. The organic world invades and contaminates the domestic. The woman goes to the woods to search for "containers."

In the latter half of the film, compelling, enigmatic images predominate. No written texts order this world, and the woman's voice merges with the cacophony of the outdoors. Overexposed high-contrast film depicts her lying in the mud, initially indistinguishable from the ground, perhaps drinking water from a puddle. Discovered by the camera, she bounds off, her bright white clothing patterned with dirt and stains. She peruses domestic artifacts scattered in a field as a voice repeats incessantly, "I only wanted to say, I only wanted to say . . ." Meaning becomes a mantra, a drone blending with the sounds of frogs and insects. Hemmed in by foliage, the woman sets a mock table, placing a worm and a frog on a plate as an almost incoherent, reverberating voice recites the proper placement of knives and spoons.

Gruben contrasts the two halves of her film by whimsically repeating and remotivating certain motifs of order. A high-contrast shot of the woman pushing an empty shopping cart recklessly through a field provides a humorous visual analogue to the opening of the film, where the woman's wrists are described as "white" from the strain of holding bulky grocery bags while she struggles to get into the house. The dull repetition characteristic of housework finds its counterpart in the echoes that render the aural atmosphere of the woods. The pattern of stains on the woman's white blouse visually recalls the dirty footprint so industriously scrubbed off the white floor in an earlier sequence. Much of the play between the two sections derives from Gruben's strategy of recontextualizing the film's motifs. The dresser and shopping cart, embedded in a fairy tale and found in the woods, become objects of curiosity and fascination, deprived of their familiar surroundings and utilitarian functions. The reverberating instructions for setting a proper table sound ludicrous and strange when we see the woman carefully following the rules as she lays out a table in the forest. Gruben invokes a visual pun as the woman scoops a worm out of a can for dinner. Literally a *grub*, the worm writhes on the plate as "grub," or food.

Gruben further distinguishes the two worlds of her film by tone or mood. Initially she uses images or texts that consist of abstract, schematic sets of instructions — the floor plan, the carpenter's drawing, the recipe — to represent the ordering of a domestic space. These "objective" or scientific documents function both as instructions and as representations, involving a perspective, a point of view, a way of knowing based on causality, reason, explication, and consensual means of transmitting knowledge. In the woods, however, the filmmaker manipulates the images and the sound track to articulate a very different kind of textuality. In the first half of the film Gruben documents housework, but in the second half she "plays house." She renders setting a table and pushing a shopping cart fantastic and nonsensical acts simply by moving them outdoors. If the first section stresses the rationality, the drudgery, and the humorlessness of housework, the second invents a whimsical fantasy from housekeeping practices. There is no center, no emotional quality or coherent subjectivity that unifies the two parts of the film; instead, Gruben moves from one world to the other by following the contradictory imperatives of the housewife's duties — to clean, to feed, to cultivate.

The narrative moves from indoors to outdoors according to a deconstructive logic that illuminates the differing senses of the words *cultivation*, *cultivate*, and *culture*. Deriving from the same Latin stem as *culture* and almost synonymous with it, *cultivate* means to till the soil, to plow and fertilize, to dig the soil around growing plants. It also means to foster or nourish and, finally, to refine or polish. Gruben uses the differing meanings of this term to reveal paradoxes relating to dirt, to food, to depth and surface, and to indoors and outdoors that all affect the "character" of housewifery, the home, and, by implication, women who keep house. To cultivate out of doors, as Gruben's film illustrates, involves getting dirty, getting beneath the surface, and concerning oneself with growth, roots, and fertility. The cultivation practiced indoors, by contrast, implies ridding oneself of dirt and vulgarity, cleaning and polishing all aspects of one's person (physical, mental, and social), and obsessively concerning oneself with surfaces and appearances. While the cultivation one practices outdoors often produces food, indoors one cultivates the intangible nourishments associated with a refined sensibility. Cultivation in its sense of "refinement" implies activities of purification and discrimination; fertility, however, requires the mixing of disparate elements. Beginning with the implied oppositions that structure the opening sequences of the film, between the grocery store and the garden, between the sterility the housewife should strive for within the home and the messy fertility that is a necessary component of nourishment, *The Central Character* playfully explores the plethora of contradictions, both actual and symbolic, that are managed and provisionally effaced by the activities of housework.

The film opens. As stills of the broom sweeping the patio dissolve one on top of the other, the woman's voice informs us that "the patio must be swept every day to reclaim it from the out of doors." Margins are problematic; the patio, outdoors yet part of the home, borders on the woods and requires vigilant daily attention. As the stills of a sweeping broom continue, the housewife notes the superimposition of the patio, of the cultural surface, onto the natural one: "The clay bricks are set directly into the earth in the extensive backyard." This attention to the cultural function of surfaces dominates the first half of the film, the half that concerns the indoors, the domestic; furthermore, most of the early images are flat, two-dimensional (a white floor, a floor plan on graph paper, a drawing of cabinets). These surfaces must be kept clean, free from the material that characterizes the outdoors (dirt), from all residue that indicates the work done in the kitchen (food particles), and from the signs of human presence itself (fingerprints and footprints). Significantly, the presence of the housewife is conveyed strictly by her hand, her voice, or scrolling text.

The housewife performs these tasks of erasure and purification that keep indoors separate from outdoors, activity separate from its effects or residue and the body and traces of the body separate from the work involved in satisfying its needs. One of the housewife's chores is to efface the signs of her own work (food particles) and those of her role as worker (fingerprints). Another is to make manifest a system of spatial distinctions. In this regard her work resembles primitive ritual in that it provides a literal frame for culture. As I have noted in another context, Mary Douglas equates our secular housecleaning with ritual:

> When we honestly reflect on our busy scrubbings and cleanings . . . we know that we are not mainly trying to avoid disease. We are separating, placing boundaries, making visible statements about the home we are intending to create out of the material house.[4]

While Gruben's film illustrates the role cleaning plays in establishing cultural boundaries and distinctions, it also suggests the fragility of these boundaries and the profound interdependency of the two realms created by them. The film visually suggests the degree to which the ideas of "nature" and "culture" depend on the practices that maintain this supposedly natural division. Although the housewife creates these distinctions and keeps them "neat," she herself inhabits or comes to embody their paradoxical connection.

As a result of the imperatives of purity implied in various aspects of housework, the housewife is placed in what Mary Douglas would call a "dangerous" cultural position. In order to clean, to separate, to keep dirt (nature) out, the housewife must "get her hands dirty," do the "dirty work." As a cultural cleaning agent, she must come into contact with and handle the very pollutions she protects others from; she therefore runs the risk of being tainted with them herself. But she also must avoid being too clean, or becoming overzealous and maniacal like Craig's wife. Douglas remarks that

> the quest for purity is pursued by rejection. . . . [W]hen purity is not a symbol but something lived, it must be poor and barren. Purity is the enemy of change, of ambiguity and compromise . . . it is an attempt to force experience into logical categories of non-contradiction. But experience is not amenable and those who make the attempt find themselves led into contradiction.[5]

We can see the housewife's liminal and paradoxical situation represented in advertisements for cleansers, soaps, dishwashing liquids, or floor-cleaning products, where the same contradictions between inside and outside, between "nature" and "culture," shape the character of the product. Ad copy stresses that the effects of housework are effects of erasure, yet an erasure that leaves traces in its wake—a gleam, a shine, the scents of lemon or pine. Cleaning products promise not only to evacuate dirt, grime, and germs, aspects of the "natural" that are dirty and dangerous, but also to import the scent and freshness of the outdoors, leaving olfactory traces of vegetal or floral growth.[6] Thus nature or the natural, coded as the source of the dirty and taboo, is also commodified and chemically reproduced as a signifier of cleanliness that opens up and refreshes indoor domestic space. Significantly, the purity promoted by these ads derives from a complex process of transformations enacted between the "natural" and the "cultural," not from an oppositional relation between them.

As the agent of these paradoxical transformations, the housewife, like the cleaning product, contains contradictory significations that affect the coherence of her identity. Gruben's film shows how a woman's various household duties influence her own (unstable) image. The same instability exists in cultural constructions of female gender and sexuality. Historically and culturally relegated to perform tasks that establish the distinctions between the natural and the cultural, women, generalized in the "feminine," come to represent extremes of both.[7] "The feminine" therefore signifies conflicting polarities that articulate not an opposition to a male other but an enclosure, a parenthesis in which "he" figures as norm/neutral/neither. Women, writes Catherine Clément, "are double. They are allied with what is regular, according to the rules, since they are wives and mothers, and allied as well with those natural disturbances, their regular periods, which are the epitome of paradox, order and disorder."[8] While Clément locates the source of this doubling in women's physical, biological functions, Gruben's film argues that the gender coding of certain highly symbolic activities—cleaning, cooking, feeding—also helps create the frame in which we read biological differences. Furthermore, the ideological pressure of such a frame is evident in considerations of housekeepers' and, by inference, women's sexuality.

As a worker whose practices create, police, and maintain the cultural border between purity and impurity, whose actions determine what comes close to the bodies of her family and what is kept at a distance, who supervises what goes in and comes out of those bodies, the housekeeper finds that her own body is subject to stringent limitations and cultural controls. These controls monitor the cleanliness of both her body and her sexuality. If we look at narratives about housewives, we can see that the stories they tell are often marked by a confusion of literal and metaphorical cleanliness. In accounts of bad or mad housewives, the woman is associated either with a "dirty" sexuality and slovenly housewifery or with frigidity and obsessive orderliness. Codes of personal cleanliness and sexuality are bound up with the diverse chores of the housewife, infusing cultural constructions of her sexuality with hygienic concerns: a "slut" is both a slovenly housewife and a promiscuous woman. The housewife's role as cleaner becomes associated with her role as sexual partner, a phenomenon treated in *Craig's Wife* and critiqued in *Jeanne Dielman*. The good housewife must negotiate a position that includes some of both roles and all of neither. She must manage and contain contradiction.

The Central Character exposes the paradoxical character of housekeeping by muddying conventional distinctions between meanings and between spaces. Her poetic

meditation on the nature-culture divide adopts this essentialist binary only to deconstruct it on its own terms. In transgressive and playful ways, Gruben's film undercuts
the cultural practices that keep things separate by revealing the cracks and contradictions in the language and imagery of housekeeping.

Differentiating Domesticities: Zeinabu Davis's *Cycles*

Zeinabu Davis's film *Cycles* (1988) uses the many implications of its title to organize
a very different meditation from Gruben's on the natural and cultural implications of
housekeeping in relation to women's bodies and the spaces they inhabit. Her film
uses irony rather than poetry to mock (as both mimic and critique) significations of
nature and culture in women's domestic lives. Over the title sequence we hear chant-
ing, as visuals depict the word "CYCLES" written out over the simultaneous chalk
drawing of a voodoo inscription. Lines in the shape of a cross branch out into a heart
shape, which is then traced over with lines and ornament. The word *cycle* invokes an
array of meanings: "an interval of time during which a sequence of a recurring suc-
cession of events or phenomena is completed"; "a course or series of events or operations that recur regularly and usually lead back to the starting point"; "a group of
poems, plays, novels, or songs treating the same theme"; "a circular or spiral arrangement . . . whorl, orbit, ring."[9] The word proposes a kind of temporal paradox: the
cycle is both a figure of repetition and its termination or closure. It is within this
paradox that Davis articulates her film, opening and closing it with the same
sequence whose meaning changes because of the text that inhabits the interval
between its repetition.

The cycles to which Davis's title applies include women's menstrual patterns, the
character of housework, and the structuring of reproduction and narrative in relation to these cyclic domestic events. Both reproduction and narrative are only *apparently* linear patterns which are ultimately predicated on meaningful repetition—that
is, repetition interrupted or closed down by alterity or difference. Davis's film invokes
a system under which these disparate "cycles" are integrated, that of spiritual ritual
as it pertains to domesticity, fertility, reproduction, and tradition.

But her invocations of spirituality and mysticism are not at all naive or apolitical.
Intervening both in standardized, commodified, mainstream representations of
housekeeping and in some white feminist reappropriations of it, Davis's *Cycles* insists
on underrepresented domestic arrangements, styles, and, most important, histories.
The film's protagonist is African American, single, without children, maintaining her
own home. The film inscribes its difference at the intersection of familial, hetero-
sexist, reproductive, and racial biases that underpin conventional representations of
"home."

Drawing a chalk heart in the title sequence, Davis alludes to a cultural icon saturated with sentimental heterosexual feminine meanings and concerns. Yet this image
is immediately overlaid with puzzling, enigmatic ornamentation that precludes any
easy association with conventional romantic meanings. The voodoo inscription
belongs to a cultural tradition and history of love and domesticity very different from
that of Saint Valentine and his secularized sentimental commodity offspring. Voodoo

signifies slavery, West Africa, the Middle Passage; the decimation of peoples, families, and tradition; spiritual resilience, a pronounced reverence for (lost) ancestors, and the assimilation of the spiritual to the everyday; the necessity of tricks, magic, and deception in the master-slave relation; the possibility of power sources beyond logic and an unacceptable reality.[10] But because this host of associations remains tacit in the image, the inscription marks the opening of the film with a culturally and historically inflected enigma.

Following a dedication and directorial credits, the screen reads: "for the goddess within us all." Davis refers to a theme in New Age or spiritualist feminism—the goddess—here situated within a specific cultural context. As we hear South African women's choral music, the film begins with a handheld camera slowly tilting down the profile of an African fertility goddess, then panning across other objects, in extreme close-up, on what appears to be an ancestral altar: an old family photo, a calendar, candles, a bowl of fruit and nuts, a burning incense stick. The African icon visually disappropriates the abstract "white" feminist goddess perhaps conjured up in the previous sequence and gives her flesh and a history. Like a musical overture or prologue, this sequence alludes, though very enigmatically, to the film's thematic concerns. Not directly a part of the "narrative," the sequence is very puzzling on first viewing (it also closes the film), though the ensuing narrative explicates some of its meanings. Rather than give the audience generalized, immediately accessible narrative information, the sequence provides ambiance, connotation, and arcane significations.

The screen fades to black; the music ends. From black, we cut to a long shot, whose foreground contains an African American woman in profile, sitting by a large picture window, slowly and intently dusting the goddess icon, which she holds in front of her. A nondiegetic clock ticks loudly, keeping time in the manner of a metronome. Outside the window a man walks away, but it is unclear whether he has come from this woman's apartment or another in the complex. The contrast in the image is striking: the woman seems flat and one-dimensional, her image collapsed on the glass, while the man moves through the depth and space rendered by the shot's deep focus outside the window. She is completely still; he is going somewhere. Her space is flat, his expansive and deep. With stunning visual acuity and economy Davis gives us within this one shot a stereotypical gender narrative as old as Penelope and Odysseus. Seemingly in accord with the "he goes, she waits" motif, a voice-over recounts:

> She had been waiting for two weeks now, but it had not arrived. She didn't know what to do, whether to prepare or not. So she did the only thing she knew to do to keep her mind from the anticipated moment. She had no one to talk to so she indulged herself in her humble surroundings.

As the quote suggests, the rest of Davis's film reverses or undoes the signification of this shot. Rather than follow the man out into what is usually the "world" of narrative, we move into the dynamics and the depth of the woman's domestic space.

In the next shot the woman sits at the kitchen table reading Toni Morrison's *Beloved,* a bag of potato chips open in front of her. Morrison's novel, which subsequently garnered its author the Nobel Prize for literature, tells a story about blood, loss, slavery, murder and the horror of maternity, of tradition, if that tradition, that maternal bequest, is slavery. It narrates the problem of living with impossible memories, intolerable histories. Like the title and opening altar sequence, *Beloved* (its type enlarged so we can see the book title in the long shot in which it is depicted) gives a wealth of associational significations that are never anchored or given specific motivation in the minimalist narrative of this film. The woman puts the book down and begins to "indulge herself in her surroundings." In *Cycles* the narrative becomes incidental (in all senses) as the film explores traces of ritual traditions and meanings in banal repetitions of everyday life. These pointed cultural allusions (ancestral altar, voodoo symbol, Morrison's novel) provide a thematic matrix within which the narrative of domesticity occurs. This tactic reverses the usual relation between theme and narrative, wherein the former emerges from the logic of the latter. Correlatively, Davis's thematic allusions tacitly challenge family of man universalities about family, motherhood, fatherhood, and so on, conventionally rooted in gendered, reproductively rationalized domestic arrangements. Instead her allusions insist on domesticity conceived within historical boundaries. American history, including slavery and racism, shaped the traditions, the homes, and the families of some Americans, and the traces of this history still remain.

As we learn in the ensuing sequences, the indulgence of which the narrator speaks is housework. The body of *Cycles* consists of two contiguous parts: a series of shots depicts the woman cleaning her home and herself; this is followed by a dream sequence that occurs when she lies down to rest after her labors. Within the cognitively dissonant frame of indulgence, then, the film represents housekeeping acts. Not only the narrator and the protagonist but the film's director as well transform what are usually represented as boring, banal, hopelessly trivial acts into sensuous visions of special pleasures, which I want to describe in some detail.

The housekeeping scenes alternate between moving film and stills; the sound track is silent save for the rhythmic ticking of the clock, keeping time. We see the woman strip her bed, take clothes out of a hamper and sort them, vacuum, mop the floor, clean the toilet, wash the sink. Among these activities we get suggestions of narrative. After stripping the bed, the woman sits on the edge of the mattress, in long shot, and pulls clothes out of the hamper. Taking out a couple of items, she comes upon a man's large sweater; she holds it up against her body, caressing it lovingly, then suddenly crumples it up and throws it on the floor. As she interacts with the sweater, the camera slowly moves in, ending on a tight close-up of her face, downcast and dejected.

Fade. She begins to clean. Keeping the camera at ground level, Davis depicts only the woman's feet and the vacuum cleaner as they negotiate the space of the carpet. Fade. A series of stills render a mop in a bucket, then the sequential actions of squeezing the mop out, all seen from an overhead angle. Then we see, at floor level, the mop tendrils in various positions. Throughout, the cuts between stills occur with each tick of the clock. Fade. A moving image renders the actions of making the bed. The voice-over tells us the woman has chosen fresh white linen and that "progress is being made." Switching to stills again, a series of images, taken from overhead, show her cleaning the toilet, her dark muscular shoulders cutting across the gleaming white oval of porcelain. The series culminates in stills rendering the woman cleaning white shower tiles, her body movements shifting from cleaning gestures to dance as the stills become moving images and then rapidly projected stills that give the illusion of dance movements. On the sound track an audio sampling of Louis Armstrong, looped in a repeated jazz chant, dictates the rhythm of the cleaning-dancing movements and the cutting and repetition of the film stills.

Using rhythmic and graphic contrasts, Davis frames the woman's housekeeping activities such that the aesthetic and formal values of her bodily movements, the image itself, and the cutting are foregrounded. In black-and-white film stock, the whiteness of the sheets, the toilet, and the shower tile set off the beauty of the woman's skin. Davis enhances this visual contrast in the sensuous distinctions she articulates in the images between skin and porcelain, muscle and fabric. The film renders these contrasts within more abstract rhythmic and audio alternations: between silence and sound, silence and music; between moving and still images. Setting oppositions in play, Davis cleverly demonstrates the power of context and representational tactics over the interpretation of any event. Housekeeping becomes indulgence in surroundings as the relentless ticking of a clock—which might indicate boredom, the endlessness of tasks, the loss of valuable time—becomes the beat that determines the rhythm of the cutting, and that keeps time and leads into the Louis Armstrong piece. In *Cycles*, work becomes play, labor dance, housekeeping an indulgence.

A pan throughout the clean living space provides the segue to the next part of the film. As a shot depicts the woman looking in a mirror, a voice-over states, "You're doing O.K. and you're gonna get better." Another voice, with a West Indian accent, follows, saying, "It was no time for the obvious. Who could live in a clean house without a clean body? Time to attend to herself now." The next several shots render the woman brushing her teeth, taking a bath, putting on a nightshirt, and rubbing oil on her feet, legs, and hands. As she does so, other voices recount her actions in the third person: "She then stepped into the bathtub and stayed there for what seemed an eternity." The clock continues to tick; the woman sits in front of her altar, incense burning, as rhythmic choral music replaces the clock. She leaves a flower on the altar and gets into bed as a series of chants begins. These chants and a shot of the woman closing her eyes, her head on a pillow, signal the beginning of the dream sequence.

The world of the dream contrasts sharply with that of the narrative that has preceded it. It takes place, save for one shot, outside, on the streets of South Central Los Angeles. The protagonist is with friends; they window-shop, laugh, and talk, although we do not hear anything in synchronized sound. Rather, the silence and incessant ticking that constituted the sound track earlier is replaced by a series of chants, two African percussion instruments (one clanks like a cow bell, and the other makes a sandy sound) keeping time, and the repetition of three phrases, conveying admonishments and advice. Repeated in different contexts during the dream, the phrases are "You're doin' all right and you're gonna get better," "Progress is being made," and "We get what we really ask for." In the dream, the agents of this advice are anonymous voices as well as the woman's friends.

The arrangement of shots represents a different kind of alternation from that in the earlier section of the film. We see Rasheeda (we learn her name when her friend hails her) sleeping, sometimes smiling on her pillow at what we are given to under-stand are her inner thoughts. Yet these inner thoughts are articulated not in the first person, as her inner speech, but rather in the second and third person. The voices narrate or direct the protagonist's activities, give her advice, relay to the audience her thoughts and feelings. Insinuating an array of cultural, personal, narrative, and historical influences, the voices perhaps mimic those of the elders, telling fragments of stories, giving advice, framing the picture.

The narrative of the dream is reassuring. Rasheeda and her two friends walk down a street window-shopping. In some of these scenes the footage is pixelated, a technique that formally enhances their playful narrative character.[11] As a street musician walks by, Rasheeda dances after him, only to be "rescued" by her friends, who laugh and chide her for her boldness. Their voices are not synchronized with the image; rather, they have the quality of memory, being temporally divorced from and mapped, disembodied, over the visuals. Throughout these shots, cutaways show a man constructing the voodoo inscription of the title sequence on a sidewalk in front of a graffitied wall. The wall, like the writing pad of the unconscious, like the thematic structure of the film, contains an array of complicated, allusive information: the name of a Los Angeles street gang, the brand name of the film camera Davis is using (Bolex), and other arcane inscriptions. The dream sequence alternates shots of the three women dancing with one another or with the street drummer, walking down railroad tracks, standing at an intersection, with shots detailing the completion of the voodoo inscription, which Rasheeda and her friend dance on. A clap of thunder, a quick image of Rasheeda in the bath, and the dream ends. Rasheeda gets up out of bed and goes to the bathroom, the camera lingering on the small spot of blood now staining her sheets. Over the image the voices chant, "You're doin' all right and you're gonna get better," "We get what we really ask for . . ." The opening pan across the ancestral altar is repeated and the film ends. Over the credit sequence a group of women's voices recount the kinds of food obsessions that they experience around the time of their periods.

Cycles operates allusively, weaving together myriad information in very little screen time. Davis cuts frequently, quickly, rhythmically in the first part of the film and more symbolically in the dream sequence. She fills images with significations that exceed narrative functions, that always gesture to the world outside the film. The dream sequence employs an array of visual puns involving movement, traffic, walking the tracks, being at an intersection, which humorously exploit dream logic to deconstruct the implicit gender dichotomies introduced by the opening sequence of the narrative: male/female, outside/inside, leaving/waiting. The film's final joke — that Rasheeda was waiting for her period—completely undoes the gender narrative in one way (she was not waiting for *him*) and ties it up in another (she is not pregnant). The pun on *period*—an ending (of a sentence or film), a duration, a part of the menstrual cycle (a red dot on the sheet)—brings together all the levels of the film's ruminations. Completely adhering to trivial occurrences and representations, Davis manages to assimilate the spiritual, the cultural, and the historical to the everyday in an unprepossessing film whose economic significations greatly exceed their terse and timely presentation.

If Gruben and Davis explore housekeeping by way of a poetic "narration," they do so within a realm outside commercial cinema, for the most part to an audience at film festivals and in university classrooms. Thus, if their allusions are more far reaching, their audience is also much more limited. Yet within the context of these audiences, the films speak to crucial differences and changes in feminism and its priorities. While Gruben's film remotivates scientific and fantastic understandings of cultivation from a woman's point of view, one that had been grossly underexplored before the advent of feminism, Davis's *Cycles* speaks from within the differences hidden in gender difference. Her witty film astutely invokes and reframes the dangerous relationship feminism has had with biology by taking women's menstrual cycles as the occasion, the structure, and the end point for a mythic story whose cinematic imagining bring it emphatically into a very particular place, time, and sociohistorical milieu. If her characters experience something all women do, she makes it clear that they do it differently.

In this book I have tried to bring a scholarly observation (the lack of domestic labor in Hollywood melodramas), a personal artifact (my family photograph), and a professional error (what I could not see in its image) into relation with one another and with history, while at the same time avoiding recourse to (my) identity as a mode of explanation. I have not written a history of domesticity as lived practice, nor are my arguments about domestic labor, representation, and class based on certifiable demographics and populations. Instead I have attempted to trace the history and construction of a profoundly influential and hegemonic idea—that of normative domestic femininity—at key historical moments within diverse discourses while looking at the forces this construction has served rather than the subjectivity it presumably represents.

Although I am a feminist film scholar, I have written a historical account of my research concerns which does not conform to their conventional object or mode of study. Feminist film theory has tended to confound the turn to history with spectatorship, a focus that necessarily produces subjective rather than systemic or discursive insights about gender. Because I wanted to investigate the archaeology of my own feminist blindness, I could not look through the lens of the "historical female spectator," a research trope predicated on a universal conception of gender. Instead, I considered domestic femininity through representations (or the lack thereof) of domestic labor, an approach that came at gender construction through a social and discursive rather than subjective lens. I wanted to discover whether domestic femininity in the United States had always functioned to render domestic labor invisible and how this femininity related to my own theoretically informed feminism. Ultimately, I wanted to investigate the possible connection between the invisibility of women's domestic labor in representation and the ways a feminist focus on women has served to make other social differences difficult to see, if not invisible.

I found the roots of this connection in domestic housekeeping manuals of the nineteenth century. In their increasingly insistent concern with the importance of (white middle-class) women's unlabored appearance, a concern they relate to these women's central role in the formation and perpetuation of the nation, these manuals quite explicitly theorize the role of white bourgeois women in the privatization and sentimentalization of civic and economic inequality. In Catharine Beecher's rationale, white women of this class stand for the necessary inequality of equality, an inequity thus embodied and feminized in public representations of the private sphere. Domestic femininity thereby becomes one significant means by which the profound contradictions between capitalism and democracy are managed and resolved, by being gendered and construed across two very distinct social spheres.

The invisibility of bourgeois women's domestic labor and any of its traces on their bodies is crucial to this system. In their fragile, delicate, dependent appearance, bourgeois white women physically represent and emotionally inhabit the conversion effected by the cult of domesticity; their enforced legal subjection and material dependency are transformed into their bio-spiritual and highly idealized physical and emotional dependency, a state labeled "true" femininity or womanhood. "True" womanhood distinguishes the white bourgeois woman from working-class and slave women, who must labor, but the terms of the distinction convert what are differences in class, in race, and in labor to standards of appearance predicated on women's presumably biological and highly valued "delicacy." This conversion is especially striking in pedagogical texts authored by women that deal precisely with women's domestic labor. In the purview of these texts, successful domesticity involves eradicating all traces of household labor from the body of the laborer. Class distinctions (only aristocratic women have genuinely unlabored bodies) thereby become the standards of successful gender performance. Thus nineteenth-century American domesticity developed an invisible style wherein the bourgeois domestic woman labors to appear not to labor, and the home becomes a leisured haven where no work is presumably ever done.

These pedagogical texts provide a highly significant context for an underexplored and relatively untheorized area of film studies: the representation of domestic labor. In our own time the moralized appearance standard of leisured white femininity incorporates the responsibility to consume; and in cinematic melodramas, domestic labor came to be represented as antithetical to the duties of wife and mother, which were to love and suffer well, to look good, and to shop a lot. While feminist writings on classical Hollywood melodrama have focused on representations of gender, Hollywood films have consistently represented differences in class and race as they relate to gender difference in accordance with the appearance standards laid down in the nineteenth century. That is, this history demonstrates that labor—or, better, the *lack* of a labored appearance—as well as sexuality and castration inform white women's function as erotic icons in the classical cinema. These melodramas, with their avoidance of domestic labor and their moralized focus on white femininity, become particularly explicit about women's social function when their narratives directly address domesticity. They repeat and act out the concerns of nineteenth-century domestic writers, now shaped and altered by the twentieth-century imperatives levied on bourgeois white women concerning moralized consumption and iconic affectivity. In these culture industry texts, white middle-class domestic femininity and its unlabored appearance and spectacular morality continue to keep other social differences organized and ultimately swept out of sight.

Finally, feminist filmmakers' astute reconsiderations of domesticity attempt to make its labor and its profound social effects visible. Yet material, industrial, and cultural constraints relating to film distribution and theoretical paradigms relating to the critical reception of films obscure some of the truths these films tell. In reviewing the early works that constituted a feminist film canon in the United States, I have attempted to historicize the tension between academic feminist film theory and the aesthetic renovations and observations on domesticity and domestic femininity fashioned by feminist filmmakers. These filmmakers make use of housework to invent a different formal approach to narrative filmmaking; to tell a story about the enlightenment of a middle-class psychiatrist who encounters a working-class housewife's trenchant silence when she attempts to treat her with the "talking cure"; to reinvestigate the nature-culture split, utterly confounding it through the operation and considerations of housekeeping; or to use the specificity of housework to underscore the historical relativity of any biological, social, cultural, or aesthetic universals pertaining to women. Each film produces knowledge about domesticity differently, and each answers back to the tradition of representation I have laid out in parts I and II. What the feminist film texts share is a studied resistance to emotional and sexual abandonment, to representations of women being swept away, and a passionate engagement with depicting women's housework: the sweeping, the broom, the laboring female body, and their profound aesthetic, social, and ideological effects. As Chantal Akerman says, these things are "never, almost never shown."

Throughout this book I have attempted to identify the complex discursive configuration that has promoted the visibility of some ideas (white femininity, the affective moral transcendence of the middle-class home and family, the fiction of the personal and the private sphere) at the expense of others (domestic labor, the profound interrelation of all social differences, identities, and inequities). To sort through this complexity, I first set out to investigate the discursive construction of domesticity vis-à-vis labor rather than to consider the construction of female subjectivity vis-à-vis domesticity. What I found is that if the female subject, whether feminine or feminist, cannot see (her own) class and race as among the differences that constitute (her) gender identity, American domesticity has made that so. The key to unlocking these complicated relationships was to follow the chronic suppression of representations of domestic labor.

I am not dismissing feminist work on historical female spectatorship; I have in fact drawn a great deal of information and inspiration from that scholarship. But in changing the filter through which I was viewing representations of femininity— from subjectivity to domestic labor— my research extended outside filmic representation per se (to nineteenth-century women's texts on domestic labor) and reoriented femininity as a research object. This reorientation allowed me to approach gender construction beyond its conventional containment within categories of identity and subjectivity and to look instead at its disciplinary, political, and social contexts. Domestic femininity emerged as a compelling and persistent fiction, comprising an interrelated matrix of identity constructions relating to class, race, and gender, the last (gender) positioned to override and subsume the significance of the former (class and race) through the fantasy of an undifferentiated and unlabored feminine ideal.

Although I have addressed these issues diachronically in this book, my latest research adopts a more synchronic approach to similar problems in the classical and contemporary cinema. Using the trope of women's automobility, I consider how cinematic representations of diverse identities (marked by gender, race, sexuality, and class) depend on and draw from industrial contexts—in this instance, those of the cinema and the automobile industry.[1] Yet while the conceit of women taking the wheel does indicate significant changes in the representation of domestic femininity and women's autonomy, I find that the concerns of the home nevertheless haunt privileged white women's public life, in representations both real and narrative, even as the dramatic reality of class and racial inequities are still hidden behind her skirts. In an astute commentary on the "Nannygate" controversy in the early months of the Clinton administration, L. S. Kim notes that it was consistently professional white women who suffered politically for hiring undocumented workers as nannies, while white male politicians who had done the same thing easily evaded sanction by blaming the transgression on their wives.[2] Domesticity is still women's business, their moral and legal responsibility, even if they work outside the home. By the same token, men need not worry about these issues. Thus, gender continues to mediate the complex social and economic relationships of privilege and difference that underwrite modern domesticity in such a way that questions of domestic labor and laborers are still getting lost.

Notes

1. Neither Marx nor Freud can account for housework because they divide the public and private spheres, Freud positioning work as a sublimation of sexuality and Marx assessing labor strictly in its relation to capital. Thus, housework cannot be defined even as unproductive labor or barter because its defining characteristic is that it has no relation to capital. See Margaret Coulson, Branka Magaš, and Hilary Wainwright, "'The Housewife and her Labour under Capital': A Critique," *New Left Review*, no. 89 (1975): 59–71; Frederick Engels, *The Origin of the Family, Private Property and the State, in Light of the Researches of Lewis H. Morgan* (New York: International Publishers, 1942); Terry Fee, "Domestic Labour: An Analysis of Housework and Its Relation to the Production Process," *Review of Radical Political Economy* 8, no. 1 (1976): 1–8; Susan Himmelweit and Simon Mohun, "Domestic Labour and Capital," *Cambridge Journal of Economics* 1 (1977): 15–31. Many theorists and social historians have also investigated the limitations of psychoanalytic theory in relation to domestic labor and class by investigating the social and symbolic implications of the maid's or governess's presence in the bourgeois home. See Peter Stallybrass and Allon White's discussion in *The Politics and Poetics of Transgression* (Ithaca: Cornell University Press, 1986), 163–65; Jane Gallop, *The Daughter's Seduction* (Ithaca: Cornell University Press, 1982), 142–48; and Gilles Deleuze and Felix Guattari, *Anti-Oedipus* (Minneapolis: University of Minnesota Press, 1983), 352–55. In film studies, Chuck Kleinhans, "Notes on Melodrama and the Family under Capitalism," *Film Reader* 3 (February 1978): 40–47, lays out many of the relevant problems and issues.

2. The feminism of the sixties and seventies, both academic and otherwise, has been critiqued for what in retrospect seems an obvious oversight: interrelations between race and sexuality or gender. For examples of recent attempts to address this oversight, see Mary Anne Doane, "Dark Continents: Epistemologies of Racial and Sexual Difference in Psychoanalysis

and the Cinema," in *Femmes Fatales: Feminism, Film Theory, and Psychoanalysis* (New York: Routledge, 1991), 209–248; Jane Gaines, "White Privilege and Looking Relations: Race and Gender in Feminist Film Theory," in *Issues in Feminist Film Criticism*, ed. Patricia Erens (Bloomington: Indiana University Press, 1990), 197–214; Tania Modleski, "Cinema and the Dark Continent," in *Feminism without Women* (New York: Routledge, 1991), 115–34. Interestingly, a certain split persists insofar as it is white feminists who theorize the "field" while feminists of color critique it from particular subject positions. See Jacqueline Bobo's work on black female spectatorship: "*The Color Purple*: Black Women as Cultural Readers," in *Female Spectators: Looking at Film and Television*, ed. E. Deidre Pribram (New York: Verso, 1988), 90–109, and "Reading through the Text: The Black Woman as Audience," in *Black American Cinema*, ed. Manthia Diawara (New York: Routledge, 1993), 272–87. Also in Diawara's *Black America Cinema*, see bell hooks, "The Oppositional Gaze: Black Female Spectators," 288–302, and Michele Wallace, "Race, Gender, and Psychoanalysis in Forties Film: *Lost Boundaries, Home of the Brave*, and *The Quiet One*," 257–71.

3. On American domesticity, Glenna Matthews's "*Just a Housewife*": *The Rise and Fall of Domesticity in America* (New York: Oxford University Press, 1987) and Jeanne Boydston's *Home and Work: Housework, Wages, and the Ideology of Labor in the Early Republic* (New York: Oxford University Press, 1990) have provided comprehensive (Matthews) and specific (Boydston) histories of housework, while Phyllis Palmer's *Domesticity and Dirt: Housewives and Domestic Servants in the United States, 1920–1945* (Philadelphia: Temple University Press, 1989) and Ruth Schwartz Cowan's *More Work for Mother: The Ironies of Household Technology from the Open Hearth to the Microwave* (New York: Basic Books, 1983) have addressed the cultural implications of certain aspects of domesticity. In this work I make a very distinct contribution to scholarship on domesticity in several ways. Its interdisciplinary character allows me to connect the nineteenth-century domestic woman to the woman-to-be-looked-at of twentieth-century feminist film theory in historically rigorous ways and to show how both of these women are connected to a nationalist ideology. Methodologically, my book most resembles Nancy Armstrong's *Desire and Domestic Fiction* (Oxford: Oxford University Press, 1987), but as I focus on American rather than British domesticity, my book provides an important counterpart to hers.

4. David James has written extensively on class and representation. See his introduction, "Is There a Class in this Text?", to *The Hidden Foundation: Cinema and the Question of Class*, a collection which he edited with Rick Berg (Minneapolis: University of Minnesota Press, 1996), and his collection *Power Hits: Essays across (Un)Popular Culture* (New York: Verso Press, 1996), especially the introduction and chaps. 2, 7, and 12.

5. Hazel Carby in *Reconstructing Womanhood: The Emergence of the Afro-American Woman Novelist* (New York: Oxford University Press, 1987), especially her account of the influence of the cult of domesticity and white women's appearance on constructions of race and class difference in her chapter "Slave and Mistress: Ideologies of Womanhood under Slavery," 20–39, has inspired mine.

6. Thomas Streeter, *Selling the Air: A Critique of the Policy of Commercial Broadcasting in the United States* (Chicago: University of Chicago Press, 1996), 276. Domestic labor and its relationship to gender, constructions of the public and private, and mass entertainment have already been investigated in television studies. See, for example, Lynn Spigel, *Make Room for TV* (Chicago: University of Chicago Press, 1992), and Tania Modleski, "The Search for Tomorrow in Today's Soap Operas," *Loving with a Vengeance* (New York: Methuen, 1984 [1982]), 85–109.

7. Although my argument shares many concerns with that of Thorstein Veblen in *The Theory of the Leisure Class* (Toronto: Dover Publications, 1994 [1899]), I set out to explain the "curious inversion" that he remarks but cannot incorporate within the terms of his overall

argument: how it is that middle-class women rather than men come to bear the burden of representing conspicuous consumption and leisure when that privilege has always been accorded to superior males in the history he recounts and within the cultures he studies. See especially chap. 4, "Conspicuous Consumption," 50–51.

8. My overall project is to give psychoanalytic theories of sexuality in the cinema a history and a material context through investigations of domesticity and domestic labor and to open up film texts to readings of difference that include but are not limited to gender and sexuality. In this I am following in the footsteps of Judith Halberstam's insightful treatment of the gothic in *Skin Shows: Gothic Horror and the Technology of Monsters* (Durham: Duke University Press, 1995).

9. Paul Gilroy lays out this series of concerns in *The Black Atlantic: Modernity and Double Consciousness* (Cambridge: Harvard University Press, 1993), 85.

10. The question is Rachel Blau DuPlessis's in *The Pink Guitar: Writing as Feminist Practice* (New York: Routledge, 1990), 6.

CHAPTER ONE

1. Barbara Welter, "The Cult of True Womanhood: 1800–1860," *American Quarterly* (Summer 1966): 151–74; Nancy Cott, *The Bonds of Womanhood: "Woman's Sphere" in New England, 1780–1835* (New Haven: Yale University Press, 1977). Cott and other historians refer to these terms interchangeably. See Cott's introduction to *The Bonds of Womanhood* and the chapter titled "Domesticity," pp. 1–18, 63–100, respectively.

2. Jane Tompkins, *Sensational Designs: The Cultural Work of American Fiction, 1790–1860* (New York: Oxford University Press, 1985).

3. Carolyn L. Karcher's comprehensive and critically nuanced *The First Woman in the Republic: A Cultural Biography of Lydia Maria Child* (Durham: Duke University Press, 1991) was an invaluable resource to me in conceiving and articulating the argument of this chapter. She summarizes Child's extensive accomplishments on pages xi–xiii.

4. Quoted ibid., 12. Child published *Hobomok*, her first novel, in 1824. Another novel, short stories, a journal for children, and an array of essays established her reputation before she published *The Frugal Housewife* in 1829.

5. Child's reform efforts extended to Native Americans, women, prostitutes, the elderly, prisoners, the poor, and immigrants. Her most pressing commitment, however, was to abolition and to alleviating the oppressions suffered by "free" African Americans in the North. Following the publication of *An Appeal in Favor of That Class of Americans Called Africans* in 1833, her popularity plummeted, severely affecting her income. See Karcher, *First Woman in the Republic*, xiii, 5, and chaps. 7–9.

6. Michel Foucault, *Discipline and Punish*, trans. Alan Sheridan (New York: Vintage Books, 1979), 219.

7. Ann Douglas, *The Feminization of American Culture* (New York: Avon, 1978), 96–97.

8. Karcher, *First Woman in the Republic*, 3.

9. Matthews, "*Just a Housewife*," 23. See also Karcher, *First Woman in the Republic*, chaps. 5 and 6.

10. Charles Grier Sellers, *The Market Revolution: Jacksonian America, 1815–1846* (New York: Oxford University Press, 1991), 137–39.

11. Nancy Cott asserts that the changes in women's experience between 1780 and 1830 "outran that for considerably more than a century preceding and half a century following." Cott, *Bonds of Womanhood*, 4.

12. Karcher's biography includes careful and insightful readings of Child's fiction, relating narrative outcomes to Child's polemical and political positions on issues involving Native

Americans, African Americans, and women. See, for example, Karcher's reading of *Hobomok* in relation to the interracial marriage plot and Child's ideas about eradicating racism in *First Woman in the Republic*, chap. 1.

13. Ibid., 127–28; quotation from Child, 127.

14. Ibid., 129.

15. The original title of the book was *The Frugal Housewife*, a title Child changed to *The American Frugal Housewife* because, as she explains in the 1836 edition, "there is an *English* work of the same name, not adapted to the wants of this country." See Lydia Maria Child, *The American Frugal Housewife*, ed. Alice Geffen (New York: Harper and Row, 1972 [1835]), 2.

16. Ibid., vii.

17. Karcher, *First Woman in the Republic*, 128–29.

18. Child, *American Frugal Housewife*, 3. All further references to this source will be given parenthetically in the text.

19. Boydston, *Home and Work*, 84.

20. Ibid., 53.

21. See Douglas's discussion of homespun in *Feminization of American Culture*, 58–59.

22. See Boydston, *Home and Work*, 124.

23. Ibid., 137.

24. Ibid., 137–39.

25. Max Weber, *The Protestant Ethic and the Spirit of Capitalism*, trans. Talcott Parsons (New York: Scribners, 1958), 48.

26. Franklin quoted ibid., 48–49.

27. He advises the man who is in debt, "The sound of your hammer at five in the morning, or eight at night, heard by a creditor, makes him easy six months longer." Quoted ibid., 49.

28. Though related to labor in this context, this quality fosters the home's identity as spiritually outside pressure and duress in the cult of domesticity and also seems related to the nostalgia that accrues to the domestic.

29. Sellers, *Market Revolution*, 5–19.

30. E. P. Thompson, "Time, Work-Discipline, and Industrial Capitalism," *Past and Present* 38 (1967): 60.

31. Ibid., 60, 79. Of course the neat dichotomy between housewife and tradesman leaves out the industrial worker who, according to Thompson, is paid in increments of disciplined time and has no share in the profits she or he produces for a tradesman or capitalist employer. While the tradesman can make money with time, the worker cannot.

32. Weber, *Protestant Ethic*, 53 and chap. 2, passim.

33. Ibid., 53.

34. Pierre Bourdieu, *Outline of a Theory of Practice*, trans. Richard Nice (Cambridge: Cambridge University Press, 1977), 175.

35. Claude Lévi-Strauss, *The Savage Mind* (London and Chicago: Weidenfeld and Nicolson and the University of Chicago Press, 1966), 17.

36. Karcher, *First Woman in the Republic*, 133.

37. Jack Goody, *The Domestication of the Savage Mind* (Cambridge: Cambridge University Press, 1977), 75–79. As is also the case with Lévi-Strauss, Goody's title and text refer to Western anthropological biases and qualitative evaluations of different modes of cognition which have since been extensively critiqued.

38. Ibid., 81.

39. Ibid., 136.

40. See Michael Warner's cogent critique of Goody, Ong, and the tradition of thinkers

who argue that print, in and of itself, has democratizing effects outside social and political relations. Michael Warner, "The Cultural Mediation of the Print Medium," in *The Letters of the Republic: Publication and the Public Sphere in Eighteenth-Century America* (Cambridge: Harvard University Press, 1990), 5–8. I am examining the construction of a certain kind of femininity in relation to print, authorship, and prevailing social relations.

41. Goody, *Domestication of the Savage Mind*, 81.

42. See Karcher's discussion in *First Woman in the Republic* of Fenimore Cooper and Child's book *Hobomok* and the opening chapter of Sellers, *Market Revolution*.

43. Christine Gledhill, "The Melodramatic Field: An Investigation," in *Home is Where the Heart Is*, ed. Christine Gledhill (London: BFI, 1987), 24.

44. Karcher, *First Woman in the Republic*, 131.

45. Ibid., 133.

46. Boydston, *Home and Work*, 131.

CHAPTER TWO

1. Kathryn Kish Sklar makes this point, arguing that the comprehensiveness of Beecher's text "standardized American domestic practices," in *Catharine Beecher: A Study in American Domesticity* (New York: W. W. Norton, 1973), 151–52.

2. Matthews, *"Just a Housewife,"* 47–48; Douglas, *Feminization of American Culture*, 65; Karcher, *First Woman in the Republic*, 610; Cott, *Bonds of Womanhood*, 50n. In part, Beecher's success derives from her compatibility with the cult of domesticity, a compatibility that Child did not share. See Karcher's chapter "The Frugal Housewife," 129–31.

3. Michel Foucault, *Power/Knowledge: Selected Interviews and Other Writings, 1972–1977* (New York: Pantheon Books, 1980), 115.

4. Sklar, *Catharine Beecher*, xiii.

5. Feminist historians—Nancy F. Cott, Carroll Smith-Rosenberg, and Barbara Welter, for example—are obviously exceptions. But insofar as they restrict their analyses to the relevance of the cult of domesticity to the lives of women and their gendered relationships with men, the larger implications of the cult remain unexplored.

6. Ellen Carol DuBois, "Taking Law into Their Own Hands: Voting Women during Reconstruction," in *Voting and the Spirit of American Democracy*, ed. Donald W. Rogers (Urbana: University of Illinois Press, 1992), 68, emphasis added.

7. Nancy Armstrong makes this point astutely in *Desire and Domestic Fiction*, 27: "I have tried to defamiliarize the division of discourse that makes it so difficult to see the relationship between the finer nuances of women's feelings and the vicissitudes of a capitalist economy run mainly by men."

8. How these vital distinctions are arbitrated by the culture industry in the twentieth century is the topic of section 2.

9. The cult of domesticity positioned women as moral guardians to their families and consequently to the nation. See the discussion of Beecher later in this chapter; also Sara M. Evans, *Born for Liberty: A History of Women in America* (New York: Free Press, 1989), esp. chaps. 4 and 6. On influence, see Douglas, *Feminization of American Culture*, 77–93.

10. Sellers, *Market Revolution*, chap. 1; see Sean Wilentz, "Property and Power: Suffrage Reform in the United States, 1787–1860," in Rogers, *Voting and the Spirit of American Democracy*, 31–41; John B. Kirby, "Early American Politics—The Search for Ideology: An Historiographical Analysis and Critique of the Concept of 'Deference,'" *Journal of Politics* 32, no. 4 (November 1970): 808–38.

11. Sklar cites an unpublished paper by Kenneth Lockridge concerning literacy in the colonial period. His quantitative research suggests that "gender identity became increasingly func-

tional" throughout the seventeenth and eighteenth centuries in New England, while class identity diminished in importance. She asserts that the tendency of gender to replace class "as a building block of social structure was not an invention of the nineteenth century, but it was first given ideological articulation during that period." My argument exceeds hers in scope insofar as I assert that the cult of domesticity weds gender to issues of *citizenship*. In doing so it brings together and organizes issues of literacy, private property, religious ideologies, and political conflicts that include both class and race, orienting them all toward questions of identity rather than privilege and property ownership. See Sklar, *Catharine Beecher*, 308n19.

12. Historians agree that the years from the 1780s to the 1840s were a period of profound historical change in the United States unrivaled by any other. See Carroll Smith-Rosenberg, *Disorderly Conduct: Visions of Gender in Victorian America* (New York: Knopf, 1985), 79. See also Cott, *Bonds of Womanhood*, Intro. and chap. 1; Douglas, *Feminization of American Culture*.

13. Evans, *Born for Liberty*, 55.

14. Ibid., 56.

15. Christopher Collier, "The American People as Christian White Men of Property: Suffrage and Elections in Colonial and Early National America," in Rogers, *Voting and the Spirit of American Democracy*, 23.

16. According to the laws of coverture, the legal principle inherited from British common law, a woman's legal subjectivity became null when she married; it was absorbed and represented by her husband (see the next section of this chapter). And most women did marry. Smith-Rosenberg, *Disorderly Conduct*, 81.

17. Collier, "White Men of Property," 22; Sellers, *Market Revolution*, 127.

18. Collier, "White Men of Property," 24.

19. Wilentz, "Property and Power," 33.

20. Sellers, *Market Revolution*, 127.

21. This was true of gender to a lesser extent because the policy of coverture already rationalized the limitations on women's rights. This legal precedent was successfully challenged, however, in 1830.

22. See Barbara Jeanne Fields, "Slavery, Race, and Ideology in the United States of America," *New Left Review* 181 (1990): 95-118, for a stunning exposition of the relation between slavery and the construction of race and racial difference in America. She argues that "American racial ideology is as original an invention of the Founders as is the United States itself" (101).

23. The disestablishment of colonial state churches, completed in 1833, subjected them to the foibles of the market; once able to rely on state support, clergy were now forced to generate their own income and any funds they might need to construct and maintain their churches. For a variety of complex reasons, the economic privatization of religion fostered the development of a pronounced discursive affinity among middle- and upper-class women and the churches, their theology, and their clergy. Ann Douglas argues that this affinity, facilitated by increasing literacy and the rise of mass media, made itself manifest in the plethora of magazines, novels, memoirs, and religious tracts published at the time by "ministers and mothers." All their work, she asserts, served as literary propaganda for a "sentimentalized culture." See Douglas, *Feminization of American Culture*, 17-139. Mary Ryan points out that 80 percent of the women in the Female Missionary Society had husbands who maintained businesses at venues separate from the home. These women's affluence relieved them from onerous domestic responsibilities and left them time for benevolent activities. See Mary Ryan, *Cradle of the Middle Class: The Family in Oneida County, New York, 1790-1865* (New York: Cambridge University Press, 1981), chap. 2. Douglas argues that economic dependency feminizes the clergy. Ryan's less polemical position articulates how religious concerns are domesticated.

24. Ryan, *Cradle of the Middle Class*, 102.

25. Ibid., 101; Douglas, *Feminization of American Culture*, 97–100.

26. Gerda Lerner, "The Lady and the Mill Girl: Changes in the Status of Women in the Age of Jackson," *Midcontinent American Studies Journal* 10, no. 1 (Spring 1969): 5–15.

27. See Ruth Bloch's discussion of the feminization and privatization of virtue in "The Gendered Meanings of Virtue in Revolutionary America," *Signs* 13, no. 1 (1987): 37–58.

28. The public and private spheres of this period do not correspond exactly with public and private distinctions in classical Greece (where all economic activity was considered private and only speech, debate, and civic deliberation by the citizenry was considered public) or with how they are theorized and understood today. For these terms as they applied to the Greek city-state and how they were altered by the rise of the modern nation-state, see Hannah Arendt, "The Public and the Private Realm," in *The Human Condition* (Chicago: University of Chicago Press, 1958), 22–78.

29. Sklar, *Catharine Beecher*, 152.

30. Ibid., 151–84.

31. See Matthews, *"Just a Housewife,"* 146; Sigfried Giedion, *Mechanization Takes Command* (New York: W. W. Norton, 1969 [1948]), 513–14; Witold Rybczynski, *Home: A Short History of an Idea* (New York: Penguin Books, 1987), 158.

32. The cult of domesticity draws from a long European tradition associating women with spirituality, an association that justified their designation as unequal. John Locke classifies women as among those "who cannot know and therefore must believe." Beecher's call for women to be educated affirms their spirituality but insists it be buttressed by knowledge and education. Locke quoted in Rosalind Delmar's "What Is Feminism," in *What Is Feminism?*, ed. Juliet Mitchell and Ann Oakley (Oxford: Basil Blackwell, 1986), 31n28.

33. In *The Novel and the Police* (Berkeley: University of California Press, 1988), D. A. Miller discusses the home as a disciplinary space in Foucauldian terms, which it is in certain respects. As I point out, however, there are crucial differences, especially when the housewife is considered a laborer.

34. In "Docile Bodies," in *Discipline and Punish*, 141n1, Foucault states, "I shall choose examples from military, medical, educational and industrial institutions. Other examples might have been taken from colonization, slavery, and childrearing." In so doing, he implies that disciplinary structures unproblematically cross the public-private divide without actually having to defend that assertion. The institutions he chooses as examples distinguish themselves in part precisely because they are not private or familial in structure.

35. Ibid., 135–69.

36. Catharine Beecher, *A Treatise on Domestic Economy* (New York: Source Book Press, 1970 [1841]), 144. All further references to this source will be given parenthetically in the text.

37. Foucault, *Discipline and Punish*, 143, 141–49.

38. Ibid., 136.

39. Glenna Matthews, in *"Just a Housewife,"* 150, makes this point in connection with the professionalization of housework, which did involve disparaging and discounting traditional forms of knowledge.

40. Foucault, *Discipline and Punish*, 160–61.

41. Lerner, "Lady and the Mill Girl," 11–13.

42. Sklar, *Catharine Beecher*, 158–61. Sklar writes that Beecher, who drew many of her ideas from Tocqueville, very consciously promoted gender hierarchy as a solution to the myriad tensions that riddled the United States in the 1840s: "By removing half the population from the arena of competition and making it subservient to the other half, the amount of antagonism the society had to bear would be reduced to a tolerable limit. Moreover by defining gender identity as more important than class, regional, or religious identity, and by ignor-

ing altogether the imponderables of American racial divisions, she promoted the belief that the society's only basic division was that between men and women" (156).

43. Specifically from James Marston Fitch and Sigfried Giedion, noted in Rybczynski, *Home*, 159.

44. Ibid., 160-61.

45. Hazel Carby relates the cult's representation of true womanhood's delicate appearance to distinctions in race and class in "Slave and Mistress: Ideologies of Womanhood under Slavery," in *Reconstructing Womanhood*, 25.

46. Making this point in a slightly different way, historian Jeanne Boydston observes that, in this period, middle-class women's labor came to include "status" work, tasks involved in the creation "of a household's *gentility*" which ultimately reflected not a woman's labor but the power of her husband's income. She remarks, "Because of this way of seeing, status production—a responsibility that wives assumed not instead of, but in addition to their other work—became an invisible component of most of the unpaid domestic labor that women performed." Boydston, *Home and Work*, 135.

47. The economic changes articulated and transformed in the cult of domesticity coincided historically with manhood's increasingly being "identified with wage-earning." The instability of the economy at the turn of the century strengthened that identification and fostered "the cult of the male 'breadwinner.'" Boydston notes that, as this identity intersected with and inflected men's traditional (and universal) roles as husbands and fathers, it "crossed the lines of the emerging classes, characterizing the self-perceptions and social claims of both laboring and middle-class men." Ibid., 137.

48. See, for example, Cott, *Bonds of Womanhood*; Ryan, *Cradle of the Middle Class*; Smith-Rosenberg, *Disorderly Conduct*. For the very different effects of domestic discourses on slave women, see Angela Davis, "The Legacy of Slavery: Standards for a New Womanhood," in *Women, Race and Class* (New York: Vintage Books, 1981), 3-29.

49. On coverture, see Delmar, "What Is Feminism?" 31n28. See Evans, *Born for Liberty*, 76-77, 102-3, on the contestation and reform of these laws.

50. Hortense J. Spillers, "Mama's Baby, Papa's Maybe: An American Grammar Book," *Diacritics* 7, no. 2 (Summer 1987): 78.

51. I thank Lisa Duggan for this wording, and also for pointing out the regionalism of the cult of domesticity.

52. Spillers, "Mama's Baby, Papa's Maybe," 74.

53. "Certainly if 'kinship' were possible, the property relations would be undermined, since the offspring would then 'belong' to a mother and father." Ibid., 75.

54. Fields, "Slavery, Race, and Ideology," 101.

55. Ibid., 99. The history textbook in question is Winthrop D. Jordan, Leon F. Litwack, et al., *The United States*, 5th ed. (Englewood Cliffs, N.J., 1982), see p. 144.

56. Ibid., 114.

57. Ibid., 115.

58. Jane Tompkins, "Sentimental Power: *Uncle Tom's Cabin* and the Politics of Literary History," in *Feminisms*, ed. Robyn Warhol and Diane Herndl (New Brunswick, N.J.: Rutgers University Press, 1991), 20-39.

59. See Rachel Bowlby's incisive reading of Stowe's construction of femininity in "Breakfast in America—*Uncle Tom's* Cultural Histories," in *Nation and Narration*, ed. Homi Bhabha (New York: Routledge, 1990), 197-212. Although she presents a very nuanced and careful reading of Stowe, I am interested in the broader or more general relations the novel constructs between genders and races. For a consideration of the displacements and interrelations Stowe articulates between race and gender in relation to visibility, see Robyn Wiegman's discussion

in "The Alchemy of Disloyalty," in *American Anatomies: Theorizing Race and Gender* (Durham: Duke University Press, 1995), 193–201.

60. Harriet Beecher Stowe, *Uncle Tom's Cabin; or, Life among the Lowly*, ed. Ann Douglas (New York: Penguin, 1981), 88.

61. Ibid., 207.

62. Anti-porn feminists, in both their aims and their rhetoric, are resolutely Victorian. Nor are their legal collusions with right-wing Christian groups an accident. Such extremists frequently rely on sentimentalized images of home and family, but most particularly of women, to promote and justify crudely racist and misogynist forms of social control. See Douglas's discussion of influence and sentimentalism in *Feminization of American Culture*.

CHAPTER THREE

1. Quoted in Gwendolyn Wright, *Moralism and the Model Home* (Chicago: University of Chicago Press, 1980), 235.

2. Writing on this period in American history, Sara Evans observes: "Modern America had a violent birth, and although perpetrators and victims of class and racial violence were predominantly male, women shared men's conflict-shaped environment and their ideas of race and class position. Severe depression, bloody labor disputes, racist terrorism, and the demise of populism punctuated the 1890s. It seems ironic that within these turbulent and violent times science—with its emphasis on rationality, methodological processes, and objectivity—should be in ascendancy. But there it was, the underpinning of new technologies as well as a new worldview. . . . Science meshed with the rational, secular worldview of the middle class and promised the capacity to restore order and rationality to their own highly disordered world. In the service of these middle class values, science could be used to buttress traditional prejudices." Evans, *Born for Liberty*, 146.

3. For an extended consideration of "Americanism" from a Marxist point of view, see "Americanism and Fordism" in *Selections from the Prison Notebooks of Antonio Gramsci*, ed. and trans. Quintin Hoare and Geoffrey Nowell Smith (New York: International Publishers, 1971), 277–320. See Matthews, *"Just a Housewife,"* on the professionalization of home economics, and Gwendolyn Wright, "Model Housewives and Model Houses," in *Moralism and the Model Home*, 150–71, on affiliations between new academic disciplines.

4. For other discussions of Mary Pattison, Christine Frederick, domestic engineering, and their relation to film culture, see Patricia Mellencamp, *A Fine Romance: Five Ages of Film Feminism* (Philadelphia: Temple University Press, 1995), 207–9; and Constance Balides's more extensive consideration of Frederick in *Making Dust in the Archives: Feminism, History, and Early American Cinema* (Minneapolis: University of Minnesota Press, forthcoming), 175–98.

5. Christine Frederick, *The New Housekeeping: Efficiency Studies in Home Management* (Garden City, N.Y.: Doubleday, Page and Company, 1913 [1912]), 10. All further references to this source will be given parenthetically in the text.

6. Mary Pattison, *Domestic Engineering: Or the What, Why, and How of a Home* (New York: Trow Press, 1915), 148. All further references to this source will be given parenthetically in the text.

7. Rosalind Williams, *Dream Worlds: Mass Consumption in Late Nineteenth-Century France* (Berkeley: University of California Press, 1982), 9–10.

8. Susan Strasser, *Never Done: A History of American Housework* (New York: Pantheon Books, 1982), 203.

9. Ibid., 206.

10. Glenna Matthews discusses the ethnocentrism of the Progressives and the influence

their social doctrines had on the emerging discipline of home economics in *"Just a Housewife,"* 163–64.

11. This rhetoric was not limited to home improvement. Writing on the cult of the expert during this period, Gwendolyn Wright states, "In the cities the rallying cry of all reformers became that of efficiency. The way to achieve it was through rational organization and scientific standards." See Wright, "Expert Advice," chap. 9 in *Moralism and the Model Home*, 260.

12. For more on the discourse of the "two worlds" in American historiography, see David W. Noble, *The End of American History: Democracy, Capitalism, and the Metaphor of Two Worlds in Anglo-American Historical Writing, 1880–1980* (Minneapolis: University of Minnesota Press, 1985).

13. Gramsci, "Americanism and Fordism," 277–320.

14. See Stephen Kern, *The Culture of Time and Space: 1880–1918* (Cambridge: Harvard University Press, 1983).

15. Strasser, *Never Done*, 207.

16. Matthews, *"Just a Housewife,"* 150.

17. Ibid., 151.

18. Matthews's book contains several short biographies of aspiring chemists who all became pioneering home economists instead—by necessity rather than design. Ibid., 146–48.

19. Ibid., 148.

20. Frederick Winslow Taylor, *The Principles of Scientific Management* (New York: Harper & Row, 1911), 36–40.

21. Ibid., 101–4.

22. Ibid., 46.

23. The domestic engineering books were written at the same time that a major transformation was occurring in the ethnic configurations and structuring of domestic servitude in America. During this period (1890–1920), the immigrant population shifted to groups from eastern Europe toward whom there was particular mistrust. In every area but the South, the proportion of African American servants grew and for the first time eclipsed the percentage of immigrant servants employed. Each group constituted a larger fraction of those employed as domestic servants than did native white servants, and this had been the case since the latter years of the nineteenth century. At the same time, the trend in employment was shifting from live-in servants to day workers. For the statistics without knowing analysis (note his title), see Daniel E. Sutherland, *Americans and Their Servants: Domestic Service in the United States from 1800 to 1920* (Baton Rouge: Louisiana State University Press, 1981), 47–58, 183. For more politically aware work on domestic servitude and issues of class and race, see Mary Romero, *Maid in the U.S.A.* (New York: Routledge, 1992), particularly chaps. 1–4. Elizabeth Clark-Lewis, *Living In, Living Out: African American Domestics in Washington, D.C., 1910–1940* (Washington, D.C.: Smithsonian Institution Press, 1994), presents the opinions of the servants themselves on the question of living in versus living out. For them, living out meant more freedom and less exploitation (148, 185–87). For more general accounts of domestic economy, immigration, and domestic servants, see Strasser, *Never Done*, 162–79; Matthews, *"Just a Housewife,"* 95–97.

24. For a critique of the assertion that appliances ease housework, see Cowan, *More Work for Mother*, 99–101.

25. See Frederick, *New Housekeeping*, 228–34; Pattison, *Domestic Engineering*, 196–97.

26. See Constance Balides's discussion of the housewife's interiority, which developed as a consequence of this organization and how it affected her turn toward consumerism, in *Making Dust in the Archives*, 195–97.

27. On the sexualization of movement in early cinema, see Linda Williams, "Film Body: An Implantation of Perversions," in *Narrative, Apparatus, Ideology*, ed. Phil Rosen (New York: Columbia University Press, 1986), 507–34.

28. Constance Balides discusses how the domestic engineers imbricated women's individuality—an individuality articulated in opposition to feminism—with their skills as consumers. My argument does not present the construction of domestic femininity as solely related to women; rather I see it as implicated in issues of class, individuality, and the mystification effected by public and private spheres for everyone, regardless of gender. See Balides, *Making Dust in the Archives,* 181–82.

29. Laura Shapiro, *Perfection Salad: Women and Cooking at the Turn of the Century* (New York: Henry Holt, 1986), 176–77.

CHAPTER FOUR

1. My argument differs from that of Nick Browne in "Griffith's Family Discourse: Griffith and Freud," in Gledhill, *Home is Where the Heart Is,* 223–34, because he does not go far enough. He sees the family solely as the preeminent "subject matter" that the cinema developed a visual language to represent. In my view, American domesticity had already developed a rhetoric of representation based exactly on what should and should not be seen, which was then assimilated by the cinema.

2. David Bordwell, Janet Staiger, and Kristin Thompson, *The Classical Hollywood Cinema: Film Style and Mode of Production to 1960* (New York: Columbia University Press, 1985), 114–15.

3. See Anne Friedberg, *Window Shopping* (Berkeley: University of California Press, 1993), esp. chaps. 1 and 2, in which she examines the synthesis of visual apparatuses and commodification in relation to alterations in subjectivity and time.

4. For very nuanced accounts of this process and how it related to class and spectatorship, see Tom Gunning, *D. W. Griffith and the Origins of American Narrative Film* (Urbana: University of Illinois Press, 1991), chaps. 4–6; Miriam Hansen, *Babel and Babylon: Spectatorship in American Silent Film* (Cambridge: Harvard University Press, 1991), chaps. 1 and 2.

5. For insightful considerations of D. W. Griffith's work and its import with regard to representations and constructions of racial difference in the United States, see Daniel Bernardi, "The Voice of Whiteness: D. W. Griffith's Biograph Films, 1908–1913," in *The Birth of Whiteness: Race and the Emergence of the U.S. Cinema,* ed. Daniel Bernardi (New Brunswick, N.J.: Rutgers University Press, 1996), 103–28; Thomas Cripps, *Slow Fade to Black: The Negro in American Film, 1900–1942* (New York: Oxford University Press, 1977); Julia Lesage, "Artful Racism, Artful Rape: Griffith's Broken Blossoms," in Gledhill, *Home is Where the Heart Is,* 235–54; Chon A. Noriega, "Birth of the Southwest: Social Protest, Tourism, and D. W. Griffith's *Ramona,*" in Bernardi, *Birth of Whiteness,* 203–26; Michael Rogin, "'The Sword Became a Flashing Vision': D. W. Griffith's *The Birth of a Nation,*" *Representations* 9 (Winter 1985): 150–95; Clyde Taylor, "The Re-birth of the Aesthetic in Cinema," *Wide Angle* 13, nos. 3–4 (July–October 1991): 12–30.

6. Scott Simmon, "'The Female of the Species': D. W. Griffith, Father of the Woman's Film," *Film Quarterly* 46, no. 2 (Winter 1992–93): 10.

7. See Kathy Peiss, *Cheap Amusements: Working Women and Leisure in Turn-of-the-Century New York* (Philadelphia: Temple University Press, 1986), 163–85, for the ways in which the sexuality of working-class women was observed by middle-class reformers and critics, many of whom were also women breaking away from a traditional domestic role in the interests of philanthropy. Chief among their concerns were the public visibility of these women, the mixed gender venues, such as dance halls and nickelodeons, that they frequented, and their frank conversations among themselves about sexuality and romantic issues. That is, these women did not observe the middle-class codes regulating women's discretion, sexual ignorance, and public modesty and reserve, even if they were often very strict about what

kinds of specific sexual behaviors they would participate in. See also Kathy Peiss, "'Charity Girls' and City Pleasures: Historical Notes on Working-Class Sexuality, 1880–1920," in *Passion and Power: Sexuality in History*, ed. Kathy Peiss and Christina Simmons (Philadelphia: Temple University Press, 1989), 58–61.

8. I am thinking here of the panics about "white slavery," misegenation, and the derogation of immigrants that characterized this period, evidenced in the representational dynamics of Griffith's *The Birth of a Nation*, which I discuss later in this chapter.

9. These standards of visibility or lack thereof have everything to do with class distinction, as I discussed in relation to nineteenth-century domesticity in part I of this book.

10. Tom Gunning states that by 1908 "comedies as well as melodramas centered increasingly on the bourgeois home." Gunning, *D. W. Griffith and the Origins of American Narrative Film*, 141.

11. Ibid., 13; Hansen, *Babel and Babylon*, 44.

12. This was defined by Tom Gunning and André Gaudreault as the "primary motive force" of early cinema, which consisted precisely in its alluring aspects that were related not to storytelling but rather to its capacity "to show something." See Gunning, *D. W. Griffith and the Origins of American Narrative Film*, 41, and also his essay "The Cinema of Attraction: Early Film, Its Spectator, and the Avant-Garde," *Wide Angle* 8, nos. 3–4 (1986): 63–71.

13. Constance Balides, "Scenarios of Exposure in the Practice of Everyday Life: Women in the Cinema of Attractions," *Screen* 34, no. 1 (Spring 1993): 24–26 (reprinted as chap. 2 of Balides, *Making Dust in the Archives*, 65–122).

14. Ibid., 28–29.

15. Roland Barthes, "Diderot Brecht Eisenstein," in Rosen, *Narrative, Apparatus, Ideology*, 172.

16. Miriam Hansen discriminates between audiences for vaudeville (new urban white-collar workers and upwardly mobile working class) and those for nickelodeons (immigrants and working class), both venues for early cinema. Hansen, *Babel and Babylon*, 61–65. Tom Gunning also mentions the heterogeneity of the audience for early cinema. Gunning, *D. W. Griffith and the Origins of American Narrative Film*, 87.

17. Lary May, *Screening Out the Past: The Birth of Mass Culture and the Motion Picture Industry* (New York: Oxford University Press, 1980), 28. See also Tom Gunning, "From the Opium Den to the Theater of Morality: Moral Discourse and the Film Process in Early American Cinema," *Art & Text* 30 (September–November 1988): 30–40.

18. May, *Screening Out the Past*, 28.

19. Matthews, *"Just A Housewife,"* 119.

20. May, *Screening Out the Past*, 49.

21. Quoted ibid.

22. Ibid., 50–51.

23. Matthews, *"Just A Housewife,"* 163–64.

24. Again, the family and domesticity became the anchor for paradoxical political constructions, as the Progressives attempted to conserve "familial" values against the onslaught of certain kinds of progress by invoking, in some cases, "engineered" morality. Another, more troubling manifestation was the compatibility of eugenics with the scientific reform celebrated in the Progressive era. The Progressive president of the University of Wisconsin, Charles R. Van Hise, asserted, "We know enough about eugenics so that if the knowledge were applied, the defective classes would disappear within a generation." Quoted in Diane B. Paul, *Controlling Human Heredity: 1865 to the Present* (Atlantic Highlands, N.J.: Humanities Press, 1995), 78.

25. May, *Screening Out the Past*, 51.

26. Ibid., 46–51; Matthews, *"Just a Housewife,"* 163–64.

27. Gunning, "From the Opium Den to the Theater of Morality," 31–35.

28. Ibid., 39.

29. Ibid., 32–34.

30. Gunning, *D. W. Griffith and the Origins of American Narrative Film*, 77–78. See also Scott Simmon, *The Films of D. W. Griffith* (Cambridge: Cambridge University Press, 1993), 76.

31. Simmon, *Films of D. W. Griffith*, 13.

32. As Scott Simmon argues, the reasons for focusing on Griffith include the extraordinary number of his films that survived; the fact that Griffith promoted himself and the cinema in highly successful ways; that he saw himself as a reformer; and that he set the model for the feature film in this country. Film history has for all of these reasons been fashioned around him. Ibid., 22.

33. Christine Gledhill, "The Melodramatic Field: An Investigation," in *Home is Where the Heart Is*, 24.

34. Nick Browne makes this point in "Griffith's Family Discourse," 226.

35. See Virginia Wright Wexman's discussion of these threats to women in Griffith's films and the contemporaneous political struggles for women's rights in "Star and Auteur: The Griffith-Gish Collaboration and the Struggle over Patriarchal Marriage," in *Creating the Couple: Love, Marriage, and Hollywood Performance* (Princeton: Princeton University Press, 1993), 42–43.

36. Many critics focus on Griffith's psyche and his sexuality. See, for example, Kenneth S. Lynn, "The Torment of D. W. Griffith," *American Scholar* 59, no. 2 (1990): 255–64; Rogin, "The Sword Became a Flashing Vision."

37. Lynn, "The Torment of D. W. Griffith," 255–64.

38. See Gunning, "From the Opium Den to the Theater of Morality," 36–37; Hansen, *Babel and Babylon*, 90.

39. Clyde Taylor, whose discussion of *The Birth of a Nation* has informed mine, expresses this point succinctly: "The immanent violation of a White woman has played so large a role in the American cinema as compared to others as to seem an American obsession." See Taylor, "The Re-birth of the Aesthetic in Cinema," 25.

40. Michael Rogin quotes Lillian Gish on Griffith's decision to cast her rather than Blanche Sweet as Elsie Stoneman in *The Birth of a Nation* after she rehearsed a scene with the Silas Lynch character: "I was very blonde and fragile-looking. The contrast with the dark man evidently pleased Mr. Griffith, for he said in front of everyone, 'Maybe she would be more effective than the mature figure I had in mind.'" See Rogin, "The Sword Became a Flashing Vision," 164.

41. For a discussion of how Griffith celebrated whiteness in his use of lighting, particularly on Lillian Gish, see Richard Dyer, "The Colour of Virtue: Lillian Gish, Whiteness, and Femininity," in *Women and Film: A Sight and Sound Reader* (Philadelphia: Temple University Press, 1993), 1–9.

42. See G. J. Baker-Benfield, "The Spermatic Economy: A Nineteenth-Century View of Sexuality," *Feminist Studies* 1, no. 1 (Summer 1972): 45–74.

43. I am grateful to Linda Williams for identifying the dance as an apache dance.

44. I thank Ron Green for mentioning these films to me.

45. In "'The Female of the Species': D. W. Griffith, Father of the Woman's Film," Scott Simmon discusses films that deal with the problem of the "idle woman." Simmon, *Films of D. W. Griffith*, 14.

46. For discussions of white femininity and racism in *The Birth of a Nation*, see Dyer, "The Colour of Virtue"; Rogin, "The Sword Became a Flashing Vision"; and Taylor, "The Re-birth of the Aesthetic in Cinema."

47. James Baldwin, *The Devil Finds Work: An Essay* (New York: Dell, 1990 [1976]), 49.

48. Ibid., 49.

49. For example, the Whoopi Goldberg character in *Corrina, Corrina* (1994).

50. See Daniel Bernardi's valuable discussion of the racist content of these and other of Griffith's Biograph films in "Voice of Whiteness," 115–17. While Bernardi emphasizes the effect of Griffith's films as always positioning the white man at the top of the "social and moral ladder," my argument is that the white woman's domesticity and delicacy are the linchpin of this system. The perverse logic of the white man–white woman–black man triangle Griffith constructs to assert the value of white womanhood above all else reveals itself in the cabin scene near the end of *The Birth of a Nation*, where white fathers and husbands savagely grip their daughters and wives by the hair, rifle butts and stones poised to bash their heads in to "protect" them from "a fate worse than death." My point is that in the U.S. cultural imaginary, articulated so cogently by Griffith, white women and their delicate domesticity have no value in and of themselves. That value is always instrumental within overarching but repressed proprietary rights related to racial and class differentiation. And that delicacy depends on an unlabored appearance.

51. See Lesage, "Artful Racism, Artful Rape."

52. Thomas Burke, "The Chink and the Child," in *Limehouse Nights* (New York: Grosset & Dunlap, 1927). The tension between a violent white working-class man and a Chinese merchant who is depicted as successful if unambitious and fond of opium would strike familiar chords in an affluent white American audience, especially in California and the Southwest. The Chinese Exclusion Law, passed in 1882, renewed in 1892, and extended indefinitely in 1902, was based on fears that "a yellow proletariat" would deprive an angry and racist white working class of work. See Ronald T. Takaki, *Iron Cages: Race and Culture in Nineteenth-Century America* (Seattle: University of Washington Press, 1979), 215–49, and *A Different Mirror: A History of Multicultural America* (Boston: Little, Brown, 1993), 204–9. For Griffith's attempts to avoid both charges of anti-Orientalism and comparison to de Mille's *The Cheat* in his very "class conscious" marketing of *Broken Blossoms*, see Vance Kepley, Jr., "Griffith's 'Broken Blossoms' and the Problem of Historical Specificity," *Quarterly Review of Film Studies* 3, no. 1 (1978): 37–47.

53. Dudley Andrew, "Broken Blossoms: The Art and the Eros of a Perverse Text," *Quarterly Review of Film Studies* 6, no. 1 (Winter 1981): 86.

54. Ibid., 87.

55. Nick Browne argues that the film secularizes Cheng Huan's worship of Buddha "into a Religion of Love whose object of worship is Woman." Browne, "Griffith's Family Discourse," 225.

56. See Virginia Wright Wexman's discussion of this film in "Star and Auteur: The Griffith-Gish Collaboration and the Struggle over Patriarchal Marriage," in *Creating the Couple*, 39–66.

57. Scott Simmon, in *Films of D. W. Griffith*, discusses the fatal consequences of being gazed at in a number of Griffith's films, but his line of analysis is more plot focused than mine.

58. Iris Barry, *D. W. Griffith, American Film Master* (New York: Plantin Press, 1965), 30.

59. Quoted ibid.

60. Molly Haskell, "The Twenties," in *From Reverence to Rape: The Treatment of Women in the Movies* (Baltimore: Penguin Books, 1974), 49.

CHAPTER FIVE

1. Ally Acker, *Reel Women: Pioneers of the Cinema, 1896 to the Present* (New York: Continuum, 1991), 7–12. Acker actually asserts that Blaché, rather than Meliès, "arguably" deserves the title of first narrative director, but this assertion is a matter of dispute.

2. Sincere thanks to Ramona Curry for suggesting that I take a look at this film and Lois Weber's *Too Wise Wives*.

3. This iconography is particularly interesting, given that the Statue of Liberty was a gift from the French government, presented to the United States in 1885 and dedicated on October 28, 1886, during Blaché's lifetime. Although it may be only a coincidence, Blaché made this film in October 1912. More substantively, the statue's installation in the United States coincided with a shift in immigration from the Irish, English, Germans, and Scandinavians who made up earlier waves of immigrants to those from eastern and southern Europe in the late nineteenth and early twentieth centuries. See Evans, *Born for Liberty*, 130–31.

4. As I will discuss in chapter 6, the illusions on which these multiple invisibilities are predicated break down in a film such as Douglas Sirk's 1959 *Imitation of Life*.

5. A substantial tradition of film scholarship deals with the relationship between films, women, and consumption, though not always in relation to domesticity per se. See Mary Ann Doane, "The Economy of Desire: The Commodity Form in/of the Cinema," in *The Desire to Desire: The Women's Film of the 1940s* (Bloomington: Indiana University Press, 1987), 22–33, for a cogent discussion of these issues. She credits Charles Eckert's essay "The Carole Lombard in Macy's Window," *Quarterly Review of Film Studies* 3, no. 1 (Winter 1978): 1–22, for raising these issues in relation to the cinema. See also Jeanne Allen, "The Film Viewer as Consumer," *Quarterly Review of Film Studies* 5, no. 4 (Fall 1980): 481–99; Elizabeth Ewen, "City Lights: Immigrant Women and the Rise of the Movies," *Signs* 5, no. 3, suppl. (Spring 1980): S45–S65; Jane Gaines, "The Queen Christina Tie-Ups: Convergence of Show Window and Screen," in "Female Representation and Consumer Culture," ed. Jane Gaines and Michael Renov, *Quarterly Review of Film and Video* 11, no. 1 (1989): 35–60.

6. Of these women, detailed in Acker, *Reel Women*, Lois Weber, Ida Lupino, and Dorothy Arzner were the most famous, successful, and prolific.

7. In 1950 a remake titled *Harriet Craig* featured Joan Crawford in the lead. Rather than focusing on Harriet's housework and cleanliness, this version emphasizes Harriet's acquisitiveness and her sexual control over her husband. The later Harriet is also much more dishonest, and so the nuances about the demonization of domestic labor itself, consistent with the very transformation in women's roles that the earlier film documents so well, are no longer present.

8. See Acker, *Reel Women*, 21–29.

9. Griffith's family history and his psychosexual profile in relation to his father, his older sister, and the actresses he was involved with are regularly invoked in discussions of the meanings of his films. Arzner's identity as lesbian informs much of the critical work on her.

10. Two early pieces are Claire Johnston, "Dorothy Arzner: Critical Strategies," 36–45, and Pam Cook, "Approaching the Work of Dorothy Arzner" 46–56, both in *Feminism and Film Theory*, ed. Constance Penley (New York: Routledge, 1988). More recently, Judith Mayne provocatively readdresses Arzner's work in "Female Authorship Reconsidered," 89–123, in *The Woman at the Keyhole* (Bloomington: Indiana University Press, 1990).

11 See Jacqueline Suter, "Feminine Discourse in *Christopher Strong*," in Penley, *Feminism and Film Theory*, 89–103.

12. In *Shot/Countershot: Film Tradition and Women's Cinema* (Princeton: Princeton University Press, 1989), 153, Lucy Fischer argues that Judy in *Dance, Girl, Dance* "rejects the role of fetishistic object."

13. "*Craig's Wife*," *Variety*, September 13, 1936.

14. "*Craig's Wife*: Character Drama," *Motion Picture Herald*, September 19, 1936.

15. James Naremore, *Acting in the Cinema* (Berkeley: University of California Press, 1988), 87.

16. Robert B. Ray, *A Certain Tendency of the Hollywood Cinema, 1930–1980* (Princeton:

Princeton University Press, 1985), 57; Thomas Elsaesser, "Tales of Sound and Fury: Observations on the Family Melodrama," in Gledhill, *Home is Where the Heart Is*, 45–47.

17. Columbia press release synopsis, *Craig's Wife* clippings file, Academy of Motion Picture Arts and Sciences Archive, Beverly Hills.

18. Arzner had a significant amount of control over the production of *Craig's Wife*. Harry Cohn had been wanting her to work for Columbia since 1927. Arzner instigated contract negotiations with him in 1936, demanding and receiving producer's status and exemption from Cohn's story conferences on his yacht. Cohn was nevertheless furious with her for hiring Rosalind Russell without his approval, and he retaliated by ordering a set, "Columbia fashion," for the film. Arzner simply hired interior decorator William Haines, and the two of them "sneaked into the studio at night and transformed the set according to Arzner's wishes." From *Features and Directors: Films by Women* (Chicago, 1974), 6–7, *Craig's Wife* clippings file, Academy of Motion Picture Arts and Sciences Archive, Beverly Hills.

19. George Kelly, *Craig's Wife* (New York: Samuel French, 1925), 7.

20. Arzner favored classical motifs and wanted *Craig's Wife* to have "the appearance of a modern Greek tragedy. *Features and Directors*, 7.

21. Beth Bailey, *From Front Porch to Back Seat* (Baltimore: Johns Hopkins University Press, 1988), 77–78.

22. Elaine Tyler May, *Great Expectations: Marriage and Divorce in Post-Victorian America* (Chicago: University of Chicago Press, 1980), 60–62.

23. "*Craig's Wife*," *Variety*, 5.

24. Mary Douglas, *Purity and Danger* (London: Routledge and Kegan Paul, 1966), 7.

25. Ibid., 68.

26. Ibid., 35.

27. Palmer, *Domesticity and Dirt*, 6–7.

28. Stephen Mintz and Susan Kellogg, *Domestic Revolutions: A Social History of American Family Life* (New York: Free Press, 1988), 115.

29. Matthews, "*Just a Housewife*," 181–82.

30. Ibid., 183.

31. T. J. Jackson Lears, "From Salvation to Self-realization: Advertising and the Therapeutic Roots of the Consumer Culture, 1880–1930," in *The Culture of Consumption*, ed. Richard Wightman Fox and T. J. Jackson Lears (New York: Pantheon, 1983), 4–6.

32. Ibid., 9–10.

33. Ibid., 16–17.

34. Stasser, *Never Done*, 253.

35. Lears, "From Salvation to Self-realization," 21–22.

36. Ibid., 22–27.

37. In "The Hegemonic Female Fantasy in *An Unmarried Woman* and *Craig's Wife*," *Film Reader* 5 (1982): 91, Julia Lesage observes that Arzner changed Kelly's play by enhancing the roles of the secondary women characters. Judith Mayne considers the emphasis on female characters in her discussion of lesbian inflections in Arzner's films in *Woman at the Keyhole*, 113.

38. Peter Brooks, *The Melodramatic Imagination: Balzac, Henry James, Melodrama, and the Mode of Excess* (New Haven: Yale University Press, 1976), 27.

39. Gledhill, "Melodramatic Field," 24.

40. Elsaesser, "Tales of Sound and Fury," 46.

41. According to Sutherland, *Americans and Their Servants*, 59, in 1890, 45 percent of domestic servants were immigrants (39 percent Irish), 27.5 percent were African American, and 26 percent were native white; by 1920, 38 percent were African American, 24 percent were native white, and 22 percent were immigrants. The category "native white" is as problematic as the title of this work.

42. Nor perhaps were they representationally normative for the cinema in the thirties. Donald Bogle, in *Toms, Coons, Mulattoes, Mammies & Bucks: An Interpretive History of Blacks in American Films* (New York: Continuum, 1973, 1989), 35–38, argues that during the depression, the use of African Americans as servants in the movies skyrocketed, thus creating a "golden age" for black actors.

43. For the significance of horizontal relations among groups of people vis-à-vis gender and class identity, see Nancy Armstrong's introduction to *Desire and Domestic Fiction*, 3–27, and, in relation to the construction of nations, Benedict Anderson's introduction to *Imagined Communities* (New York: Verso, 1991 [1983]), 1–7.

44. Although Mammy in *Gone With the Wind* is granted a certain degree of wisdom, both conventional femininity and maternity are withheld from her, and of course Melanie completely exceeds her in affective wisdom and its agency.

45. This organization accounts for the fact that though there are many African American servants in classical Hollywood cinema, and some single mothers, autonomous African American families are very rare.

46. Acker, *Reel Women*, 10.

47. Ibid., 13–15.

48. Ibid., 27.

49. Ibid., 15.

50. Ibid., 21.

51. See the entries for Blaché, Weber, and Arzner, ibid., 7–12, 12–16, 21–29.

CHAPTER SIX

1. See Christian Vivani, "Who Is without Sin: The Maternal Melodrama in American Film, 1930–1939," in *Imitation of Life*, ed. Marcia Landy (Detroit: Wayne State University Press, 1991), 170–71.

2. See Eckert, "Carole Lombard in Macy's Window."

3. For example, see, on *Stella Dallas*, E. Ann Kaplan, "The Case of the Missing Mother: Maternal Issues in Vidor's *Stella Dallas*," in Erens, *Issues in Feminist Film Criticism*, 126–36; Linda Williams, "'Something Else besides a Mother': *Stella Dallas* and the Maternal Melodrama," in Gledhill, *Home is Where the Heart Is*, 299–325; on *Imitation of Life*, see Lauren Berlant, "National Brands/National Body: *Imitation of Life*," in *Comparative American Identities: Race, Sex, and Nationality in the Modern Text*, ed. Hortense J. Spillers (New York: Routledge, 1991), 110–40; Marina Heung, "'What's the Matter with Sara Jane?': Daughters and Mothers in Sirk's *Imitation of Life*," *Cinema Journal* 26, no. 3 (Spring 1987): 21–43; On *Mildred Pierce*, see Joyce Nelson, "*Mildred Pierce* Reconsidered," *Film Reader* 2 (1977): 65–70; and Linda Williams, "Feminist Film Theory: *Mildred Pierce* and the Second World War," in Pribram, *Female Spectators*, 12–30.

4. See Sara Evans, "Flappers, Freudians, and All That Jazz," in *Born for Liberty*, 175–78.

5. Williams, "Something Else besides a Mother," 308.

6. The novel *Stella Dallas* articulates Laurel's development and the class problematic in much more nuanced terms than the film. In the novel, Stella uses all her extra money and goes without a lot of things for herself to provide Laurel with riding lessons, swimming lessons, dancing lessons, lessons "in every sport which her mother considered fashionable and in which instructions could be bought." Her father takes her camping and introduces her to literature. Rather than characterizing Laurel's suitability for her ultimate social position as innate, the novel suggests it is the result of both her parents' attentions. Olive Higgins Prouty, *Stella Dallas* (New York: Harper and Row, 1990 [1923]), 45.

7. In the period between the two wars, the United States surged "well ahead of Britain

and the rest of the world" in the development of factory-produced ready-to-wear fashion. Technological innovations, the vast market, and the literally immense areas that could be covered by production runs all contributed to this success. The mass media influenced the concept and implementation of ready-to-wear because they created "uniformity of standards of taste among the populace." Significantly, what had inhibited technical developments in the fashion industry immediately after the war had been mercurial changes in fashion and women's "desire for individuality." See Elizabeth Ewing, "Developments in Fashion Manufacture between the Wars, 1918–1939," in *History of Twentieth-Century Fashion* (London: B. T. Batsford, 1974), 119–38.

8. "*Stella Dallas*," *Time*, August 9, 1937.

9. Lauren Berlant's essay "National Brands/National Body: *Imitation of Life*" has informed my discussion substantially. Berlant considers the novel and both films for the way the very different feminine bodies contained in each narrative are distributed and represented across public and private spheres.

10. See Berlant's discussion of Delilah's fractured body, ibid., 119–22.

11. In Hurst's novel, Delilah has contributed a great deal of money to churches and other associations in Harlem, though she has not been socially present there.

12. Peola's dilemma extended to the actress who played her, Fredi Washington. Donald Bogle writes that casting Washington was always a problem because she "looked white," and that the very "spectacular looks" that made a film career initially a possibility for her also made that career finally impossible because there were no romantic lead roles for African American women. See Bogle, *Toms, Coons, Mulattoes, Mammies & Bucks*, 60–62.

13. The extensive critical literature on "passing" includes Berlant, "National Brands/National Body"; Jennifer DeVere Brody, "Clare Kendry's 'True' Colors: Race and Class Conflict in Nella Larsen's *Passing*," *Callaloo* 15, no. 4 (Fall 1992): 1053–65; Judith Butler, "Passing, Queering: Nella Larsen's Psychoanalytic Challenge," in *Bodies That Matter: On the Discursive Limits of Sex* (New York: Routledge, 1993); Carby, *Reconstructing Womanhood*; Richard Dyer, "White," *Screen* 29, no. 4 (Autumn 1988): 44–64; Harryette Mullen, "Optic White: Blackness and the Production of Whiteness," *Diacritics* 24, nos. 2–3 (Summer–Fall 1994): 71–89; Valerie Smith, "Reading the Intersection of Race and Gender in Narratives of Passing," *Diacritics* 24, nos. 2–3 (Summer–Fall 1994): 43–57; and Carole-Anne Tyler, "Passing: Narcissism, Identity, and Difference," *differences* 6, nos. 2–3 (1994): 212–48.

14. See Pam Cook, "Duplicity in *Mildred Pierce*," in *Women in Film Noir*, ed. E. Ann Kaplan (London: BFI, 1996 [1978]), 68–82.

15. Williams, "Feminist Film Theory," 13.

16. See Sara Evans, "Surviving the Great Depression" in *Born for Liberty*, 197–219.

17. Bailey, *From Front Porch to Back Seat*, 104.

18. Paul Skenazy, *James M. Cain* (New York: Continuum, 1989), 67.

19. Citing the work of several economic experts, Glenna Matthews observes, "Industrial capitalism requires a high level of consumer spending—optimally of a rather indiscriminate nature—and this task has been ascribed to women." Matthews further finds that "there began to be a pervasive male fear that women were getting off too easy, reflected in literature in the interwar years and more generally in the society after World War II." The economic and cultural dichotomies that distinguish producers from consumers obscure the perception that, for housewives, shopping is work. Matthews, *"Just a Housewife,"* 187–202.

20. Linda Williams uses *Mildred Pierce* to outline a mode of historical analysis that apprehends the "contradictory situation of the historical female spectator" and avoids the repression/reflection binary that has characterized feminist psychoanalytic-semiotic and sociological approaches to film, respectively. Drawing from Fredric Jameson, she reads *Mildred Pierce* for

how it reflects and represses its historical moment, which she identifies as determined by the Second World War. She ends her analysis, however, by referring to the two women scrubbing the floor in the final sequence of the film, asserting that "this film is not their story." While my analysis is concerned not with spectatorship but with a combination of Foucauldian discourse analysis and social history, Williams's argument, by its own logic, would suggest that *Mildred Pierce* is precisely about working-class women, since it is their history that the film represses. My analysis attempts to show how the film organizes the working class of different races by pointing to the disastrous consequences of the white middle-class woman's being out of place. See Williams, "Feminist Film Theory," 12–30.

21. For a consideration of how these ambivalences translated into highly contradictory narrative messages to women in postwar film noir, see Michael Renov, "*Leave Her to Heaven*: The Double Bind of the Post-war Woman," in *Journal of Film and Video* 35, no. 1 (Winter 1983): 13–36.

22. Nelson, "*Mildred Pierce* Reconsidered"; Williams, "Feminist Film Theory."

23. For commentary on Lana Turner's performance and how it frames Mahalia Jackson's appearance within the film's promotion of "the cultural authenticity of blacks," see Richard Dyer, "Four Films of Lana Turner," in *Imitations of Life: A Reader on Film and Television Melodrama*, ed. Marcia Landy (Detroit: Wayne State University Press, 1991), 423–28; and Marina Heung's discussion of Jackson's singing as "a documentary performance within a fiction film," in "What's the Matter with Sara Jane?" 21–43, esp. 37–38.

CHAPTER SEVEN

1. Silvia Bovenschen, "Is There a Feminine Aesthetic?" trans. Beth Weckmueller, *New German Critique* 10 (Winter 1977): 132.

2. Ibid., 132–33.

3. On melodramas of the fifties, see Jackie Byars, *All That Hollywood Allows: Re-reading Gender in 1950s Melodrama* (Chapel Hill: University of North Carolina Press, 1991).

4. By this comment I do not mean that that binary was secure and unchanging during this period, merely that inordinate attention has been paid to its maintenance and institution, particularly during times of economic or social crisis.

5. See Lisa Duggan and Nan D. Hunter, *Sex Wars: Sexual Dissent and Political Culture* (New York: Routledge, 1995), 1–80.

6. For an invaluable historical description of the rise of feminist film production and theory in relation to alternative cinemas in the United States in the sixties, see David James, "Cinema and Sexual Difference," in *Allegories of Cinema: American Film in the Sixties* (Princeton: Princeton University Press, 1989), 304–14.

7. Teresa de Lauretis, "Rethinking Women's Cinema," in *Technologies of Gender* (Bloomington: Indiana University Press, 1987), 128. De Lauretis is summarizing the trajectory of feminist film theory from content-based to formal critiques.

8. De Lauretis's argument in "Rethinking Women's Cinema" inspired this approach. She asserts that "the time has come to re-think women's cinema as the production of a feminist social vision" and feminism itself as a productive discourse which has "conceived a new social subject, women: as speakers, writers, readers, spectators, users, and makers of cultural forms." Ibid., 134–35.

9. Critical judgments concerning what type of film *Jeanne Dielman* is vary. Marsha Kinder finds that the film uses "a conventional plot" to express "a radical vision" in "Reflections on *Jeanne Dielman*," *Film Quarterly* 30, no. 4 (1977): 3. Judith Mayne considers its relation to early cinema's primitive techniques and the avant-garde in "Revising the Primitive," in *Woman at the Keyhole*, 207–8. Kaja Silverman, discussing Jacqueline Suter's work, calls the

film "experimental," in *The Acoustic Mirror: The Female Voice in Psychoanalysis and Cinema* (Bloomington: Indiana University Press, 1988), 208.

10. Kinder, "Reflections on *Jeanne Dielman*," 2.

11. Janet Bergstrom, "*Jeanne Dielman, 23 Quai du Commerce, 1080 Bruxelles* by Chantal Akerman," *Camera Obscura* 2 (Fall 1977): 118.

12. Rachel Blau DuPlessis, "For the Etruscans: Sexual Difference and Artistic Production—the Debate over a Female Aesthetic," in *The Future of Difference*, ed. Hester Eisenstein and Alice Jardine (New Brunswick, N.J.: Rutgers University Press, 1988), 135.

13. Ibid., 135.

14. Judith Mayne has an extensive discussion of the types of ambivalence that structure this film and prevent any comprehensive resolution in "Revising the Primitive," 203–11. My argument differs from hers, however, in that I see the aesthetic of *Jeanne Dielman* as drawn from the material experience of women's housework, whereas she relates it to early cinema and avant-garde notions of the primitive.

15. This emphasis on noise over speech, discussed by Marsha Kinder in "Reflections on *Jeanne Dielman*," 7, reverses the tendency of the classical narrative film, in which, David Bordwell asserts, "speech appears to occupy the foreground, noise the background." David Bordwell, *Narration in the Fiction Film* (Madison: University of Wisconsin Press, 1985), 118.

16. Bergstrom, "*Jeanne Dielman*," 118.

17. Ibid., 119.

18. Kinder, "Reflections on *Jeanne Dielman*," 4.

19. David Bordwell has written extensively on the components of the classical film narrative and their interrelationship with film style and spectatorship. What he calls the "canonical story format" consists of a causal chain of events motivated by the goals of a protagonist who is thwarted from realizing his or her aims by various complicating actions. The protagonist's attempts to overcome these obstacles move the story forward to an outcome and ending. Bordwell, *Narration in the Fiction Film*, 35.

20. Ruth Perlmutter, "Feminine Absence: A Political Aesthetic in Chantal Akerman's *Jeanne Dielman*," *Quarterly Review of Film Studies* 4, no. 2 (Spring 1979): 132.

21. Bergstrom, "*Jeanne Dielman*," 119.

22. Kinder, "Reflections on *Jeanne Dielman*," 3. See also Mayne's discussion of the primal scene and the displacement of the son's desire by the daughter's, "Revising the Primitive," 208–10.

23. Mary Ann Doane, "Woman's Stake: Filming the Female Body," *October* 17 (Summer 1981): 34–35.

24. Ibid., 33–34. See also Vivian Sobchack's phenomenological approach to spectator responses, which makes an end run around these vexing binaries, in *The Address of the Eye: A Phenomenology of Film Experience* (Princeton: Princeton University Press, 1992).

25. Bordwell, *Narration in the Fiction Film*, 38.

26. For a more conventional discussion of the uncanny in relation to this film, see Danièle Dubroux, "Le familier inquiétant (*Jeanne Dielman*)," *Cashiers du cinéma*, no. 265 (March–April 1976): 17–20.

CHAPTER EIGHT

1. Lucy Fischer, "*A Question of Silence*: Ritual in Transfigured Time," in *Shot/Countershot: Film Tradition and Women's Cinema* (Princeton: Princeton University Press, 1989), 292.

2. In Fischer's chapter on this film, she includes information about criminologists' profiles of women who kill. Ibid., 297.

3. Jeanette Murphy, "*A Question of Silence*," in *Films for Women*, ed. Charlotte Brudson (London: BFI, 1986), 102.

4. Stanley Kaufmann, "Jaundice Posing as Justice," *New Republic*, September 3, 1984.

5. See Fischer, "*A Question of Silence*"; Mary Gentile, "Feminist or Tendentious: Marleen Gorris's *A Question of Silence*," in Erens, *Issues in Feminist Film Criticism*, 396; Murphy, "*A Question of Silence*," 102–3. Murphy astutely observes that the film's violence presents problems for feminists who take a politicized and gendered position against violence. Rather than focusing on the film's violence, Linda Williams notes how *A Question of Silence* documents the conditions, including housework, which perpetuate women's silence and allow them only the most circumscribed forms of speech in "A Jury of their Peers," *Multiple Voices in Feminist Film Criticism*, ed. Diane Carson, Linda Dittmar, and Janice R. Welsch (Minneapolis: University of Minnesota Press, 1994), 432–40.

6. Gentile, "Feminist or Tendentious," 398.

7. Ibid., 397.

8. Sarah Montgomery, "Cinematic Silence," *Feminist Review* 18 (November 1984): 40.

9. See Mary Ann Doane, "Clinical Eyes: The Medical Discourse," in *The Desire to Desire*. Fischer makes this connection also in "*A Question of Silence*," 285.

10. Murphy, "*A Question of Silence*," 100.

11. Ray, *A Certain Tendency of the American Cinema*, 56–57.

12. Gentile, "Feminist or Tendentious," 401.

13. Fischer, "*A Question of Silence*," 286.

14. Peter Brooks associates muteness with melodrama in *The Melodramatic Imagination*.

15. See Gledhill, "Melodramatic Field," and Elsaesser, "Tales of Sound and Fury," both in Gledhill, *Home is Where the Heart Is*, 5–42, 43–69.

16. Freud's case studies would be exemplary in this regard, as he "reads," writes, and explains these women's complaints about seduction and incest as narratives or fantasies that trace the contours of the unconscious.

17. Elsaesser, "Tales of Sound and Fury," 46.

18. Laura Mulvey, "Visual Pleasure and Narrative Cinema," in Rosen, *Narrative, Apparatus, Ideology*, 199.

19. In "Some Films Men and Women Can't Talk About," Molly Haskell notes: "The psychiatrist, who represents (a little too neatly) the civilized, elitist, sheltered point of view, comes to understand and honor the perfect clarity of the women's awareness of what they have done and their lack of guilt . . . even as the filmmaker wisely makes no attempt to mitigate their crime." *Ms.* 12 (May 1984): 17.

20. For an interesting reading of this film in relation to the history of shoplifting, see Ketura Persellin, "'A High-Heeled Army of Furies': Shoplifting in Marlene [*sic*] Gorris's *A Question of Silence*," *Spectator* 16, no. 1 (Fall/Winter 1995): 23–31.

21. Montgomery, "Cinematic Silence," 41.

22. For an excellent summary of the issues involved in female identification and spectatorship and different theoretical positions on these questions, see the debate between Mary Ann Doane and Tania Modleski on these points: Mary Ann Doane, "Film and the Masquerade: Theorising the Female Spectator," *Screen* 23, nos. 3–4 (September–October 1982): 175–89; Tania Modleski, "Rape vs. Mans/Laughter: *Blackmail*," in *The Women Who Knew Too Much: Hitchcock and Feminist Theory* (New York: Routledge, 1989), 17–30; and Mary Ann Doane, "Masquerade Reconsidered: Further Thoughts on the Female Spectator," in *Femmes Fatales*, 33–43.

23. B. Ruby Rich, "Up Against the Kitchen Wall: Chantal Akerman's Meta-Cinema," *Village Voice*, March 29, 1983.

CHAPTER NINE

1. Yoko Ono, *Instruction Paintings* (New York: Weatherhill, 1995).

2. Ono's performances are foundational to the establishment of performance art as a genre. She experiments with the use of her own body and voice in antitheatrical spaces, acts not necessarily overtly labeled as feminist but with obvious implications for later feminist work. See Barbara Haskell and John G. Hanhardt's cogent monograph *Yoko Ono: Arias and Objects* (Layton, Utah: Peregrine Smith, 1991). For recent reconsiderations and exhibitions of American feminist art on domesticity from the seventies onward, see *Dirt and Domesticity: Constructions of the Feminine*, exhibition catalogue (New York: Whitney Museum of American Art at the Equitable Center, 1992); *Division of Labor: Women's Work in Contemporary Art*, exhibition catalogue (New York: Bronx Museum of the Arts, 1995); *Mechanical Brides: Women and Machines from Home to Office*, exhibition catalogue (New York: Cooper-Hewitt, National Museum of Design, Smithsonian Institution, 1993); *Pleasures and Terrors of Domestic Comfort*, exhibition catalogue (New York: Museum of Modern Art, 1991). Judy Chicago's *Dinner Party* has been taken as exemplary of 1970s' feminist artwork on the domestic. For an exhibition that considers and contextualizes its status, see Amelia Jones, ed., *Sexual Politics: Judy Chicago's Dinner Party in Feminist Art History*, exhibition catalogue (Los Angeles: Armand Hammer Museum of Art and Cultural Center and University of California Press, 1996).

3. Oscar Wilde, "The Decay of Lying," in *Literary Criticism of Oscar Wilde* (Lincoln: University of Nebraska Press, 1968), 117.

4. Douglas, *Purity and Danger*, 68.

5. Ibid., 161–62.

6. I am grateful to Jon McKenzie for pointing out the odd significance of the scents of many cleaning products.

7. The woman's alignment with nature in traditional thought is described in Susan Griffin's *Woman and Nature: The Roaring inside Her* (New York: Harper and Row, 1978). But the highly cultured is also seen as feminine, as in the stereotype of the effeminate man. See also Jacques Lacan's provocative closure to "Guiding Remarks for a Congress on Feminine Sexuality," in which, commenting on "feminine sexuality and society," he alludes to the particularly refined and cultured quality of groups of women. See Jacques Lacan, *Feminine Sexuality: Jacques Lacan and the école freudienne*, ed. Juliet Mitchell and Jacqueline Rose, trans. Jacqueline Rose (New York: W. W. Norton, 1982), 88–98.

8. Catherine Clément, *The Newly Born Woman*, trans. Betsy Wing (Minneapolis: University of Minnesota Press, 1975), 8.

9. *Webster's Ninth New Collegiate Dictionary* s.v. *cycle*.

10. Luisah Teish's "Women's Spirituality: A Household Act" sketches the rise, history, and logic of voodoo. I have borrowed my list of significations from her account in *Home Girls: A Black Feminist Anthology*, ed. Barbara Smith (New York: Kitchen Table/Women of Color Press, 1983), 331–51.

11. I thank Ramona Curry for pointing this out to me.

EPILOGUE

1. See Kathleen McHugh, "Women in Traffic: L.A. Autobiography," *South Atlantic Quarterly* 97, no. 2 (Spring 1998).

2. L. S. Kim, "Maid in Color: The Figure of the Racialized Domestic in American Television" (Ph.D. diss., University of California, Los Angeles, 1997), 222–23.

Bibliography

Acker, Ally. *Reel Women: Pioneers of the Cinema, 1896 to the Present.* New York: Continuum, 1991.

Albee, Edward. *Who's Afraid of Virginia Woolf? A Play.* New York: Antheneum, 1962.

Allen, Jeanne. "The Film Viewer as Consumer." *Quarterly Review of Film Studies* 5, no. 4 (Fall 1980): 481–99.

Anderson, Benedict. *Imagined Communities.* New York: Verso, 1991 [1983].

Andrew, Dudley. "Broken Blossoms: The Art and the Eros of a Perverse Text." *Quarterly Review of Film Studies* 6, no. 1 (Winter 1981): 81–90.

Arendt, Hannah. *The Human Condition.* Chicago: University of Chicago Press, 1958.

Armstrong, Nancy. *Desire and Domestic Fiction.* New York: Oxford University Press, 1987.

Bailey, Beth. *From Front Porch to Back Seat.* Baltimore: Johns Hopkins University Press, 1988.

Baker-Benfield, G. J. "The Spermatic Economy: A Nineteenth-Century View of Sexuality." *Feminist Studies* 1, no. 1 (Summer 1972): 45–74.

Baldwin, James. *The Devil Finds Work: An Essay.* New York: Dell, 1990.

Balides, Constance. *Making Dust in the Archives: Feminism, History, and Early American Cinema.* Minneapolis: University of Minnesota Press, forthcoming.

———. "Scenarios of Exposure in the Practice of Everyday Life: Women in the Cinema of Attractions." *Screen* 34, no. 1 (Spring 1993): 19–37.

Barry, Iris. *D. W. Griffith, American Film Master.* New York: Plantin Press, 1965.

Barthes, Roland. "Diderot Brecht Eisenstein." *Narrative, Apparatus, Ideology.* Ed. Phil Rosen. New York: Columbia University Press, 1986.

———. *S/Z.* Trans. Richard Miller. New York: Hill and Wang, 1974.

Baudrillard, Jean. *The Mirror of Production.* Trans. Mark Poster. St. Louis: Telos Press, 1975.

Beecher, Catharine. *A Treatise on Domestic Economy.* New York: Source Book Press, 1970 [1841].

Benjamin, Walter. *Charles Baudelaire: A Lyric Poet in the Era of High Capitalism.* Trans. Harry Zohn. London: NLB, 1973.

———. "Paris, Capital of the Nineteenth Century." In *Reflections.* Trans. Edmund Jephcott. New York: Schocken Books, 1986.

Bergstrom, Janet. "*Jeanne Dielman, 23 Quai du Commerce, 1080 Bruxelles* by Chantal Akerman." *Camera Obscura* 2, (Fall 1977): 114–21.

Berlant, Lauren. "National Brands/National Body: *Imitations of Life.*" In *Comparative American Identities: Race, Sex, and Nationality in the Modern Text.* Ed. Hortense J. Spillers. New York: Routledge, 1991.

Bernardi, Daniel. "The Voice of Whiteness: D. W. Griffith's Biograph Films, 1908–1913." In *The Birth of Whiteness: Race and the Emergence of U.S. Cinema.* Ed. Daniel Bernardi. New Brunswick, N.J.: Rutgers University Press, 1996.

———. *The Birth of Whiteness: Race and the Emergence of U.S. Cinema.* New Brunswick, N.J.: Rutgers University Press, 1996.

Bhabha, Homi, ed. *Nation and Narration.* New York: Routledge, 1990.

Bloch, Ruth. "The Gendered Meanings of Virtue in Revolutionary America." *Signs* 13, no. 1 (1987): 37–58.

Bobo, Jacqueline. "*The Color Purple*: Black Women as Cultural Readers." In *Female Spectators: Looking at Film and Television.* Ed. E. Deidre Pribram. New York: Verso, 1988.

———. "Reading through the Text: The Black Woman as Audience." In *Black American Cinema.* Ed. Manthia Diawara. New York: Routledge, 1993.

Bogle, Donald. *Toms, Coons, Mulattoes, Mammies & Bucks: An Interpretive History of Blacks in American Films.* New York: Continuum, 1989 [1973].

Bordwell, David. *Narration in the Fiction Film.* Madison: University of Wisconsin Press, 1985.

Bordwell, David, Janet Staiger, and Kristin Thompson. *The Classical Hollywood Cinema: Film Style and Mode of Production to 1960.* New York: Columbia University Press, 1985.

Bourdieu, Pierre. *Outline of a Theory of Practice.* Trans. Richard Nice. Cambridge: Cambridge University Press, 1977.

Bovenschen, Sylvia. "Is There a Feminine Aesthetic?" Trans. Beth Weckmueller. *New German Critique* 10 (Winter 1977): 111–37.

Bowlby, Rachel. "Breakfast in America—Uncle Tom's Cultural Histories." In *Nation and Narration.* Ed. Homi Bhabha. New York: Routledge, 1990.

Boydston, Jeanne. *Home and Work: Housework, Wages, and the Ideology of Labor in the Early Republic.* New York: Oxford University Press, 1990.

Brody, Jennifer DeVere. "Clare Kendry's 'True' Colors: Race and Class Conflict in Nella Larsen's *Passing.*" *Callaloo* 15, no. 4 (Fall 1992): 1053–65.

Brooks, Peter. *The Melodramatic Imagination: Balzac, Henry James, Melodrama, and the Mode of Excess.* New Haven: Yale University Press, 1976.

Browne, Nick. "Griffith's Family Discourse: Griffith and Freud." In *Home is Where the Heart Is.* Ed. Christine Gledhill. London: BFI, 1987 [1981].

Burke, Thomas. *Limehouse Nights.* New York: Grosset and Dunlap, 1927.

Butler, Judith. *Bodies That Matter: On the Discursive Limits of Sex.* New York: Routledge, 1993.

Byars, Jackie. *All That Hollywood Allows: Re-reading Gender in 1950s Melodrama.* Chapel Hill: University of North Carolina Press, 1991.

Carby, Hazel. *Reconstructing Womanhood: The Emergence of the Afro-American Woman Novelist.* New York: Oxford University Press, 1987.

Child, Lydia Marie. *The American Frugal Housewife*, ed. Alice Geffen. New York: Harper and Row, 1972 [1835].

Clark-Lewis, Elizabeth. *Living In, Living Out: African American Domestics in Washington, D.C., 1910–1940.* Washington, D.C.: Smithsonian Institution Press, 1994.

Clément, Catherine. *The Newly Born Woman.* Trans. Betsy Wing. Minneapolis: University of Minnesota Press, 1986.

Collier, Christopher. "The American People as Christian White Men of Property: Suffrage and Elections in Colonial and Early National America." In *Voting and the Spirit of American Democracy.* Ed. Donald W. Rogers. Urbana: University of Illinois Press, 1992.

Cook, Pam. "Approaching the Work of Dorothy Arzner." In *Feminism and Film Theory.* Ed. Constance Penley. New York: Routledge, 1988.

———. "Duplicity in *Mildred Pierce*," in *Women in Film Noir,* ed. E. Ann Kaplan (London: BFI, 1996 [1978]), 68–82.

Cott, Nancy. *Bonds of Womanhood: "Woman's Sphere" in New England, 1780–1835.* New Haven: Yale University Press, 1977.

Coulson, Margaret, Branka Magaš, and Hilary Wainwright. "'The Housewife and Her Labour under Capital': A Critique." *New Left Review,* no. 89 (1975): 59–71.

Cowan, Ruth Schwartz. *More Work for Mother: The Ironies of Household Technology from the Open Hearth to the Microwave.* New York: Basic Books, 1983.

Craig's Wife. Columbia press release synopsis, clippings file, Academy of Motion Picture Arts and Sciences Archive, Beverly Hills.

"*Craig's Wife*: Character Drama." *Motion Picture Herald,* September 19, 1936.

"*Craig's Wife.*" *Variety,* September 13, 1936.

Cripps, Thomas. *Slow Fade to Black: The Negro in American Film, 1900–1942.* New York: Oxford University Press, 1977.

Daly, Mary. *Gyn/ecology: The Metaethics of Radical Feminism.* Boston: Beacon Press, 1978.

de Lauretis, Teresa. *Technologies of Gender.* Bloomington: Indiana University Press, 1987.

———, ed. *Feminist Studies/Critical Studies.* Bloomington: Indiana University Press, 1986.

Davis, Angela Y. *Women, Race and Class.* New York: Vintage Books, 1881.

Deleuze, Gilles, and Felix Guattari. *Anti-Oedipus.* Minneapolis: University of Minnesota Press, 1983.

Delmar, Rosalind. "What Is Feminism?" In *What Is Feminism?* Ed. Juliet Mitchell and Ann Oakley. Oxford: Basil Blackwell, 1986.

Derrida, Jacques. "Choreographies." *Diacritics* 12, no. 2 (Summer 1982): 66–76.

———. *Spurs: Nietzsche's Styles.* Trans. Barbara Harlow. Chicago: University of Chicago Press, 1979.

Diawara, Manthia, ed. *Black American Cinema.* New York: Routledge, 1993.

Dirt and Domesticity: Constructions of the Feminine. Exhibition catalogue. Whitney Museum of American Art at the Equitable Center, 1992.

Division of Labor: Women's Work in Contemporary Art. Exhibition catalogue. New York: Bronx Museum of the Arts, 1995.

Doane, Mary Ann. *The Desire to Desire: The Women's Film of the 1940s.* Bloomington: Indiana University Press, 1987.

———. *Femmes Fatales: Feminism, Film Theory, and Psychoanalysis.* New York: Routledge, 1991.

———. "Film and the Masquerade: Theorising the Female Spectator." *Screen* 23, nos. 3–4 (September–October 1982): 175–89.

———. "Women's Stake: Filming the Female Body." *October* 17 (Summer 1981): 23–36.

Douglas, Ann. *The Feminization of American Culture.* New York: Avon Books, 1977.

Douglas, Mary. *Purity and Danger.* London: Routledge and Kegan Paul, 1966.

DuBois, Ellen Carol. "Taking the Law into Their Own Hands: Voting Women during Reconstruction." In *Voting and the Spirit of American Democracy.* Ed. Donald W. Rogers. Urbana: University of Illinois Press, 1992.

Dubroux, Danièle. "Le familier inquiétant (*Jeanne Dielman*)," *Cahiers du cinéma*, no. 265 (March–April 1976): 17–20.

Duggan, Lisa, and Nan D. Hunter. *Sex Wars: Sexual Dissent and Political Culture*. New York: Routledge, 1995.

DuPlessis, Rachel Blau. "For the Etruscans: Sexual Difference and Artistic Production—the Debate over a Female Aesthetic." In *The Future of Difference*. Ed. Hester Eisenstein and Alice Jardine. New Brunswick, N.J.: Rutgers University Press, 1988.

———. *The Pink Guitar: Writing as Feminist Practice*. New York: Routledge, 1990.

Dyer, Richard. "The Colour of Virtue: Lillian Gish, Whiteness, and Femininity." In *Women and Film: A Sight and Sound Reader*. Philadelphia: Temple University Press, 1993.

———."Four Films of Lana Turner." In *Imitations of Life: A Reader on Film and Television Melodrama*. Ed. Marcia Landy. Detroit: Wayne State University Press, 1991.

———. "White." *Screen* 29, no. 4 (Autumn 1988): 44–64.

Eckert, Charles. "The Carole Lombard in Macy's Window." *Quarterly Review of Film Studies* 3, no. 1 (Winter 1978): 1–22.

Elsaesser, Thomas. "Tales of Sound and Fury: Observations on the Family Melodrama." In *Home is Where the Heart Is*. Ed. Christine Gledhill. London: BFI, 1987.

Engels, Frederick. *Condition of the Working Class*. Trans. W. O. Henderson and W. H. Chalmer. London: Blackwell, 1958.

———. *The Origin of the Family, Private Property, and the State, in Light of the Researches of Lewis H. Morgan*. New York: International Publishers, 1942.

Erens, Patricia, ed. *Issues in Feminist Film Criticism*. Bloomington: Indiana University Press, 1990.

Evans, Sara M. *Born for Liberty: A History of Women in America*. New York: Free Press, 1989.

Ewen, Elizabeth. "City Lights: Immigrant Women and the Rise of the Movies." *Signs* 5, no. 3, suppl. (Spring 1980): S45–S65.

Ewing, Elizabeth. "Developments in Fashion Manufacture between the Wars, 1918–1939." In *History of Twentieth-Century Fashion*. London: B. T. Batsford, 1974.

Features and Directors: Films by Women. Chicago, 1974. Program of a film festival sponsored by the Film Center of the Art Institute of Chicago with the *Chicago Tribune*. Clippings file, Academy of Motion Picture Arts and Sciences Archive, Beverly Hills.

Fee, Terry. "Domestic Labour: An Analysis of Housework and Its Relation to the Production Process." *Review of Radical Political Economy* 8, no. 1 (1976): 1–8.

Fields, Barbara Jeanne. "Slavery, Race, and Ideology in the United States of America." *New Left Review* 181 (1990): 95–118.

Fischer, Lucy. *Shot/Countershot: Film Tradition and Women's Cinema*. Princeton: Princeton University Press, 1989.

Forty, Adrian. *Objects of Desire: Design and Society from Wedgewood to IBM*. New York: Pantheon Books, 1986.

Foucault, Michel. *Discipline and Punish*. Trans. Alan Sheridan. New York: Vintage Books, 1979.

———. *Power/Knowledge: Selected Interviews and Other Writings, 1972–1977*. New York: Pantheon Books, 1980.

Fox, Richard, Wightman, and T. J. Jackson Lears, eds. *The Culture of Consumption*. New York: Pantheon, 1983.

Fraser, Nancy. "Rethinking the Public Sphere." *Social Text*, nos. 25–26, (1990–91): 56–80.

———. "Social Criticism without Philosophy." In *Universal Abandon? The Politics of Postmodernism*. Ed. Andrew Ross. Minneapolis: University of Minnesota Press, 1988.

Frederick, Christine. *The New Housekeeping: Efficiency Studies in Home Management*. Garden City, N.Y.: Doubleday, Page and Company, 1913.

Freud, Sigmund. *Civilization and Its Discontents.* In *The Standard Edition of the Complete Psychological Works of Sigmund Freud.* Vol. 21. Trans. James Strachey. London: Hogarth Press, 1953.

———. "Femininity." In *New Introductory Lectures on Psychoanalysis.* Trans. and ed. James Strachey. New York: W. W. Norton & Co., 1965.

———. "The Wolfman: From the History of a Case of an Infantile Neurosis." In *Three Case Histories.* Trans. James Strachey. Ed. Philip Rieff. New York: Macmillan, 1963.

Friedberg, Anne. *Window Shopping.* Berkeley: University of California Press, 1993.

Gaines, Jane. "The Queen Christina Tie-Ups: Convergence of Show Window and Screen." In "Female Representation and Consumer Culture." Ed. Jane Gaines and Michael Renov. *Quarterly Review of Film and Video* 11, no. 1 (1989): 35–60.

———. "White Privilege and Looking Relations: Race and Gender in Feminist Film Theory." In *Issues in Feminist Film Criticism.* Ed. Patricia Erens. Bloomington: Indiana University Press, 1990.

Gallop, Jane. *The Daughter's Seduction.* Ithaca: Cornell University Press, 1982.

Gentile, Mary. "Feminist or Tendentious? Marleen Gorris's *A Question of Silence.*" In *Issues in Feminist Film Criticism.* Ed. Patricia Erens. Bloomington: Indiana University Press, 1990.

Giedion, Sigfried. *Mechanization Takes Command.* New York: W. W. Norton & Company, 1969 [1948].

Gilbert, Sandra, and Susan Gubar. *Madwoman in the Attic: The Woman Writer and the Nineteenth-Century Literary Imagination.* New Haven: Yale University Press, 1984.

Gilroy, Paul. *The Black Atlantic: Modernity and Double Consciousness.* Cambridge: Harvard University Press, 1993.

Gledhill, Christine, ed. *Home is Where the Heart Is.* London: BFI, 1987.

Goody, Jack. *The Domestication of the Savage Mind.* Cambridge: Cambridge University Press, 1977.

Gramsci, Antonio. *Selections from the Prison Notebooks of Antonio Gramsci.* Ed. and trans. Quintin Hoare and Geoffrey Nowell Smith. New York: International Publishers, 1971.

Griffin, Susan. *Woman and Nature: The Roaring inside Her.* New York: Harper and Row, 1978.

Gunning, Tom. "The Cinema of Attraction: Early Film, Its Spectator, and the Avant-Garde." *Wide Angle* 8, nos. 3–4 (1986): 63–71.

———. *D. W. Griffith and the Origins of American Narrative Film.* Urbana: University of Illinois Press, 1991.

———. "From the Opium Den to the Theater of Morality: Moral Discourse and the Film Process in Early American Cinema." *Art & Text* 30 (September–November 1988): 30–40.

Halberstam, Judith. *Skin Shows: Gothic Horror and the Technology of Monsters.* Durham: Duke University Press, 1995.

Hansen, Miriam. *Babel and Babylon: Spectatorship in American Silent Film.* Cambridge: Harvard University Press, 1991.

Haskell, Barbara, and John G. Handhardt. *Yoko Ono: Arias and Objects.* Layton, Utah: Peregrine Smith, 1991.

Haskell, Molly. *From Reverence to Rape: The Treatment of Women in the Movies.* Baltimore: Penguin Books, 1974.

———. "Some Films Men and Women Can't Talk About." *Ms.* 12 (May 1984): 17–19.

Heidegger, Martin. "Building Dwelling Thinking." *Poetry Language Thought.* Trans. Albert Hofstader. New York: Harper and Row, 1971.

Heloise. *Hints for a Healthy Planet.* New York: Perigree Books, 1990.

———. *Hints from Heloise.* New York: Avon Books, 1980.

Heung, Marina. "'What's the Matter with Sara Jane?': Daughters and Mothers in Sirk's *Imitation of Life.*" *Cinema Journal* 26, no. 3 (Spring 1987): 21–43.

Himmelweit, Susan, and Simon Mohun. "Domestic Labour and Capital." *Cambridge Journal of Economics* 1 (1977): 15–31.

Homer. *The Odyssey.* Trans. Robert Fitzgerald. New York: Doubleday, 1963.

hooks, bell. "The Oppositional Gaze: Black Female Spectators." In *Black American Cinema.* Ed. Manthia Diawara. New York: Routledge, 1993.

Horowitz, Daniel. *The Morality of Spending.* Baltimore: Johns Hopkins University Press, 1985.

James, David. "Is There a Class in this Text?" *The Hidden Foundation: Cinema and the Question of Class.* Minneapolis: University of Minnesota Press, 1996.

———. *Allegories of Cinema: American Film in the Sixties.* Princeton: Princeton University Press, 1989.

———. *Power Hits/Misses: Essays across (Un)Popular Culture.* New York: Verso Press, 1996.

Jardine, Alice. Gynesis: *Configurations of Women and Modernity.* Ithaca: Cornell University Press, 1985.

Jennings, Diane. "Heloise." *Dallas Morning News,* July 9, 1989: E1–3.

Johnston, Claire. "Dorothy Arzner: Critical Strategies." In *Feminism and Film Theory.* Ed. Constance Penley. New York: Routledge, 1988.

Jones, Amelia, ed. *Sexual Politics: Judy Chicago's Dinner Party in Feminist Art Theory.* Exhibition catalogue. Los Angeles: Armand Hammer Museum of Art and Cultural Center and University of California Press, 1996.

Kaplan, E. Ann. "The Case of the Missing Mother: Maternal Issues in Vidor's Stella Dallas." In *Issues in Feminist Film Criticism.* Ed. Patricia Erens. Bloomington: Indiana University Press, 1990.

Karcher, Carolyn L. *The First Woman in the Republic: A Cultural Biography of Lydia Maria Child.* Durham: Duke University Press, 1991.

Kauffmann, Stanley. "Jaundice Posing as Justice." *New Republic,* September 3, 1984: 24–25.

Kelly, George. *Craig's Wife.* New York: Samuel French, 1925.

Kepley, Vance, Jr. "Griffith's *Broken Blossoms* and the Problem of Historical Specificity." *Quarterly Review of Film Studies* 3, no. 1 (1978): 37–47.

Kern, Stephen. *The Culture of Time and Space: 1880–1918.* Cambridge: Harvard University Press, 1983.

Kim, Lahn Sung. "Maid in Color: The Figure of the Racialized Domestic in American Television." Ph.D. diss., University of California, Los Angeles, 1997.

Kinder, Marsha. "Reflections on *Jeanne Dielman.*" *Film Quarterly* 30, no. 4 (1977): 2–8.

Kirby, John B. "Early American Politics—The Search for Ideology: An Historiographical Analysis and Critique of the Concept of 'Deference.'" *Journal of Politics* 32, no. 4 (November 1970): 808–38.

Kleinhans, Chuck. "Notes on Melodrama and the Family under Capitalism." *Film Reader* 3 (February 1978): 40–47.

Kristeva, Julia. "Woman Can Never Be Defined." Trans. Marilyn August. In *New French Feminisms.* Ed. Elaine Marks and Isabelle de Courtivron. New York: Schocken Books, 1981.

———. "Women's Time." In *Feminist Theory: A Critique of Ideology.* Chicago: University of Chicago Press, 1982.

Lacan, Jacques. *Feminine Sexuality: Jacques Lacan and the école freudienne.* Ed. Juliet Mitchell and Jacqueline Rose. Trans. Jacqueline Rose. New York: W. W. Norton, 1982.

Landy, Marcia, ed. *Imitation of Life.* Detroit: Wayne State University Press, 1991.

Laplanche, Jean, and J.-B. Pontalis. *The Dictionary of Psychoanalysis.* New York: W. W. Norton, 1973.

Lears, T. J. Jackson. "From Salvation to Self-realization: Advertising and the Therapeutic Roots of the Consumer Culture, 1880–1930." In *The Culture of Consumption.* Ed. Richard Wightman Fox and T. J. Jackson Lears. New York: Pantheon, 1983.

Lerner, Gerda. "The Lady and the Mill Girl: Changes in the Status of Women in the Age of Jackson." *Midcontinent American Studies Journal* 10, no. 1 (Spring 1969): 5–15.

Lesage, Julia. "Artful Racism, Artful Rape: Griffith's *Broken Blossoms*." In *Home is Where the Heart Is*. Ed. Christine Gledhill. London: BFI, 1987.

———. "The Hegemonic Female Fantasy in *An Unmarried Woman* and *Craig's Wife*." *Film Reader* 5 (1982): 83–94.

Lévi-Strauss, Claude. *The Savage Mind*. Chicago: University of Chicago Press, 1966.

Lovell, Terry. *Consuming Fiction*. New York: Verso Press, 1987.

Lourde, Audre. "The Master's Tools Will Never Dismantle the Master's House." In *This Bridge Called My Back*. Ed. Cherrie Moraga and Gloria Anzaldúa. New York: Kitchen Table: Women of Color Press, 1983.

Lynn, Kenneth S. "The Torment of D. W. Griffith." *American Scholar* 59, no. 2 (1990): 255–64.

Marx, Karl. *Capital: A Critical Analysis of Capitalist Production*. Ed. Frederick Engels. Trans. Samuel Moore and Edward Aveling. London: Sonnenschein, 1903.

Marx, Karl, and Frederick Engels. *The German Ideology*. Ed. C. J. Arthur. New York: International Publishers, 1970.

Matthews, Glenna. *"Just a Housewife": The Rise and Fall of Domesticity in America*. New York: Oxford University Press, 1987.

May, Elaine Tyler. *Great Expectations: Marriage and Divorce in Post-Victorian America*. Chicago: University of Chicago Press, 1980.

May, Lary. *Screening Out the Past: The Birth of Mass Culture and the Motion Picture Industry*. New York: Oxford University Press, 1980.

Mayne, Judith. *The Woman at the Keyhole*. Bloomington: Indiana University Press, 1990.

Mechanical Brides: Women and Machines from Home to Office. Exhibition catalogue. New York: Cooper-Hewitt, National Museum of Design, Smithsonian Institution, 1993.

McHugh, Kathleen. "Women in Traffic: L.A. Autobiography." *South Atlantic Quarterly* 97, no. 2 (Spring 1998).

Mellencamp, Patricia. *A Fine Romance: Five Ages of Film Feminism*. Philadelphia: Temple University Press, 1995.

Miller, D. A. *The Novel and the Police*. Berkeley: University of California Press, 1988.

Mintz, Stephen, and Susan Kellogg. *Domestic Revolutions: A Social History of American Family Life*. New York: Free Press, 1988.

Mitchell, Juliet, and Ann Oakley, eds. *What Is Feminism?* Oxford: Basil Blackwell, 1986.

Mitchell, Juliet, and Jacqueline Rose, eds. *Feminine Sexuality: Jacques Lacan and the* école freudienne. Trans. Jacqueline Rose. New York: W. W. Norton, 1982.

Modleski, Tania. *Feminism without Women*. New York: Routledge, 1991.

———. *The Women Who Knew Too Much: Hitchcock and Feminist Theory*. New York: Routledge, 1989 [1988].

———. *Loving with a Vengeance*. New York: Methuen, 1984 [1982].

Montgomery, Sarah. "Cinematic Silence." *Feminist Review* 18 (November 1984): 39–41.

Mullen, Harryette. "Optic White: Blackness and the Production of Whiteness." *Diacritics* 24, nos. 2–3 (Summer–Fall 1994): 71–89.

Mulvey, Laura. "Visual Pleasure and Narrative Cinema." In *Narrative, Apparatus, Ideology: A Film Theory Reader*. Ed. Phil Rosen. New York: Columbia University Press, 1986.

Murphy, Jeanette. "*A Question of Silence*." In *Films For Women*. Ed. Charlotte Brudson. London: BFI, 1986.

Naremore, James. *Acting in the Cinema*. Berkeley: University of California Press, 1988.

Nash, Jay Robert, and Stanley Ralph Ross. *The Motion Picture Guide, 1927–1983*. Chicago: Cinebooks, 1986.

Nelson, Joyce. "*Mildred Pierce* Reconsidered." *Film Reader* 2 (1977): 65–70.

Noble, David W. *The End of American History: Democracy, Capitalism, and the Metaphor of Two Worlds in Anglo-American Historical Writing, 1880–1980*. Minneapolis: University of Minnesota Press, 1985.

Noriega, Chon A. "Birth of the Southwest: Social Protest, Tourism, and D. W. Griffith's *Ramona*." In *The Birth of Whiteness*. Ed. Daniel Bernardi. New Brunswick, N.J.: Rutgers University Press, 1996.

Nugent, Frank. "*Craig's Wife*." In *The New York Times Film Reviews*. New York: *New York Times* and Arno Press, 1970.

Ono, Yoko. *Instruction Paintings*. New York: Weatherhill, 1995.

Palmer, Phyllis. *Domesticity and Dirt: Housewives and Domestic Servants in the United States, 1920–1945*. Philadelphia: Temple University Press, 1989.

Pattison, Mary. *The Principles of Domestic Engineering: Or the What, Why, and How of a Home*. New York: Trow Press, 1915.

Paul, Diane B. *Controlling Human Heredity: 1865 to the Present*. Atlantic Highlands, N.J.: Humanities Press, 1995.

Peiss, Kathy. "'Charity Girls' and City Pleasures: Historical Notes on Working-class Sexuality, 1880–1920." In *Passion and Power: Sexuality in History*. Ed. Kathy Peiss and Christina Simmons. Philadelphia: Temple University Press, 1989.

———. *Cheap Amusements: Working Women and Leisure in Turn-of-the-Century New York*. Philadelphia: Temple University Press, 1986.

Peiss, Kathy, and Christina Simmons, eds. *Passion and Power: Sexuality in History*. Philadelphia: Temple University Press, 1989.

Penley, Constance, ed. *Feminism and Film Theory*. New York: Routledge, 1988.

Perlmutter, Ruth. "Feminine Absence: A Political Aesthetic in Chantal Akerman's *Jeanne Dielman*." *Quarterly Review of Film Studies* 4, no. 2 (Spring 1979): 125–33.

Persellin, Ketura. "'A High-Heeled Army of Furies': Shoplifting in Marlene [*sic*] Gorris's *A Question of Silence*." *Spectator* 16, no. 1 (Fall–Winter 1995): 23–31.

Pleasures and Terrors of Domestic Comfort. Exhibition catalogue. New York: Museum of Modern Art, 1991.

Pribram, E. Deidre, ed. *Female Spectators: Looking at Film and Television*. New York: Verso, 1988.

Prouty, Olive Higgins. *Stella Dallas*. New York: Harper and Row, 1990 [1923].

Ray, Robert B. *A Certain Tendency of the Hollywood Cinema, 1930–1980*. Princeton: Princeton University Press, 1985.

Renov, Michael. "*Leave Her to Heaven*: The Double Bind of the Post-War Woman," *Journal of Film and Video* 35, no. 1 (Winter 1983): 13–36.

Rich, B. Ruby. "*Lady Killers*: It's Only a Movie, Guys!" *Village Voice*, August 7, 1984: 51–54.

———. "Up Against the Kitchen Wall: Chantal Akerman's Meta-Cinema," *Village Voice*, March 29, 1983.

Rogers, Donald W., ed. *Voting and the Spirit of American Democracy*. Urbana: University of Illinois Press, 1992.

Rogin, Michael. "'The Sword Became a Flashing Vision': D. W. Griffith's *The Birth of a Nation*." *Representations* 9 (Winter 1985): 150–95.

Romero, Mary. *Maid in the U.S.A.* New York: Routledge, 1992.

Rosen, Phil, ed. *Narrative, Apparatus, Ideology*. New York: Columbia University Press, 1986.

Ross, Andrew, ed. *Universal Abandon? The Politics of Postmodernism*. Minneapolis: University of Minnesota Press, 1988.

Rubin, Lillian Breslow. *Worlds of Pain: Life in the Working-Class Family*. New York: Basic Books, 1976.

Ryan, Mary. *Cradle of the Middle Class: The Family in Oneida County, New York, 1790–1865.* New York: Cambridge University Press, 1981.

Rybczynski, Witold. *Home: A Short History of an Idea.* New York: Penguin Books, 1987.

Sellers, Charles Grier. *The Market Revolution: Jacksonian America, 1815–1846.* New York: Oxford University Press, 1991.

Shapiro, Laura. *Perfection Salad: Women and Cooking at the Turn of the Century.* New York: Henry Holt, 1986.

Silverman, Kaja. *The Acoustic Mirror: The Female Voice in Psychoanalysis and Cinema.* Bloomington: Indiana University Press, 1988.

Simmon, Scott. "'The Female of the Species': D. W. Griffith, Father of the Woman's Film." *Film Quarterly* 46, no. 2 (Winter 1992–93): 8–20.

———. *The Films of D. W. Griffith.* Cambridge: Cambridge University Press, 1993.

Skenazy, Paul. *James M. Cain.* New York: Continuum, 1989.

Sklar, Kathryn Kish. *Catharine Beecher: A Study in American Domesticity.* New York: W. W. Norton, 1973.

Smith, Barbara, ed. *Home Girls: A Black Feminist Anthology.* New York: Kitchen Table/ Women of Color Press, 1983.

Smith, Valerie. "Reading the Intersection of Race and Gender in Narratives of Passing." *Diacritics* 24, nos. 2–3 (Summer–Fall 1994): 43–57.

Smith-Rosenberg, Carroll. *Disorderly Conduct: Visions of Gender in Victorian America.* New York: Knopf, 1985.

Sobchack, Vivian. *The Address of the Eye: A Phenomenology of Film Experience.* Princeton: Princeton University Press, 1992.

Spigel, Lynn. *Make Room for TV.* Chicago: University of Chicago Press, 1992.

Spillers, Hortense J., ed. *Comparative American Identities: Race, Sex, and Nationality in the Modern Text.* New York: Routledge, 1991.

———. "Mama's Baby, Papa's Maybe: An American Grammar Book." *Diacritics* 7, no. 2 (Summer 1987): 65–81.

Stallybrass, Peter, and Allon White. *The Politics and Poetics of Transgression.* Ithaca, N.Y.: Cornell University Press, 1986.

"*Stella Dallas.*" *Time*, August 9, 1937.

Stowe, Harriet Beecher. *Uncle Tom's Cabin; or, Life among the Lowly.* Ed. Ann Douglas. New York: Penguin, 1981.

Strasser, Susan. *Never Done: A History of American Housework.* New York: Pantheon Books, 1982.

Streeter, Thomas. *Selling the Air: A Critique of the Policy of Commercial Broadcasting in the United States.* Chicago: University of Chicago Press, 1996.

Suter, Jacqueline. "Feminine Discourse in Christopher Strong." In *Feminism and Film Theory.* Ed. Constance Penley. New York: Routledge, 1988.

Sutherland, Daniel E. *Americans and Their Servants: Domestic Service in the United States from 1800 to 1920.* Baton Rouge: Louisiana State University Press, 1981.

Takaki, Ronald T. *A Different Mirror: A History of Multicultural America.* Boston: Little, Brown, 1993.

———. *Iron Cages: Race and Culture in Nineteenth-Century America.* Seattle: University of Washington Press, 1979.

Taylor, Clyde. "The Re-birth of the Aesthetic in Cinema." *Wide Angle* 13, nos. 3–4 (July–October 1991): 12–30.

Taylor, Frederick Winslow. *The Principles of Scientific Management.* New York: Harper & Row, 1911.

Teish, Luisah. "Women's Spirituality: A Household Act." In *Home Girls: A Black Feminist Anthology.* Ed. Barbara Smith. New York: Kitchen Table/Women of Color Press, 1983.

Thompson, E. P. "Time, Work-Discipline, and Industrial Capitalism." *Past and Present* 38 (1967): 56–97.

Tompkins, Jane. *Sensational Designs: The Cultural Work of American Fiction, 1790–1860.* New York: Oxford University Press, 1985.

———. "Sentimental Power: *Uncle Tom's Cabin* and the Politics of Literary History." In *Feminisms.* Ed. Robyn Warhol and Diane Herndl. New Brunswick, N.J.: Rutgers University Press, 1991.

Tyler, Carole-Anne. "Passing: Narcissism, Identity, and Difference." *differences* 6, nos. 2–3 (1994): 212–48.

Veblen, Thorstein. *The Theory of the Leisure Class.* Toronto: Dover Publications, 1994.

Vivani, Christian. "Who Is without Sin: The Maternal Melodrama in American Film, 1930–1939." In *Imitation of Life.* Ed. Marcia Landy. Detroit: Wayne State University Press, 1991.

Wallace, Michele. "Race, Gender, and Psychoanalysis in Forties Film: *Lost Boundaries, Home of the Brave* and *The Quiet One.*" In *Black American Cinema.* Ed. Manthia Diawara. New York: Routledge, 1993.

Warhol, Robyn, and Diane Herndl, eds. *Feminisms.* New Brunswick, N.J.: Rutgers University Press, 1991.

Warner, Michael. *The Letters of the Republic: Publication and the Public Sphere in Eighteenth-Century America.* Cambridge: Harvard University Press, 1990.

Weber, Max. *The Protestant Ethic and the Spirit of Capitalism.* Trans. Talcott Parsons. New York: Scribners, 1958.

Welter, Barbara. "The Cult of True Womanhood: 1800–1860." *American Quarterly* 18 (Summer 1966): 151–74.

Wiegman, Robyn. *American Anatomies: Theorizing Race and Gender.* Durham: Duke University Press, 1995.

Wilde, Oscar. "The Decay of Lying." In *Literary Criticism of Oscar Wilde.* Lincoln: University of Nebraska Press, 1968.

Wilentz, Sean. "Property and Power: Suffrage Reform in the United States, 1787–1860." In *Voting and the Spirit of American Democracy.* Ed. Donald W. Rogers. Urbana: University of Illinois Press, 1992.

Williams, Linda. "A Jury of Their Peers: Marleen Gorris's *A Question of Silence.*" In *Multiple Voices in Feminist Criticism.* Ed. Diane Carson, Linda Dittmar, and Janice Welsch. Minneapolis: University of Minnesota Press, 1994.

———. "Feminist Film Theory: *Mildred Pierce* and the Second World War." In *Female Spectators: Looking at Film and Television.* Ed. E. Deidre Pribram. New York: Verso, 1988.

———. "Film Body: An Implantation of Perversions." In *Narrative, Apparatus, Ideology.* Ed. Phil Rosen. New York: Columbia University Press, 1986.

———. "Something Else besides a Mother: *Stella Dallas* and the Maternal Melodrama." In *Home is Where the Heart Is.* Ed. Christine Gledhill. London: BFI, 1987.

Williams, Rosalind. *Dream Worlds: Mass Consumption in Late Nineteenth-Century France.* Berkeley: University of California Press, 1982.

Wright, Gwendolyn. *Moralism and the Model Home.* Chicago: University of Chicago Press, 1980.

Wright Wexman, Virginia. *Creating the Couple: Love, Marriage, and Hollywood Performance.* Princeton: Princeton University Press, 1993.

Index

Adams, John, 38
Addams, Jane, 87
advertising, 121, 122
advice books, 15. *See also* domestic discourses
Advice to a Young Tradesman (Franklin), 22
Akerman, Chantal, 10, 11, 155–157, 159, 162, 166, 167, 179, 193
Alcott, Louisa May, 15
Alden, Mary, 97
Alger, Horatio, 132, 142
All That Heaven Allows (Sirk, 1955), 115
Althusser, Louis, 168
American domesticity, 16, 17
   as distinct from European models, 16
   influence of production methods on, 61
   in turn-of-the century domestic discourses, 60
   See also Child, Lydia; domesticity; housework
American Dream, 142
The American Frugal Housewife (Child, 1829), 17–35, 42
   construction of American domesticity of, 18, 31

critical reception of, 33
structural and discursive format of, 19, 27–29
See also Child, Lydia
The American Woman's Home (Stowe, 1869), 42
"Americanism," 60, 61
   and women, 110
Andrew, Dudley, 101
appearance,
   and class difference, 67
   and domestic labor, 5, 11, 50
   in early cinema, 82
   ethos of, 60
   in maternal melodrama, 133
   as a secularized moral imperative, 74–75
   in silent cinema, 105
   of women, 5, 11,
   See also appearance standard
appearance standard,
   class and race based, 7, 76, 77
   equated with moral standards, 93–94
   in film, 81, 92
   secularized, 81